THE BAHA'IS OF IRAN

The Baha'i community of Iran is the country's largest non-Muslim religious minority. This collection of essays presents a comprehensive study of the social and historical development of the Baha'i community, and its role in shaping modern Iran.

Central to this study is the pioneering character of the Baha'i community in the late 19th and early 20th century, with chapters examining the role of women in the Baha'i community; the impact of Baha'i-run schools on Iranian society, Baha'i contributions to public health initiatives; and the influence of Baha'i thought and the actions of individual Baha'is on the Constitutional Revolution of 1906–1911.

Conversion to the Baha'i Faith is another important theme: contributors investigate the remarkable trend of conversion to the Baha'i faith, not only from a Shi'i background, but also from ancient, persecuted, non-Muslim minority communities such as Iranian Jews and Zoroastrians.

Finally, although persecution of the Baha'is has drawn the attention of the Western media, until now few scholars working in the field of Iranian studies have chosen to write on the history or details of this persecution. Here, five prominent figures in the field redress this balance.

This book will be of interest to students and scholars of Iranian studies, Middle Eastern studies and comparative religion, and with many chapters authored by leading academics in Iranian studies, *The Baha'is of Iran* addresses both a gap in academic literature on the Baha'i faith, and in the study of modern Iran in general.

Dominic Parviz Brookshaw is Lecturer in Persian Studies and Iranian Literature at the University of Manchester.

Seena B. Fazel is Clinical Senior Lecturer in Forensic Psychiatry at the University of Oxford and an honorary Consultant Psychiatrist.

ROUTLEDGE ADVANCES IN MIDDLE EAST AND ISLAMIC STUDIES

1 IRAQI KURDISTAN
Political development and emergent democracy
Gareth R. V. Stansfield

2 EGYPT IN THE TWENTY FIRST CENTURY
Challenges for development
Edited by M. Riad El-Ghonemy

3 THE CHRISTIAN-MUSLIM FRONTIER
A zone of contact, conflict or cooperation
Mario Apostolov

4 THE ISLAMIC WORLD-SYSTEM
A study in polity-market interaction
Masudul Alam Choudhury

5 REGIONAL SECURITY IN THE MIDDLE EAST
A critical perspective
Pinar Bilgin

6 POLITICAL THOUGHT IN ISLAM
A study in intellectual boundaries
Nelly Lahoud

7 TURKEY'S KURDS
A theoretical analysis of the PKK and Abdullah Ocalan
Ali Kemal Özcan

8 BEYOND THE ARAB DISEASE
New perspectives in politics and culture
Riad Nourallah

9 THE ARAB DIASPORA
Voices of an anguished scream
Zahia Smail Salhi & Ian Richard Netton

10 GENDER AND SELF IN ISLAM
Etin Anwar

11 NIETZSCHE AND ISLAM
Roy Jackson

12 THE BAHA'IS OF IRAN
Socio-historical studies
Dominic Parviz Brookshaw and Seena B. Fazel

THE BAHA'IS OF IRAN

Socio-historical studies

Edited by
Dominic Parviz Brookshaw
and Seena B. Fazel

LONDON AND NEW YORK

First published 2008
by Routledge
2 Park Square, Milton Park, Abingdon, Oxon, OX14 4RN

Simultaneously published in the USA and Canada
by Routledge
270 Madison Ave, New York NY 10016

Routledge is an imprint of the Taylor & Francis Group, an informa business

Transferred to Digital Printing 2010

Typeset in 10/12pt Times New Roman
by Graphicraft Limited, Hong Kong

British Library Cataloguing in Publication Data
A catalogue record for this book is available
from the British Library

Library of Congress Cataloging in Publication Data
The Baha'is of Iran : socio-historical studies / Dominic Parviz Brookshaw and Seena B. Fazel.
p. cm. — (Routledge Advances in Middle East and Islamic Studies)
Includes bibliographical references and index.
1. Bahais—Iran. 2. Iran—Religion. 3. Bahais—Persecutions—Iran. 4. Bahai Faith—Relations. I. Brookshaw, Dominic Parviz. II. Fazel, Seena.
BP330.B337 2007
297.9′30955—dc22
2007004839

ISBN10: 0-415-35673-3 (hbk)
ISBN10: 0-415-58322-5 (pbk)
ISBN10: 0-203-00280-6 (ebk)

ISBN13: 978-0-415-35673-2 (hbk)
ISBN13: 978-0-415-58322-0 (pbk)
ISBN13: 978-0-203-00280-3 (ebk)

TO OUR MATERNAL GRANDMOTHERS

Ṭal‘at Khalīlī-Qazvīnī, née Mudabbir and
Hoovieh Foadi-Avaregan, née Nabil-Akbar

CONTENTS

ILLUSTRATIONS

Figures

Tables

CONTRIBUTORS

Abbas Amanat is Professor of Modern Middle East History at Yale University. His publications include *Pivot of the Universe: Nasir al-Din Shah Qajar and the Iranian Monarchy* (I.B. Tauris, 1997), *Resurrection and Renewal: The Making of the Babi Movement in Iran* (Cornell University Press, 1989) and, as editor, *Imaging the End: Visions of Apocalypse from Ancient Middle East to Modern America* (I.B. Tauris, 2002), and *Crowning Anguish: Memoirs of Taj al-Saltana from the Harem to Modernity* (Mage, 1993). His forthcoming book, *In Search of Modern Iran: Authority, Identity and Nationhood*, will be published by Yale University Press. He is also currently writing a biography of the preeminent woman Babi, Ṭāhira Qurrat al-ʻAyn, which will be published by Oneworld.

Mehrdad Amanat received his PhD in History from UCLA in 2006. His publications include, 'Prelude to Exile: Nationalism and Social Change in Contemporary Iran' in R. Kelley (ed.) *Irangeles: Iranians in Los Angeles* (University of California Press, 1998) and co-authoring 'Iran Under the Late Qajars, 1848–1922' in *The Cambridge History of Iran*, vol. VII (Cambridge University Press, 1991). He has also contributed to the *Oxford Encyclopaedia of the Modern Islamic World.*

Reza Afshari is Professor of History and Human Rights, Pace University. His articles have appeared in a variety of academic journals such as the *International Journal of the Middle East Studies* (*IJMES*) and *Human Rights Quarterly*. He co-edited (with Janet Afary) a special issue of the journal *Iran Nameh* on human rights violations of non-Muslim Iranians (Winter–Spring 2001), and in the same year published *Human Rights in Iran: The Abuse of Cultural Relativism* (University of Pennsylvania Press, 2001). Reza Afshari is a member the editorial review board of *Human Rights Quarterly*.

Dominic Parviz Brookshaw teaches Persian literature and language at the Institute of Islamic Studies, McGill University, Montreal. Before arriving at McGill, he taught medieval Persian literature at the University of

Oxford from 2002 to 2005. He was trained in Persian and Arabic Studies at the Oriental Institute, Oxford, and has published articles in *Middle Eastern Literatures, Iran* (the Journal of the British Institute of Persian Studies), and *Encyclopaedia Iranica.* He is the Assistant Editor of *Iranian Studies* and from August 2007, he will be Lecturer in Persian Studies and Iranian Literature at the University of Manchester. His monograph, *Hafiz and His Contemporaries: a Study of fourteenth century Persian Love Poetry* will be published by I.B. Tauris in 2008.

H.E. Chehabi is Professor of International Relations and History at Boston University. Before coming to Boston University he taught at Harvard University and UCLA. His publications include *Iranian Politics and Religious Modernism: the liberation movement of Iran under the Shah and Khomeini* (Cornell University Press, 1990), *Distant Relations: Iran and Lebanon in the last 500 years* (I.B. Tauris, 2006), and co-author of *Sultanistic Regimes* (Johns Hopkins University Press, 1998). His articles have appeared in numerous academic journals, including: *Aus Politik und Zeitgeschichte, Daedalus, Diplomacy and Statecraft, Government and Opposition, International Journal of the History of Sport, IJMES, Iranian Studies* and *Political Science Quarterly.*

Seena B. Fazel is a Clinical Senior Lecturer at the Department of Psychiatry, University of Oxford. His publications on Baha'i-related topics include co-editing *Search for Values: Ethics in Baha'i Thought* (Kalimat, 2004) and *Reason and Revelation: New Directions in Baha'i Thought* (Kalimat, 2002). He was founding editor of the *Baha'i Studies Review*, which he co-edited from 1990–2002.

Minou Foadi is Honorary Senior Lecturer at Imperial College School of Medicine, University of London, and was previously Senior Lecturer and Consultant in Haematology at the Imperial College School of Medicine. She has published on Baha'i history in Persian-language Baha'i periodicals and in *Encyclopaedia Iranica.* She is currently editing *Tārīkh-i amrī-yi Khurasan* by Hasan Foadi Bushrui ('Aṣr-i-Jadīd, forthcoming). In addition, she has published in *Nature, Journal of The American Medical Association*, and many other scientific journals.

Kavian S. Milani co-authored 'The History and Provenance of an Early Manuscript of the *Nuqṭat al-kāf* dated 1268 (1851–52)' in *Iranian Studies* (2004). He has also contributed to *Encyclopaedia Iranica* and is the editor of Goftman-Iran (www.goftman-iran.org), a weekly e-magazine that studies Iranian culture, arts, history and sociology.

Moojan Momen is an independent scholar with a special interest in the history and doctrine of the Babi and Baha'i religions, as well as Shi'ism. His publications include: *An Introduction to Shi'i Islam* (Yale University

Press, 1985), *The Babi and Baha'i Faiths 1844–1944: Some Contemporary Western Accounts* (George Ronald, 1982), *Selections from the Writings of E.G. Browne on the Babi and Baha'i Religions* (ed.) (George Ronald, 1987), and *The Phenomenon of Religion* (Oneworld, 1999). He has contributed articles to *Encyclopaedia Iranica* and the *Oxford Encyclopaedia of the Modern Islamic World* and published in *IJMES*, *Iran*, *Iranian Studies* and *Religion*. Moojan Momen is a Fellow of the Royal Asiatic Society.

Eliz Sanasarian is Professor of Political Science at the University of Southern California, where she specializes in comparative ethnic politics, women in international development, and Middle East and comparative politics. Her publications include *Religious Minorities in Iran* (Cambridge University Press, 2000) and *The Women's Rights Movement in Iran: Mutiny, Appeasement, and Repression from 1900 to Khomeini* (Praeger, 1982). She has also contributed articles to the *Holocaust and Genocide Studies Journal*, *Diaspora*, *Journal of Developing Societies*, and the *Oxford Encyclopaedia of the Modern Islamic World.*

Mohamad Tavakoli-Targhi is Professor of History and Near and Middle Eastern Civilizations at the University of Toronto and the Chair of the Department of Historical Studies at the University of Toronto-Mississauga. Since 2002 he has served as the editor of *Comparative Studies of South Asia, Africa and the Middle East*. His publications include *Refashioning Iran: Orientalism, Occidentalism and Nationalist Historiography* (Palgrave, 2001) and *Tajaddud-i būmī* ('vernacular modernity') (2003). His articles include: 'The Homeless Texts of Persianate Modernity', in *Iran – Between Tradition and Modernity* (Lexington Books, 2004); and 'From Patriotism to Matriotism: A Tropological Study of Iranian Nationalism, 1870–1909', in *IJMES* (2002).

Fereydun Vahman is Professor Emeritus, University of Copenhagen. He studied with Professors Barr and Asmussen at Copenhagen, and MacKenzie and Boyce at London. His publications include: *Ardā Wiraz Nāmag: the Iranian "Divina Commedia"*, (edited Pahlavī text with English translation and commentary) (Curzon, 1986), *Farhang-i mardum-i Kirman* (ed. based on the materials collected by D.L. Lorimer) (Bunyād-i Farhang-i Iran, 1975). He is also the co-author (together with Professor G Asatrian, University of Yerevan) of *Notes on the language and ethnography of the Zoroastrians of Yazd* (2002) and *The Poetry of the Baxitaris* (1995). He is a member of the Advisory Board of the *Great Pahlavi Dictionary*, and the chairman of the Danish-Iranian Society.

NOTE ON TRANSLITERATION, DATES AND NAMES

Any system of transliteration will have its critics. We have tried to standardize the transliteration throughout this volume. We have used the system adopted by the *Encyclopaedia of Islam* with some modifications: *j* replaces *dj*, *q* replaces *ḳ*, *ch* replaces *č*, and *v* replaces *w* (in most cases). The underlining of *dh*, *sh*, etc. is omitted. The *iḍāfa* is written as *–i* after consonants, and *–yi* after vowels and the silent final *h*. The silent *h* at the end of Persian words is transliterated as *a*, e.g. *nāma-yi tu*. As in the *Encyclopaedia of Islam*, the short vowels are represented by *a*, *i*, and *u*, and the long vowels as *ā*, *ī*, and *ū*. The diphthongs are represented by *ay* and *aw*.

Dates are only given in CE form, unless the Islamic lunar or solar date is deemed absolutely necessary.

If place names have a commonly-used Latinized form (e.g. Tehran), it is this which is used. Most other Iranian place names appear in a transliterated form minus the diacritics (e.g. Isfahan), unless the town or village is rather obscure (e.g. Tākur). We have elected not to transliterate fully a number of words which appear frequently, so as not to clutter the text, e.g.: Baha'i, Babi, Shi'i, Shi'ism, Sunni, Sunnism, Qajar, shah, *'ulama*, *mulla*, Ayatullah, *sharī'a*, Shaykhi, Sufi, Qur'an. We have used Baha'i Faith most frequently (rather than Baha'ism) as this is the more commonly used name for the religion founded by Baha'ullah. The names of the Babi-Baha'i leaders appear in this book in the following, simplified form: the Bab, Baha'ullah, 'Abdu'l-Baha. All other Persian and Arabic names are fully transliterated. Proper names which have the suffix *-allah* appear thus: Hidāyatullāh, Faḍlullāh. Titles with Arabic suffixes appear thus: Nāṣir al-Dīn, Mushāvir al-Mamālik, Intiẓam al-Salṭana.

INTRODUCTION

The Iranian Baha'i community emerged in the 1860s and 1870s out of the remnants of the Babi movement. From the late nineteenth century to the 1920s, it expanded significantly in size and influence. A number of factors are likely to have contributed to its growth. Written correspondence and personal contact with the prophet-founder of the Baha'i Faith, Mīrzā Ḥusayn-'Alī Nūrī, Baha'ullah (1817–1892), and his eldest son and successor as leader of the community, Mīrzā 'Abbās Nūrī, 'Abdu'l-Baha (1844–1921) provided encouragement to Iran's Baha'is and co-ordination of the community's activities.

Both in the thousands of letters Baha'ullah wrote to individual Baha'is in Iran, and in his conversations with the many Iranian Baha'i pilgrims that visited him in his successive exiles to Baghdad, Istanbul, Edirne and later 'Akka, Baha'ullah urged his followers to unite, live moral lives, and propagate their religion both inside and outside of Iran. As Smith points out, most of the Babis who survived the massacres and upheavals that ensued after the public execution of their prophet, Sayyid 'Alī-Muḥammad Shīrāzī, the Bab in Tabriz in 1850, became Baha'is: 'Faced with a combination of competent leadership, efficient communication, a reassertion of claims to charismatic leadership, and an appropriate ideology, the Babis rallied to Baha'u'llah' (Smith 1987: 88).

The Iranian Baha'i community of the late nineteenth century was not only drawn from the remaining Babi faithful, though. Baha'ullah encouraged his followers to travel to parts of the country where there were no Baha'is in order to establish new local communities. With its mix of messianic and modernizing beliefs, combined with the personalities of many enthusiastic and charismatic teachers, the Baha'i Faith experienced a steady expansion in its numbers during the lifetime of Baha'ullah. Foreign visitors attested to this growth. In 1889, a British diplomat in Iran wrote to E.G. Browne of the 'increasing multitudes' who were attracted to the Baha'i teachings, and Lord Curzon, who was visiting Iran around that time, speculated that 'If Babism continues to grow at its present rate of progression, a time may conceivably come when it will oust Mohammedanism from the field in Persia' (Browne 1918: 203; Curzon 1892: 503).

The Baha'i community of Iran grew steadily until the 1920s, and by the late nineteenth/early twentieth century the Baha'is had embarked upon a number of education and health initiatives, reflecting their confidence and optimism for future expansion. In numerical terms, it is estimated that there were at least 100,000 Baha'is in the 1880s, which represented 1–2 per cent of Iran's population of between 5 and 8 million at the time (Smith 1984). As the twentieth century unfolded, the proportion of Baha'is in the population grew gradually smaller, especially after 1979 as the birth rate among Baha'is was below the average and many Baha'is emigrated to the West to escape persecution.[1] Nevertheless, it is estimated that there remain at least 300,000 Baha'is in Iran today, equating to around 0.5 per cent of the population.

In this volume of essays, our intention is to present a series of studies on aspects of the social and historical development of Iran's Baha'i community. This volume addresses both a gap in academic literature on the Baha'i Faith, and in the study of modern Iran in general. In contrast to a number of important studies of history on the Babi movement,[2] English-language scholarship on the history of the Baha'is of Iran is surprisingly limited. There are very few books that contain chapters discussing the Baha'i community of Iran in any detail. One such volume is *In Iran: Studies in Babi and Baha'i History* (Smith 1986).[3] A number of chapters in Cole's *Modernity and the Millennium*, and scattered articles in other volumes and journals are noteworthy contributions, but even these have rarely dealt with the development of the Iranian Baha'i community in the twentieth century.[4]

There are three broad themes to this volume. The first is conversion to the Baha'i Faith. Although most Iranian Baha'is came from a Shi'i background, large numbers of Iranian Jews and Zoroastrians also converted – much to the dismay of their clergy and the surprise of foreign commentators. That Iranians from these ancient, persecuted, non-Muslim minority communities would voluntarily convert to a new religion that emerged from a messianic Shi'i milieu and which was subject to even worse persecution is a phenomenon requiring serious study. Mehrdad Amanat explores the conversion of Iranian Jews to the Baha'i religion, and presents new historical evidence to suggest that social factors, rather than merely religiously-motivated ones, were prominent in this process. In addition, Amanat provides for the first time an overview of the geographic spread of these conversions, with particular reference to Kashan and Hamadan. Fereydun Vahman examines the reasons Zoroastrians were attracted to the Baha'i teachings, and presents a novel approach to this issue arguing for importance of the 'Iranianness' of these teachings. Many fewer conversions among the Christians of Iran have been noted,[5] in part because they were less demoralised and more socioculturally separate than the Jews and Zoroastrians (Maneck 1990). There were also a small number of conversions from among other groups, such as the 'Aliyullāhīs and Sufis.

The second theme is the contribution of the Baha'i community to the wider life of the Iranian nation. Women played a prominent part in this and Dominic Parviz Brookshaw explores the role that correspondence from Baha'ullah and 'Abdu'l-Baha to individual Baha'i women are likely to have played in mobilizing Iranian Baha'i women to action both within their religious community and broader Iranian society as a whole. The Baha'i women of Iran have been the subject of research interest before (e.g. Momen 2005; Cole 1998) but this is the first close textual analysis of letters that were addressed to individual women. Under this second theme, there are also essays on the educational initiatives and health reforms pioneered by Baha'is. The importance of education is a significant theme in Baha'i texts, and Baha'is founded a large number of schools throughout Iran in both major urban centres as well as remote villages from around 1890 to 1930. In this volume, Moojan Momen, for the first time, provides a comprehensive list of these schools and discusses their innovative practices, which he argues influenced state schools. The overwhelming majority of these Baha'i-run schools (which were attended by boys and girls of all religious and ethnic backgrounds) were closed by the Iranian government in 1934. Seena B. Fazel and Minou Foadi write on Baha'i health reforms, and demonstrate how Baha'is appear to have introduced an interesting range of novel initiatives from introducing showers into public bathhouses, to building hospitals that hired women doctors to work in the specially built women-only wards. There is considerable inter-relation between health and education reforms, and many of the key health care professionals worked in the Baha'i-run schools as well. In this section of the volume, Kavian S. Milani examines the influence of Baha'i thought and the actions of individual Baha'is on the Constitutional Revolution of 1906–1911. Ever since E.G. Browne wrote on this at the time, there has been considerable speculation on the Baha'i involvement. Milani discusses some Baha'i texts, which have not been fully exploited by previous researchers. Milani highlights the changing attitude of the Iranian Baha'i community to the Revolution, thereby questioning attempts by other scholars to argue that the Baha'is adopted a monochrome approach to the constitutional movement in early twentieth century Iran. Other notable contributions of the Baha'is to Iranian society, that we have not had the opportunity to discuss in this volume, include artistic and literary ones, agricultural reforms,[6] and innovative business practices.

The third broad theme of this book is the persecution of the Baha'is. As an article in the *New York Review of Books* put it in 1982, 'the threat of genocide hangs over the Baha'is of Iran' – it has done so since its inception and continues to do so (Kazemzadeh 1982: 43). Although this persecution has drawn the attention of the Western media,[7] few scholars working in the field of Iranian Studies have chosen to write on the history or details of this persecution. In this section of the book there are chapters by five leading figures in Iranian Studies. Eliz Sanasarian compares the precarious case of the Baha'i community in Iran with that of the country's other 'recognized' and 'unrecognized' religious minorities; Abbas Amanat discusses the historical roots of the persecution of the Babis and then the Baha'is in Iran, and examines the complex intersection of the competing interests of the clergy, the state and the mob in these attacks; Mohamad Tavakoli-Targhi highlights the inseparability of the Islamist movement and anti-Baha'ism in Iran, and shows how Islamist groups were particularly active in smaller towns and villages where a sizeable number of the local population had converted to the Baha'i Faith; H.E. Chehabi looks at the phenomenon of secular anti-Baha'ism, particularly in the late Pahlavi period, and tries to uncover why many Iranian intellectuals attacked the Baha'is in their works; and, finally, Reza Afshari presents a detailed account of the persecution of the Baha'is in Iran from shortly before the Revolution of 1978–79 until the present day. Afshari shows how the persecution of the Baha'is in the Islamic Republic has morphed over the past quarter of a century, and seems to have moved on from a more violent period of detention, torture and summary execution to one of more systematic denial of basic human rights, including access to higher education.

Dominic Parviz Brookshaw and
Seena B. Fazel

Notes

1 This emigration was sizeable from the mid-1950s. In addition to persecution, other factors that contributed included moving abroad to study, and to assist new Baha'i communities (Momen 1991: 28).
2 Academic literature on the history of the Babi movement is more extensive (see works by Amanat 1989, Momen 1981, Smith 1987).
3 The volume *Iran im 19. Jahrhundert und die Entstehung der Baha'i-Religion* (Bürgel and Schayani 1998) contains two essays on the history of the Baha'i Faith.
4 A notable exception is Smith 1987.
5 For example, Ibrahim, an Assyrian (Nestorian) priest, in Adharbayjan converted (Momen 1998: 46).
6 One example is the reforms instituted in Māhfurūzak, which included the setting up of a co-operative to sell cotton (Momen 1998: 41).
7 The first Western newspaper account of the Babi religion was an 1845 report in *The Times* of London of Babi persecutions (cited in Momen 1981: 69).

Bibliography

Amanat, A. (1989) *Resurrection and Renewal: The Making of the Babi Movement in Iran, 1844–1850*, Ithaca: Cornell University Press.

Browne, E.G. (comp.) (1918) *Materials for the study of the Babi religion*, Cambridge: Cambridge University Press.

Burgel, J.C. and Schayani, I. (eds) (1998) *Iran im 19. Jahrhundert und die Entstehung der Baha'i-Religion*, Hildesheim: George Olms Verlag.

Cole, J.R.I. (1998) *Modernity and the Millennium: The Genesis of the Baha'i Faith in the Nineteenth-Century Middle East*, New York: Columbia University Press.

Curzon, G.N. (1892) *Persia and the Persian Question*, vol. 1, London: Cass.

Kazemzadeh, F. (1982) 'The terror facing the Baha'is', *New York Review of Books* (13 May 1982): 43–44.

Maneck, S.S. (1990) 'The conversion of minorities to the Baha'i Faith in Iran: some preliminary observations,' *Journal of Baha'i Studies* 3:3: 35–48.

Momen, M. (1981) *The Babi and Baha'i Religions, 1844–1944: Some Contemporary Western Accounts*, Oxford: George Ronald.

—— (1991) 'The Baha'i community of Iran: patterns of exile and problems of communication,' in A. Fathi (ed.) *Iranian Refugees and exiles since Khomeini*, Costa Messa, California: Mazda.

—— (1998) 'A preliminary survey of the Baha'i community of Iran during the nineteenth century', in J.C. Burgel and I. Schayani (eds) *Iran im 19. Jahrhundert und die Entstehung der Baha'i-Religion*, Hildesheim: George Olms Verlag.

Smith, P. (1984) 'A note on Babi and Baha'i numbers,' *Iranian Studies* 17: 295–301.

—— (ed.) (1986) *In Iran: Studies in Babi and Baha'i History*, volume 3, Los Angeles: Kalimat Press.

—— (1987) *The Babi and Baha'i Religions: From Messianic Shi'ism to a World Religion*, Cambridge: Cambridge University Press.

1

MESSIANIC EXPECTATION AND EVOLVING IDENTITIES

The conversion of Iranian Jews to the Baha'i faith[1]

Mehrdad Amanat

In 1878, two physicians and early Jewish converts to the Baha'i Faith from Hamadan travelled to Tehran to bring the message of their new faith to Ḥakīm Nūr Maḥmūd, an influential Jewish physician. An all-night debate was held over Jewish prophecies and the rabbinic authority 'on condition that no one else present should say a word'. Though their host never openly confessed the new faith, their message did raise fundamental questions in the mind of another young Jewish enthusiast. Rayḥān Rayḥānī (1859–1949), a peddler apprentice from Kashan carefully listened to the heated discussions from behind a closed door. By dawn, according to one source, he was infuriated at the Baha'is' questioning the rabbinic authority to the point of being ready to attack them. Yet he could not find answers to claims the Baha'is had made about the coming of the Messiah and had trouble negotiating the labyrinth of identities he had encountered. As an orphaned teenager in Tehran, he was exposed to ideas of Christian missionaries and, perhaps through connections with Sufis, had even accepted the prophet Muḥammad as a messenger of God. For the following five years, which he described as years of 'desperate confusion', Rayḥānī intensely struggled to root out contradictions and inconsistencies in his beliefs, which he later deemed 'fallacies and superstitions' (*khurāfāt va mawhūmāt*). He had witnessed and was moved by public execution of Babis and Baha'is. His fears of not recognizing the Messiah compelled him to persist in his search and instilled in him a desire to meet more Baha'is. In this pursuit, he was unaffected by eccentric believers and the unscrupulous pretenders he came across. His agonies came to an end following his conversion experience in the form of a dream, a milestone in his evolving identity. Though as a Baha'i he experienced persecution and discrimination, he was also an accepted member of the community of mostly Muslim converts in Kashan.[2]

During the late nineteenth and the first half of the twentieth century, a substantial number of Iranian Jews converted to the newly founded Baha'i Faith which grew out of the messianic Babi movement and had attracted a large number of mostly Shi'i Muslim followers. In many ways, the attraction to the Baha'i Faith was a novel phenomenon among Iranian Jewry. Despite their close historical ties with other sectarian movements, Iranian Jews never converted in large numbers to religions other than Islam. Although it was common among followers of any minority religion to adopt the dominant culture and the religion of the majority population, the story of the disadvantaged Iranian Jews who converted to the even more persecuted Baha'i Faith presents an important if not a unique exception.

Although reliable statistics are hard to locate, a number of foreign observers have made estimates about the number of Jewish Baha'i converts. Ephraim Neumark, a Jewish traveller, gives the exaggerated estimate of two million followers of the new religion in 1884, including 'many Jews' (Neumark 1947: 80). The British diplomat Lord Curzon's estimates in the 1880s, prior to the early-twentieth century wave of conversions, are perhaps more representative of converts who publicly confessed their Baha'i convictions. His figures for Kashan, Hamadan and Tehran are 50 to 100 to 150 Jewish families respectively. His estimate that as many as 75 per cent of the Gulpāygān Jewish population 'formally joined the Baha'i movement and their numbers have since increased considerably' indicates mass conversions among the Jews (Curzon 1892: 496).[3] Some 50 years later, the Jewish scholar Abraham Brawer estimated the number of followers in the mid-1930s to be 'thousands and perhaps ten thousand of Jews'. He reported the number of converts to be 'around a quarter of the Jews of Hamadan' whom he estimated to be 8,000. He also reported that as many as seven hundred Jews in Tehran had converted to the Baha'i Faith (Brawer 1937–8: 22, 24, 31). These figures at first may seem inflated, yet given the fluidity and range of Jewish-Baha'i identity in this period, from sympathizers to propagators, these estimates may not be entirely unreasonable.[4]

Any assessment of the number of converts is complicated by the fact that many converted as migrants away from their hometowns. A more recent study extending to the 1950s contains an expanded list numbering some 150 families and individuals originally from Kashan most of whom converted outside their city of origin, and over 600 families and individual converts from Hamadan including members of extended families. These figures compare to an estimated Jewish population of 5,000 around the turn of the century and 8,000 by mid-1930s in Hamadan. Kashan's Jewish population (including converts), prior to the mid-twentieth-century wave of migration to Tehran, is estimated at around 400 Jewish individuals and heads of households.[5]

Among Western observers and scholars who have attempted to tackle the question of Jewish Baha'i conversions, some earlier interpretations have attributed the Baha'i Faith's appeal to its 'cosmopolitan outlook on life' and its belief in 'peaceful relations between the different faiths' (Fischel 1934). More recent views attribute the general trend of Jewish conversions to Islam and the Baha'i Faith to the 'humiliation and persecution, suffering and torture' and the Jews' 'ignorance in matters of religion' (Cohen 1973: 54, 162–3). Such common charges of 'ignorance' and 'simplemindedness' are influenced by the views of nineteenth century observers. These often drew a one-dimensional picture of isolated and persecuted Jewish communities. Indigenous Jewish Iranian traditions, at variance with traditional European Rabbinic Judaism, did not allow the European Jews to identify with them. Another, more careful, study by a Baha'i writer has generally played down the role of social and economic factors in conversion (Maneck 1991).[6]

A brief historical overview may assist a more in-depth understanding of the roots and causes of conversion among the Jews. Throughout their age-old presence in Iran (as early as 700 BC) the Persian Jews made wide-ranging contributions to Iranian society and culture.[7] Mutual influences between Judaism and Iranian religions are evident within numerous Jewish and Iranian sectarian movements as well as mainstream orthodoxy.[8] Though often unrecognized, the role of the Jews was crucial in maintaining diversity in an environment often under pressures of cultural and religious conformity. During the Islamic period, the Jews of Iran helped fill gaps in some vital spheres of the economy discouraged under Islamic law (*shari'a*), such as long distance trade, money lending and the trade and manufacture of precious metals. As wine makers, musicians and entertainers free from the restrictions of the conservative *'ulama*, as well as scientists and scholars familiar with Hebrew and the Biblical tradition, they helped preserve and enrich Iran's artistic and intellectual heritage (Loeb 1972).[9] Iranian Jews were also important in the fields of Persian language and literature. The first known examples of written modern Persian are written in Hebrew script (Elwell-Sutton 1983: 20–1).[10]

Prior to the Safavid period, the overall record of treatment of Jews in Iran, at least in comparison with much of Europe in the medieval period, was one of relative tolerance.[11] Despite their long presence and extensive engagement with other Persians, mass conversions were not widespread among Persian Jews. However, pressures for conversion to Islam increased during the Safavid period (1501–1722) when Twelver Shi'ism became the state religion and its main source of political legitimacy. Even though many non-Muslims experienced periods of economic prosperity, a distinct change can be observed in the interfaith relations and the treatment of non-Muslims. The forced conversion of Sunni Muslims to Shi'ism became commonplace, while on occasion Jews were forced to convert to Islam – though in many instances communities of converts reverted to Judaism (Matthee 1999: 20, 42; Amanat 2006: 60–2).

During the Qajar period, the most notable case of forced conversion took place in 1839, when following a riot, the entire Jewish community of

Mashhad was forced to convert to Islam. Despite rigorous pressure to publicly conform to Islamic practice, including regular attendance of public prayers, many converts continued to practise Judaism in secret for generations, only to openly confess Judaism some one hundred years later under secular Pahlavi rule.[12]

The rise of legalistic Shi'ism under Safavid rule brought forth another fundamental change in the condition of the Jews, namely the prevalence of the doctrine of ritual 'impurity' (*nijāsat*) which was present in Sunni Islam but more emphatically so in Shi'ism and more strictly applied to the Jews. This doctrine underpinned the relations between Muslims and non-Muslims with consequences that went beyond restricting social interaction. Though unevenly enforced during the Qajar period, these limits created major economic obstacles for the Jews who in many cities were banned from having shops in the main Bazaar. Such discriminatory practices were supposed to protect believers from the 'impurity' resulting from close physical contact with Jews. More significantly, they eliminated competition from Jewish merchants and contributed to a gradual decline in the Jews' socio-economic status. Trends towards cultural participation became more restrained and were limited to occasional participation in Sufi orders, where Jews were more tolerated (Soroudi 1994: 164–5; Williams 1994: 72–89).

By the nineteenth century, regional and global factors led to a major economic dislocation making Iran more dependent on global trends, including recessions and currency devaluations. These developments caused further deterioration in the condition of the Jews in communities like Kashan, a centre of Baha'i conversion, where the Jews were an important part of a thriving textile industry and trade that suffered the onslaught of cheap industrial-age European goods and experienced a marked decline.

Increased contact with the West brought forth improved communications, notably print and telegraph, and a dramatic rise in the volume of foreign trade but also military defeat, diplomatic humiliation, monetary crises and financial dependency.[13] At a time when Iran was deeply affected by war, famine and epidemics, political uncertainties and weakening central authority, faith was one of the few anchors of personal stability and community support.

Yet, the economic changes in nineteenth-century Iran also included more constructive processes. An expansion of domestic markets leading to the emergence of a national economy by the twentieth century was partly fuelled by new trade routes and an increased European demand for Iran's products, such as carpets. Some members of the Jewish community, even those with little capital, benefited from these conditions by forming trading partnerships for domestic trade.

Hamadan's rapid expansion into a major economic centre after the opening of the Basra trade in 1865 and Arak's rapid growth in the 1870s as a carpet distribution centre attracted many internal immigrants and these cities became conversion centres. Many younger Jewish immigrants with no family and community support had to cope with new work environments and faced new challenges to their conventional beliefs. Hamadan also saw the establishment of a number of European-style schools, which helped open horizons and introduced doubts about traditional norms and values.

Conflicting modes of modernity accompanied overwhelming and deep-rooted changes in Iran. These challenges tended to reinforce religious conviction while at the same time posed fundamental questions about traditional belief systems and helped create a climate of religious ambiguity. Like some other Iranians who were attracted to a variety of unconventional belief systems ranging from messianic Babism to reformist Shi'ism, agnosticism, secular nationalism and later socialism, the Jews tried to confront what they viewed as their overwhelming economic and intellectual backwardness in conditions of crisis and turmoil by experimenting with unconventional beliefs and adopting new religious identities such as Christianity and the Baha'i Faith.

One important aspect of religious ambiguity can be observed in the acceleration of a primordial trend in the history of Persian Jewry, namely a sense of expectation for the coming of a saviour or Messiah (*Mashiyah*). Western missionary activities, though they attracted fewer converts, revitalized messianic fervour and introduced new options in terms of religious conviction. According to the Christian missionary Henry Stern, who visited Iran in the 1850s, the prominent Jewish physician Ḥakīm Hārūn had confessed that 'Christian salvation was in perfect harmony with the Scripture, and far superior to the fanciful system of Rabbinism'. Stern further claims that Hārūn assured him that many of the Jews of Kashan would 'as intensely love Christ and his Gospel, as they formerly rejected the one and despised the other' (Stern 1854: 254–60).[14] Even if one discounts the enthusiasm of the reporter, these statements may point to the strengthening of a deep-rooted sense of messianic expectation among the Jews.

A more visual representation of the presence of messianic memory in Kashan during this period was the customary practice of Jews to pray from their rooftops on the Sabbath for the capacity to recognize the Messiah at the time of his return (Māzandarānī 1973: 713).[15] Prior to the forced conversions in Mashhad in 1839, some Jews there had voluntarily yet secretly converted to Islam (Jadhdhāb n.d.: 2–4; Sulaymānī 1976a: 451–2). In one instance, a rabbi in Tehran even encouraged his followers to convert to Islam if the Messiah did not appear by the impending date of 1884 (Amanat 2006: 134). It is not unlikely that the coming of the year 5600 (1840) in the Jewish calendar awakened a sense of millennial anticipation in many Jews. As in other instances in Jewish (and Islamic) history, the clerical establishment stood against any expectation of messianic advent. Nevertheless, the activities of Christian missionaries and the rise of the Babi movement gave rise to a new discourse in messianic expectation.

This environment of messianic expectation and religious ambiguity, together with the pressing questions and changes related to the advent of modernity, provided fertile grounds for the spread of a new religious identity among the Jews. For those attracted to the Baha'i Faith, the coming of the saviour instilled a new sense of optimism and hopes for an end to age-old miseries and persecution. Becoming a Baha'i was to become a respected member of a community that promoted equality and was a way out of the archaic mindset and the limits of an impoverished and marginalized community. Conversion, one might argue, was a way for people to abandon retrograde and parochial divisions and embrace a common culture.

Yet for many, it was the novelty of the Baha'i religious message that had the greatest appeal. In the latter part of the nineteenth century, the Baha'is were among the first to introduce a new discourse in Iran's otherwise conservative Islamic environment, stressing the need for the renewal of religion, the unity of humanity, social and political equality, ethnic and gender harmony, and the acceptance of religious minorities. In a society where identities were primarily religious, a new faith that called for rationality and the equality of all races and creeds proved attractive to an emerging cosmopolitan class in search of alternatives to traditional identities.

The Baha'i message recognized and attempted to reconcile the increasingly pervasive presence of modernity. Its all-inclusive approach to past religions accepted the validity of all past prophets as 'manifestations' (*maẓāhir*) of the 'Divine Truth' whose mission was to renew the Divine 'Covenant' (*'ahd*). Baha'ullah's heralding of the 'coming of the New Era' (*ẓuhūr-i dawr-i badīʿ*) created a sense of messianic urgency in the minds of underprivileged Jews seeking salvation and escape from their persecuted past. The Baha'i Faith had elements of a modern religion: its universalistic outlook was inclusive of all races and ethnic groups; its emphasis on 'Progressive Revelation' gave believers much latitude to accept the validity of Islam and Christianity without having to deny their belief in Judaism; its deep indigenous roots tapped into cultural reservoirs shared by Iranian Jews; and it was in harmony with a more Iranian identity.

As such, conversion can be seen as a reconciliation of the new faith with the fundamentals of deeply held Jewish convictions. The Jewish belief system was now seen in a new light, through the rejection of what were believed to be extraneous traditions and 'superstitions' that had developed over the centuries under the dominance of clerical authority. This purist view, which depreciated the rabbinic tradition and instead upheld the Torah as the primordial source of religious inspiration, had deep roots among Iranian Jews, perhaps through the influence of the medieval, anti-rabbinic Karaite movement which rejected the authority of Talmudic law as being unchanging and relied instead on a Shiʿi-style interpretation of the Torah by living experts.[16]

However, the break with rabbinic tradition was more extensively developed in Baha'i texts that reintroduced the old Perso-Shiʿi notion of the renewal of the age and the coming of the 'New Era' with the advent of the new 'manifestation'. The non-literal and hermeneutical Baha'i reading of the text, a familiar theme in the Persian mystical tradition, appealed to the emerging rationalist trends influenced by modernity. Deeply rooted in Iran's mystical and literary tradition, the Baha'i writings were an important avenue for assimilation through Persian high culture.[17]

In a variety of ways the Baha'i community reflected principles of cultural assimilation. Baha'i schools, which emphasized Persian literature and Arabic language served as an important conduit of this cultural transformation for second generation converts.[18] In addition to their religious content, Baha'i meetings (sing. *maḥfil*) conveyed what can be characterized as a Baha'i cultural language. Their meetings included group musical recitations of prayers and poems as well as readings from Baha'i texts in Persian and Arabic. The discussion of polemical arguments, grounded in the fulfilment of the prophecies of the Hebrew Bible, missionary experiences and conversion accounts equipped the participants in Baha'i debates (Sulaymānī 1976b: 485). Baha'i gatherings, which also attracted a sizeable number of Jewish migrants, offered not only hospitality but also a universal message of tolerance and equality with Baha'is of Muslim descent who would otherwise have considered the Jews 'impure' and avoided close interaction with them.

The new Baha'i image, especially at the turn of the twentieth century, was manifested in modern attire and a modern dress code, in a standardized Persian vernacular free from provincial and communal vocabulary and intonations, as well as in an emphasis on personal health and hygiene. These were in compliance with the emerging modern Iranian identity that stressed national homogeneity and an aversion to signs of a parochial past. In the early 1920s, when Iranians had to embrace a new identity by choosing a family name, many Baha'is replaced their Jewish given names and made choices that specifically denoted their religious conviction.[19]

Aside from Kashan, Hamadan, Arak and Tehran, conversion also took place on a smaller scale among Jews from other cities and towns affected by forces of change such as Kirmanshah, Malāyir and Yazd, while it was almost non-existent in other Jewish population centres, most notably Isfahan and Shiraz, where Jews experienced little social mobility. A sizeable number of Mashhad *jadīd*s, 'neo-converts' to Islam, also became Baha'is. By the turn of the century, they reportedly numbered 60 heads of households in Mashhad and many others were scattered around Khurasan and Central Asia. However, by 1930, the community shrunk in size after many converts reverted to their 'new-Muslim' identity, reportedly disappointed because they had experienced persecution instead of empowerment against their Muslim aggressors.[20] Among Mashhad converts one notable Baha'i was 'Azizullāh Jadhdhāb, a poet and scholar who corresponded with the Cambridge Orientalist, Edward G. Browne, and was appointed by 'Abdu'l-Baha to visit Count Leo Tolstoy (Jadhdhāb n.d.: 3; Sulaymānī 1976a: 451–2; Balyuzi 1985: 175–90).

Conversion patterns among women varied in various communities. In contrast to the Jewish women of Kashan who remained in their hometowns, stayed at home and were not exposed to education, the new economy or the evolving structure of the workforce, many among the Jewish women of Hamadan became dedicated Baha'is. According to Isabella Bird, a Christian British woman who visited Hamadan around 1890, 'Some of the Jewish women, who have become *Babis*, ask to have the New Testament read to them in the hope of hearing something which they may use in the propagation of their new faith' (Bird 1891: 163).[21]

The paradox of embracing a persecuted religion

Unlike earlier incidents of collective forced conversion to Islam, conversions to the Baha'i Faith were grounded in individual convictions and private experiences. As such, the Baha'i conversions present a seemingly paradoxical question of why – notwithstanding intellectual, cultural and socio-economic grounds – an already persecuted minority would choose to join a new religion that was subject to even harsher persecution, rather than seek the relative security of conversion to Islam. In an environment particularly hostile to Baha'is, where even the murder of an infidel could be justified as religiously sanctioned or permissible, becoming a Baha'i could only increase the potential for humiliation and add the risk of anti-Baha'i persecution to an already precarious existence.

The answer may be sought in Iran's deep-rooted religious and cultural characteristics. Becoming a Muslim required cutting all family ties and all connections to the Jewish community. The stigma and loss associated with conversion in exchange for tenuous, quasi-Muslim, recognition as a 'new convert' (*jadīd al-Islām*) with all of its derogatory connotations could not have been much of a bargain. Such humiliating practices towards converts may explain why many younger Jews chose to accept the risk of persecution in return for becoming equal members of a movement that saw itself as the fulfilment of the prophecies of all religions and the leading edge of modernity. It may also explain the relatively common pattern in Baha'i conversions of Jews who had become Muslims prior to becoming Baha'is.[22] This pattern can be seen as the expression of a trend among those who were seeking new alternatives but were ill at ease with the second-class designation of *jadīd al-Islām*.[23] Even devout Muslims whose ancestors converted generations ago cannot, up to this day, completely rid themselves of their Jewish past.[24]

In contrast, the Baha'is, in theory and to a reasonable extent in practice, accepted Jewish converts as equal members. The Baha'i writings called for the elimination of religious and racial prejudice and the rejection of the idea of 'ritual purity' (*nijāsat*). Nevertheless, putting the Baha'i idea of racial unity into practice was not always an easy task, as age-old anti-Jewish prejudices at times proved to be resilient. Signs of such age-old views can be traced in 'Abdu'l-Baha's repeated warnings against racial prejudice among Baha'is.[25]

Unlike Muslims, the Baha'is at least initially tolerated fluid or flexible religious identities. The adoption of a Baha'i identity did not necessitate abandoning deep-rooted social ties involving many kinship, marriage and business relationships. Most Jewish converts continued to attend Sabbath services and observe the rituals of Yom Kippur. According to one account, a number of converts, especially those in clerical positions, together with their numerous 'followers', reclaimed their Jewish identities (Amanat 2006: 214–15). Intermarriage between Baha'i families of divergent backgrounds did not occur in Kashan until around 1929, although it gradually became common.[26] For a short while, in order to raise funds for the newly established Baha'i school in Kashan, Jewish Baha'is even ran a kosher butchery in competition with the one run by the rabbis (Amanat 1998: 36–8).

In Tehran, Jewish Baha'is had separate Baha'i Spiritual Assemblies for some years before 'Abdu'l-Baha put an end to the practice. As late as 1903, the 'Spiritual Assembly of Israelites of Tehran' expressed their solidarity with the American believers by quoting biblical passages as proof of their new religious conviction in a letter addressed to the 'Christian Baha'is of Chicago'.[27] Baha'i tolerance of dual identities allowed for a wide range of believers and sympathizers, ranging from ardent propagandists and active community leaders to those who, in line with the Shi'i practice of dissimulation of faith (*taqiyya*) and esoteric (*bāṭinī*) identity, remained discreet about their faith and maintained only distant ties to the community of believers.

Early Jewish converts

Even though most conversions to the Baha'i Faith among Jews took place during the ministry of 'Abdu'l-Baha (1892–1922), their earliest encounter with the new religion goes back to the early years of the Babi movement. In 1847 the notable female Babi leader Ṭāhira Qurrat al-'Ayn stayed shortly at the house of the Jewish physician Elezar (Lāla-zār) (d. 1881) in Hamadan before his family expressed concerns over possible trouble, including anti-Jewish riots sparked by the dangers of a rebellious Muslim woman being associated with a Jewish family.[28] Although Elezar never openly confessed his belief, his Babi sympathies or secret beliefs later found expression in at least one of his open-minded associates.

The exact circumstances of many early conversions to the Baha'i Faith can not be determined with certainty. The earliest known Jewish Babi convert in Tehran, according to Baha'i sources, is a physician whose name, Ḥakīm Masīḥ (Mashiah=Christ), may suggest an earlier conversion to

Christianity or Islam.[29] Originally from Khvānsar, he first became a Babi sympathizer in 1848 when he attended Ṭāhira's debates with Shi'i scholars in Baghdad. In 1861 he openly confessed his Babi beliefs after he came into contact with the Babi and later Baha'i leader Mulla Ṣādiq Muqaddas Khurāsānī while attending to the latter's sick child (Ibn-i Aṣdaq) in a Tehran prison. His conversion demonstrates an early universalistic view, at least by some Babi leaders, of the Babi mission going beyond Islamic confines.[30]

The prominent physician Ḥakīm Āqā Jān (d. 1298/1881) is known to be the first believer of Jewish descent in Hamadan (Ḥāfiẓī n.d.: 21). Āqā Jān was reportedly first attracted to Babis and Baha'is in 1877 when he was invited to treat a patient in the Narāqī household, a faction of the prominent *'ulama* and merchant family from Narāq near Kashan, who had moved to Hamadan after becoming Babis. According to these accounts, the young Ḥakīm Āqā Jān was impressed by the family's expression of respect towards him, their disregard for laws of purity and their willingness to share food with him. The family's sympathetic attitude did not change even after Āqā Jān gave their patient the wrong medication. Though medical mishaps were more common in the traditional setting, a case of medical malpractice would nevertheless have created much risk for a Jewish physician.[31] Moved by the Narāqīs' lenience and tolerance, Āqā Jān reportedly enquired about their beliefs, a process which resulted in his eventual acceptance of the Babi-Baha'i message.

The new message soon spread through family networks and Ḥakīm Āqā Jān's closely connected cousin Rahamim, an influential physician later known as Raḥīm Khān Hāfiẓ al-Ṣiḥḥa (1844–1942), became an active Baha'i and later, a community leader. His father Elyahu was an influential self-made physician with an uncommon knowledge of Persian (in addition to Judeo-Persian) and was a protégé of the aforementioned early Babi sympathizer, Elezar.

Āqā Jān's other cousin Āqā Ḥayyim Lāla-zār, a watchmaker 'of meagre means', also became a Baha'i but soon recanted his conviction and became a Christian missionary.[32] Such identity swings were not unusual as the early spread of the Baha'i message in Hamadan in the late 1870s and 80s was intertwined with the spread of Christianity which shared the message of the coming of a promised *Mashiah*. Many Jewish converts held multiple identities; they attended Sunday church ceremonies and sent their children to the short-lived American Presbyterian mission school before it was closed down by Qajar authorities.[33]

Aside from genuine conviction, such double identities were, according to a Baha'i source, meant to protect the new converts against the wrath of the authorities who still considered Babis as dangerous agitators and were particularly hostile towards them (Ḥāfiẓī n.d.: 23–4). However, expectations of being protected did not last long in the face of the governor's indiscriminately abusive attitude towards non-Muslims. Unimpressed by the foreign missionaries' appeals and telegraphs to foreign embassies, the cash-strapped or corrupt local governor imprisoned and bastinadoed the new Christians and demanded heavy fines before releasing them.[34]

Within two years (1877–79), with the help of other itinerate Baha'i propagators (*sing-muballigh*) of the Baha'i message – Āqā Jān and Raḥīm Khān were able to attract some fifty Jews to the nascent community in Hamadan. According to one convert's account, their arguments, a reflection of the still developing Baha'i message, were focused on challenging the bases of rabbinic tradition and the necessity of the coming of the *Mashiah* by arguing that fundamental laws of the Torah, such as the rite of sacrifice, could not be observed in the absence of the Jerusalem temple (Amanat 2006: 184–6).

Yet, much of the Baha'is initial success seems to have been based on the earlier work of the Christian mission. The missionaries' apparent decline in membership may be explained by the Baha'is' acceptance of Islam, thereby allowing the converts to adopt an Islamic identity without having to repudiate their families and community ties. A break with the Christian community came about gradually but was finalized in 1887 when the prominent Baha'i scholar, Abū'l-Faḍl Gulpāygānī arrived in Hamadan and debated with Christian leaders. It was through similar debates that Gulpāygānī helped articulate the Baha'i message (Ḥāfiẓī n.d.: 28).[35]

Beginning in the late 1870s and 1880s, the Baha'i Faith spread from Hamadan, a centre of early Jewish conversion, to a number of other Jewish communities including Kashan and Tehran. In an attempt to spread the Baha'i message, the two early Jewish converts from Hamadan, Ḥakīm Āqā Jān and Ḥāfiẓ al-Ṣiḥḥa travelled to Tehran and met with Ḥakīm Nūr Mahmūd, a highly educated and influential Jewish physician in Tehran and a secret convert to Islam. Though the latter never openly confessed his Baha'i belief, a number of his relatives became sympathizers and prominent Baha'is.[36]

Among Nūr Maḥmūd's relatives, his notable nephew and son-in-law, the influential physician Mīrzā Khalīl ('Aqiba), reflects the complexities of identity among many early believers. Mīrzā Khalīl's case was complicated by a variety of financial (family inheritance) and personal issues. When some time in the 1880s his proposed marriage to Nūr Maḥmūd's daughter, Khānum, faced opposition from her family, the two took sanctuary (*bast*) in the royal stable, converted to Islam and consecutively performed Jewish and Muslim marriage ceremonies. Later, around 1897, Kahlīl served in one of Tehran's first Baha'i Assemblies while a few years later, in 1906, he was an unsuccessful candidate to become the Jewish representative to Iran's first Constitutional Assembly (*majlis*). His is a fascinating picture of someone negotiating a labyrinth of identities at a time of emerging modernity. His manoeuvring was facilitated by the family's position of privilege but was also cluttered by financial and family inheritance disputes.[37]

Yet, not all early believers came from privileged backgrounds. An early Baha'i, the enigmatic Ḥājjī Elyahu Kāshānī, was another eccentric who is described as 'the most skilful and accomplished' professional thief in Kashan before his conversion. As an early Baha'i, he received a tablet from Baha'ullah encouraging him in his services as a Baha'i teacher. When he travelled to Palestine to meet Baha'ullah, according to one source, he admitted to 'Abdu'l-Baha that he was devoid of any useful skills, as in his previous life he had been but a common thief. Upon 'Abdu'l-Baha's recommendation, he served for a while as a guide to some European travellers who had come to visit Baha'ullah. Yet Ḥājjī Elyahu's demands (including monetary ones) on other Baha'is and Baha'i leaders, supposedly for his services as an itinerant Baha'i advocate, present an unconventional image of a convert whose moral transformation had definite limits. He later moved to Egypt where, in his enigmatic way, he dissolved into oblivion and not much more is known about him.[38]

Despite his weaknesses, Ḥājjī Elyahu was a rather successful Baha'i propagator. It appears that in the 1880s and '90s many Jewish converts went through a two-tier conversion process. Teachers such as Ḥājjī Elyahu mainly argued the validity of Christ and left the next stage of conversion to other Baha'i teachers more familiar with Islamic arguments. As a result of his activities, Ḥājjī Elyahu suffered much hardship in the hands of Tehran's Jewish traditionalists. He was even considered 'ritually impure' (*nesekh*) by other Jews. On one occasion around 1894, a religious debate with Jewish contenders led to a dispute and a subsequent gang attack 'with the intention of killing him'.[39] Other Baha'is such as the above-mentioned Mīrzā Khalīl who held Baha'i debates in his house were forced to move out of the Tehran's Jewish quarter reportedly due to harassment and consideration for safety ('Azīzī 1994: 34).

Among those influenced by Ḥājjī Elyahu's message was a certain Isḥāq later named 'Azīzullāh (1873–1950), son of Mulla Daniel, a literate Jewish peddler of meagre means from Tehran. As a traditionalist, Mulla Daniel even opposed the Alliance school for teaching the students non-Jewish material ('Azīzī 1994: 38). Isḥāq dreaded his family's poverty, his low social status, the miserable and unsanitary conditions of the Jewish ghetto and the humiliation the Jews suffered as the 'ritually impure'. He became a tailor, an unconventional choice for Jews of his time yet a conscious first step toward social mobility ('Azīzī 1994: 19–27). His experiment with a new religious identity as a 'semi-Baha'i' who frequented Tehran's Sufi circles known for their tolerance of non-Muslims, finally led to full acceptance of the optimistic Baha'i message which prophesized a future of advancement and progress for the Jews ('Azīzī 1994: 49, 54).

Isḥāq's final break with the Jewish community came not over religious disagreements but through a more potent symbolic change in his behaviour. His professional success and his association with the Baha'is, including some from more privileged groups, had made him more mindful of his attire and hygiene. What was truly objectionable to traditionalist Jews and led to his eventual estrangement from the Jewish community was his refusal to conform to the customary practice of shaving his head and growing facial hair. Not shaving one's head was sanctioned by Baha'ullah but was also a statement of commitment to modernity ('Azīzī 1994: 36–7).[40]

Unlike Hamadan where the Baha'i message experienced an initial rapid growth in the 1880s and 1890s, relatively fewer Jews joined the Baha'i Faith in Tehran. This may in part be explained by the activities of the Presbyterian mission in Hamadan which prepared the ground – especially among younger Jews – by responding to their messianic tendencies, a primordial trend among Iranian Jews. Aside from their successful institutions, including schools and a hospital, which attracted a number of traditional physicians, the success of the Christian, and to a larger extent the Baha'i message may be in part attributed to Hamadan's social environment.

Hamadan's booming economy, a product of the growing Baghdad trade in the last quarter of the nineteenth century, attracted a wide variety of immigrants from other Jewish communities throughout Iran as well as a community of affluent and Westernized Iraqi Jews.[41] Immigration entailed new occupations and work environments and a departure from traditional bonds guarded by ancient communities. More significantly, immigration meant a breakdown of the traditional Jewish mentality guarded by the Jewish quarter (*maḥalla*). Unlike in Tehran and Kashan, Jews in Hamadan were less restricted in their choice of neighbourhood and were more dispersed throughout the city. This meant less communal control and a more cosmopolitan identity.

Opposition and independence

The dramatic success of the two Baha'i physicians in Hamadan in the late 1870s led to tensions within the Jewish community. Some of these tensions may be traced to old professional rivalries among Hamadan physicians spanning over generations. Beginning in the mid-nineteenth century, a new group of physicians, many with knowledge of Persian – and many of whom later became Christians and Baha'is – challenged more traditional colleagues who claimed an inherited right to the profession.[42] Divisions and estrangements, even within extended families, were not limited to Baha'i conversions. One Jewish enthusiast who formally complained to the governor against his own relative who was a Christian convert reportedly went as far as threatening, 'We must re-crucify Christ over again' (Ḥāfiẓī n.d.: 28).

Tension with the Baha'i converts of Hamadan manifested itself early on in 1877, when Jewish leaders complained to the governor and accused one of the converts, a certain Ḥājjī Yari (d. 1918–19), of offending the Jews by openly criticizing their beliefs and customs as superstitions. This early opposition points to older tensions within the community, which probably predated the Baha'is' conversions. A crowd of Jews gathered in the town's main square and grew to a thousand after urban crowds, ready to engage in collective behaviour, joined them. As the main ingredients for an anti-Babi riot were forming, the Baha'is became particularly alarmed when Jewish leaders rejected their offer to resolve their internal differences without involving the Muslims. Perhaps as a sign of desperation, Rahīm Khān Ḥāfiẓ al-Ṣiḥḥa tried to defuse the situation by turning the tables against the vulnerable contenders and repeated a familiar charge about bloodthirstiness, imported from Europe, used as liable against the Jewish community.[43] Once the contenders felt the excitement within the pliant crowds, they feared for their own security and dispersed while street fighting, reminiscent of Babi skirmishes, ensued. The governor then ordered the party's elders to debate the issue but took offence in the allegation that the new converts had violated Jewish law by 'eating the [non-Kosher] bazaar food'. The affair came to an end with the usual payment of a fine, supposedly for sacrilege (Ishrāq-Khāvarī 2004: 44–6; Ḥāfiẓī n.d.: 26–8).

Later, in 1881, tensions with the Jews of Hamadan relating to continuing Baha'i conversions resulted in persecution. In a move similar to the earlier measures against converts to Christianity, the governor, responding to concerns voiced by Jewish leaders, arrested a number of Baha'is only to release them upon payment of a fine.[44] Other repeated complaints to the authorities, mostly relating to the Baha'is' consumption of non-Kosher food had familiar connotations with Muslim laws of impurity and proved offensive to Muslim authorities. In one instance in 1890, in front of the Hamadan town council, the Jews insisted on severing all ties with Baha'is unless they conformed to all Jewish practices. The Baha'is responded by accusing the rabbis of obstructing the laws of the Torah and making innovations contrary to the Torah (Ishrāq-Khāvarī 2004: 78–9).[45]

The Jewish leaders' insistence on what many saw as a narrow definition of religion based on strict observance of details of Jewish ritualistic practices may be an indication of why so many Jews were willing to endure stigmatization and persecution in return for a new identity. The traditionalist rabbis who saw their role as protectors of Jewish traditions could not tolerate such a break and repeatedly defined Baha'is as being outside of the acceptable boundaries of Judaism. On the occasion of the death of Ḥakīm Āqā Jān in 1880, the Jewish leaders at first disallowed his burial in the Jewish cemetery only to be dissuaded by 'the wealthy *(a'yān)* among the Baha'is' (Ishrāq-Khāvarī 2004: 47).

Yet the enforcement of Jewish laws varied according to the religious climate and to personal relationships. On one occasion, the governor of Hamadan ignored the Jewish elders' complaints relating to breaking the laws of Sabbath.[46] In more conservative Kashan, where Jewish leaders were under pressure by the Shi'i *'ulama* to fully enforce Jewish law or accept conversion to Islam, similar charges had more serious consequences.[47] The outspoken Mulla Mūsā, who publicly proclaimed the coming of the promised saviour, was the first convert in Kashan to publicly defy Jewish law by opening his shop on the Sabbath. The Jewish elders demanded a punishment that included the death sentence in accordance with the law of the Torah.[48] Mulla Mūsā was arrested, imprisoned and beaten, but eventually released upon the intercession of his relatives with the condition that he would leave Kashan. He moved to Lahijan where he was murdered in 1905, apparently by an anti-Baha'i gang. He is considered to be the first Jewish convert who paid with his life for openly advocating his beliefs (Māzandarānī 1976: 713–15; Amanat 1988: 70).[49]

By the turn of the century, the traditionalist rabbis at times found a new, more modern ally in their opposition to Baha'i conversions. Concerned with Baha'i success in Hamadan, an agent of Alliance Israelite Universelle, an organization dedicated to promotion of the status and education of less privileged Jews, tried to discourage Jews from attending – and even tried to disband – Baha'i gatherings by putting pressure on the local authorities and even demanded that his superiors in Tehran pressure the governor of Hamadan to administer corporal punishment (the bastinado) to the new converts. He also tried, without much success, to stop the rabbis from presiding over marriages involving new converts.[50] Some Baha'i gatherings held in Sanandaj in Kurdistan on Saturday afternoons, for example, attracted Jewish enthusiasts and thus became a cause for concern for the agents of the Alliance.[51]

In some ways, opposition from the traditionalist leaders helped define the Baha'is as a separate community with their own distinct institutions. By 1911, Baha'is who were denied access to Muslim and Jewish cemeteries took steps towards establishing their own cemetery and bathhouse (Ishrāq-Khāvarī 2004: 137–40).[52] In 1901, Baha'i students temporarily boycotted the Alliance school after school officials put them under pressure to closely observe traditional Jewish practices. This incident may be seen as a starting point for the formation of the Ta'īd boys' school in 1907 and the Mawhibat girls' school in 1910. The two schools later served as the community's beacons of modernity and independence (Ishrāq-Khāvarī 2004: 105, 116–25, 128).[53]

Yet, despite the traditionalists' opposition, many Jews continued to convert, become recognized Baha'is and were elected to Baha'i assemblies (sing. *maḥfil-i rawḥānī*). As propagators, they helped introduce the Baha'i Faith to others, even including some members of the *'ulama*. A notable example was a member of a leading *'ulama* family of Hamadan and later a leading Baha'i scholar and teacher, Ḥājjī Sayyid Aḥmad Ṣadr al-'Ulamā, entitled by 'Abdu'l-Baha as Ṣadr al-Ṣudūr (1868–1907) who learned about the Baha'i Faith around 1898 through his Jewish-Baha'i physician (Rastigār 1948: 21–8; Māzandarānī 1976: 480–1). As converts, their contribution to scholarship was limited to a few treatises on prophecies and polemical discourse. However, as later generations became more assimilated, their contribution to scholarship became more significant.[54]

External opposition notwithstanding, the daunting changes in the internal dynamics of the Baha'i community played a critical role in defining the boundaries of Baha'i identity. Beginning in the 1930s, under the leadership of Shoghi Effendi, the Guardian of the Baha'i Faith (1922–1957), multiple identities and loose associations, which had been key elements in the growth of the movement, were challenged by an increasingly well-defined and institutionalized form of religious identity. This process of consolidation, which was influenced by prevailing Western trends, made it more difficult to sustain multiple religious identities and produced a more tightly-knit Baha'i community in which membership in other religious communities and attendance at mosque and synagogue services were no longer considered normal.[55] This crucial transition in the development of Iran's Baha'i community was accompanied by an equally significant process of institutionalization that placed elected administrative bodies much more firmly in control of religious and daily life. Through these institutions, new rules for formal 'enrolment' (*tasjīl*) were established and Baha'i laws such as those relating to marriage, the prohibition against working on Baha'i holidays and even occasional temporary travel restrictions were more vigorously enforced.[56] This trend towards institutionalization coincided with and may in part explain the decline in the rate of growth of the Iranian Baha'i community by the 1950s.[57]

Baha'i conversions were also affected by developments within the Jewish community. Iran's first Zionist committee was formed in Hamadan in 1912, probably in reaction to the Baha'is' overwhelming success at converting Jews there (Netzer 1980: 225). Zionism and later the establishment of the state of Israel in 1948 instilled a new sense of self-confidence in Iran's Jewish community and provided a vital psychological boost to this distressed community. Many Persian Jews now saw the successes of their coreligionists in the Promised Land as a fulfilment of their messianic aspirations and an end to their miseries as an impoverished and disadvantaged minority. Iran's Jewish community gradually adopted a more westernized version of Judaism, less preoccupied with issues of messianic expectation and more engaged with Zionism.

A large number of those who chose to confirm their belief in the Baha'i Faith made important contributions to the Baha'i community. Beginning in the 1920s, many Jewish converts experienced substantial social mobility and economic enhancement, often using community networking in what amounted to a form of 'ethnic economy'. Some even sought and received guidance from 'Abdu'l-Baha in starting their business.[58] Others were philanthropists and became known as major donors to the Baha'i community.[59]

A number of mostly second-generation Baha'is benefited from the higher level of education they received in modern (including Baha'i) schools and joined the growing educated middle class of the Pahlavi period. Many advanced in business and as professionals. One leading Baha'i and highly respected professor of medicine, Manūchihr Ḥakīm (1910–81), was murdered in his Tehran office, ostensibly for his Baha'i activities.[60] Many more used their education to become successful professional entrepreneurs.[61]

Among the converts' descendants, a few became leading innovators and industrialists, important agents of modernity and major contributors to Iran's economy and industry. One notable innovator and industrialist, Khalīl Arjumand (d. 1944), an engineering professor, founded Arj industries (1937) and was responsible for introducing the manufacturing of a number of vital industrial products to Iran. Ḥabīb Thābit was a well-known industrialist and mega entrepreneur whose ventures included the establishment of Iran's first television stations (1959).[62]

Conclusion

The conversion of a substantial number of Jews to a persecuted minority religion was a unique phenomenon in Islamic Iran, if not the entire Muslim world. The converts added colour to an already diverse community of followers that mostly consisted of the disadvantaged but also including the educated elite, radical revolutionaries and eccentrics. Within a relatively short time period, the Baha'i Faith evolved from a popular messianic anti-establishment movement to an institutionalized faith. The experience of the converts also included elements of change and continuity. Those from within the isolated and deprived Jewish community who joined the Baha'i Faith maintained patterns of economic activity in line with their Jewish relatives. As they became more assimilated and adopted a more Iranian identity, they also tended to be more educated and their social mobility was geared towards professional patterns.[63]

Today, decades after the wave of emigration of non-Muslims following the 1979 Islamic Revolution, Iran's diverse cultural heritage, once a vital aspect of its survival, is again under the threat of cultural conformity. The hegemony of Islamic legalistic tradition resists engagement with other religious or secular traditions. Even alternative readings of Islam, more engaged with modernity, are often considered non-Islamic. The Islamic Republic's efforts to showcase the religious freedoms of 'recognized' minorities are contradicted by its treatment of the Baha'is who have become a silenced 'other' belonging to a forbidden memory. A vital question for Iran's future might be whether it is able to rejuvenate within itself the sense of cultural diversity that historically has enhanced its culture.

Notes

1 This study is indebted to the work of my late father Mousa Amanat without whose tireless efforts in collecting historical material and composing a narrative,

this study would not have been possible. The editors are grateful to Heather Empey for her help in editing this chapter.

2 For details of life and times of Rayḥān Rayḥānī including a translation of his memoirs, see Amanat 2006: 189.

3 Neumark's estimate of the number of Babi/Baha'is is most likely an exaggeration. Only a few families of Gulpāygān Jewish Baha'is can be traced in Baha'i sources. One can only speculate that they may have retracted their Baha'i identity. See also Fischel 1934: 54.

4 See also Brawer 1944–46: 146–53, cited in Cohen 1973: 162. I am indebted to Daniel Tsadik for translating selected passages from Hebrew.

5 For list of Jewish Baha'i families in Kashan and Hamadan, see Amanat 1988 and 2000. For details on Kashan's Jewish population, see Yerushalaymi 1985. For Hamadan's Jewish population, see Brawer 1937–8: 22 and the sources cited in Sarshar 2003.

6 Susan Maneck's work, one of the first studies of the subject, cites historical accidents in explaining Baha'i conversions. In her view, Hamadan's increasing economic prosperity and social mobility, arguably an important motive for conversion, is viewed as evidence to refute conventional arguments citing the poverty and ignorance of the Jews as factors in their conversion.

7 For general surveys on the history of Jews in Iran, see Fischel 1937, Moreen 2000 and Spector 1975.

8 For an introductory survey of the subject, see Foltz 2004.

9 A close reading of studies of Persian music, such as that of Ruḥullāh Khāliqī (1956), reveals many references to Jewish musicians and instructors.

10 These first examples of modern Persian, written in Hebrew script, date back to the eighth and ninth centuries and were discovered in north-western China.

11 Persia is the only nation referred to favourably in the Hebrew Bible and Cyrus the Great is referred to as 'the anointed one' (the Messiah). With the exception of periods during Sasanian rule, Jews enjoyed relative tolerance in pre-Islamic Iran. At least when compared to medieval Europe, the Jews under Islamic rule were favoured more positively. During the Īlkhānid period, they even rose to positions of political prominence.

12 For the Mashhad conversions, see Levy 1998, Patai 1997: 51–64, Pīrnaẓar 2001 and Fischel 1949. For an alternative view of the circumstances leading to anti-Jewish riots, see Amanat 2006: 69–91.

13 On famines, see Okazaki 1986. For the state of the economy, including the adverse effects of European influence, see Issawi 1971: 70–151 and 258–309. For treatments of Iran's social and political conditions in the mid-nineteenth century, see Cole 1998: introduction, and Amanat 2004.

14 For details about multiple conversions (including to the Baha'i Faith) among Ḥakīm Hārūn's family, his son – the aforementioned Ḥakīm Nūr-Maḥmud – and other family members, see Amanat 2006: 135n and 146–51. For a study of Baha'i debates with Christian missionaries, see Momen 1982.

15 This practice is reported to have taken place in the latter part of the nineteenth century.

16 On the Karaites see *Encyclopaedia Judaica*, s.v. 'Karaites' and 'Persia' and Netzer 1997. For a collection of Islamic Karaite writings, see Nemoy 1952. For the influence of the Karaites in Kashan through the twentieth century and in Baha'i conversions, see Amanat 1998.

17 For a study of the influences of Persian literature on Baha'i writings, see Lewis 2002.

18 As the leading edge of modern education in Iran, Baha'i schools (including girls' schools) were established in a number of Baha'i population centres in the early

1900s, mostly through local initiatives and with encouragement from 'Abdu'l-Baha. See Momen's chapter in this volume. See also Thābit 1997. Tehran's first official 'modern' school was opened in 1898 by the reformist educator Ḥājjī Mīrzā Ḥasan Rushdiyya, under the supervision of the Anjuman-i Ma'ārif, see *Encyclopaedia Iranica*, s.v. 'Anjoman-e Ma'aref'. See also Ringer 2001.

19 Some Jewish converts to the Baha'i Faith did change their given names, e.g. Mithāqullāh for Elyas, Khalīl for 'Aqiba and Rayḥān for Ruben.

20 For details of Mashhad Muslim convert Baha'is including a list of many community members, see Foadi-Bushrū'ī 1931.

21 I am grateful to Daniel Tsadik for bringing this source to my attention.

22 One indication of the stigma attached to conversion may be observed in the Jews of Mashhad who nominally converted to Islam in 1839 but reverted to Judaism in the first half of the twentieth century. To this day, they generally do not intermarry with Jews from other communities, even after emigrating outside Iran (Patai 1997: 104).

23 For another example of conversion to Islam involving a financial dispute and leading in turn to a Baha'i conversion, see Iqrari 2004: 22.

24 A contemporary example of the stigmatization of a Muslim with alleged Jewish ancestry is the case of the current opposition leader 'Abbās Amīr-Intiẓām who, among other 'accusations', has had his faith to Islam questioned due to his alleged Jewish family connections going back to 1839, a 'charge' he has denied. See Amir-Intiẓām (n.d.). It is worth noting that the Registry Code of the Islamic Republic of Iran recognizes the title *jadīd al-Islām* as an official category. I am indebted to Jalāl Jalālī and Dr. Khūbrū-Pāk respectively for bringing these facts to my attention.

25 For one such letter by 'Abdu'l-Baha, see Ishraq-Khavari (n.d.).

26 The first two known cases of marriage between Baha'is of Muslim and Jewish backgrounds in Kashan (one involving Rayḥānī's daughter) took place around 1929. Correspondence with Ms. Bāhira Rastigār, 11 January 2005.

27 Letter dated 2 June 1903 in *Najm-i Bākhtar (Star of the West)*. I am grateful to Dr. Fereydun Vahman for pointing out this source to me.

28 Elezar moved to Baghdad, where he died from an alcohol overdose (Ḥāfiẓī n.d.: 12 and 36). For details of Ṭāhira's stay in Hamadan, see Ishrāq-Khāvarī 2004: 28–30 and Amanat 1989: 315.

29 The subtle difference between Mashiah, a rather common choice of name among Iranian Jews and Masīḥ (Christ), together with the physician's interest in Islamic concerns and Babi debates, points to an unconventional believer or perhaps a convert to Christianity or Islam.

30 For details of Ḥakīm Masīḥ's conversion, see an account by Mīrzā 'Alī-Muḥammad Ibn-i Asdaq, son of Mulla Ṣādiq Muqaddas, in Rafati 2005: 395. See also Balyuzi 1985: 18. Some members of Ḥakīm Masīḥ's family became committed Baha'is and his grandson, Luṭfullāh Ḥakīm, was elected to the Universal House of Justice in 1963.

31 Ḥakīm Āqā Jān must have been mindful of such risks, as his own maternal grandfather, Mūsā, died from injuries after being beaten by the family members of a Muslim patient after fellow competing Jewish physicians ruled that the patient's death was due to medical malpractice (Hafizi n.d.: 5–6).

32 Ḥāfiẓī (n.d.: 2) reports his cousin's salary from the Presbyterian mission as being three to four *tūmāns* per month.

33 Ḥāfiẓī (n.d.: 22–3) reports that by 1878, 'a small group of Jews were attracted first in the name of Christianity but in reality to the cause of Baha'u'llah'. Some missionaries went so far as to demand that prospective members denounce the

Baha'i Faith before being accepted to the congregation. See Richards as cited in Maneck 1991.

34 Ḥāfiẓī (n.d.: 25) reports fines of ten *tūmāns* per person being imposed on the prisoners. At least some Jews were extremely hostile to Christian conversions.

35 Ḥāfiẓī's telescoped narrative of the process of breaking with the Christian community minimizes its significance. A more reliable account by Abū'l-Faḍl Gulpāygānī dates the final break to 1887, some ten years after the first Baha'i conversions. See Mihrābkhānī 1975: 130. For Gulpāygānī's articulation of the Baha'i debate, see Gulpāygānī 1898.

36 Nūr Maḥmūd's son Ayyūb visited 'Abdu'l-Baha who sent him a number of tablets. Ayyūb was an accomplished calligrapher, and he transcribed a number of Baha'i writings into works of art. The author has seen some of this artwork which is in the possession of his descendants. For details on Nūr Maḥmūd and his family, see Amanat 2006: 134–6.

37 For a detailed discussion of the complexities of conversion, with all its financial and social dimensions, over the generations in Nūr Maḥmūd's family, see Amanat 2006: 145–50.

38 For details of Ḥājjī Elyahu's life, including his medical problems and financial demands on other Baha'is, see Amanat 2006: 201–5. According to Rayḥānī, his sons remained active Baha'is.

39 For an account of Hajji Elyahu's activities and persecution in Tehran at the hands of other Jews, see 'Azīzī 1994: 28–9. Baha'ullah's tablet addressed to Ḥājjī Elyahu also appears in 'Azīzī 1994: 27a.

40 On another occasion in 1887, the Jewish leaders of Hamadan, offended that the Baha'i men were growing their hair, used physical force to cut it. See Ishrāq-Khāvarī 2004: 71.

41 For an excellent study of Jews in the Qajar period with particular emphasis on Hamadan, see Sahim 2005. For a history of Iraqi Jews in Iran, see Arleen Dallalfar's chapter in *Esther's Children.*

42 For an account of rivalries between Raḥīm Khān's father, Ḥakīm Elyahu, and the family of Hamadan physicians who had an exclusive claim to the profession, see Ḥāfiẓī n.d.: 15.

43 The myth of Jews killing Gentile children to use their blood to make matzos has deep roots in medieval Europe and may have been introduced to Iran by sixteenth-century Christian missionaries.

44 This incident took place on 14 March 1881, see Ishrāq-Khāvarī 2004: 140.

45 The sources do not specify which laws Baha'is (or Christians) defied other than the Kosher and Sabbath observances.

46 Ḥājjī Yari's defiance of the Sabbath in Hamadan in 1380/1890–1 caused considerable uproar among the Jewish leaders who complained to the governor. However, in a dramatic turn of events and for unexplained reasons, the governor 'Izz al-Dawla instead ordered the beating of the Jewish claimants. See Ishrāq-Khāvarī 2004: 44–6.

47 'Either convert to Islam or obey your own clergy', is how Rayḥānī reports the Shi'i *'ulama* drew the line with the Jewish rabbis. See Amanat 2006: 251.

48 Although there are numerous provisions for capital punishment in the Torah, they are distinctly rare in the Talmud, even for those who deliberately commit murder. See Moreen 1987: 72ff.

49 No exact date is given in the sources for the Sabbath controversy in Kashan. One can only speculate that it took place around the turn of the century.

50 See Bassan to President, 'Babism' (5 December 1901), Archive of the Alliance Israelite Universelle, Paris.

51 The Sabbath ritual was conducted on Friday evenings and Saturday mornings, leaving the afternoon for leisure.
52 The Baha'i cemetery first became functional in 1915–6, see Ishrāq-Khāvarī 2004: 148.
53 For a detailed list of Baha'i schools founded in the years immediately after the Constitutional Revolution, see Momen's chapter in this volume.
54 For an example of Jewish-Baha'i debate written by a convert, see Arjumand 1982. Since this study is not concerned with contemporary personalities, the issue of Jewish-Baha'is' contributions to the field of scholarship would have to be dealt with in a separate study.
55 Shoghi Effendi discouraged Baha'is from attending non-Baha'i religious ceremonies such as *rawḍa-khvānī*. See Ishrāq-Khāvarī 1960: 14.
56 Baha'i marriage laws include requirements for the consent of both parties as well as their parents, the attainment of the minimum legal age of 15, the limitation of the engagement period to 95 days and the performance of the Baha'i ceremony in the presence of two lay witnesses. See Ishrāq-Khāvarī 1980: 159–88. The Baha'i holidays during which work must be suspended consist of nine days which include the commemoration of festivals such as Nawrūz (21 March) and the first, ninth and twelfth days of Riḍvān (21 and 29 April, and 2 May), as well as the commemoration of the birth, proclamation and martyrdom of the Bab (20 October, 23 May and 9 July, respectively) and of the birth and passing of Baha'ullah (12 November and 29 May). Travel restrictions included a prohibition for Iranian Baha'is to travel to the U.S. beginning in the mid-1940s through the mid-1950s.
57 For a survey of transitions in the Baha'i community, see Smith 1987.
58 In a visit to Palestine around 1920, Isḥāq Anvar (d. 1975), a Jewish convert to the Baha'i Faith from Hamadan, asked for 'Abdu'l-Baha's guidance to improve his family's dire economic condition. He was advised to move to Tehran where using Baha'i contacts, he built a successful business distributing modern medicines. See his autobiography in the Mousa Amanat archives.
59 'Abd al-Mīthāq Mīthāqiyya (1893–1981), a nephew of the aforementioned Ḥakīm Nūr Maḥmūd, is known to have donated most of his fortune, which he earned in Tehran's post-World War II real estate market, to religious and philanthropic causes including a major Tehran hospital in his name in 1945 and a nursing school. See his autobiography in the Mousa Amanat archives. Also see article in this volume by Fazel and Foadi.
60 Manūchihr Ḥakīm was a descendant of the aforementioned Ḥakīm Masīḥ. For more details on his life and services, see Hakim-Samandari 1982.
61 For account of one such Baha'i physician and medical entrepreneur, see Iqrārī 2004.
62 Both Khalīl Arjumand and Ḥabīb Thābit were descendants of the aforementioned ambitious physician Mīrzā Khalīl. See Arjumand 2002: 38–48 and 62–6. See also Thābit 1993.
63 In a survey of Iranian immigrants to Los Angeles based on the 1980 Census data, Baha'is ranked second in education level after Muslims (many Muslims were foreign students who chose to stay in the US). See Borzorgmehr 1993: 73.

Bibliography

Amanat, A. (1989) *Resurrection and Renewal: The Making of the Babi Movement in Iran, 1844–1850*, Ithaca, NY: Cornell University Press.

—— (2004) 'Introduction', in C.J. Wills, *In the Land of the Lion and Sun*, Costa Mesa: Mazda Publishers.

Amanat, Mehrdad. (2006) 'Negotiating Identities; Iranian Jews, Muslims and Baha'is in the memoirs of Rayhan Rayhani (1859–1939)', unpublished Ph.D. thesis, University of California, Los Angeles.

Amanat, Mousa. (1988) 'Abnā'-i Khalīl-i Kāshān', unpublished manuscript.

—— (2000) 'Aḥibbā-yi Kalīmī-nijād-i Hamadān', unpublished manuscript.

Amīr-Intiẓām. A. (n.d.) *Ān sū-yi ittihām*, np: np.

Arjumand, A. (2002) *Chirāgh-i pur-furūgh*, Ontario: np.

Arjumand, M. (1982) *Gulshan-i ḥaqāyiq*, Los Angeles: Kalimat.

'Azīzī, A. (1994) *Khāṭirāt-i 'Azīzullāh 'Azīzī, yā Tāj-i vahhāj*, New Delhi: Baha'i Publishing Trust.

Balyuzi, H. (1985) *Eminent Baha'is in the Time of Baha'u'llah*, Oxford: George Ronald.

Bird, I. (1891) *Journeys in Persia and Kurdistan*, vol. 2, London: John Murray.

Bozorgmehr, M. (1993) 'Beyond Nationality: Religo-ethnic Diversity', in R. Kelley (ed.) *Irangeles, Iranians in Los Angeles*, Berkeley: University of California Press.

Brawer, A.J. (1937–8) *Mi-Parashat Mas'otay be-Paras*, Jerusalem: np.

—— (1944–46) *Avak derakhim*, Tel Aviv: 'Am 'Oved.

Cohen, H.J. (1973) *The Jews of the Middle East: 1860–1972*, New York: John Wiley & Sons.

Cole, J.R.I. (1998) *Modernity and the Millennium: the genesis of the Baha'i Faith in the nineteenth-century Middle East*, New York: Columbia University Press.

Curzon, G.N. (1892) *Persia and the Persian Question*, London: Longmans, Green, and Co.

Elwell-Sutton, L.P. (ed.) (1983) *Bibliographical Guide to Iran*, Suffolk: The Harvester Press.

Fischel, W.J. (1934) 'The Baha'i Movement and Persian Jewry', *Jewish Review*, 7: 47–55.

—— (1937) *Jews in the Economic and Political Life of Medieval Islam*, London: Royal Asiatic Society.

—— (1949) 'Secret Jews of Persia', *Commentary* 7: 28–33.

Foltz, R.C. (2004) *Spirituality in the Land of the Noble: How Iran Shaped the World's Religions*, Oxford: Oneworld.

Fu'ādī Bushrū'ī, H. (1931) 'Tārīkh-i Amrī-yi Khurāsān', unpublished manuscript, Iranian National Baha'i Archives.

Gulpāygānī, A. (1898) *Dalā'il al-Bahiyya*, Cairo: np.

Hāfiẓī, Y.K. (n.d.) 'Tārikh-i zindagānī-yi Ḥājj Yuḥannā Khān Ḥāfiẓī', photocopy of typed manuscript, Mousa Amanat Archives.

Hakim-Samandari, C. (1982) *Les Baha'is: ou victoire sur la violence*, Paris: Editions Pierre-Marcel Favre.

Iqrārī, A. (2004) *Panjāh va haft bahār*, Los Angeles. np.

Ishrāq-Khāvarī, 'A. (1960) *Mā'ida-yi Āsamānī*, Tehran: Mu'assasa-yi Millī-yi Maṭbū'āt-i Amrī.

—— (1980) *Ganjīna-yi ḥudūd va aḥkām*, New Delhi: Baha'i Publishing Trust.

—— (2004) *Tārīkh-i amrī-yi Hamadān*, V. Ra'fatī (ed.) Hofheim: Baha'i-Verlag.

Issawi, C. (ed.) (1971) *The Economic History of Iran, 1800–1914*, Chicago: University of Chicago Press.

Jadhdhāb, M.A. (n.d.) 'Tafṣīl-i fawz ba īmān-i haḍrat-i abavī', known as 'Khāṭirāt-i Jadhdhāb', photocopy of manuscript, Mousa Amanat Archive.

Khāliqī, R.A. (1956) *Sargudhasht-i mūsīqī-yi Īrān*, 2 vols, Tehran: Chāpkhāna-yi Firdawsī.

Levy, A. (1998) *The Jews of Mashhad*, Jerusalem: A. Levy.

Lewis, F. (2002) 'Scripture as Literature', in S. Fazel and J. Danesh (eds) *Reason and Revelation: New Directions in Baha'i Thought*, Los Angeles: Kalimat Press.

Loeb, L.D. (1972) 'The Jewish Musician and the Music of Fars', *Asian Music* 4: 3–14.

Maneck, S. (1991) 'The conversion of Religious Minorities to the Baha'i Faith in Iran: Some Preliminary Observations', *Journal of Baha'i Studies* 3.3: 35–48.

Matthee, R.P. (1999) *The Politics of Trade in Safavid Iran: Silk for Silver, 1600–1730*, Cambridge, UK: Cambridge University Press.

Māzandarānī, A.F. (1976) *Tārikh-i ẓuhūr al-ḥaqq*, vol. 8.2, Tehran: Mu'assasa-yi Millī-yi Maṭbū'āt-i Amrī.

Mihrābkhānī, R. (1975) *Sharḥ-i aḥvāl-i jināb-i Mīrzā Abū'l-Faḍl-i Gulpāygānī*, Tehran: MMMA.

Mīthāqiyya, 'A. (1977) 'Khulāṣa'i az khāṭirāt-i jināb-i Mīthāqiyya va namūna'i az nīkūkārī-hā-yi īshān', M.A. Fayḍī (ed.) xeroxed manuscript, Mousa Amanat archives.

Momen, M. (1982) 'Early Relations between Christian Missionaries and the Babi and Baha'i Communities', in M. Momen (ed.) *Studies in Babi and Baha'i History*, vol. 1, Los Angeles: Kalimat Press.

Moreen, V. (1987) *Iranian Jewry's Hour of Peril and Heroism: A Study of Babai ibn Lutf's Chronicle, 1617–1662*, New York: American Academy for Jewish Research.

—— (2000) *In Queen Esther's Garden*, New Haven: Yale University Press.

Neumark, E. (1947) *Masa'be-erets ha-qedem*, with Introduction and Notes by A. Ya'ari, Jerusalem: ha-Ahim Levin-Epshtin.

Nemoy, L. (1952) *Karaite Anthology: Excerpts from the Early Literature*, New Haven: Yale University Press.

Netzer, A. (1980) 'Iran', in M. Davis (ed.) *Zionism in Transition*, New York: Arno.

—— (1997) 'Sayrī dar tārīkh-i Yahūd-i Īrān', in A. Netzer (ed.) *Padyavand*, vol. 2, Costa Mesa: Mazda Publishers.

Okazaki, S. (1986) 'The Great Persian Famine of 1870–71', *Bulletin of the School of Oriental and African Studies* 49: 183–92.

Patai, R. (1997) *Jadīd al-Islām: The Jewish 'New Muslims' of Meshed*, Detroit: Wayne State University Press.

Pīrnaẓar, J. (2001) 'Yahūdiyān-i jadīd al-Islām-i Mashhad', *Irān-nāma* 19.1–2: 41–60.

Ra'fatī, V. (ed.) (2005) *Payk-i rāstān*, Darmstadt: 'Aṣr-i Jadīd.

Rastigār, N. (1948) *Tārīkh-i haḍrat-i Ṣadr al-Ṣudūr*, Tehran: np.

Ringer, M. (2001) *Education, Religion, and the Discourse of Cultural Reform in Qajar Iran*, Costa Mesa: Mazda Publishers.

Sahim, H. (2005) 'Jews of Iran in the Qajar Period', in R. Gleave (ed.) *Religion and Society in Qajar Iran*, London: RoutledgeCurzon.

Sarshar, H. (2003) 'Hamadan Jewish community', in *Encyclopedia Iranica*, vol. 11: 615–23.

Smith, P. (1987) *The Babi and Baha'i Religions*, Cambridge: Cambridge University Press.

Soroudi, S. (1994) 'The Concept of Jewish Impurity and Its Reflection in Persian and Judeo-Persian Traditions', *Irano-Judaica* 3: 142–70.

Spector, D.E. (1975) 'A History of the Persian Jews', unpublished Ph.D. thesis, University of Texas.

Stern, H.A. (1854) *Dawnings of Light in the East*, London: O.H. Purday.

Sulaymānī, A. (1976a) *Maṣābīḥ-i hidāyat*, vol. 7, Tehran: Mu'assasa-yi Millī-yi Maṭbū'āt-i Amrī.

——(1976b) *Maṣābīḥ-i hidāyat*, vol. 9, Tehran: Mu'assasa-yi Millī-yi Maṭbū'āt-i Amrī.

Thābit, A. (1997) *Tārīkhcha-yi Madrasa-yi Tarbiyat-i Banīn*, New Delhi: Mir'āt.

Thābit, Ḥ. (1993) *Sargudhasht-i Ḥabīb-i Thābit ba qalam-e khud-i īshān*, Costa Mesa: Mazda.

Williams, A.V. (1994) 'Zoroastrian and Judaic Purity Laws: Reflections on the Viability of a Sociological Interpretation', *Irano-Judaica* 3: 72–89.

Yerushalaymi, Y. (1985) 'Sharḥ-i qismī az Yahūdat-i Kāshān va sāyir-i shahristānhā-yi kishvar-i Iran', photocopy of manuscript, Mousa Amanat Archive.

2

THE CONVERSION OF ZOROASTRIANS TO THE BAHA'I FAITH

Fereydun Vahman

The conversion of a considerable number of the Zoroastrians of Iran to the Baha'i Faith is of significant socio-historical importance for a number of reasons. Firstly, Iran's non-Muslim religious minorities were extremely conservative and for centuries adhered faithfully to the religion of their ancestors. Secondly, due to the longstanding hostility and persecution from their Muslim countrymen for centuries, resentment against Islam and anything Arabic was commonplace. That they accepted almost whole scale a new religion born in an Islamic country does not appear to have been adequately explained.

Apocalyptical texts in Zoroastrianism

Zoroastrianism, a religion almost 3,000 years old, has a rich apocalyptic literature. In this section, I will not survey these texts but will highlight the importance of these texts in the conversion of Zoroastrians to the Baha'i Faith.

In these texts, time is divided into four periods of 3,000 years each. At the beginning of each period, one of the three posthumous sons of Zarathustra will reveal himself: Ushedar, Ushedar-māh and Saoshyant (Wiedengren 1995: 32–62). They are from the seed of the prophet Zoroaster kept in Lake Kayanish, where they are guarded by Anahita, the Goddess of Water. At the beginning of each period a virgin will go to Lake Kayanish to bathe; while bathing the glory (of Zoroaster) will enter her body, and she will bear a child. And so, his sons will be born, each at his predestined time. Saoshyant, the highest and the greatest of them, is as bright as the sun. He brings about the perfection of the creation and the annihilation of Ahrīman (the devil, creator of evil). Through the coming of Saoshyant, sickness, old age, and death will disappear from the world, as will greed, tyranny, heresy and related evil.

At each revelation there will be signs warning believers of the end of one period and inauguration of a new one. These include the sun standing still; a fierce animal in the form of a savage wolf or snake that will cause devastation to the world; there will be drought, severe cold and other natural calamities. Religious people will suffer; corruption, untruthfulness, and injustice will be rife (Boyce 1968: 45–51).

Saoshyant, according to the Dēnkard (Book 5, Ch. 2: 14), will renew religion, convert unbelievers, bring everlasting happiness to the people, and free them from afflictions (Āmūzgār & Tafaḍḍulī 2000: 30). He is a prince from the lineage of the legendary Iranian dynasty Kayanids, and on the night he is born a star will fall from the sky. The other titles of the saviour are Hushēdar and Shah Bahrām (*Shāh Vahrām-i varjāvand* ('with miraculous power')) (West 1880: 190–235; Jamasp-Asana 1897: 160–61; Blochet 1916: 9–10).

The prophecies of the coming of the saviour are also found in other Zoroastrian texts. One good example is the writings of Ādhar Kayvān (approximately 1529–1609 AD) and his disciples, who founded the Zoroastrian *Ishrāqī* or Illumination School. He moved from Fars to India and settled in Patna. Ādhar Kayvān and his disciples believed that they received visionary dreams with apocalyptic content (Corbin 1989: 187). These apocalyptical visions culminate in the final victory of Saoshyant.[1]

Zoroastrian communities in later centuries

Before the Safavid era (1502–1736 AD), the number of Zoroastrians residing in Iran has been estimated at between one and three million (Amīnī 2001: 385). This number seems to have declined dramatically by the Qajar period (1794–1925 AD) to about only 8,000.[2] Persecution, together with the burden of paying the *jizya* (poll tax) in spite of widespread poverty among Zoroastrians, resulted in the emigration of a large number to India, and the conversion to Islam of many of those who remained in Iran. Islamic laws governing the religious minorities were another cause of distress and misery. For example, if a murderer who had killed a Zoroastrian was brought to justice he could go free after paying an insignificant amount of money. Inheritance laws also allowed a former Zoroastrian who converted to Islam to be considered the only heir disregarding all other relatives of the deceased one. The Zoroastrians were not even allowed to repair the dilapidated fire temples and *dakhma*s so essential to the religious life of their society.[3]

Part of what made this situation bearable was the hope of the coming saviour to assist the community and bring about the glory of the Zoroastrian faith. Zoroastrians diligently and patiently observed the tenets of their faith and introduced it to their children. To non-Zoroastrians they were generally known as modest, humble, honest and trustworthy people (Boyce 1979: 181–2).

The Zoroastrian community was divided into two groups: the priests (sing. *dastūr* or *mobad*) and laymen (*beh-dinan*). Priesthood was a hereditary office. The duty of the priest was to attend the religious ceremonies, perform weddings and rituals concerning death, and offer sacrifice to the holy fire on behalf of individuals. In recent centuries, the priests were mostly unable to read and understand the holy scripture, the *Avesta*. Not being in touch with the changing times and the challenges facing the community, their main concern was to observe old rituals and retain their apparent superiority in the community.

Manekji and the improvement of the situation

The sad news of the condition of the Zoroastrians of Iran reached their fellow believers (the Parsis) in India and they decided to send an envoy to Iran to monitor the situation at first hand and extend help to improve the situation. The first emissary was Manekji Limji Hatari, a tireless and devoted Parsi, whose ancestors were Iranians. He arrived in April 1854 at Yazd, where he settled and started his mission.[4] He soon won the respect and confidence of the local authorities and even the Muslim clergy. His gentle behaviour, honesty and the generous gifts he gave to the authorities and *mulla*s were important elements in his success. He repaired the fire temples and *dakhma*s, and prevented the Zoroastrians from practising customs such as polygamy, and the sacrifice of animals, which, he argued, were alien to their faith. Later on Manekji took residence in Tehran and this helped him to come in contact with a wide range of Iranian dignitaries. He encouraged Zoroastrians to start trading with India, an initiative which changed the condition of the Zoroastrians and created a well-to-do class. He had to deal with many difficulties, not only caused by the hostile Muslim environment but also those fomented by the Zoroastrian priests, who opposed his reforms and who resisted change in the direction of modernity.

Manekji's greatest achievement, which took him 25 years of hard work, was the official abolishment of the *jizya*. This was achieved in July 1882 after obtaining a verdict from the religious authorities and a royal decree, from Nāṣir al-Dīn Shah (Amīnī 2001: 8–10). Manekji died in Tehran in 1890.

During his first stay in Iran, Manekji most likely heard of the Babi movement. The tales of the heroism and the shared history of persecution of the Babis and early Baha'is must have aroused the interest of Manekji. On his way to India in 1862, Manekji visited Baha'ullah who then resided in Baghdad. Baha'ullah received Manekji warmly and showed him considerable respect. Some years later in Tehran, Manekji employed Mīrzā Abū'l-Faḍl Gulpāygānī, a renowned Baha'i scholar, to teach at the Zoroastrian school founded by him. Abū'l-Faḍl also acted as his personal secretary.[5] Abū'l-Faḍl excelled at writing Persian prose without borrowed words from Arabic (*fārsī-yi sara*, or so-called 'pure' Persian), a fashionable pursuit of the Iranian intellectuals of that period, and a style that was attractive to Zoroastrians who traditionally disliked all things Arabic. Manekji corresponded with Baha'ullah through Abū'l-Faḍl and asked him several questions regarding the signs of the coming of the promised one (*Yārān-i Pārsī* 1998: 19–45). Evidence shows that that he continued to correspond with Baha'ullah throughout his life (Amīnī 2001: 8–10).

Manekji also asked his other Baha'i secretary, Mīrzā Ḥusayn Ḥamadānī, to write a history of the Babi religion. This work is commonly known as the *Tārikh-i jadīd*.[6] There is also evidence that Manekji used to invite Baha'is to his home, where they would discuss religious subjects (Safīdvash 1999: 49). It is not certain to what extent Manekji's correspondences with Baha'ullah and his contact with other Baha'is had any direct impact on the conversion of the Zoroastrians to the Baha'i Faith. But one thing is certain: his friendly and positive attitude towards the new religion must have influenced the people around him.

Conversions to the new religion

The conversion of considerable numbers of Iranian Zoroastrians to the Baha'i religion (and to a lesser degree of Parsis in India) largely took place between the early 1880s and the late 1920s. There are no statistics available for these conversions except the figures given by the high priest of the Zoroastrians, Dastūr Dhalla (1875–1956) who visited Iran in 1920. He estimated that 4,000 Zoroastrians in Iran and 1,000 in India had converted to the Baha'i Faith (Dhalla 1975: 703, 725). The shift to the new religion mostly happened in Yazd, Kirman, Kashan and Tehran and affected almost all the Zoroastrian families of Iran. When Dhalla visited Qazvin, he found that 'all Iranians credited as Zoroastrians had already become Baha'is.' The majority of these converts were either merchants or young, better-educated individuals working in Zoroastrian-owned businesses.[7]

Contrary to popular belief that the conversions were a means of securing their prosperity and safety, the reverse was true. According to the renowned Zoroastrian scholar Mary Boyce:

> Just as life was becoming safer and more prosperous for them (the Zoroastrians), a relatively large number of their community were attracted by the preaching of the Baha'is. For centuries the Zoroastrians had had to grieve for those of their fellows who were lost to Islam, but at least these had achieved by their apostasy a better worldly lot; now they had to mourn their relatives and friends who on embracing this new religion met persecutions as harsh as any that the Zoroastrians themselves had known during the worst years of oppression.
>
> (Boyce 1979: 212)

The real reasons for the conversions of so many Zoroastrians were perhaps the search for modernity and the need to come to terms with the new age. The demand for change which was felt in Iran during the time of Nāṣir al-Dīn Shah also affected young Zoroastrians. They saw in their own community a people headed by priests clinging to the rituals of the past, largely ignorant of the tenants of their own religion and out of touch with the developments of the modern world. The efforts of Manekji had helped the community in many ways but did not succeed in reconciling it ideologically with modernity. Boyce's evaluation of the situation of the Zoroastrian community of Iran before the coming of Islam to Iran (around 651 AD) could have just as well been written for the nineteenth century as a whole:

> After many ecclesiastical and ritual developments of the period, Zoroastrianism was ripe for reform, and a return to the simpler usage of earlier days, when each man's hope of salvation lay more measurably within his own; but what in fact sprang up for the faith was not the reviving breeze of reformation, to give new life and strength but instead the withering tempest of militant Islam.
>
> (Boyce 1979: 143)

The same hope of renewal existed in the nineteenth century and the community was vulnerable to embrace modernity and face the intellectual challenges of the time. They found the new religion in harmony with their own beliefs, fulfilling the dreams of the coming of Saoshyant. The Baha'i Faith was perceived as modern, practical, progressive and with spiritual doctrines. And unlike the surrounding Muslim society, Zoroastrians were accepted by the Baha'is on equal terms and with respect.[8] We can summarize the reasons for conversion into the following main themes:

1 The impact of the sufferings and persecution of the Baha'is.
2 The fulfilment of prophecies.
3 Baha'i universalism and ethics.
4 Iranian elements in the Baha'i teachings.
5 Baha'ullah's and Abdu'l-Baha's letters to Zoroastrians.[9]

The impact of the sufferings and persecutions of Baha'is

Among the values which Jews and Zoroastrians adopted from Shi'i Muslims was the attitude they held towards suffering, persecution and oppression. The Shi'is regarded persecution in the path of God as an indication of legitimacy. The Jews and Zoroastrians found this motif uniquely suited to their own situation, for if suffering and persecution lent legitimacy to a religion, then their own legitimacy was proven. But, by the same token, the Baha'is could be seen as even more legitimate. No single factor proved more impressive to those who converted than the persecution that Baha'is endured at the hands of Muslims (Stiles 1990–91: 7). A number of individual accounts support this. For example, there is a report of a Zoroastrian who saw the public humiliation of a Babi merchant in the bazaar of Kashan, and converted to Babism the very same day (Abdu'l-Baha 1980: 21).[10]

Mulla Bahrām Akhtar-Khāvarī, one of the most prominent Baha'is of Zoroastrian heritage, is said to have heard of the killing of three Baha'is for refusing to recant before he seriously started investigating the new religion (Sulaymānī 1959: 412–413).[11]

Fulfilment of prophecies

The expectation of the coming of the promised one was always present in the Zoroastrian community of Iran. But the more the community suffered under the difficult conditions imposed on it, the greater was the yearning for the appearance of the saviour. Already in 1626 AD a priest from Iran wrote to the Parsis of India: 'The millennium of *Ahrīman*[12] is ended, and the millennium of *Ohrmazd*[13] is at hand, and we look to see the face of the glorious King of Victory, and Hushēdar and Pashotan will come without doubt' (Dhabhar 1913: 593–4). This expectation was fulfilled in the nineteenth century both in Iran and partly among the Parsis of India. For many people, whether laymen or the priests, the coming of the promised one was imminent. Many prayed and read in anticipation *Bahrām Yasht*, the Avestan hymn praising the deity Bahrām.[14]

Chardin, a European who visited Isfahan during the time of Shah 'Abbās (d. 1628 AD), noted that 'one of their [the Zoroastrians'] most constant traditions is that their religion will again be paramount . . . and that empire will once more be theirs. They sustain themselves and their children with this hope' (cited in Boyce 1979: 181–2). At the end of the nineteenth century the expectation was so high that the head of the Zoroastrian priests of Yazd, *dastūr* Tīrandāz, made a wager with Jalāl-al Dawla, the governor of the province, on the appearance of Shah Bahrām within six months. He lost the wager and had to send the governor a grilled lamb with 'a barrel' of wine (Farīdānī 1998: 5).[15]

It is unlikely that the average Zoroastrian during the late Qajar period knew much of the details of this rich apocalyptical literature. The abundance of the prophecies and their divergent motifs did not make it easy for the expectant masses to concentrate on one specific event. Thus, hearsay and tales of the ancestors played their role. In all these prophecies the central precondition was the physical presence of Shah Bahrām or Saoshyant. The occurrence of the other signs such as the sun standing still in the middle of the sky, or the falling of the stars could clearly contribute to the truth of the claim. There are many stories about those Zoroastrians who were inspired or had visions of the signs telling them about the coming of the promised one. Some Zoroastrians wrote letters to Baha'ullah and 'Abdu'l-Baha asking explicitly about the fulfilment of prophecies, and how the signs and happenings foretold in them could match the appearance of the Baha'i religion. Before giving examples of such questions and their responses, it is helpful to consider the hermeneutical framework that informs the reading of Baha'i texts. Franklin Lewis, suggests that some statements in the Baha'i writings are:

> . . . couched in the terms of particular discourse, or intellectual traditions, of the text's immediate audience. As such, these statements may assume some of the premises of the addressee, passing over them without necessarily seeking to challenge or affirm those premises in an absolute sense, in order to make an argument which the addressee can accept. Such premises may sometimes be factually true, in an empirical sense, while sometimes they may not be propositionally true, but may rather be true in a metaphoric and symbolic sense. This being the case, recovering the nature of the discourse being employed, or the intellectual context of the statement, can help to evaluate whether a given statement is meant to convey a propositional fact or a rhetorical truth.
>
> (Lewis 2004: 51)

With this in mind, the writings of Baha'ullah on Zoroastrian prophecies can be seen as the reiteration of the truths and principles of his faith, and figuratively responds to the questions posed to him.[16] For example, with the negative attitudes of Zoroastrians towards Arabs and the Arabic language on the one hand, and Islam and the prophet Muhammad on the other, when they posed the question to Baha'ullah whether Muhammad was a true prophet, Baha'ullah urges the writers of these letters to believe in the truth of *all* the prophets of the past (*Yārān-i Pārsī* 1998: 10). Baha'ullah interprets 'hell' and 'paradise' as nearness to God or being deprived of God's favour; and interprets the day of judgement to be the time of the coming of a new revelation (*Yārān-i Pārsī* 1998: 11). When asked about different signs that shall mark the coming of the saviour, Baha'ullah writes that the world is replete with the 'glad tidings of the eternal paradise' (*Yārān-i Pārsī* 1998: 11). At the same time, using different terms, he emphatically repeats that in this age the 'Lord' has appeared, and in so doing he challenges ancient beliefs of Zoroastrian eschatology on the detailed conditions of the coming of the promised one.[17]

In response to a prophecy that the saviour will be a prince from the lineage of the legendary Iranian dynasty, the Kayānids, and that he shall bring back to Iran its ancient glory, Baha'ullah referred the inquirer to the genealogy drawn up by Abū'l-Faḍl Gulpāygānī (*Yārān-i Pārsī* 1998: 11). In this genealogy Baha'ullah's ancestry is shown to reach the last Sasanian king of Iran, Yazdigird III.[18] The falling of stars on the night of the birth of the saviour was a prophecy that helped a number of Zoroastrians to accept the Baha'i Faith. They had either seen it happen themselves, or had heard about this extraordinary event from their fathers warning them the nearness of the advent of the saviour.[19] Similarly, 'Abdu'l-Baha answers a question asked by an inquirer about the prophecy concerning the sun standing still in the sky for ten, twenty and thirty days, employing metaphoric and symbolic language.[20] Christopher Buck, discussing this prophecy, makes an important point about Baha'i interpretations of prophecies:

> Baha'ullah's fulfilment of Zoroastrian prophecy was never meant to bear the test of textual and hermeneutical scrutiny. The new revelation was the new divine standard, the fresh locus of authority, the touchstone of truth, past and present. The fulfilment motif provided the eschatological climax at the crescendo of salvation-history. The old prophecies served as bridges into the Baha'i era, and the dawn of a new chiliasm or eschatological millennium. The old, mantic and vatic texts had served their purpose in the eyes of the Zoroastrian Baha'is. Prophecies, in the post-conversion experience, were only referentially meaningful. At first, Baha'ullah was validated by the prophecies, when Zoroastrians embraced Baha'ullah as the promised Shah Bahrām. After becoming Baha'is, the reverse was true: It was Baha'ullah who validated the prophecies concerning Shah Bahrām. In effect, Baha'ullah redefined the role of Shah Bahrām.
>
> (Buck 1998)

Baha'i universalism and ethics

The writings of Baha'ullah on unity and his injunctions to consort with all religions with love and friendliness are thought to have removed some of the barriers that had isolated Zoroastrian society for centuries. Whether they converted to the new religion or not, Baha'is are reported to have treated Zoroastrians with respect and kindness, invited them to their homes and established friendly ties. For centuries Zoroastrians had been humiliated and insulted, considered by the Muslims to be *najis* (religiously unclean) and thus untouchable. They were also barred from entering certain trades and professions. The behaviour of Baha'is, therefore, was novel and proved attractive to many Zoroastrians.

The evidence for this is necessarily anecdotal and from Baha'i sources. For example, Mulla 'Abd al-Ghanī of Ardakān, a former *mulla* who became a Baha'i, reportedly invited Zoroastrian youths to his home, received them with respect, and would let them sit in the upper portion of the room where the guests of honour normally sat. He is said to have instructed these youths in the Arabic writings of Baha'ullah, as well as in the Qur'an (Farīdānī 1998: 16).[21] Another historian of the Baha'i religion notes:

> One element that increased their [the Muslims'] enmity was the way the Baha'is treated the Zoroastrians. The former Muslims and the Zoroastrians sitting together like brothers was to them a major and unpardonable sin. A young man, Āqā 'Abd al-Rasūl, the son of Ustād Mihdī from the village of Dih-bālā was accused of being a Baha'i and the mob clamoured for his death. Most of the *mulla*s were not sure whether he was a Baha'i or not. Two persons gave witness saying they had seen him eating food with a Zoroastrian; this being only characteristic of the Baha'is, who did not avoid socialising with Zoroastrians. That reason was sufficient to put him to death.
>
> (Āvāra 1924: 103, 132)

Baha'i universalism shared many similarities but also widened the Zoroastrian worldview. Lack of prejudice, love of humankind, kindness to animals and respect for nature were all familiar motifs which appealed to Zoroastrians.

Iranian elements in the Baha'i teachings

Zoroastrians had always regarded themselves as 'true' and 'pure' Iranians. As such, they felt a kind of guardianship for ancient Persian culture and identity. The fact that the Baha'i Faith was born in Iran was in itself an attractive element. Baha'ullah's ancestry and lineage, which reportedly stretched back to the pre-Islamic Sasanian dynasty, not only fulfilled one of their prophecies but added a stronger Iranian identity to the new religion.

A closer study of Baha'i scriptures reveals many elements which reflect ancient Iranian religious motifs. For example, there is an injunction by the Bab in his book the *Bayān-i 'Arabī* that requires Babis to go outside each Friday and welcome the sun by chanting a special verse in praise of light. This is reminiscent of the respect and worship of the sun in Mithraism and early Zoroastrianism (Ekbal 1998: 110–124).

In addition to the Iranian elements in the Baha'i Faith previously discussed, the strong emphasis in the Baha'i Faith on being virtuous, and even achieving excellence in all manners of life perhaps reflects the three most important Zoroastrian motifs: good thoughts, good manners, and good words. Cleanliness in all manners of life is another shared element in both religions. The Baha'i teachings abhor lies and deceitfulness and consider them to be the greatest sin. 'Abdu'l-Baha considers a lie to be worse than blasphemy (*Mā'ida-yi āsamānī* 1971: 169). The same is true in Zoroastrianism where a lie is symbolized by *Ahrīman*, the hostile spirit and the counterpart to the good god, *Ohrmazd*, great lord of wisdom. *Ahrīman* spreads lies and devastation in the world and it is only defeated by Saoshyant who comes to the world by the will of *Ohrmazd*. The emphasis in the Baha'i Faith on mercy and kindness to animals brings to mind the Zoroastrian deity Vahman, who is the guardian of animals. Protecting and respecting nature are shared elements of the two religions. In Zoroastrianism, there is a deity *Ameretat* who is the guardian of plants and ensures their growth. The importance of being happy and content under all circumstances is another point of similarity between the teachings of these two religions.

The Baha'i calendar is another link to ancient Persian culture. Since the inception of Islam the official calendar of the country was the Islamic lunar calendar, in which the year begins with the first day of the month of Muḥarram. The Baha'i calendar, like the Zoroastrian one, preserved the solar system and vernal equinox, with the first day of spring as the beginning of the New Year (Nawrūz). In both religions the days of the month bear a name, one of the attributes of God. The names of the days of the months are likewise either the name of one of the holy deities (in Zoroastrianism) or one of God's attributes (in the Baha'i religion). Whenever the name of the day coincides with the name of the month, Zoroastrians arrange a feast, a kind of religious ceremony. A similar monthly celebration, known as the 'nineteen-day feast' marks the start of every Baha'i month.

Other clear similarities are in their moral teachings, the emphasis by Baha'ullah on the importance of agriculture, the profession of most Zoroastrians of the time, and the Baha'i worldview on the establishing the universal peace in a united world which echoes the founding of eternal bliss by Saoshyant.[22] Boyce remarks: 'Baha'ism developed a claim to be world-faith, and offered the Iranian Zoroastrians, as theosophy did the Parsis in India, membership of a wider common community, in which they would have an honoured place' (Boyce 1979: 212).

Letters from Baha'ullah and 'Abdu'l-Baha to Zoroastrians

The stream of letters to Zoroastrians from Baha'ullah and 'Abdu'l-Baha had an important role in their conversion. They were sent to Zoroastrians of all ages and social classes. For example, a poor Zoroastrian farmer who sent greetings to Baha'ullah received a letter from him in return (Safīdvash 1999: 61–63). For the new converts, these letters were sources of affirmation and support when they were encountering opposition to their conversion from their close relatives and the Zoroastrian priests. These letters may have also played a role in the emergence of a distinct Baha'i identity among converts from the Zoroastrian community.

Baha'ullah's letters are written in a beautiful yet simple Persian, some without any Arabic words, and others with a limited amount of Arabic phrases and words. In these letters Baha'ullah expounds upon the tenets of the new religion and answers the questions posed to him. One of Baha'ullah's best known letters to a Zoroastrian individual is the *Lawḥ-i haft pursish* (the Tablet of Seven Questions), addressed to Ustād Javānmard, a knowledgeable Zoroastrian. Javānmard was already a Baha'i when he asked these questions, but the answers he received seemed to have encouraged many other Zoroastrians to convert to the Baha'i religion.[23]

'Abdu'l-Baha's letters to Zoroastrians are excellent examples of Persian prose. His style is easy to comprehend, while being rich in the use of rhythm and rhyme. 'Abdu'l-Baha incorporates a fair number of rhetorical flourishes that make his letters intrinsically Persian in their intimacy and musicality. He extensively uses images and metaphors related to Zoroastrian religion such as fire, the fire temple, *Sorosh* (the angel), and the names of different deities. An example is where 'Abdu'l-Baha responds to a question about the lack of the centrality of fire in the Baha'i Faith. 'Abdu'l-Baha answers by saying the real meaning of 'fire' is 'the fire of love of God' and the 'fire place' as 'the heart, the abode of the burning fire of love' whose 'light' is 'the light of knowledge' (*Yārān-i Pārsī* 1998: 5, 6, 91).

As most Zoroastrians' given names were the names of historical personalities of pre-Islamic Iran, 'Abdu'l-Baha often associated the addressee with the historical or mythological name he or she bore, and conveyed his message in the context of the related history or mythology. To a man called Rustam (a hero of ancient Iran), he expresses the hope that he too would become a conqueror, and conquer the 'land of faith and certitude' (*Yārān-i Pārsī* 1998: 78). For a man called Kayūmarth (the first legendary king of Iran), 'Abdu'l-Baha wishes that he would likewise establish a kingdom in this world, the 'eternal kingdom of servitude' (*Yārān-i Pārsī* 1998: 83). For a man named Nūshīravān (a king who was famous for justice), 'Abdu'l-Baha wishes that he will act with the same fairness and sense of justice (*Yārān-i Pārsī* 1998: 174, 195, 432).

These letters had a great impact on Zoroastrians and facilitated their understanding of Baha'i literature. Susan Stiles Maneck asserts that by using less Arabic words and phrases in their correspondence with the Zoroastrians, Baha'ullah and 'Abdu'l-Baha played down the Islamic background of the religion and highlighted its Persian aspects (Stiles 1984: 70). Further, these letters were written in a very sympathetic tone, in particular some letters by 'Abdu'l-Baha, in which he shares with the Zoroastrian recipients their sorrow at the invasion of Iran by the Arabs and the devastation of Iran's glorious past (*Yārān-i Pārsī* 1998: 115, 131, 141, 166).

Some early converts

Kay-Khusraw Khudādād (Paymān) was by all accounts the first Zoroastrian who accepted the Baha'i Faith, around 1880. He was a merchant from Yazd, but lived in Kashan and was a close relative of two other Zoroastrian merchants, the above-mentioned Suhrāb Pūr-Kāvūs who previously had accepted the Bab (see note 10) and one Mihrabān Kāvūs (most likely Suhrāb's brother). In the Qajar period, Zoroastrian tradesmen used to go to different cities in groups of three or four, where they lived together due to the hostile attitudes of others. It seems that Kay-Khusraw and the two others had contact with other Babis of Kashan. Kay-Khusraw, who was born in 1848, died in Yazd in 1925 (Safīdvash 1999: 59).

The process of promoting the Baha'i Faith among Zoroastrians soon accelerated. It was mostly the new converts from a Zoroastrian background who undertook this work. They could easily contact their relatives and friends and some of them had the necessary knowledge of the Zoroastrian sacred texts. One such individual was the above-mentioned Mulla Bahrām Akhtar-Khāvarī, who after becoming a Baha'i devoted all his life to teaching the new religion to both Zoroastrians and Muslims. In particular, he travelled extensively to villages around Yazd where he talked to the people about the new religion; his home was also always open to receive people. Twice he had to flee to India in order to save his life because of the enmity of both the Zoroastrian and Muslim priests. He received many letters from Baha'ullah and 'Abdu'l-Baha in which he is addressed as: 'the heavenly Bahrām', 'the light of the assembly of the friends', 'the blessing of God' and 'the bounty of heaven'.[24]

Some Baha'is from a Muslim background also played a role in converting Zoroastrians to the Baha'i religion. Ḥājjī Āqā Muḥammad 'Alāqband used to go most mornings to the outskirts of Yazd to contact interested Zoroastrians who were on their way to town to tell them about the Baha'i religion. Those relatives of the Bab resident in Yazd, the Afnān family, provided financial support for another learned Baha'i for the same purpose (Farīdānī 1998: 53, 76). Ḥājjī Muḥammad Ṭāhir Mālmīrī, the famous Baha'i teacher of Yazd, was successful in converting many Zoroastrians in Yazd and the surrounding villages to the Baha'i Faith.

The reluctance of the priests to explain Zoroastrian texts, compared with the readiness of the Baha'is to explain and expound their understanding of the meaning of Zoroastrian scriptures and prophecies, were additional factors that influenced conversions (Farīdānī 1998: 175–7). The call of 'Abdu'l-Baha to the new believers to travel and bring the message to other people, especially to Zoroastrians, resulted in significant teaching activity by new converts in and around Yazd, particularly in Zoroastrian-dominated villages. This pattern was later repeated in other towns and cities in Iran with significant Zoroastrian populations.[25] Jamshīd of Ḥusaynābād who had witnessed the killing of seven Baha'is in Yazd, was reportedly astonished by their steadfastness and courage. He converted to the new religion after meeting some Baha'is and soon started to teach the religion to the people of his village, with the assistance of some learned Baha'is from Yazd. Gradually all the Zoroastrian families of Ḥusaynābād, apart from one, accepted the Baha'i Faith, together with some Muslims, among whom were two *mulla*s (Safīdvash 1999: 92–3).

Stiles Maneck has observed:

> These conversion stories share a number of factors in common. All of the early converts were drawn from the new educated elite which Manekji's reforms, growing trade relations with Bombay, and changing conditions within Iran had combined to create. Some were professionals, others merchants, while still others were the more prosperous agriculturists. These conversions were catalytic to other conversions among the poorer peasants who associated with others. Relatives converted soon after the conversion of these key individuals, who formed the leadership of the Zoroastrian Baha'is.
> (Stiles 1984: 75)

Conflict with *Dastūrs*

Unlike converting to Islam, which normally required converts to change their given names, their style of dress, their customs, and which often carried with it pressure to sever links with Zoroastrian relatives and the Zoroastrian community, those Zoroastrians who converted to the Baha'i Faith kept their given names (although many of them adopted new 'surnames', such as Majdhūb or Anvarī), their mode of dress, their customs; they were for many years simultaneously members of both the Zoroastrian *and* Baha'i communities. Gradually, the 'Zoroastrian Baha'is' began to adhere more strictly to Baha'i law, and to interact freely with Baha'is from Muslim and Jewish backgrounds.

Following the death of Manekji in 1890, another envoy Kay-Khusrawjī Ṣāḥib arrived from India. In order to improve the conditions of the Zoroastrians and to represent the community when dealing with the authorities, he established administrative committees (each known as *Anjuman-i Nāṣirī*) of prominent Zoroastrians in Yazd, Kirman and Tehran (Amini 2001: 283–85).[26] In Yazd, the majority of the members of this society were either Baha'is, or else individuals who were sympathetic to the Baha'i Faith.[27] Kay-Khusrawjī Ṣāḥib, who was aggravated by what he saw as the corruption and inability of the priests, asked the *Anjuman* to supervise the *dastūr*s and their activities. The Zoroastrian priests were angered by this, and accused the Baha'is of being the cause of the trouble. Without any evidence they started to spread shameful rumours about the Baha'is, and encouraged the mobs to attack them (Farīdānī 1998: 32; Safīdvash 1975: 197).

Some incidents gradually strengthened the Baha'i identity of the new believers and led to the open conflict between the *dastūr*s and the Baha'is. One such incident was the wedding of a Zoroastrian Baha'i and the refusal of the *dastūr*s to preside over it. Eventually the *Anjuman* intervened and agreed that two Zoroastrian laymen should perform the ceremony in accordance with Zoroastrian law. This decision was supported by the *dastūr*s of Kirman and the vice-governor of Yazd. The wedding ceremony was performed according to Zoroastrian law, observing all the required rituals. This incident, which was a clear departure from traditional practices, weakened the position of the *dastūr*s in Yazd. Following this incident, the weddings of most Baha'is of Zoroastrian heritage were performed by laymen, paving the way for observing Baha'i law in future marriage ceremonies.

Another achievement of the Zoroastrian Baha'is of Yazd was the acquisition of a Baha'i cemetery. The process through which land was secured for the Baha'i cemetery was a long and complicated one. The *dastūr*s tried twice to damage this cemetery, once by ruining a part of the outer wall and then by setting fire to the entrance of the cemetery (Safīdvash 1999: 125–6).

In order to oppose the liberals and halt reform, the *dastūr*s formed a society named *Majma'-i ḥaqq-shinās va ḥaqq-gū-yi Yazd* ('The Society of Truth-Knowers and Truth-Speakers of Yazd') (Amīnī 2001: 408). One of the main tasks of this society was to oppose the activities of the Baha'is. A plot was devised to assassinate Fīrūz Fīrūzmand, one of those who had performed the above-mentioned wedding ceremony, and Master Khudābakhsh, who was one of the most respected Zoroastrians of Yazd and who for years had served as the president of the city's *Anjuman*, as well as the headmaster of the Kay-Khusravī school. Master Khudābakhsh had lived in India for 14 years and had studied the sacred books of Zoroastrians. He was very sympathetic to the Baha'i Faith and helped the Baha'is on many occasions, including assisting in the establishment of the Baha'i cemetery. The *dastūr*s hired a man by the name of Farīdūn Rustam of Kirman, to assassinate both Fīrūz Fīrūzmand and Master Khudābakhsh.

One night in September 1917, Farīdūn Rustam shot Fīrūz Fīrūzmand but did not succeed in killing him. The following morning he shot Master Khudābakhsh in the head with five bullets, while he was on his way to the Kay-Khusravī school. An English doctor, Henry White, arrived at the scene, only to find Master Khudābakhsh dead in a pool of blood (Farīdānī 1998: 62). The Zoroastrians later built on the site a memorial with burning light. The assassin was eventually arrested but he escaped from prison in Tehran, allegedly with the financial help of Dastūr Rustam and Arbāb Kay-Khusraw, the representative of the Zoroastrians in the Majlis (Safīdvash 1975: 127–28). 'Abdu'l-Baha revealed a prayer in honour of Master Khudābakhsh and considered him to be a martyr (*Yārān-i Pārsī* 1998: 226, 229).

As Stiles points out, the assassination proved a serious miscalculation on the part of the conservatives, and irreparably undermined the moral credibility of the Zoroastrian clergy (Stiles 1984: 89). From this point on, the power and authority of the priesthood collapsed rapidly and the *Anjuman* assumed almost complete leadership of the Zoroastrian community (Safīdvash 1975: 127–8).

Fostering a Baha'i identity

By learning more about the Baha'i teachings, while keeping themselves within Zoroastrian society, the new converts gradually and cautiously strove to move towards a distinctive Baha'i identity. As we have seen, their wedding ceremonies were officiated by laypersons but the actual ceremony was performed within the confines of Zoroastrian laws and norms. Again, they succeeded in avoiding laying the dead in *dakhma*s and instead buried them in graves (although it should be noted that the graves were built in accordance with Zoroastrian law). Each year an increasing number of Zoroastrians converted to the Baha'i Faith, and tried together with Baha'is from Muslim and Jewish backgrounds to shape their own Baha'i community. Converts from the Zoroastrian community were active in promoting the Baha'i religion among members of their extended families. They arranged large meetings and invited Zoroastrians to participate and hear about their new religion. When they learnt of the emphasis on the importance of universal education in the Baha'i scriptures, they established schools for both boys and girls.[28]

Gradually the Zoroastrian Baha'is were integrated into the wider Baha'i community of Iran. They took an active role alongside Baha'is of Jewish and Muslim heritage in community activities, such as propagating the Baha'i Faith,[29] donating funds, and serving on elected Baha'i councils which, in the absence of clergy, administered the affairs of the community. Intermarriage between Baha'is of Muslim, Jewish and Zoroastrian backgrounds gradually became more commonplace, and seems to have been relatively common by the late 1930s.

It is worth noting that both 'Abdu'l-Baha and Shoghi Effendi invited a number of Zoroastrian Baha'is to settle in Palestine. Many of these individuals farmed Baha'i-owned land, or helped with the running of Baha'i-owned properties (Farīdānī 2000: 415–17). Other notable achievements of Zoroastrian Baha'is include those of Sīāvash Safīdvash, who in 1926 succeeded in procuring a large piece of land for the first Baha'i centre (Haẓīrat al-Quds) of Tehran. Later on he helped the community acquire land north of Tehran for the purpose of building a Baha'i house of worship (Safīdvash 1999: 127). In 1945, Rustam Mihshāhī started a kindergarten for the Baha'i children of Panchgani in India. This kindergarten started with a handful of children and is now a large educational establishment with hundreds of students (Safīdvash 1999: 226) Likewise the Parsi Baha'is of India played a significant role in purchasing the land for the Baha'i temple in New Delhi, India.[30]

Three large trading companies were set up by Zoroastrian Baha'is in Iran in the twentieth century: Pārsiyān, Paymān and Pāyanda. The founders of these companies were young, Zoroastrian Baha'is who had previously worked in trading companies belonging to Zoroastrians. They started their businesses with limited capital and asked 'Abdu'l-Baha for his blessings for the success of their companies. These companies became successful with branches throughout Iran and with trading ventures abroad. All these companies were confiscated following the Islamic revolution in 1979.[31]

In the aftermath of the revolution of 1978–1979, and the severe persecution of the Baha'i community that followed, 12 Baha'is of Zoroastrian heritage were among more than 200 Baha'is who were killed for refusing to recant their religious beliefs.[32]

The Pahlavi period

For the ancient, conservative Zoroastrian community of Iran, the message of the Baha'i Faith brought the promise of renewal and progress. In the mid-1920s, Riḍā Shah Pahlavi had firmly established control of Iran and he set about modernizing Iran by constructing roads and railways, establishing an efficient postal service, opening government schools for boys and girls, and, later, by founding a university in Tehran. During his time, Iran was gripped by nationalistic fervour, particularly for the history of ancient, pre-Islamic Iran. The Zoroastrian religion, because of its roots in Iran's ancient past, enjoyed increasing esteem among the Shi'i Muslim majority. In some circles there were even rumours that Zoroastrianism would once again become the state religion of Iran. For the first time in many centuries, Zoroastrian Iranians enjoyed almost equal rights with their Shi'i compatriots. Riḍā Shah's reforms were so popular with some Zoroastrians that they came to view him as one of the promised redeemers.

Seeing their dream of redemption coming true with these reforms, and with more contact with the West and modern ideologies, many Zoroastrians, in particular those residing in Tehran and larger urban centres, adopted more liberal lifestyles and loosened their ties with traditional society. This manifested itself in a number of ways, such as the increased incidence of mixed marriages (with Muslims or Baha'is), and a preference for the burying of the dead in graves over the use of *dakhmas*. Consequently, these reforms had an impact on the conversion of Zoroastrians to the Baha'i religion, which appear to have slowed from the 1930s onwards.

Notes

1 Ādhar Kayvān's book, *Dasātīr*, although composed very late in the history of Zoroastrianism, had a considerable impact on Zoroastrian society and influenced the individual Zoroastrian's conception of the coming of the saviour. Some of these prophecies are also quoted in the early works written by Baha'is to validate the truth of the claims of the Bab and Baha'ullah.

2 Gobineau in *Trois Ans en Asie* (1859: 378) gives a total figure of 8,000 for the Zoroastrian population of Iran in the mid-nineteenth century of men, women and children.

3 A place on the mountain top where, according to Zoroastrian customs, the dead bodies were laid to be devoured by vultures.

4 Being a British citizen, Manekji obtained letters of introduction from the British authorities in India to the British authorities in Iraq and Iran. On a boat to Iran he met Mīrzā Ḥusayn Khān, Sipahsālār, who later became the Iranian Ambassador to the Ottoman Empire and the Grand Vizier of Naṣir al-Dīn Shah. It turned into a close friendship, which helped Manekji in his efforts to improve the condition of the Zoroastrians in Iran (Amīnī 2001: 4, 47).

5 Prior to his conversion to the Baha'i Faith in 1876, Abū'l-Faḍl was the headmaster at a religious seminary in Tehran. He appears to have been employed by Manekji some time between his expulsion from the seminary on account of his conversion to the Baha'i religion, and before 1881 when Abū'l-Faḍl left Tehran to travel throughout Iran to preach the Baha'i message.

6 For the full story of the composition of this peculiar work see Abū'l Faḍl's statement in *Risāla-yi Iskandariyya*, translated by Browne (Browne 1893b: xxxix–xliii).

7 Due to the lack of any demographic statistics the accuracy of the figures given by Dhalla is questionable. Approximately 70 years prior to Dhalla's visit to Iran, the French consul in Iran, Gobineau, in a rather exact calculation estimated that the Iranian Zoroastrians numbered 8,000 (Gobineau 1859: 378). If Gobineau's and Dhalla's figures are correct, it would seem that somewhere from around one third to half of Iran's Zoroastrians converted to the Baha'i religion in the late nineteenth/early twentieth centuries.

8 For detailed accounts of the conversion of Zoroastrian individuals to the Baha'i Faith, see Farīdānī 1989; Safīdvash 1975 and Safīdvash 1999.

9 For a discussion of the letters of 'Abdu'l-Baha to Zoroastrian Baha'is, see Brookshaw's chapter in this volume.

10 The man was Suhrāb Pūr Kāvūs, a merchant who knew the victim Ḥājjī Muḥammad Riḍā Kāshānī to be a trustworthy and well-respected merchant of Kashan, see Faizi 1994: 137.

11 When questioned by the governor of Yazd as to why he, a Zoroastrian, had become a Baha'i, he is reported to have said: 'I saw with my own eyes how those holy souls gave their most precious possessions, their lives, to vindicate the truth of this revelation. This miracle is higher than all other miracles and this proof is the strongest arguments' (Sulaymānī 1959: 412–13).

12 'The Evil Spirit'.

13 'The Good Spirit', or 'the Wise God'.

14 There are in all 21 *Yashts* or hymns praising the deities of Indo-Iranian peoples.

15 The same *dastūr*, who was not well disposed towards the Baha'is, had assured Edward G. Browne during the latter's sojourn in Iran (1887–88) that Shah Bahrām, the Zoroastrian saviour, would appear before the Iranian New Year (Nawruz) of the same year (Browne 1893b: 442).

16 For the texts of 28 letters written by Baha'ullah to Zoroastrians, see *Yārān-i Pārsī* 1998: 1–61.

17 For the word 'Lord' Baha'ullah has used four Persian terms in one sentence: *jahān-khudā, jahān-kadkhudā, jahān-bārī*, and *jahān-panāh* (*Yārān-i Pārsī* 1998: 44). Thus without challenging the four varieties of the name of the saviour in Zoroastrian tradition (Hushēdar, Saoshyant, Pashotan and Shah Bahrām), he asserted the realization of all four in his revelation.

18 For more on this, see Majdhūb 1993: 180.

19 For the examples of the Zoroastrians who have witnessed the falling of stars, see Safīdvash 1999: 93–4; Farīdānī 1998: 187.

20 Quoted by Shoghi Effendi 1969: 101–02. See also Shoghi Effendi's letter dated 7 August 1934, published in (American) *Baha'i News* No. 87, September 1934: 1.

21 Fīrūz Tīrandāz, whose only objection to the Baha'i Faith was accepting Muḥammad as a prophet of God, studied the Qur'an for two years with Mulla 'Abd al-Ghanī until his doubts were dispelled (Farīdānī 1998: 215–16).
22 There are more points of similarities in doctrinal and moral issues which require detailed study. They include the praising the wisdom (*khirad*); the role of human beings in the advancement of civilization; and the importance of the covenant with God. Certainly not all Zoroastrians or Baha'is of that period were aware of these similarities.
23 For the Persian text of this letter, see *Yārān-i Pārsī* 1998: 8–12; for an English translation, see Razavi (1993) 'The Tablet of the Seven Questions of Baha'ullah (*Lawh-i haft pursish*) An Introductory Note and Provisional Translation', *Baha'i Studies Bulletin* 7.3–4: 48–59. For an example of a Zoroastrian who converted to the Baha'i Faith after having studied this tablet, see Farīdānī 1998: 81–2.
24 *Bahrām-i āsamānī, sham'-i anjuman-i yārān, raḥmat-i rahmān*; and *ni'mat-i āsamānī* (*Yārān-i Pārsī* 1998: 249).
25 For examples of such letters, see *Yārān-i Pārsī* 1998: 75–76.
26 Manekji in his lifetime tried to establish similar *anjumans* in Yazd and Kirman but failed to receive the support of the *dastūr*s and the Zoroastrian elders.
27 For the names of the Baha'i members of the *Anjuman-i Nāṣirī* of Yazd, see Sulaymānī 1951: 405. Among them was Kay-Khusraw Khudādād, the first Zoroastrian Baha'i, Mulla Bahrām Akhtar-Khāvari, and Ustād Javānmard, the addressee of the *Tablet of Seven Questions*. For a photograph of this *anjuman*, see Farīdānī 1998: 12. 'Abdu'l-Baha revealed a prayer for the success of this *anjuman* (*Yārān-i Pārsī* 1998: 74).
28 When he learnt about the importance given to the education of girls in the Baha'i scriptures, Hūshang Hūshangī, a Zoroastrian Baha'i businessman, established a girls' school in Yazd in 1924. This school first started at his home, but soon moved to a larger building. It was headed by a Gulchir Farīdānī, and was the second girls' school in Yazd after the school run by the Christian missionaries. The Hūshangī school enrolled girls from all religious backgrounds and was renowned for its high moral and educational standards. Hūshangī also established endowments to secure the future financial needs of the school which at its height had more than one hundred pupils. The Hūshangī school was closed by the order of the government in 1934, along with all other Baha'i-run schools throughout Iran. There was also a Baha'i-run school in the village of Maryamābād, near Yazd (Farīdānī 2002: 213). On the Baha'i schools of Yazd and the surrounding villages, see the chapters by Momen and Brookshaw in this volume.
29 A number of Baha'is from a Zoroastrian background even emigrated to Arabic-speaking countries to assist with the development of Baha'i communities in those countries. This shows the influence of the Baha'i teachings, which reduced the traditional dislike of Arabs and the Arabic language among those Zoroastrians who converted.
30 *Payām-i Baha'i* April-May 1987: 36–7.
31 For more details on these companies, see Farīdānī 2002: 147–149, 157–8, 421–424.
32 For a list of these martyrs, see Farīdānī 2002: 430.

Bibliography

'Abdu'l-Baha (1993) *A Traveller's Narrative*, Wilmette: Baha'i Publishing Trust.

Amini, T. (2001) *Asnādī az Zartushtiyān-i mu'āṣir-i Iran* ['Some Documents on the Contemporary Zoroastrians of Iran'], Tehran: Iran National Archives Organization.

Āmūzgār, J. and Tafaḍḍulī, A. (2000) *Le Cinquième Livre du Dēnkard*, Paris: Association pour l'avancement des études Iraniennes.
Āvāra, A. (1924) *al-Kawākib al-Durriyya*, vol. 2. Cairo.
Blochet, E. (1895) 'Text pehlvis inédits III', Suppl. Pers. *RHR*, Paris.
Boyce, M. (1968) 'Middle Persian Literature' in *Handbuch der Orientalistik*, Band: Iranistik, no. 2. Abschnitt: 48–51.
—— (1979) *Zoroastrians: Their Religious Beliefs and Practices*, London & New York: Routledge and Kegan Paul.
Browne, E.G. (1893a) *A Year Amongst the Persians*, Cambridge: The University Press.
Browne, E.G. (1893b) *The New History of Mírzá 'Alí Muhammad the Báb (Táríkh-i Jadid)* (trans.& ed.) Cambridge: The University Press.
Buck, C. (1998) 'Baha'ullah as Zoroastrian saviour', *Baha'i Studies Review*, 8: pp. 15–33.
Corbin, H. (1989) 'Āzar Keyvān', in *Encyclopaedia Iranica*, vol. III, London & New York: Routledge and Kegan Paul.
de Gobineau, A. (1859) *Trois Ans en Asie*, Paris.
Dhabhar, B.N. (1913) *The Pahlavi Rivayat*, Bombay.
Dhalla, M.N. (1975) *The saga of a soul: an autobiography of Shams-ul-ulama Dastūr Dr. Maneckji Nusserwanji Dhalla*, trans. H.J. Rustomji, Karachi: Gool & Behram Sohrab.
Ekbal, K. (1998) 'The Maid of Heaven and the Tablet of the Holy Mariner', in *Safīna-yi 'Irfān*, volume 1, Darmstadt, Germany: 'Aṣr-i Jadīd Publishers.
Farīdānī, S. (2002) *Dūstān-i Rāstān*, Hofheim, Germany: Baha'i Verlag.
Jamasp-Asana, J.M. (1897–1913) *Pahlavi Texts*, Bombay.
Lewis, F. (2004) 'Discourses of knowledge in the Baha'i writings', in J. Danesh and S. Fazel (eds) *Search for Values: Ethics in Baha'i Thought*, Los Angeles: Kalimat Press.
Mā'ida-yi āsamānī, volume 5 (1971) Comp. A.H. Ishrāq-Khāvarī, Tehran: Baha'i Publishing Trust.
Majzūb, N. (1993) 'Jamāl-i aqdas-i abhā, niyākān va ajdād-i mubārak' in *Maḥbub-i 'ālam*, Canada: 'Andalíb Editorial Board.
Safīdvash, I. (1999) *Tanī chand az pīshgāmān-i Pārsī-nijād dar 'ahd-i rasūlī*, Dundas, Ontario: Persian Association of Baha'i Studies.
Safīdvash, S. (1975) *Yār-i dīrīn*, Tehran: Baha'i Publishing Trust.
Stiles Maneck, S. (1990–1991) 'The Conversion of Religious Minorities to the Baha'i Faith in Iran', *Journal of Baha'i Studies*, 3.3: 35–48.
Stiles (Maneck), S. (1984) 'Early Zoroastrian Conversions to the Baha'i Faith in Yazd, Iran', in J.R. Cole and M. Momen (eds) *From Iran East and West, Studies in Babi and Baha'i History*, vol. 2, Los Angeles: Kalimat Press.
Sulaymānī, A. (1951) *Maṣābīḥ-i hidāyat*, vol. 4. Tehran: Baha'i Publishing Trust.
West, E.W. (1880) (trans.) 'Zand-i Vohuman Yasan (or Bahman Yasht)' in *Sacred Books of East*, vol V, part 1. Oxford.
Wiedengren, G. (1995) 'Les Quatre Ages du Monde' in G. Widengren, A. Hultgård and M. Philomonenko (eds) *Apocalyptique Iranienne et Dualisme Qoumránie*, Paris: Librarire Adrien Maisonneuve.
Yārān-i Pārsī (1998) *Majmū'a-yi alvāḥ-i mubāraka-yi Jamāl-i aqdas-i abhā va haḍrat-i 'Abdu'l-Baha bi-iftikhār-i Bahā'iyān-i Pārsī*, Hofheim, Germany: Baha'i Verlag.

3

INSTRUCTIVE ENCOURAGEMENT

Tablets of Baha'ullah and 'Abdu'l-Baha to Baha'i women in Iran and India

Dominic Parviz Brookshaw

Introduction

To date, most studies concerning early Babi and Baha'i women of Iran have focused on the biographies of individuals.[1] This trend has, in part, been dictated by the nature of the sources available to researchers, which tend to focus on the achievements of individuals, rather than collective activities or community developments.[2] Individual studies of Khadīja Baygum (the wife of the Bab) and Āsīya Khānum (Baha'ullah's first wife and mother of 'Abdu'l-Baha) have appeared, but are both very slight and fail to draw on all the available sources (Balyuzi 1981 and Rouhani Ma'ani 1993).[3] A volume of writings about and to Bahiyya Khānum ('Abdu'l-Baha's full sister) by Baha'ullah, 'Abdu'l-Baha and Shoghi Effendi has been published together with a selection of letters written by her (BWCRD 1982), and the brief memoirs of Munīra Khānum ('Abdu'l-Baha's wife) have also appeared in English translation together with a few of her letters (Munīra Khānum 1986), but no in-depth academic study of either of these leading female Baha'i figures exists. Ṭāhira Qurrat al-'Ayn has received much more attention, some scholarly,[4] although much of what has been written about the pre-eminent woman of the Babi movement is semi-academic at best. Some individual Baha'i women have begun to receive the attention they deserve from historians of nineteenth- and early-twentieth-century Iran,[5] but there is much work to be done before an accurate picture of the role played women in the development of the community in this early stage will emerge.

In this study I have chosen to focus on the tablets of Baha'ullah and 'Abdu'l-Baha written to women in Iran and India, a vital source for those writing the history of the Baha'i women of these countries from 1870 to 1921.[6] This study highlights the richness and diversity of these texts (both in terms of content and style) and shows how they can be used to better understand the role played by the average Baha'i woman in the development of the Baha'i communities of Iran and India in this period.[7] These tablets also shed light on how Baha'ullah and 'Abdu'l-Baha viewed the position of women in the Baha'i community, and in what areas they encouraged them to be active participants.

Baha'ullah is estimated to have composed 15,000 tablets and 'Abdu'l-Baha 27,000, a staggering total of 42,000 individual texts. Based on the collections used for this study, I would estimate that between 10–20 per cent of these tablets were addressed to women, i.e. approximately 4,200–8,400 tablets. This study is based on a close reading of more than 250 of these tablets, many of which have only recently been published. I have divided my study into three sections: 1) tablets addressed to the women of several prominent Babi-Baha'i families (those of Ibn-i Aṣdaq, Samandar and Nabīl ibn-i Nabīl); 2) tablets to female Baha'is in two provincial towns with sizeable Baha'i communities, Hamadan and Najafabad; and, 3) tablets to women of Zoroastrian heritage who converted to the Baha'i Faith in Iran and India.

Tablets to the women of some prominent Baha'i families

The family of Ibn-i Aṣdaq

Mulla Ṣādiq, Ibn-i Aṣdaq and their families received many tablets from Baha'ullah and 'Abdu'l-Baha.[8] Mulla Ṣādiq Muqaddas Khurāsānī (d. 1874) was born into a clerical family in Mashhad, where he became known as 'Muqaddas' ('holy', 'sanctified'). In the 1830s he studied under the Shaykhi leader, Sayyid Kāẓim Rashtī, rising to the rank of *mujtahid* shortly before his teacher's passing. Mulla Ṣādiq met the Bab on several occasions in Iraq, and he was one of the first prominent Shaykhis to align himself with the Babi movement. Mulla Ṣādiq, Quddūs and Mulla 'Alī-Akbar Ardistānī, were the first Babis to be tortured publicly in Iran for their faith (Shiraz, 1845). Mulla Ṣādiq fought at Shaykh Ṭabarsī and was one of the very few Babis to survive. He visited Baha'ullah in Baghdad in 1861 with his wife, Jināb-i Bībī (d. 1901) who was also a Babi, and their son, Ibn-i Aṣdaq. Mulla Ṣādiq is thought to have been one of the first Babis to recognize Baha'ullah as 'He whom God shall make manifest' (*man yuẓhiru-hu Allāh*), and he received the title 'Ismullāh al-Aṣdaq' ('the name of God, the most-truthful') from Baha'ullah. He visited 'Akka in 1874, and died in Hamadan shortly after returning to Iran. After his death, Mulla Ṣādiq was named a 'Hand of the Cause' by 'Abdu'l-Baha.[9]

Mīrzā-'Alī Muḥammad, Ibn-i Aṣdaq (1850–1928) was the eldest son of Mulla Ṣādiq. In 1861, Ibn-i Aṣdaq visited Baha'ullah in Baghdad with his father, and from 1862 to 1864, father and son were imprisoned in Tehran. In prison, Ibn-i Aṣdaq fell ill and was treated by Ḥakīm Masīḥ, who became one of the first Jews to accept the new religion.[10] Ibn-i Aṣdaq wrote to Baha'ullah expressing his desire for martyrdom, and in 1882 Baha'ullah conferred upon him the title, 'Shahīd, Ibn-i Shahīd' ('martyr, son of martyr'). Ibn-i Aṣdaq played an important role in the propagation of the Baha'i Faith in Iran, India, Burma, Central Asia, and the Caucasus, and in 1887 Baha'ullah named him one of the first 'Hands of the Cause of God' (*ayādī amrullāh*). Ibn-i Aṣdaq served on the first Baha'i Assembly of Tehran (established ca. 1897), and in 1919 he delivered 'Abdu'l-Baha's tablet to the Central Organization for a Durable Peace in The Hague. He made the pilgrimage to Palestine several times, and died in Tehran in 1928. Shoghi Effendi named him one of the 19 Apostles of Baha'ullah.[11]

In this section, I will discuss tablets addressed to Ibn-i Aṣdaq's wife, 'Adhrā Khānum, Ḍiyā' al-Ḥājjīya (1860–1923); his four daughters, Laqā'iyya (1886–1977), Huvīya (1890–1967), Rūḥā (1892–1982) and Ṭalī'a (1896–1958); his sister-in-law, Āqā Shāhzāda (1850–1902); and his mother-in-law, Shahanshāh Baygum (1836–1919). Āqā Shāhzāda converted to the Baha'i Faith some time in the mid-1870s,[12] following the conversion of her husband, Sayyid 'Abdullāh Intiẓām al-Salṭana (d. 1892),[13] through the family doctor, Muḥammad-Ḥusayn Munajjim-bāshī. Āqā Shāhzāda then converted her mother and her youngest sister, who was still a child. Shahanshāh Baygum was a Qajar princess, the daughter of Mīrzā Mas'ūd Anṣārī Garmrūdī (1790–1848) (twice appointed foreign minister by Muḥammad Shāh) and Ḍiyā' al-Salṭana (1797–1873), the seventh and, arguably, the most influential daughter of Fatḥ-'Alī Shah Qajar (d. 1834).[14]

Shahanshāh Baygum's first husband, Muḥammad Hāshim Qāḍī Ṭabāṭabā'ī, a relative of her father, died in 1864 and subsequently, Shahanshāh Baygum married a relative of her late husband, Mīrzā Ma'sūm Khān Anṣāri, who variously held the titles of 'Itimād al-Vizāra and Muntakhab al-Dawla. Around 1880 the family moved to Mashhad where Muntakhab al-Dawla took up a government position. Shahanshāh Baygum seems to have kept her conversion from her husband at this stage,[15] but before leaving Tehran she asked Munajjim-bāshī to introduce her to a prominent Baha'i in Mashhad. This prominent Baha'i was Ibn-i Aṣdaq, who began to visit Shahanshāh Baygum and Ḍiyā' al-Ḥājjīya clandestinely to tutor them in the Baha'i religion. Around 1881 Ibn-i Aṣdaq and Ḍiyā' al-Ḥājjīya married and moved to Tehran (Baha'ullah and 'Abdu'l-Baha 2005: 359–360). When Shahanshāh Baygum and her second husband returned to Tehran they built a large house in a garden in Khīābān-i Anṣārī where they lived together with Ḍiyā' al-Ḥājjīya and her family. Shahanshāh Baygum and Āqā Shāhzāda helped to support Ḍiyā' al-Ḥājjīya and Ibn-i Aṣdaq's family, allowing him to travel both inside and outside of Iran to promote the Baha'i Faith (Ibid.: 360).

Ibn-i Aṣdaq and Ḍiyā' al-Ḥājjīya had six children, two sons who died in childhood and four daughters: Laqā'iyya, who married Hidāyatullāh Mudabbir, Mudīr-i Khāqān (d. 1934), son of one of the first Baha'is of Rasht, Ghulām-'Alī Khān, Mudabbir al-Mamālik; Huvīya, who married 'Ināyatullāh Farzār, son of the prominent Tehrani Baha'i Ḥājjī Muḥammad Karīm-i 'Aṭṭār and Ibn-i Aṣdaq's half-sister, Shams-i Jahān Khānum; Rūḥā, who married Dr. Mūsā Khudādūst from Shiraz; and Ṭalī'a, who married Luṭfullāh Munajjim, the grandson of Munajjim-bāshī who had converted Intiẓām al-Salṭana (Ibid.: 357–367).

In 1913 Ibn-i Aṣdaq and his family were invited by 'Abdu'l-Baha to come on pilgrimage. Shahanshāh Baygum was too frail to travel and so she stayed in Tehran with her middle daughter, Khānum Shāhzāda (b. 1852), who was Muslim. Laqā'iyya was living with her husband in Rasht and could not travel because she had several young children. She took care of Huvīya's infant child so that she could join the rest of the family on pilgrimage.[16] The family spent more than seventy days in Haifa, throughout which Ḍiyā' al-Ḥājjīya and her daughters stayed in 'Abdu'l-Baha's house with Bahiyya Khānum and Munīra Khānum. Āqā Shāhzāda had passed away by 1913. It is evident from more than one of Baha'ullah's tablets to her that she had longed to go on pilgrimage, although it is unclear why she was unable to do so.[17] To date, at least 49 tablets addressed to these women have been published.[18]

Baha'ullah's tablets to these women date from the 'Akka period (1868–1892). Approximately half of the tablets are in Arabic, and most of those which are in Persian contain many Arabic phrases and sections. All of the women of Ibn-i Aṣdaq's family were literate, and his daughters were tutored by their maternal grandmother in Arabic grammar, Persian literature and calligraphy (Aṣdaq 1987: 7–8 and Baha'ullah and 'Abdu'l-Baha

Table 3.1 Tablets addressed to women

Name of addressee	*Number of tablets from Baha'ullah*	*Number of tablets from 'Abdu'l-Baha*	*Total number of tablets received*
Āqā Shāhzāda	10	6	16
Shahanshāh Baygum	2	4	6
Ḍiyā' al-Ḥājjīya	5	8	13
Laqā'iyya	3	2	5
Huvīya	2	2	4
Rūḥā	–	1	1
Ṭalī'a	–	–	0
Huvīya, Rūḥā, Ṭalī'a	–	1	1
Shahanshāh Baygum, Ḍiyā' al-Ḥājjīyya and her daughters	–	1	1
Ḍiyā' al-Ḥājjīya and her four daughters	–	2	2

2005: 515–516). It is interesting to note that Baha'ullah addressed at least three tablets to Ibn-i Aṣdaq's eldest daughter, Laqā'iyya, and another two to her younger sister, Huvīya, when they were both less than six years old.[19] By 1886, there were three generations of Baha'i women in Ibn-i Aṣdaq's immediate family.[20]

On the significance of receiving tablets

In a tablet to Āqā Shāhzāda, Baha'ullah says he is addressing her from the prison in 'Akka with a call that is sweeter than sugar and more luminous than the sun and moon. Baha'ullah says that she has drunk the wine of revelation, and taken hold of his tablets and writings (Baha'ullah and 'Abdu'l-Baha 2005: 208). In another tablet to her, Baha'ullah likens his words to precious gems and pearls which were hidden and which he has now revealed for her.[21] Elsewhere, Baha'ullah tells Shahanshāh Baygum that she has been mentioned at the throne (*'arsh*) of God, and that her name has been recorded in the tablets, and that he has revealed verses for her so that from them she might perceive the scent of the shirt of her Lord (a reference to the story of Joseph; ibid.: 205). It is impossible to know how many of the tablets originally revealed for these women have been lost. In a tablet to Ḍiyā' al-Ḥājjīya, Baha'ullah says she has repeatedly received divine verses (Ibid.: 219), and in a tablet to her from 'Abdu'l-Baha we read that she received many tablets (*alvāḥ-i muta'addada*) during the time of Baha'ullah (Ibid.: 294).[22]

Praise for their recognition of Baha'ullah

The significance of these women's recognition of Baha'ullah as a prophet is a theme which weaves through many of these tablets. In a tablet to Shahanshāh Baygum, 'Abdu'l-Baha says that few men of learning have recognized Baha'ullah, but that she is one of the very few who has (Ibid.: 298). To Āqā Shāhzāda, Baha'ullah writes that she has experienced the endless rains of God's mercy in the 'days of God', and has drunk from the cup of mystical knowledge (*'irfān*; ibid.: 210). To Laqā'iyya, Baha'ullah emphasizes the importance of recognizing the prophet during his lifetime, and he says she has achieved that which most of the clergy and rulers of the world have not (Ibid.: 221). Āqā Shāhzāda, Ḍiyā' al-Ḥājjīya and Shahanshāh Baygum all converted to the Baha'i Faith from Shi'i Islam, a brave and daring move for any woman in Qajar Iran. In a tablet to Rūḥā, 'Abdu'l-Baha speaks of the comparative ease with which she has accepted Baha'ullah, having been born into a devout Baha'i family:

> O thou illumined leaf!
>
> A hundred thousand maidservants, who for countless years engaged in divers arduous devotions, and who, with fervent longing and

tearful lamentation, supplicated the threshold of Divine Oneness that they might live for but a moment in these Days and perceive the merest glimmer of the Sinaitic fire, expired at last in the wilderness of separation, and, with infinite regret, laid down their lives in love's arena. Thou, however, having neither expended effort, nor suffered hardship, nor experienced the fatigue of arduous devotions, hast, through purest grace and bounty, become a recipient of this bestowal from Him Who is the Lord of the seen and the unseen, attained unto the Days of God, and been favored with a boundless outpouring of His mercy and loving-kindness.

(Aṣdaq 1999: preface)[23]

References to their royal heritage

Shahanshāh Baygum, who was descended from Fath-'Alī Shah through his seventh daughter, Ḍiyā' al-Salṭana, may have enjoyed a certain degree of status among the Qajar women of Tehran.[24] Her close family ties to Muslims within the ruling elite would have both helped her family escape direct persecution, and also enabled Ibn-i Aṣdaq to associate with the leading men of the day.[25] One of these influential relatives was Shahanshāh Baygum's nephew, 'Alī-Qulī Khān Mushāvir al-Mamālik, who served as Minister of Foreign Affairs on several occasions between 1915 and 1926, and who sought to represent Iran at the Paris Peace Conference in Versailles in 1919.[26] Another close relative of Shahanshāh Baygum was her first cousin, Galīn Khānum, Nāṣir al-Dīn Shah's first wife.

There are many subtle references to royalty in the tablets addressed to these women. In one very intriguing tablet, Baha'ullah says that Āqā Shāhzāda's recognition of him has raised her status above that of all queens: 'through the grace of God . . . thou hast attained unto a station which is the pride and glory of the queens of the world' (Aṣdaq 1999: 45).[27] In this same tablet Baha'ullah refers to Queen Victoria, who he says goes to church every day thinking that she is worshiping God, but how in reality she is just clinging to his name, and is essentially deprived of knowing him, like all the other empresses of the world (Baha'ullah and 'Abdu'l-Baha 2005: 207).[28] Baha'ullah sent a lengthy tablet to Queen Victoria shortly after arriving in 'Akka, in which he called on her to accept his prophetic claims, but also praised her for Britain's prohibition of the slave trade and system of parliamentary government.[29] Queen Victoria began to use the title 'Empress of India' around 1877, so this tablet probably dates from the late 1870s or early 1880s. In a similar tablet to Ḍiyā' al-Ḥājjīya, Baha'ullah says that the emperors (*qayāṣira*) and kings (*malik-hā*) eagerly awaited this day, but when it arrived they were all heedless of it (ibid.: 218–219). 'Abdu'l-Baha alludes to Ḍiyā' al-Ḥājjīya's royal heritage in both subtle and poetic terms in another tablet, saying that God has chosen her from among womankind and ennobled her head with the glittering crown of knowledge ('Abdu'l-Baha 1978: 59),[30] he explains:

> Thou hast round thy neck, in token of thy servitude unto the Ancient Beauty, a collar adorned with the jewels of the Most Great Name; and in thy ear, in token of thy thralldom unto that Embodied Spirit, thou wearest a golden ring bestowed upon thee from the loftiest Paradise.
>
> (Aṣdaq 1999: 44)[31]

In a tablet to Āqā Shāhzāda, Baha'ullah explains that all the queens and princesses of the world have sacrificed their material wealth to attain this day, but that all except a very few have been deprived of this bounty (Baha'ullah and 'Abdu'l-Baha 2005: 211).

Women vs. men

In his tablets to women, Baha'ullah often contrasts the faithful devotion of his female believers with the heedlessness of the majority of the men of their age. To Āqā Shāhzāda Baha'ullah writes that many leading men (*rijāl*) have failed to recognize him, whereas there are many women who have (Ibid.: 210). Similarly, to Shahanshāh Baygum, 'Abdu'l-Baha writes that many women have recognized God's new revelation, whilst very few men of learning have (Ibid.: 298). In a tablet to Ibn-i Aṣdaq's mother, Jināb-i Bībī, Baha'ullah says she has attained that which the majority of the prominent men of the world remain ignorant of (Ibid.: 36).[32] By employing such analogies, Baha'ullah is raising the status of his female followers to one higher than that of the clergy of their time. In a tablet to Ḍiyā' al-Ḥājjīya, he writes that the clergy (*'ulama'*) and temporal rulers (*umarā'*) have, throughout the centuries, asked God to witness this day, but that when it arrived they were unable to recognize it (Ibid.: 220).[33]

The role of women in the Baha'i community

Both Baha'ullah and 'Abdu'l-Baha encouraged Ibn-i Aṣdaq's female relatives to be active members of the Baha'i community. One of Baha'ullah's tablets to Ḍiyā' al-Ḥājjīya includes an Arabic prayer for her to recite in order to call on God to assist her and other female Baha'is to arise to serve their community (Ibid.: 219). In a tablet to Huvīya, Baha'ullah expresses the hope that she and her female relatives will play an instrumental role in guiding other women to the new religion (Ibid.: 222). Given the prominence of this family within the Baha'i community of Iran, and its strong family ties to high-ranking government officials, the women of this family would have been in a position to introduce the Baha'i religion to the wives, daughters and mothers of princes and ministers.[34] Tehran's population in 1883 has been estimated at just 100,000, and it is not unreasonable to believe, therefore, that socially prominent female Baha'is could have exerted influence on other leading women of the capital.

It is clear from a number of these tablets that both Baha'ullah and 'Abdu'l-Baha placed great emphasis on the moral conduct of Baha'i women. In a tablet to Ḍiyā' al-Ḥājjīya, Baha'ullah asks God to adorn the women believers with the ornament of chastity (*'iṣmat*) and to illumine them with the light of knowledge (*ma'rifat*). The fostering of upright, moral behaviour implies strict observance of Baha'i law, something which Baha'ullah refers to in at least two of his tablets to Ḍiyā' al-Ḥājjīya (e.g., ibid.: 219).[35] To Āqā Shāhzāda, 'Abdu'l-Baha writes that Baha'i women should arise to serve their community through the power of piety ('Abu'l-Baha 1978: 139), and he continues by reassuring her that her services are recognized by God:

> Render thou thanks unto the All-Glorious that thy services have been set down and preserved in clear characters in the records of the heavenly court of the All-Merciful, wherein a bounteous recompense hath been ordained and held in store for thee
>
> (Aṣdaq 1999: 45)[36]

In an essentially gender-segregated community, the influence of these women would have primarily been limited to that which they could exert on their female coreligionists, or female friends and relations, Baha'i or otherwise. Perhaps the most important contribution of the women of Ibn-i Aṣdaq's family to the Baha'i community of Iran was the establishment of the first classes aimed at training Baha'i women to propagate their religion (*dars-i tablīgh*).[37] Upon hearing of the establishment of this class, 'Abdu'l-Baha sent a tablet via Ibn-i Aṣdaq and his wife to all those women attending the classes. In addition to Ḍiyā' al-Ḥājjīya, her four daughters, and a sister of Ibn-i Aṣdaq (Ukht-i Shahīd, most likely Ṣamadiyya), 'Abdu'l-Baha addressed his tablet to a further fifteen women: Bigum Sulṭān, Khadīja Sulṭān, the mother of Āqā Sayyid Mihdī, Qudsiyya, Laqā'iyya, Ḍiyā'iyya, Thanā'iyya, Ḥishmat, Lamī'a, Batūl, Shawkat, Thābita, the mother of Mīrzā Zamān, the wife of Mīrzā Zamān and Galīn Khānum. 'Abdu'l-Baha congratulates them for having been the first to establish such a class and expresses the hope that in a short space of time they will become skilled in using rational proofs, decisive evidence, clear explanations, luminous proofs, eloquent speech and fluent words in the face of the learned of the world ('Abdu'l-Baha 1978: 79).[38] 'Abdu'l-Baha stresses the importance of these classes and encourages the addressees by telling them that they may even surpass men in promoting and propagating the Baha'i religion:

Confirmations from the kingdom of God will assuredly be received, enabling some radiant leaves to appear resplendent in the assemblage of this world with clear proofs and convincing reasons, which will adorn the cause of womanhood. They will prove that in this cycle women are equal to men, nay in certain aspects they will excel. Ponder ye: in this wonderful Cause numerous were the men who scaled the heights of knowledge; they had a brilliant utterance, a convincing proof, an eloquent tongue and magnificent speech, but the blessed leaf, Jinab-i Tahirih, because she was a woman, emerged with immense splendor and dumbfounded all the people. If she were a man, this would not have been so at all. Therefore, ye should know that the greatness of the Cause hath penetrated the nerves and veins of the world in such wise that if one of the leaves is attracted and gains mastery in demonstrating reasons and proofs and in uttering convincing evidences, she will shine resplendently. O radiant leaves, I swear by the Beauty of the Desire One and the Mystery of Existence that if ye work actively in this realm, the outpourings of the Blessed Beauty will reflect as the sun in the mirrors of your hearts. Your progress will astonish all.

(BWCRD 1997: 48–49)[39]

The families of Samandar and Nabīl Ibn-i Nabīl

The families of Shaykh Kāẓim-i Samandar ('Samandar') and his brother Ḥājjī Shaykh Muḥammad-'Alī ('Nabīl ibn-i Nabīl') were the recipients of a large number of tablets from both Baha'ullah and 'Abdu'l-Baha, many of which have recently been published in a collection entitled *Āyāt-i Bayyināt* (Baha'ullah and 'Abdu'l-Baha 1999).[40] Shaykh Kāẓim (1844–1918) was the son of Ḥājjī Shaykh Muḥammad, a prominent Shaykhi and later Babi of Qazvin. Shaykh Kāẓim was a staunch follower of Baha'ullah, from whom he received the title 'Samandar' ('Salamander'). He visited 'Akka a number of times and his daughter, Thurayyā, married one of Baha'ullah's sons, Ḍiyā'ullāh. Shoghi Effendi named Samandar one of the nineteen Apostles of Baha'ullah. Samandar's brother, Ḥājjī Shaykh Muḥammad-'Alī ('Nabīl ibn-i Nabīl') was a similarly devout Baha'i who resided for a considerable amount of time in Istanbul where he was a successful merchant. Nabīl ibn-i Nabīl committed suicide in 1890 in the wake of false accusations brought against the Afnāns and other leading Baha'i traders in Istanbul by the supporters of Ṣubḥ-i Azal.[41]

Āyāt-i Bayyināt contains 393 tablets (188 by Baha'ullah and 205 by 'Abdu'l-Baha), 35 (9 per cent) of which are addressed to women, including: 3 to Fāṭima Sulṭān (d. 1890), Samandar's first wife; 8 to Ma'ṣūma Farhādī (d. ca. 1918), Samandar's second wife; 1 tablet to Samandar's daughters; 3 to Ṭaraziyya Farhādī (d. 1946), Samandar's daughter-in-law and wife of Ṭarāzullāh

Samandarī; 8 tablets to Sharīfa Baygum, wife of Nabīl ibn-i Nabīl; 3 tablets to Sādhijiyya (b. 1877) and Rūḥiyya (b. 1878), daughters of Nabīl ibn-i Nabīl; 3 to Qudsiyya Ḥakīmbāshī-Farzānī and 2 tablets to 'Izziyya Arbāb Naṣīrī, both daughters-in-law of Nabīl ibn-i Nabīl. The average length of the tablets addressed to individual women by Baha'ullah is 11 lines, slightly longer than those of 'Abdu'l-Baha at 7 lines. The majority of these tablets to women are in Persian, although often interspersed with Arabic phrases. There are some which incorporate large sections in Arabic, sometimes in the form of prayers (Tablets B98, B119, B121, A76 and A93; these numbers refer to the tablets as numbered in *Āyāt-i Bayyināt*; 'B' signifies a tablet of Baha'ullah, 'A' a tablet composed by 'Abdu'l-Baha), and there are a small number purely in Arabic (Tablets B120, A86, A162 and A164). Most of the tablets in this collection carry Arabic opening invocations, but there are a number with Persian invocations.[42]

Fāṭima Sulṭān, first wife of Samandar

Baha'ullah's two tablets to Fāṭima Sulṭān date from the 'Akka period (there are no pre-1868 tablets to women in *Āyāt-i Bayyināt*).[43] Both of these tablets are in Persian, interspersed with Arabic phrases. The inclusion of phrases and whole sections in Arabic may suggest that the addressee was proficient in Arabic, but given the liturgical significance of Arabic for Baha'is from a Muslim background, it could be argued that they would have expected to be addressed at least partly in Arabic, and it does not, therefore, necessarily follow that they understood the language. In one tablet to Fāṭima Sulṭān (B96), Baha'ullah writes that women all over the world have longed to attain this day, and that the queens of the world mention the name of the Promised One in their places of worship every day, but they have been deprived of recognizing him, implying that the station of Baha'i women is above that of royalty.[44] Baha'ullah then calls on God to assist the male and female Baha'is to act in accordance with that which pleases God. Baha'ullah implies equality between the male and female members of the community, although, because of prevailing social norms, most Baha'i community activities in Iran were divided down gender lines well into the 1930s. The tablet ends with an Arabic blessing for Fāṭima Sulṭān and all the female Baha'is. In this way Fāṭima Sulṭān acted as a conduit for Baha'ullah's words to the women of her extended family and the other women Baha'is in Qazvin. In another tablet to Fāṭima Sulṭān (B118), Baha'ullah clearly states that he is writing to her from the prison of 'Akka.[45] In this tablet Baha'ullah again emphasizes the equality of men and women, saying that God mentions both his near ones (*awliyā*) and his handmaidens (*imā'*) in the prison, and he calls on God to assist all the devout male and female believers (*qānitīn va qānitāt*) in Qazvin; an important centre of Babi and then Baha'i activity from the 1840s.

In a lengthy tablet addressed to Fāṭima Sulṭān and her children written in his own hand (A76), ʻAbdu'l-Baha describes the pilgrimage of her son, ʻAbd al-Ḥusayn, to the Haifa-ʻAkka area. This tablet ends with a prayer in Arabic for the whole family, in which ʻAbdu'l-Baha refers to them as a 'blessed family' (*ʻā'ila mubāraka*). The Samandarī family was one of the leading Baha'i families not only of Qazvin, but of Iran as a whole, and it seems that ʻAbdu'l-Baha is encouraging Fāṭima Sulṭān and her children to take justified pride in their lineage.[46]

Maʻṣūma Farhādī, second wife of Samandar

Maʻṣūma Farhādī was the mother of Hand of the Cause (*ayādī amrullāh*) Ṭarāzullāh Samandarī.[47] In one of his tablets to Maʻṣūma (B97), Baha'ullah describes the declaration of his mission as an 'unveiling' (*kashf-i ḥijāb*), a poignant image for a woman in Qajar Iran. Baha'ullah says that she has drunk from the cup of knowledge (*ʻirfān*) and attained unto the writings (*āthār*) of God. He encourages her to spread the Baha'i religion and to tell other women that the Day of God has come. Baha'ullah asks Maʻṣūma to send his greetings to the female Baha'is of Qazvin and enjoin them to 'purity and holiness' (*tanzīh u taqdīs*). He continues by saying that the best garment in this world for Baha'i women is chastity.[48] Baha'ullah's other tablet to Maʻṣūma (B119) is mostly in Arabic. In this tablet Baha'ullah consoles her on the passing of a relative, saying that God's wisdom and mysteries are hidden within death. Baha'ullah calls on her and the other women believers to rejoice that they are remembered by God in this day of great joy (*yawm-i faraḥ-i akbar*).

There are also six tablets to Maʻṣūma Farhādī from ʻAbdu'l-Baha in this collection, five of which are in his own hand. In a short tablet in Persian (A92), ʻAbdu'l-Baha praises her for having been a Babi, and having subsequently given her allegiance to Baha'ullah. ʻAbdu'l-Baha then calls on her to become drunk on the wine of the Covenant (i.e. devote herself wholeheartedly to ʻAbdu'l-Baha).[49] ʻAbdu'l-Baha is highlighting the loyalty of the Farhādī and Samandarī families to the Bab, Baha'ullah and himself, and praising their Babi-Baha'i heritage. This tablet is essentially a short, personal letter, but it may well have been shared with other family members. In another tablet to Maʻṣūma (A93), ʻAbdu'l-Baha writes that in this mighty century, a number of women will be raised up to tear down the veils of the people of this world through the force of mighty proofs,[50] suggesting that some women will be at the forefront of the propagation of the new religion. This tablet also contains an Arabic prayer for Maʻṣūma to recite.[51] The prayer asks God to make her a sign of unity and the essence of knowledge among the women believers.

In another tablet (A94), ʻAbdu'l-Baha describes the pilgrimage of Maʻṣūma's son to the Baha'i shrines and how he prayed for all the family members, and for those who have passed away.[52] 'Abdu'l-Baha praises her family and says that she should be assured of Baha'ullah's special favour (*faḍl-i makhṣūṣ*). In another tablet (A95) 'Abdu'l-Baha once again praises Ma'ṣūma's family,[53] and emphasizes the fact that they have been believers since the time of the Bab. He says that he hopes they will continue to be firm in their faith, even in the face of tests and difficulties. Elsewhere (A96), 'Abdu'l-Baha once again makes reference to Ma'ṣūma's Babi-Baha'i heritage and praises her husband and his loyalty to the Covenant. In his sixth tablet to Ma'ṣūma (A97), 'Abdu'l-Baha says that she should give thanks to God for the faith of her family, calling them 'the sign of God's guidance', adding that he had sent her son Ṭarāzullāh all over Iran on missions, but that now he is sending him to Qazvin for her contentment.

Samandar's daughters: Dhikriyya, Thurayyā, Ḥubbiyya, Mihriyya and Khātūn Jān

This collection contains one tablet from Baha'ullah to the daughters of Samandar (B121). It was composed in 'Akka and opens in Persian, ending in an Arabic prayer for them to recite. The tablet ends with Baha'ullah calling on God to bestow blessings on his closest male and female believers (*muqbilīn* and *muqbilāt*) through the Hands of the Cause and Samandar, leading figures in the Baha'i community of Iran.[54]

Ṭarāziyya Farhādī, daughter-in-law of Samandar and wife of Ṭarāzullāh

In a very short tablet (A98), 'Abdu'l-Baha says that she should give thanks to God for being born into such a family. Elsewhere (A99), 'Abdu'l-Baha explains how Ṭarāzullāh is currently travelling in the area of Shiraz, and 'Abdu'l-Baha praises him for having left his loving family to teach the Baha'i religion. He says he is happy that Samandar has such a son who is following in the footsteps of his father, and that Ṭarāzullāh's relationship to his father is a true, spiritual one (*nisbat-ash ḥaqīqī ast*). 'Abdu'l-Baha recognizes that this separation is very hard for her, but consoles her by saying that she and her husband have an eternal connection.[55] In his third tablet to Ṭarāziyya (A100), 'Abdu'l-Baha thanks her for her letter, assures her of God's favours, and praises her for her time spent teaching girls.[56] In this tablet 'Abdu'l-Baha again mentions Ṭarāzullāh's extensive travels in Iran and elsewhere to promote steadfast allegiance among the Baha'is to the leadership of 'Abdu'l-Baha. He explains that Ṭarāzullāh fell ill and rested in Haifa, but that now he is sending him back to Qazvin for a few days before he dispatches him on another mission. This tablet clearly shows how 'Abdu'l-Baha directed the activities of the Baha'i *muballigh*s in Iran from Haifa.

Sharīfa Baygum, wife of Nabīl ibn-i Nabīl

In a tablet written partly in Persian, partly in Arabic (B98), Baha'ullah says that she should give thanks that she was mentioned by God in the prison of 'Akka, and he tells us something interesting about the composition process.[57] Baha'ullah says that when Jinab-i Ism-i Jūd (a prominent Qazvini Baha'i) was in his presence and the tablets were being sorted and the names of the addressees were being arranged in the notebook, it was noticed that her name was not among them, and so at that moment Baha'ullah revealed these words for her. It seems that Baha'ullah had been presented with a list of the names of those Baha'is who had requested tablets. Baha'ullah's second tablet to Sharīfa Baygum (B120) is entirely in Arabic, which suggests that she was proficient in that language. This is a tablet written to console her after the death of a relative, possibly that of her husband. Baha'ullah asks God to change her sorrow into joy, and to adorn her with the ornament of patience. Baha'ullah says death is one of the doors of God's mercy, and that death is nothing more than the ascension of the spirit from its lower station to its higher one.[58]

Six of the tablets to Sharīfa Baygum are from 'Abdu'l-Baha, five of which are in his own hand. In one short tablet (A159) 'Abdu'l-Baha says that certain Baha'i women will shine so brightly in the world that they will obliterate all mention of their ancestors and outstrip all those women who came before them.[59] 'Abdu'l-Baha says that they will have such impact because they will appear with the utmost grace and eloquence (*dar kamāl-i nadārat u faṣāḥat u balāghat mab'ūth shavand*). In another short tablet to Sharīfa Baygum (A160), 'Abdu'l-Baha urges her to remain steadfast in her faith so that she will be praised by the maidens of heaven. Elsewhere (A161), 'Abdu'l-Baha expresses his sorrow to Sharīfa Baygum in the strongest terms at the death of a child from her family.[60] 'Abdu'l-Baha consoles her, saying that this 'sapling' (*nahāl*) has been planted in the garden of God, and has been transplanted to the heavenly paradise.[61] Given the personal nature of the content, it is unlikely that this tablet would have been shared with anyone outside the family. In a shorter tablet (A162), this time in Arabic, 'Abdu'l-Baha says she should thank God for having chosen her as a believer, and for having given her a believing son. In a more substantial tablet (A163) 'Abdu'l-Baha assures her that she is remembered at the holy shrines, expresses his hope that her wishes will be fulfilled, and urges her not to be sad, saying that these difficult days will come to an end, and we will all enter a much sweeter world.[62] It is clear from these tablets that Sharīfa Baygum (and many other Baha'i women like her) felt such a strong, personal connection to 'Abdu'l-Baha that it was natural for her to write to him about the sorrows of her own life, and the sufferings of the Baha'i community of Iran as a whole.

In one tablet to Sharīfa Baygum (A167), 'Abdu'l-Baha addresses topics which would have been of interest to many women within the Persian-speaking

Baha'i community at the beginning of the twentieth century. This tablet was sent to Sharīfa Baygum when she was living in 'Ishqābād in Turkmenistan, a city which boasted a large and active Baha'i community in the time of 'Abdu'l-Baha, and where the construction of the first Baha'i House of Worship (Mashriq al-Adhkār) was completed in 1907.[63] From the text of the tablet it is clear that Sharīfa Baygum had originally written to Bahiyya Khānum with questions, and that when Bahiyya Khānum showed this letter to 'Abdu'l-Baha, he wrote this tablet in response. Sharīfa Baygum's first question was whether Baha'i women can abandon the use of the veil (it seems that she does not mean altogether, but rather in women-only gatherings).[64] 'Abdu'l-Baha says that he has heard that there has been some discussion and difference of opinion about that matter among the Baha'is, but does not pronounce judgment on the matter himself. Her second question concerns classes to train women to propagate the Baha'i religion (*dars-i tablīgh*). 'Abdu'l-Baha says he is very much in favour of such classes, adding that the women who take part must be informed of the divine proofs (*dalā'il u barāhīn-i ilāhī*) and knowledgeable as to the laws of the *Kitāb-i Aqdas* so that they can teach other women. He says that these meetings must be held in a most orderly fashion (*dar nahāyat-i intiẓām*) so that in the shortest amount of time female instructors (*mu'allama-hā*) and teachers (*muballigha-hā*) be trained.

Nabīl ibn-i Nabīl's daughters, Sādhijiyya and Rūḥiyya

In this fairly lengthy tablet to Sādhijiyya and Rūḥiyya (B127), Baha'ullah asks them not to grieve at the death of their father, whom he praises in the strongest terms. Baha'ullah then broadens the scope of his words by calling on God to set Qazvin ablaze with the fire of those who are near to God (*awliyā*) and to illumine the city with the light of knowledge (*'irfān*). In a short tablet addressed to Sādhijiyya (A71), 'Abdu'l-Baha says that through her father the whole of her family has been blessed.[65] Echoing many of his tablets to members of Samandar's family, 'Abdu'l-Baha expresses the hope that each member of the family will become one of the mighty signs (*āyāt-i kubrā*) in service to the Baha'i Faith. 'Abdu'l-Baha's praise for Sādhijiyya's family comes hand in hand with his hope and expectation that she will live up to her elders' achievements.

The daughters-in-law of Nabīl ibn-i Nabīl

There are two tablets in *Āyāt-i Bayyināt* addressed to the wife of Nabīl ibn-i Nabīl's son, Āqā Shaykh Aḥmad. These tablets are most likely addressed to Āqā Shaykh Aḥmad's second wife, Qudsiyya Hakīmbāshī-Farzānī, as his first wife, his cousin, Dhikriyya Samandarī, died in 1894. In one of these tablets (A164), which is entirely in Arabic and in the hand of 'Abdu'l-Baha, 'Abdu'l-Baha assures Qudsiyya that if she loosens her tongue in praise of God, the 'angels of inspiration' (*malā'ikat ilhām*) will instruct her in the most exceptional meanings and modes of expression. 'Abdu'l-Baha is encouraging her to take part in the teaching of her religion, and reassuring her of divine assistance if she takes the first step. In another tablet addressed to Āqā Shaykh Aḥmad and his family members (A185), 'Abdu'l-Baha says that he is writing them this letter as a sign of his heartfelt affection for them. As in many other tablets, 'Abdu'l-Baha says that he finds it difficult to answer all the letters that he receives.

Āyāt-i Bayyināt also contains two tablets from 'Abdu'l-Baha to another daughter-in-law of Nabīl ibn-i Nabīl, 'Izziyya Arbāb Naṣīrī-Qazvīnī, wife of Munīr. In one of these tablets (A190), 'Abdu'l-Baha writes that Munīr, who was on pilgrimage, has requested a separate tablet for her, and although he has no time, he is writing this letter so that her husband's request will be fulfilled. 'Abdu'l-Baha ends the tablet by saying that 'Izziyya has permission to travel to the Holy Land for pilgrimage whenever she has the means to do so.

In addition to the tablets addressed specifically to the female members of the Samandarī and Nabīlī families, there are two tablets in *Āyāt-i Bayyināt* addressed to the female Baha'is of Qazvin. In one of these tablets (A40), 'Abdu'l-Baha discusses the attacks launched against him by his half-brother, Muḥammad-'Alī. 'Abdu'l-Baha tells them how words fabricated by Muḥammad-'Alī have been attributed to him, and asks them to compare these falsely attributed writings with the tablets they have received from him in the past. 'Abdu'l-Baha says that until now he has not responded, but that recently some printed forgeries reached Haifa and so now he is compelled to write to warn the believers. The other tablet (A86) is addressed to both the male and female Baha'is of Qazvin and is essentially a prayer in Arabic for them to recite. Presumably copies of this prayer would have been made and distributed among the Baha'is in Qazvin to be recited in meetings or used for private prayer.

Tablets to Baha'i women in two provincial towns

Hamadan

This section is based on the recently published history of the Baha'i community in Hamadan, *Ta'rīkh-i amrī-yi Hamadan* by 'Abd al-Ḥamīd Ishrāq-Khāvarī, which contains a small proportion of the tablets addressed by 'Abdu'l-Baha to the Baha'i women of that town (Ishrāq-Khāvarī 2004).[66] In a tablet addressed to one male and three female Baha'is (at least three of whom seem to be of Jewish descent, as were many of the early Baha'is of Hamadan),[67] 'Abdu'l-Baha explains that, due to his heavy workload, he is only able to write in brief, but that he is writing so that they will know they are remembered at the Holy Threshold (Ishrāq-Khāvarī 2004: 21). He says that however lacking and imperfect the physical tongue and pen are, the tongue of the spirit is in constant conversation with them, and the pen of the mind is continually writing (Ishrāq-Khāvarī 2004: 21–22). In this tablet 'Abdu'l-Baha says he longs for the time when the male and female Baha'is of Hamadan will become the 'cause of the luminosity of the world of humanity'.[68] Here 'Abdu'l-Baha clearly specifies both the male Baha'is (*yārān*) and the female Baha'is (*imā'*).

The *Ta'rīkh-i amrī-yi Hamadan* contains a number of other tablets from 'Abdu'l-Baha to individual Baha'i women in Hamadan. In one such tablet, addressed to the wife of Ḥājjī Āqā Jān, 'Abdu'l-Baha says that she has received bounty from God without asking for it, and that her family is blessed (Ishrāq-Khāvarī 2004: 231). In a similarly concise tablet to the daughter of Ḥājjī Āqā Jān, 'Abdu'l-Baha says that her father has always asked for assistance and favour for her, and that she should be grateful to him and serve him in all necessary ways. There is the sense in this tablet (as there is in many of the tablets to members of the Samandarī family) that 'Abdu'l-Baha is praising the spiritual lineage of the addressee.[69]

A number of female Baha'is from Hamadan made the pilgrimage to Palestine in the time of 'Abdu'l-Baha, where they met with Baha'ullah's eldest daughter Bahiyya Khānum, and 'Abdu'l-Baha's wife, Munīra Khanum. Mīrzā 'Abd al-Raḥīm Khān, Ḥāfiẓ al-Siḥḥa, one of the prominent members of the Hamadan Baha'i community, led a large group of female and male Baha'is on pilgrimage in early 1913. They travelled via Kirmanshah by litter (*kajāva*), and they eventually arrived in Haifa several months later, around the same time that 'Abdu'l-Baha returned from his journey to Europe and America.[70]

A Baha'i-run school for girls (Madrasa-yi Mawhibat-i Banāt) was established in Hamadan in 1909 (Ishrāq-Khāvarī 2004: 127–129),[71] and was attended by pupils from Baha'i, Jewish and Muslim backgrounds.[72] All of the directors, superintendents (*nāẓim*s) and teachers at the school appear to have been women.[73] The Baha'i Assembly of Hamadan established a committee to administer the affairs of the Ta'īd (boys') and Mawhibat (girls') schools, although it is not clear from the *Ta'rīkh-i amrī-yi Hamadan* whether or not any women served on that committee. By 1919 the Baha'is had also established classes in Hamadan for women and girls aimed at deepening their knowledge of the Baha'i religion and training them to propagate it (Ishrāq-Khāvarī 2004: 354).[74]

'Abdu'l-Baha wrote several tablets to those who worked at the girls' school. In one tablet, addressed to the first two teachers, Munavvar and Ṭavūs, and the superintendent, Ḥannā, 'Abdu'l-Baha praises them and those who have established the school (Ibid.: 316).[75] 'Abdu'l-Baha says the girls' school is more important than the boys' school because young women today must have knowledge of the sciences (*'ulūm*), learning (*ma'ārif*), crafts (*ṣanāyi'*) and new inventions (*badāyi'*) of this century so that they can teach children and fully educate their own offspring from an early age. 'Abdu'l-Baha then calls on all the Baha'is in Hamadan to pay special attention to the girls' school, and praises the teachers at the school in the strongest terms for following the ordinances of Baha'ullah by arising to educate girls (Ibid.: 316).[76] 'Abdu'l-Baha says that the day will come when these girls will become mothers and will, in utmost gratitude, pray to God for their teachers' success and prosperity. It is at the end of this tablet that 'Abdu'l-Baha decrees that the school should be named 'Mawhibat' (lit. 'gift', 'bounty').

In another tablet addressed to the women teachers of the Mawhibat School, 'Abdu'l-Baha says that in the nineteenth century, girls in Iran were completely deprived of education and had no schools, no teachers and no moral educators (Ibid.: 317).[77] 'Abdu'l-Baha notes that the situation has changed and that now numerous schools for girls have opened in Iran. 'Abdu'l-Baha says that these schools are deficient, though, for they neglect moral education (*tarbiyat*), which he argues is more important than 'schooling' (*ta'līm*). 'Abdu'l-Baha says it is good that a Baha'i school for girls has opened in Hamadan so that they can educate the girls in chastity (*'iṣmat u 'iffat*), good manners and right conduct (*ḥusn-i akhlāq u ādāb*), as well as the sciences (*ta'līm-i 'ulūm*).

In a tablet to Yūsuf Muttaḥida, 'Abdu'l-Baha says he is very pleased with the performance of the pupils of the Mawhibat School in their exams, and he sends greetings to Naw-Ẓuhūr Baygum who taught at the school for some time (Ibid.: 318).[78] It seems that 'Abdu'l-Baha was kept informed about (and took a personal interest in) the progress of the school. The staff at the Mawhibat School were a diverse group: some were local Baha'i women (of Jewish and Muslim descent), and others came to Hamadan from cities such as Isfahan and Shiraz to teach at the school. Three daughters of a prominent convert to the Baha'i Faith in nearby Malāyir, the Qajar prince Mihdī-Qulī Mīrzā Mawzūn, Ṣadr al-Mulūk, Shams al-Mulūk and Akhtar al-Mulūk, taught at the school, where they seem to have been schooled. Ṣadr al-Mulūk married 'Abd al-Ḥamīd Ishrāq-Khāvarī, but she died just a few months after marriage due to medical negligence on the part of a local doctor (Ibid.: 129–132).[79]

Najafabad

This section is based on Fatḥullāh Mudarris's history of the Baha'i community of Najafabad, the *Ta'rīkh-i amr-i Baha'i dar Najafabad* (Mudarris 2004).[80] The Baha'i community of Najafabad grew out of the sizeable Babi community established there in the mid-nineteenth century. A Baha'i-run girls' school (Sa'ādat) was established in Najafabad around 1917. By 1928, a new building had been constructed next to the Baha'i boys' school to house the school for girls (Ibid.: 140). The school's popularity among Muslim inhabitants of the town can partly be explained by the fact that, at that time, no government school for girls existed in Najafabad. The Sa'ādat schools were closed in 1934 by order of the government.

Several women played an active role in the Najafabad Baha'i community from the very beginning, especially in the area of children's education. One such woman was Baygum, a niece of the prominent local Baha'i Mulla Zayn al-'Ābidīn, renamed Zayn al-Muqarrabīn by Baha'ullah (Ibid.: 176). Baygum was born in 1863 and her father, encouraged by his brother-in-law Zayn al-Muqarrabīn, took steps to have Baygum and her brothers and sisters taught to read and write Persian, and trained to read the Baha'i scriptures. When Baygum's husband passed away she wrote to 'Abdu'l-Baha and he replied with a tablet in which he expressed his sorrow at her loss, praised her husband and urged her not to grieve (Ibid.: 177). Some time after receiving this tablet, Baygum set up a small, traditional school (*maktabkhāna*) in her own home and she taught the sons and daughters of the local Baha'is to read and write (Ibid.: 177). In another tablet to her 'Abdu'l-Baha says that there are many ways of serving God, but the greatest service and the most complete reward is the education of the sons and daughters of the Baha'is, and the teaching of their orphans and children (Ibid.: 177). 'Abdu'l-Baha encourages Baygum to put the utmost effort into educating these boys and girls, so that her school will become the model school for all others (*tā ān maktab sar-rishta-yi sā'ir-i maktab-hā shavad*).

Another influential female figure in the Najafabad Baha'i community was Ustād Ḥājjīya Khānum Raḥmānī (Ibid.: 178). She is said to have played an important role in the organization of Baha'i women's gatherings and educational classes in Najafabad, for which she was praised by the Baha'i National Committee for the Advancement of Women (*lajna-yi millī-yi taraqqī-yi nisvān*).[81] Ustād Ḥājjīya Khānum Raḥmānī ran a *maktab* in her home, which seems to have functioned as a kindergarten for Baha'i children. She died in Najafabad in 1967, aged 90.

One other prominent Baha'i woman in Najafabad who took an active interest in the education of the young was Ustād Bībī Jān, also known by her pen-name, 'Makhmūra' (Ibid.: 179–181). Makhmūra was literate in both Persian and Arabic and had a good knowledge of both literatures. For many years she ran Qur'an classes at her home, until her conversion to the Baha'i Faith at the age of 60. Following her conversion she stopped her Qur'an class and instead opened a small school for Baha'i children. When the Baha'i-run girls' school opened in Najafabad, Makhmūra closed her home school. Martha Root, the prominent American Baha'i itinerant teacher, visited Najafabad in 1929 and she met Makhmūra, who composed a poem in praise of her (Ibid.: 179). Makhmūra died in Najafabad in 1935, aged around 100.

In addition to the tablets addressed to individual women, there is a lengthy tablet quoted in Mudarris's history written by 'Abdu'l-Baha to all the male and female Baha'is in Najafabad, in which he refers to Najafabad's place in Babi-Baha'i history and expresses the hope that 'that blessed region' (*ān khiṭṭa-yi mubāraka*), will continue to flourish (Ibid.: 34–35). 'Abdu'l-Baha writes that all are amazed at how the Baha'i Faith has spread in both the east and the west, and that what is even more amazing is that funds for the construction of a Baha'i House of Worship (Mashriq al-Adhkār) in Chicago are being contributed by Baha'is from all over the world.[82] He then gives the example of a poor woman from Manchester who had no money to donate to the project, and so instead cut off her hair, sold it and donated the money to the Temple fund.[83] 'Abdu'l-Baha says that he does not advise such actions, but he admires them because they are a sign of dedication and self-sacrifice. 'Abdu'l-Baha then relates a similar story of how a poor woman donated all she owned, a handful of dates, to the Prophet Muhammad to help towards funding one of his campaigns. 'Abdu'l-Baha concludes by saying that this European woman's decision to sacrifice her hair for the Mashriq al-Adhkār is a proof of how strong the Baha'i religion has become.[84]

In a long tablet addressed to a mixed group of 16 named individuals, including seven women,[85] 'Abdu'l-Baha says that those advocating parliamentary government caused such a storm in Iran and sparked such a revolution, but that this will amount to little because they have concerned themselves with worldly matters (Mudarris 2004: 38). 'Abdu'l-Baha says that the Baha'is in Najafabad should strive to distinguish themselves from the rest of their countrymen (*dar jamī'-i shu'ūn az īn khalq mumtāz bāshand*), and seek to guide them to the new religion.

In another tablet, this time addressed to all male and female Baha'is of Najafabad, 'Abdu'l-Baha emphasizes the role played by the Babis and early Baha'is in Najafabad, and he reminds them how a number of the Baha'is of their town were martyred for their faith (Ibid.: 41–42),[86] and calls on them to be firm in their faith. 'Abdu'l-Baha says that now the most important of all activities is the propagation of the religion, and adds that the old cohort of Baha'i preachers (*muballigh*s) should train a new generation. The tablet ends with a prayer in Arabic for all the Baha'is of the town, male and female.

Tablets to Baha'i women of Zoroastrian heritage in Iran and India

A large number of the tablets addressed to Baha'is of Zoroastrian heritage have recently been published in a collection entitled *Yārān-i Pārsī* (Baha'ullah and 'Abdu'l-Baha 1998).[87] This collection contains eight tablets by Baha'ullah and 735 tablets written by 'Abdu'l-Baha. None of Baha'ullah's tablets are specifically addressed to women, but 153 (21 per cent) of 'Abdu'l-Baha's tablets are addressed to women: 57 to individual women, nine to groups of women, and 87 to mixed groups of men and women.[88] Over 180 women addressees are named in this collection, the majority of whom (approximately 80 per cent) received one tablet, a further 11 per cent received two tablets, and the remaining nine per cent three tablets or more. Those women

Figure 3.1 The four daughters of Ibn-i Aṣdaq circa 1924 (left to right): Laqā'iyya, Rūḥā, Ṭalī'a, Ṭal'at (Laqā'iyya's eldest daughter), and Huvīya.

Figure 3.2 Ibn-i Aṣdaq circa 1910.

who received the largest number of tablets are: Dawlat Īrān (143, 485, 487, 492, 493, 495, 497, 500, 588, 640 and 658)[89], Dawlat Jamshīd (3, 9, 340, 367, 611, 636, 639 and 640), Dawlat Mihrabān (523, 625, 674 and 707), Dawlat Nūsh (112, 257 and 270), Fīrūza Isfandiyār (3, 77, 98 and 698), Gawhar Māndigār (112, 272 and 432), Gul Bahrām (112, 327, 418 and 618), Gul Kay-Qubād (112, 257 and 306), Murvārīd Bahrām (112, 283, 414, 417, 426, 444, 511 and 644), Murvārīd Gushtāsb (523, 645 and 707), Murvārīd Rashīd (127, 623 and 640), Shīrīn Jamshīd (9, 581, 639 and 687), Shīrīn Kay-Qubād (213, 522 and 651), Shīrīn Khudādād (112, 261, 279, 415, 420 and 640),

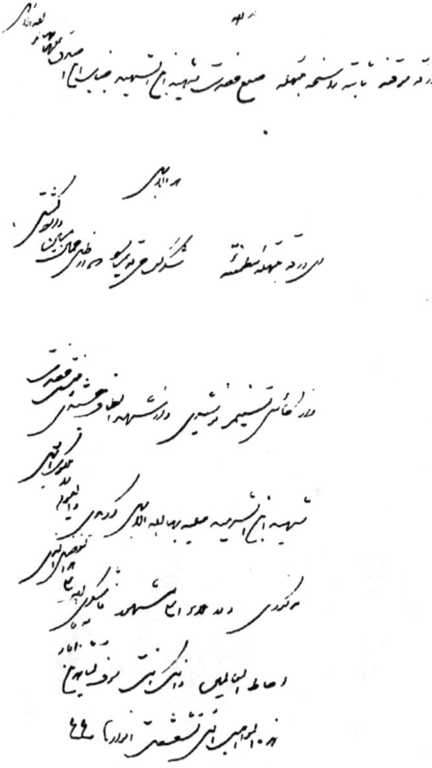

Figure 3.3 Persian tablet in the hand of 'Abdu'l-Baha addressed to Ḍiyā' al-Ḥājjīya, wife of Ibn-i Aṣdaq.

Shīrīn Mihrabān (125, 498, 501 and 707), and Zumurrud Ardashīr, 'Farrukh' (428, 640 and 734). 'Abdu'l-Baha was well aware of the effect his tablets had on those who received them. In one tablet (164) he says that he is writing so that his tablet will be the cause of their joy and that their souls and minds will be revivified through reading his words.[90] Being named in a tablet, and receiving correspondence from 'Abdu'l-Baha (especially if written in his own hand) was no doubt a great honour for the recipient.[91] Access to Baha'i scripture (in particular in Iran)[92] was rather limited and so tablets received from 'Abdu'l-Baha would most likely have been copied and distributed widely, and studied in depth by members of the community.

Geographic spread

Roughly half (349) of 'Abdu'l-Baha's 735 tablets mention the village, town or city in Iran or India where the addressee(s) resided:

Table 3.2 Geographic spread of tablets

Name of village, town or city	*Total number of tablets for that locality*	*Percentage of the 349 tablets*	*Number of tablets addressed to women*	*Percentage of tablets for that locality*
Yazd	59	17%	16	27%
Qāsimābād	10	3%	2	20%
Maryamābād	8	2%	4	50%
Ḥusaynābād	6	2%	2	33%
Khurramshāh	4	1%	–	–
Mihdīābād	3	1%	1	33%
Mārīābād	2	0.6%	1	50%
Naṣrābād	2	0.6%	–	–
Raḥmatābād	2	0.6%	–	–
Asadābād	1	0.3%	1	100%
Allāhābād	1	0.3%	–	–
'Alīābād	1	0.3%	–	–
'Aṣrābād	1	0.3%	–	–
Khayrābād	1	0.3%	–	–
Kūcha-Buyūk	1	0.3%	–	–
Murdābād	1	0.3%	–	–
Total for Yazd and villages	103	29.5%	27	26%
Taft	4	1%	1	25%
Kirman	9	3%	1	11%
Bam	1	0.3%	–	–
Bushihr	1	0.3%	–	–
Nayriz	1	0.3%	–	–
Shiraz	30	8.5%	1	3%
Isfahan	1	0.3%	–	–
Kashan	1	0.3%	–	–
Qum	4	1%	–	–
Qazvin	4	1%	1	25%
Tehran	47	13%	6	13%
Total for Iran	206	59%	37	18%
Bombay	129	36%	23	18%
Poona	13	4%	1	8%
Burma	1	0.3%	–	–
Total for India and Burma	143	41%	24	17%

How men are addressed in 'Abdu'l-Baha's tablets to Zoroastrians

The most common title used to address male recipients in these tablets (around 75 per cent) is *jināb* ('sir'). The title *jināb-i zā'ir* ('his Excellency the pilgrim') is less common, since relatively few Baha'is made the pilgrimage to the Haifa-'Akka area. The title *jināb-i zā'ir* before the addressee's given name, or *zā'ir* added afterwards functions in a similar way to Ḥājjī.[93] Titles commonly used by Muslim men in nineteenth-century Iran (e.g. *āqā, mīrzā* and *khān*) are rarely used by 'Abdu'l-Baha when addressing male Zoroastrian Baha'is. It is interesting to note that a number of Zoroastrian Baha'is used the title *mulla* before their given names, e.g., Mulla Bahrām (29, 32, 36, 38, 39, 40, 42, 45, 49, 502 and 547), Mulla Khusraw (65), Mulla Rustam Mihrabān (148), Mulla Nūshirvān Ḥusaynābādī (206), Mulla Dīnyār (382), Mulla Rustam Bahrām (729).[94] The Zoroastrian priestly title, *dastūr*, is notably much less common, although the Zoroastrian titles *mihtar* ('elder') and *sarvar* ('leader', 'head') are relatively common.[95] The fact that 'Abdu'l-Baha used these titles when addressing converts from a Zoroastrian background shows his sensitivity for their heritage.

In around 50 tablets, 'Abdu'l-Baha added *fārsī* or *pārsī* ('the Persian' or 'the Zoroastrian', 'the Parsee') to the given names of addressees in both Iran and India. In a few tablets (less than ten), 'Abdu'l-Baha added '*zardushtī*' ('the Zoroastrian') after the recipient's given name. The integration of Baha'is of Zoroastrian and Jewish heritage into the community which was initially dominated by Baha'is from a Shi'i background, was a gradual one that lasted well into the twentieth century. This perhaps explains why 'Abdu'l-Baha in tablets to Zoroastrian Baha'is often refers to them as a separate sub-group of the Baha'i community, e.g. *aḥibbā-yi pārsiyān* (1, 15), *aḥibbā-yi pārsī* (13, 96, 115), *aḥibbā-yi pārsī-yi zardushtī* (387), *aḥibbā-yi fārsiyān* (28, 166), *aḥibbā-yi fārsī* (113, 277, 394, 489, 671), *yārān-i pārsiyān* (12, 204), *yārān-i pārsī* (109), *yārān-i fārsiyān* (44, 81, 102, 122), *yārān-i fārsī-yi bahā'ī* (309), *yārān-i fārsī-yi yazdānī* (359), *dūstān-i fārsiyān* (17), *dūstān-i fārsī-yi yazdānī* (296), and *dūstān-i pārsiyān* (156, 212). A few of the tablets in this collection are addressed to Baha'is from both Zoroastrian and Muslim backgrounds, though.[96] The terms *aḥibbā'*, *yārān* and *dūstān* all literally mean 'friends' and (at least until the 1920s) were used to address groups of male Baha'is. At some later stage these terms come to be used to address male and female Baha'is collectively. That being said, a small number of these tablets are addressed to all the Baha'is in a given locality, both male and female, using either *yārān* or *aḥibbā*: tablet 341 is addressed to all the Baha'is of Ḥusaynābād and Asadābād, both male and female (*'umūm-i aḥibbā-yi Ḥusaynābād u Asadābād, 'alay-him wa 'alay-hunn al-Bahā' al-Abhā*).

In almost all of these tablets the name of the addressee is followed by the Arabic phrase, *'alay-hi Bahā'ullāh al-Abhā* ('upon him be the Glory of God, the Most-Glorious'), which is modified according to the gender and number of the recipients. In a good number of tablets this Arabic phrase is omitted and a Persian one used instead, for example, *jān-ash khush bād* ('may his soul be gladdened'),[97] *jān-ash rawshan bād* ('may his soul be illumined'; 35, 54, 231, 315 and 317), *jān-ash shād bād* ('may his soul be joyous'; 37, 54, 227, 238 and 262), *kām-ash pur nūsh bād* ('may his palate be filled with honey'; 222), *rūy-ash safīd bād* ('may his face be white'; 316), *rūy-ash chun khurshīd bād* ('may his face be like the sun; 326), *dil u ravān-ash gulistān bād* ('may his heart and soul be like a rose garden'; 570), and *bahra-ash fuzūn bād* ('may his portion increase'; 324).

How women are addressed in these tablets

The most common title used by 'Abdu'l-Baha to address Zoroastrian Baha'i women is *amatullāh* ('handmaid of God'), which is also the most common title used to address Baha'i women of Muslim or Jewish heritage. In tablets to women from a Muslim or Jewish background, the title *varaqa* (lit. 'leaf') is also very common, although in tablets to Zoroastrian Baha'i women, *varaqa* is very seldom used. The Persian title *kanīz* ('maidservant') is, however, frequently used in these tablets, appearing in various forms (in order of frequency): *kanīz-i ilāhī, kanīz-i 'azīz-i ilāhī, kanīz-i khudā, kanīz-i khudāvand, kanīz-i yazdān, kanīz-i ḥaqq* and *kanīz-i bahā'*. It could be argued that 'Abdu'l-Baha is using the Persian title *kanīz* in a conscious effort to use fewer words of Arabic origin when addressing Zoroastrian Baha'i women.

The title *zā'ira* ('pilgrim') is much less common than the male equivalent *zā'ir*, as fewer Zoroastrian Baha'i women than men made the pilgrimage to Palestine. At least one woman is addressed with the (conventionally) male title *jināb*, which, at the time, would have been a sign of great respect.[98] This use of *jināb* for women is rare in the tablets of Baha'ullah and 'Abdu'l-Baha and is generally reserved for very prominent women, such as the Babi poet Ṭāhira, Qurrat al-'Ayn.[99] In some of these tablets, 'Abdu'l-Baha addresses the recipient by her given name (e.g. Khurshīd), although most are addressed using their full name (that is their given name plus the given name of their father, e.g. Khurshīd Ardashīr). Sometimes *bint*, *ṣabīya* or *dukhtar* ('daughter') is inserted between the woman's given name and that of her father, but this is the exception rather than the rule. A minority of these women are addressed to 'wife of' or 'mother of' a named male Baha'i, something which is much more common in tablets addressed to women of Muslim heritage.[100]

How these tablets were delivered

A minority of these tablets were addressed directly to the recipient(s), and even those would most likely have been delivered via a third party. Whether a tablet was addressed directly or indirectly does not appear to be linked to the gender of the recipient or whether they resided in India or Iran. The majority of these tablets, however, are addressed to the recipient via (*bi-vāsiṭa-yi*) a named third party, often a relative or close family friend who made the pilgrimage to Palestine (and who had often solicited the tablet on the addressee's behalf), or else a prominent Baha'i (of either Muslim or Zoroastrian heritage) resident in the same locality,[101] or else a well-known Baha'i *muballigh* (itinerant propagator of the Baha'i Faith). Sending a tablet via a trusted third party increased the probability that it would reach the addressee, and it also meant that there would be someone at hand to read and explain the contents of the tablet, depending on the literacy level of the addressee, and his or her knowledge of Arabic. Some of the most prominent Baha'is of Iran are named as conduits for these tablets, including Ḥājjī Amīn,[102] Bashīr-i Ilāhī,[103] Ḥājjī Mirza Ḥaydar-'Alī,[104] Ibn-i Abhar (382, 536 and 554), Ibn-i Aṣdaq (720), Maḥmūd Zarqānī (395, 620 and 680), Jināb-i Adīb (550) and Shaykh Kāẓim-i Samandar (708). One of the tablets in this volume (721) was sent to a Zoroastrian Baha'i woman via Elizabeth Stewart, one of the American Baha'i women sent to Tehran by 'Abdu'l-Baha to assist the Baha'i community.[105] This shows that Zoroastrian Baha'is in both Iran and India were in close contact with the leading members of the Baha'i community.[106] One of the tablets in this volume (611) was sent via 'Abdu'l-Baha's full sister, Bahiyya Khānum, and a further two (460 and 664) via his eldest grandson, Shoghi Effendi, who later succeeded him as head of the Baha'i Faith. This shows that other members of Baha'ullah's family corresponded with Zoroastrian Baha'is (as they did with many other Baha'is in Iran and elsewhere).

Invocations

Most of these tablets open with the Arabic invocation *huvallāh* ('He is God'), and many others with *huva'l-Abhā* ('He is the Most-Golrious'), *Allāh-u Abhā* ('God is Most-Glorious'), or simply *hū* ('He').[107] A small number of the tablets to Zoroastrian Baha'is (approximately six per cent) open with invocations in Persian, which could be seen as another acknowledgement of the non-Muslim heritage of the recipients. These Persian invocations include phrases such as, *bi-nām-i pāk yazdān* ('in the name of the pure Lord'; 156), *ū-st rawshanā'ī-yi jahān* ('He is the light of the world'; 199), *ū-st āfarīnanda-yi farhang u hūsh* ('He is the creator of wisdom and intellect'; 204), *ū-st jān-i jahān* ('He is the soul of the world'; 234), and *ū-st dānā va tavānā* ('He is the wise, the powerful'; 227).

Tablets written in honour of deceased Zoroastrian Baha'is

One interesting feature of this collection is that it includes a large number of tablets (more than 40) written in honour of deceased male and female Baha'is.[108] These tablets are either addressed to the deceased person's relatives, or else (especially in the case of tablets written in honour of a group of deceased Baha'is) they are addressed to all the Baha'is in a given town or village.[109] These tablets would have been used in gatherings held to commemorate the dead, or in private prayer by friends and relatives. There is also one tablet (648) written in honour of a Baha'i martyr from a Zoroastrian background, Jināb-i Āqā Gūdarz.[110]

Tablets addressed to individual women

There are 57 tablets addressed to more than 20 individual women in *Yārān-i Pārsī*. Most of these women received one tablet, but a small number received more, most notably three women from Bombay, Dawlat Īrān, Dawlat Jamshīd and Murvārīd Bahrām, who each received more than four individually addressed tablets.[111] The majority of these tablets are written in a fairly standard Persian, which includes a sizeable percentage of words of Arabic origin, although perhaps a lower percentage than in tablets addressed to Baha'i women from Muslim and Jewish backgrounds. Arabic phrases and passages, which are common in tablets addressed to Baha'i women from a Muslim background, are almost totally absent from the tablets addressed to Zoroastrian Baha'is, whether male or female. A few tablets in this volume are written in so-called 'pure' Persian (*fārsī-yi sara*), but these are less in number than one might think.[112]

Of those tablets to individual women in which the home town (or village) of the recipient is indicated, five are addressed to individual women in Yazd, two to women in Qāsimābād, one to a woman in Maryamābād, three to women in Tehran and more than ten to women in Bombay. This suggests that in both Iran and India a number of Zoroastrian Baha'i women were independently active in the Baha'i community.[113] Although addressed to individual women, many of these tablets contain greetings and messages for other male and female Baha'is, and therefore cannot strictly be considered purely private or personal communication. Many of these tablets are very short (often no more than four or five lines in length).[114]

Some of these tablets have a very personal tone, and it is difficult to imagine that they would be distributed to anyone beyond the recipient's family. One such example is a short tablet (140) addressed to Mahbānū, an elderly Baha'i woman from Qāsimābād. In this tablet 'Abdu'l-Baha says that as women grow old they tend to lose the physical beauty of their youth, but that in her old age Mahbānū has freshness (*ṭarāvat*), sweetness (*ḥalāvat*), grace (*liṭāfat*), and beauty (*malāḥat*) because of her faith.

In many of his tablets to individual women, 'Abdu'l-Baha addresses them by their given names, something much less common in tablets to Baha'i women from a Muslim background, perhaps because of stricter taboos within conservative Muslim society in regard to social interaction between unrelated members of the opposite sex. In a number of these tablets, 'Abdu'l-Baha puns on the woman's given name.[115] For example, to a women named Fīrūza (lit. 'turquoise'), 'Abdu'l-Baha says she is a 'turquoise from the mine of God' (*īn fīrūz az kān-i yazdān ast*; 352), and to a woman named Dawlat (lit. 'good fortune'), he congratulates her for having attained lasting good fortune (*dawlat-i pāydār*; 500).

A number of these tablets are addressed to relatives of deceased Baha'i women (71, 255, 377, 414, 432 and 702), and a number of tablets contain words of consolation from 'Abdu'l-Baha to the recently bereaved, or words of comfort in regard to other personal hardships and difficulties (279, 538, 700 and 721). These tablets for the deceased show that within the lifetime of 'Abdu'l-Baha there was an elderly generation of Baha'is from a Zoroastrian background.

By 1920, there were often two (if not three) generations of Zoroastrian Baha'i women in many towns. This is evident from the manner in which some of the women are addressed as the grandmothers, mothers and daughters of other Baha'is. It seems that by the second and third generations a burgeoning Baha'i identity (distinct from the local Zoroastrian or Parsi identity) seems to be emerging. One manifestation of this is that a number of the second and third generation Zoroastrian Baha'i women have given names such as Riḍvāniyya and Bahiyya which are Arabic in origin and which were also popular among Baha'is of a Muslim and Jewish background.

As mentioned above, tablets were often solicited from 'Abdu'l-Baha (either by letter or else orally, through pilgrims).[116] Some tablets mention that the recipients have previously made the pilgrimage to Haifa.[117] 'Abdu'l-Baha would pray at the shrines of the Bab and Baha'ullah for those women who could not make the difficult and expensive journey to Palestine (30 and 497).

In many of these tablets, 'Abdu'l-Baha makes reference to the letters sent to him by the addressee(s).[118] To Dawlat Jamshīd of Bombay (611), 'Abdu'l-Baha says he has sent a letter to her before, but that Bahā'iyya Khānum has interceded on her behalf and asked him to send a second letter. In a tablet to Shīrīn Mihrabān of Yazd (125), 'Abdu'l-Baha praises the quality of the poems she sent to him, saying that they are eloquent and flow well.[119] In the same tablet, 'Abdu'l-Baha praises Shīrīn Mihrabān for teaching girls in the village of Qāsimābād outside of Yazd, and he assures her that she will be successful.[120] In a tablet (498) addressed to another Shīrīn Mihrabān, daughter of Dawlat Īrān of Bombay, 'Abdu'l-Baha praises the quality of some English poems she has composed, and signs the tablet 'abdul-Baha abbas' in Latin letters. Shīrīn Mihrabān of Bombay was, in 1936, the first woman to be elected to the National Spiritual Assembly of the Baha'is of India and Burma.[121]

In many of these tablets, 'Abdu'l-Baha says that because of their conversion to the Baha'i religion, Baha'i women enjoy a station which is superior to that of other women. In a tablet to Shīrīn Bahrām (157) he says that one hundred thousand women of the world have been deprived (*maḥrūm*) of this bounty, whereas she has become initiated in the divine mysteries (*maḥram-i rāz*). To Bahiyya Ḥakīm he writes that God has placed the 'crown of mystical knowledge' (*tāj-i ʿirfān*) on her head and thereby made her superior over the women of the world, and that 100,000 women should serve her for she has the diadem of servitude (*iklīl-i kanīzī*) to Baha'ullah on her brow and the robe of his love and knowledge is draped upon her (186).[122] In a tablet addressed to a Zoroastrian Baha'i woman in Tehran (649), 'Abdu'l-Baha praises the recipient for having adopted the Baha'i religion, whilst likening the other women of the world to lost sheep. Using what might strike the reader as a very Christian metaphor, 'Abdu'l-Baha says she has found the heavenly shepherd (*shabān-i āsamānī*), and entered the blessed flock of God (*galla-yi farkhunda-yi īzadī*). 'Abdu'l-Baha continues by saying that if the other women of the world knew what she had found they would all be envious of her.

In addition to praising these women for having converted, 'Abdu'l-Baha also urges them to strive to become moral leaders among women. For example, in a tablet to Shīrīn Khudadad (415), 'Abdu'l-Baha exhorts her to adorn herself with chastity (*ʿiṣmat uʿiffat*). In a similar tablet, addressed to Dawlat Iran of Bombay (485), 'Abdu'l-Baha calls on her to become an example for the women of Iran and, ultimately, for all the women of the world. He says that her name is Dawlat-i Īrān ('the good fortune of Iran'), and that her desire should be to serve Iran (*kām-at khidmat-i Iran bād*). 'Abdu'l-Baha hopes that the women of Iran will follow her example, and display such chastity, purity, nobility, wisdom and knowledge that they will become the cause of the eternal glory of the women of the world.[123] In another tablet to the same lady (497), 'Abdu'l-Baha asks her to return to India and inspire other Parsee women to follow the same path.[124]

In a tablet to the wife of Khudādād Mihrabān (549), 'Abdu'l-Baha says that the 'star' (*kawkab*) of the Zoroastrians had not shone for over one thousand years, but that now it is shining brightly and casting the rays of the bounty of God over the whole world. 'Abdu'l-Baha's praise for the Zoroastrians and their heritage is not a blind one, though, and in a tablet to Mihrbānū Bahman in Yazd, he calls on her to thank her relatives that have converted her to the Baha'i religion, and saved her from the clutches of the Zoroastrian priests.[125] 'Abdu'l-Baha ends the tablet by urging her to convert other Zoroastrian women.

Tablets addressed to groups of women

There are nine tablets addressed to groups of women in this collection. Some are addressed to the members of one family, others to women from the same locality. In a tablet addressed to three sisters, Khurshīd, Zumurrud and Shīrīn Khudābakhsh (491), 'Abdu'l-Baha says they should give thanks for having been guided to the Baha'i message. In another tablet addressed to seven Baha'i women in Bombay (640) sent through a female pilgrim, Shīrīn Khudādād, 'Abdu'l-Baha similarly calls on the addresses to rejoice in their new-found faith.[126]

As with the tablets to individual women, it is clear that many of these letters were solicited by pilgrims who visited 'Abdu'l-Baha in Palestine. In a tablet addressed to Gawhar Khudābakhsh and her three daughters (11), 'Abdu'l-Baha explains how Gawhar's husband, Burzū, insisted that 'Abdu'l-Baha write letters to every one of them.[127] To a group of five Parsee Baha'i women in Bombay (257), 'Abdu'l-Baha describes how a female pilgrim, Shīrīn (perhaps the same Shīrīn Khudādād), has arrived on pilgrimage, mentioned them all by name, and requested separate tablets for each one of them. 'Abdu'l-Baha tells them how difficult it is for him to keep up regular correspondence with the Baha'is in both the east and the west, both collectively and individually.[128] 'Abdu'l-Baha then asks these women to forgive him for writing to them as a group. It is clear from the text of some of these tablets that they were written in response to letters sent to 'Abdu'l-Baha by groups of women (e.g. 531 and 566). In a tablet addressed to a group of 12 women (707), which was delivered via a female pilgrim, Murvārīd Gushtāsb, 'Abdu'l-Baha describes how, when he read their names he wanted to write to each of them individually, but regretfully he does not have enough time to do so.

In a number of these tablets 'Abdu'l-Baha calls on the addressees to guide other Zoroastrian women to the new religion (e.g. 566 and 707). The existence of tablets addressed to groups of women is evidence that women Baha'is were engaging in collective activities as early as the first two decades of the twentieth century. One arena in which the women of the community were particularly active was that of children's education. In a tablet addressed to a group of five women in Yazd (670), 'Abdu'l Baha stresses the importance of children's education, saying that it is obligatory that children be schooled in reading (*qirā'at*), writing (*kitābat*), learning (*ta'līm*) and good manners (*ādāb*), so that they will develop at all levels. 'Abdu'l-Baha continues, saying that mothers are the first educators of their children (*avval murabbī-yi aṭfāl mādarān-and*) and that they are the ones who train their children in manners and good conduct (*mu'assis-i akhlāq u ādāb-i farzand*). 'Abdu'l-Baha concludes that in God's eyes, the greatest form of worship is the moral education of children.[129]

Tablets addressed to mixed groups of men and women

These are tablets addressed to mixed family groups, or to Baha'is residing in the same town or village. Many of the tablets addressed to mixed groups also contain information about the nature of the correspondence between 'Abdu'l-Baha and Zoroastrian Baha'is. Many tablets are responses to letters sent to 'Abdu'l-Baha,[130] or else were solicited by pilgrims,[131] and many were sent via pilgrims.[132] Frequently 'Abdu'l-Baha apologizes either for the brevity of the tablet, or that he cannot write to each of them in turn,[133] and his motivation for writing is often to reassure them that he remembers them and that they are dear to him, and that they are mentioned at the holy shrines in Palestine.[134] A large number of the tablets written in honour of mixed groups are tablets for groups of deceased Baha'is.[135] All these tablets contain the names of the deceased women and men, and in some of the tablets 'Abdu'l-Baha has skilfully weaved the deceased's given names into the body of the tablet, adding a short description of them which rhymes.[136]

Some of these tablets are addressed to a large number of Baha'is. One example is tablet 27, which is addressed to more than 50 individuals in Yazd, Shiraz, Kirman, Bombay and Poona, including 11 women who are all residents of Yazd, including Kharman Hurmuzdyār, who is believed to be the first woman from a Zoroastrian background in Yazd to convert to the Baha'i Faith. In this tablet, 'Abdu'l-Baha mentions says when he returned from the west (probably 1913) he met with some of the Zoroastrian Baha'is who had come on pilgrimage, and wrote this tablet immediately after reading the names of the addressees. 'Abdu'l-Baha may have been presented with a list of the newest converts from a Zoroastrian background in the cities mentioned.

In many of these tablets 'Abdu'l-Baha refers to the recipients' Zoroastrian heritage. In one such tablet (16), 'Abdu'l-Baha praises the addressees for having put into practice the advice and exhortations of Zoroaster (*naṣāyiḥ u vaṣāyā-yi haḍrat-i Zardusht*), implying that their adherence to the Baha'i Faith is in no way a violation of their Zoroastrian beliefs, but rather a natural extension of them. In a tablet to a mixed group from Yazd (31), 'Abdu'l-Baha says that God in this age has placed the crown of Baha'ullah's bounty upon the heads of the Zoroastrians, the gems of which will shine throughout the centuries and ages to come.[137] The Zoroastrian community of Iran was an oppressed and deprived one throughout the nineteenth century and the first few decades of the twentieth century, and such laudatory statements would have been extremely empowering for the recipients. Elsewhere (76), 'Abdu'l-Baha says the Zoroastrian Baha'is should give thanks that they have been chosen by God, and in another tablet addressed to a mixed group in Qazvin (96), 'Abdu'l-Baha reassures the recipients by saying that their ancestors (*niyākān-i pīshīniyān*) prayed that they would see this promised day would come, and that now the longing of their forefathers has been fulfilled.[138] In a tablet to a group in Maryamābād near Yazd (129), 'Abdu'l-Baha writes that the addressees have followed their ancestors (*niyākān*) and revived the names of their forefathers (*pīshīniyān*) and the pre-Islamic kings (*pīshdādiyān*). In the same tablet 'Abdu'l-Baha broadens the significance of their conversion to the Baha'i Faith by saying that soon they will see the diverse peoples of Iran, as well as both America and Africa illumined by the sun shining from Iran.[139] These statements are doubly intriguing when we remember that 'Abdu'l-Baha is writing to villagers in rural Iran at the beginning of the twentieth century.

In a tablet addressed to Zoroastrian Baha'is in Yazd and Bombay (164), 'Abdu'l-Baha discusses how the prophet Zoroaster is praised in the highest terms in numerous places in the Baha'i scriptures. He says that Zoroaster was one of the major prophets of God (one of the *maẓāhir-i ilāhī*, 'manifestations of God'), who led a mighty community (*millat-i 'aẓīma*). 'Abdu'l-Baha says that anyone who studies the teachings of Zoroaster will realize that they are divine teachings (*ta'ālīm-i āsamānī*). He sums up by saying that the lofty station of Zoroaster has been made clear in this revelation.[140] 'Abdu'l-Baha is both reassuring the converts of the station of Zoroaster in Baha'i belief, and also informing Baha'is from a Muslim or Jewish background who may also have read the tablet that they should accept Zoroaster as a divinely-guided prophet who holds the same rank as Abraham, Moses, Jesus, Muhammad, the Bab and Baha'ullah.

Elsewhere (261), 'Abdu'l-Baha highlights the sufferings of the Zoroastrians, saying that they have lived in a state of utter sorrow and anguish for a thousand years, and have suffered innumerable difficulties and woes, and been attacked and oppressed, but that now the 'star of eternal might' (*kawkab-i 'izzat-i abadī*) has shone from the horizon of the Zoroastrians, and the 'stars of eternal joy' (*akhtarān-i sa'ādat-i sarmadī*) have shone from the horizon of Iran, so that this weighty oppression may be transformed into great power and glory.[141] This image of Iran illuminating the world appears in another tablet (522) where 'Abdu'l-Baha says that the Zoroastrian Baha'is in Yazd should rejoice because the shining morning star of Iran has once again begun to sparkle and has lit the lamps of their forefathers.

In a tablet to a group in Mihdīābād (526), 'Abdu'l-Baha says their recognition of Baha'ullah as a prophet has raised them to a place of great honour within society, whereas the most learned men of the age, because they have ignored Baha'ullah's message, have been stripped of their status.[142] In another tablet addressed to a group in Bombay (546), 'Abdu'l-Baha expresses the hope that the addressees will guide all other Zoroastrians to the Baha'i religion and that the Iranians will illumine the world.

Conclusion

The most striking feature of the tablets of Baha'ullah and 'Abdu'l-Baha addressed to women is their variety, especially in terms of content. A large number of those addressed to individual women are essentially short letters of a personal nature. These were written to reassure the addressees that they were remembered by Baha'ullah or 'Abdu'l-Baha, and to inform them that prayers had been said for them at the holy shrines. A good number of these more personal tablets also contain words of consolation on the death of family members. Given the personal nature of these tablets, they are most useful as sources of information for those wishing to reconstruct individual biographies of early Baha'i women of Iran and India.

Another category of tablets where the individual addressee is the focus are those in which women are praised for having converted to the Baha'i Faith in their youth or adulthood, independently of their spouses or other family members. There are a good number of such tablets to women who converted from Zoroastrianism, and also to Ibn-i Aṣdaq's wife, Ḍiyā' al-Ḥājjīya, her sister, Āqā Shāhzāda, and their mother, Shahanshāh Baygum, who all converted to the Baha'i religion from a Shi'i background independently of their male relatives. The chief women of the families of Samandar and Nabīl ibn-i Nabīl were all born into families that had aligned themselves with the Babi movement in the 1840s and subsequently given their allegiance to Baha'ullah in the late 1860s/early 1870s. Tablets addressed to them more often contain praise for their long Babi-Baha'i heritage than for their recognition of Baha'ullah.

Another important feature of the tablets to the women of Ibn-i Aṣdaq's family, and more strikingly of those tablets addressed to the women of the Samandarī, Nabilī and Farhādī families is the collective praise of the family, their services to the Baha'i community, and the staunchness of their faith. As discussed above, this praise is often mixed with the expectation that these women will continue in the footsteps of the older members of their families and live up to their example. One fact often overlooked is that it was often the women of the household who held the family together and administered its daily affairs (often under difficult financial and social conditions) in the absence of their husbands, fathers and sons. This is particularly true in the case of Ḍiyā' al-Ḥājjīya and Ṭarāziyya Farhādī, whose husbands travelled extensively throughout Iran and beyond to promote the Baha'i religion. The difficulties these women endured are alluded to in a number of the tablets studied here, and a desire to empathize with these women seems to have been the impetus behind the composition of these tablets.

Although a minority of these tablets were addressed to women who do not appear to have played significant roles as individuals in the development of the Baha'i community, the majority of these tablets were addressed to women of prominence and influence within the Baha'i community, and, in a few cases, beyond. In the late nineteenth and twentieth centuries the most direct means through which Baha'ullah and 'Abdu'l-Baha could communicate with their female followers in Iran and India was by writing to them. Therefore, if we wish to understand how Baha'ullah and 'Abdu'l-Baha viewed the role of women in the Baha'i communities of the East, we must look to tablets addressed to women for clues as to the activities they were encouraged to devote themselves to. From the tablets penned by Baha'ullah studied here, it seems that he encouraged his female followers to be steadfast in their faith, try to convert other women from their extended family and from their local community to the Baha'i Faith, and strictly adhere to the Baha'i laws as contained in the *Kitāb-i Aqdas* and other pronouncements by Baha'ullah, most particularly in terms of chastity and personal morality. 'Abdu'l-Baha in his tablets to women reiterated all of these points, but also repeatedly encouraged women to act in two main areas: the systematic propagation of the Baha'i religion, and the education of girls. In all three sections of this study (tablets to women of three prominent Babi-Baha'i families, tablets to women of two provincial towns, and tablets to women of a common, non-Muslim heritage) there are tablets from 'Abdu'l-Baha which address both these areas. By the time of 'Abdu'l-Baha's passing in November 1921, throughout Iran, classes aimed at systematically training women propagators of the Baha'i Faith (*muballigha*s) had either been established or else were beginning to form, a fact which served to democratize the propagation of the religion, which until then had been largely restricted to a small class of well-educated and courageous men and women, often converts from (or descendants of converts from) the clergy, whether Shi'i, Jewish or Zoroastrian. As Momen's study in this volume shows, by 1921 a large number of Baha'i-run schools for girls had been established throughout Iran, often through the initiative of women within the community. Baha'ullah had emphasized the importance of the education of women at least as early as the 1870s, and many Babi-Baha'i families seem to have ensured that their womenfolk were literate in Persian, if not also in Arabic, but the formalization of the education of girls within the Baha'i community of Iran is really a phenomenon of the period of 'Abdu'l-Baha's leadership and must, at least in part, be attributed to the large volume of tablets he wrote to both women and men initially encouraging them to educate girls in a systematic manner, and then praising them for their efforts upon the establishment and successful running of girls' schools.

One method for future research on early Baha'i women in Iran and India would be to analyse all the tablets addressed to women in a given locality, and then compare them with tablets to women in other towns and cities. The study of tablets to the women of the families of Samandar and Nabīl ibn-i Nabīl presented here could easily be broadened, for example, to include all tablets addressed to the women of Qazvin. Then, by comparing the tablets to Baha'i women of Qazvin, with, say, those to Baha'i women in Yazd, patterns may emerge which shed new light on the role of women in the development of the Baha'i community in a given town or city which have been overlooked in local Baha'i histories. A comparison of the tablets addressed to the Baha'i women of one of the villages of Mazandaran with, say, those addressed to women in Tehran would no doubt highlight the divergent realities of the lives of rural and urban Baha'i women in late nineteenth century Iran. Another valuable project would be a comparative study of the tablets addressed to women of Zoroastrian heritage discussed here and those tablets addressed to women of Jewish heritage. Studies of larger groups of women (whether grouped by religious background, home town or extended family) should, in turn, facilitate a more accurate analysis of the contributions of those individual women in the Baha'i communities of Iran and India who have received the most attention to date.

Notes

1 I am very grateful to Stephen Lambden, Todd Lawson, Moojan Momen and Fereydun Vahman for their comments on an earlier draft of this chapter.
2 E.g. Arbāb 1969. Scholars now seem to be moving away from focusing on individual women's biographies and instead looking at broader trends within the evolution of the role of women in the Iranian Baha'i community, e.g. Momen 2005.
3 It is surprising that no study of either Maryam Khānum (Baha'ullah's cousin and sister-in-law) or Sāra Khānum (Baha'ullah's full sister) exists.
4 E.g. Amanat 1989: 295–331; Maneck 1989; Milani 1992: 77–99; Mottahedeh 1998; Afnān 1999; Momen 2003 and Banani 2004.
5 E.g. 'Iṣmat Khānum, 'Ṭā'ira' see Afary 1996: 197–199; Cole 1998: 180–181; and Momen 2005: 353.
6 The term 'tablets' is used by Baha'is to refer to letters written by Baha'ullah and 'Abdu'l-Baha. In Persian the term used to refer to a letter written by Baha'ullah to an individual Baha'i or a group of Baha'is is *lawḥ* (pl. *alvāḥ*), hence the English translation 'tablet'. 'Abdu'l-Baha generally uses the Persian word *nāma* (letter) to refer to his own correspondence, but Baha'is generally refer to his letters as *makātīb* (the plural of *maktūb*, an archaic word for 'letter').
7 See Momen 2005: 346. It is difficult to move beyond discussion of the most prominent women of the Baha'i community, but one way to do this is to examine the tablets of Baha'ullah and 'Abdu'l-Baha since they were addressed to a broad cross section of Baha'i women from all social classes and backgrounds.
8 Baha'ullah addressed at least 45 tablets to Ibn-i Aṣdaq, see Baha'ullah and 'Abdu'l-Baha 2005: 45–203. 'Abdu'l-Baha penned an impressive 83 tablets to Ibn-i Aṣdaq, see ibid.: 223–286.
9 For more on Mulla Ṣādiq, see 'Abdu'l-Baha 2002: 5–8; Afnān 2001: 123–129; Amanat 1989: 136–138, 260–264 and 286–289; Balyuzi 1985: 7–23; and Sulaymānī 1973: 374–418. For two of the Bab's tablets to Mulla Ṣādiq, see Baha'ullah and 'Abdu'l-Baha 2005: 3–4; and for 14 of Baha'ullah's tablets to Mulla Ṣadīq, see ibid.: 5–31.
10 For more on Ḥakīm Masīḥ and his conversion to the Baha'i Faith, see Thābitī 2004: 32–33.
11 For more on Ibn-i Aṣdaq, see 'Alā'ī 1974: 465–493; Balyuzi 1985: 171–176; and Samandar 1975: 163–171. For details of Ibn-i Aṣdaq's visit to The Hague, see De Vries 2002: 106–108, 111, 118–119 and 132.
12 Baha'ullah gave Āqā Shāhzāda the honorific 'Badī'a' ('marvellous', 'unique'). Other women in Ibn-i Aṣdaq's extended family also received tablets. His mother, Jināb-i Bībī, received five tablets from Baha'ullah and four from 'Abdu'l-Baha, see Baha'ullah and 'Abdu'l-Baha 2005: 35–37 and 287–290 respectively. Jināb-i Bībī's daughters, Ṣamadiyya and Badī'a also received tablets from Baha'ullah and 'Abdu'l-Baha, see ibid.: 42 and 290–293, as did Mulla Ṣadīq's second wife, Fāṭima Baygum, known as Hudhud Khānum (see ibid.: 37) and her daughter, Ibn-i Aṣdaq's half-sister, Shams-i Jahān Khānum, see ibid.: 38–39 and 311–313.

13 Intiẓām al-Salṭana received at least eight tablets from Baha'ullah, see Baha'ullah and 'Abdu'l-Baha 2005: 212–216. Shortly before his death he was appointed Chief of Police for Tehran. His father, Mīrzā Mūsā, and his elder brother, Mīrzā 'Īsā, both served as Minister (*vazīr*) of Tehran under Nāṣir al-Dīn Shah. Mīrzā Mūsā had been present at the interrogation of the Bab in Tabriz in July 1848.

14 Ḍiyā al-Salṭana acted as private secretary to Fatḥ-'Alī Shah and was the 'Munshī al-Mamālik' of the royal harem. She was an accomplished poet and an excellent calligrapher, see 'Aḍud al-Dawla 1997: 31–34, 175, 192, 195 and 248–249; Anṣārī 1970: 22–26; and Khāvarī 2001: 986, 1011–1013 and 1158. Mīrzā Mas'ūd Anṣārī (d. 1848) was the first Iranian official to master French. He married Ḍiyā' al-Salṭana in 1835, see Anṣārī 1970: 12–15 and 25–26; and Bāmdād 1968: 75–78.

15 It was not unheard of for the women in a family to convert to the Baha'i religion and for the men of the family not to convert, see Momen 2005: 364.

16 According to Parvin Namdar, Laqā'iyya's eldest grandchild, after returning to Iran, Huvīya related that when she and her sisters entered the presence of 'Abdu'l-Baha he said, *Laqā'iyya musharraf shud* ('Laqā'iyya has already made her pilgrimage').

17 Two of Āqā Shāhzāda's letters to Baha'ullah, and one addressed to 'Abdu'l-Baha have recently been published, see Baha'ullah and 'Abdu'l-Baha 2005: 457–459. For the texts of a number of Ibn-i Aṣdaq's touching letters written to his wife, mother-in-law, sister-in-law and daughters, see ibid.: 426–455. Rūḥā Aṣdaq has left a brief but fascinating account of their pilgrimage, see: Aṣdaq 1987 for the original Persian and Aṣdaq 1999 for the English translation.

18 For a more comprehensive discussion of these tablets than the one presented here, see Brookshaw 2004.

19 Baha'ullah addressed a tablet to Ibn-i Aṣdaq when he visited Baghdad in 1861 aged 10 years, see Balyuzi 1985: 171–172; and Baha'ullah and 'Abdu'l-Baha 2005: 45.

20 In a number of these tablets Baha'ullah points out that the addressee is the sister and/or daughter of a female Baha'i, see Baha'ullah and 'Abdu'l-Baha 2005: 222.

21 See ibid.: 211.

22 This suggests that she may have received many more tablets than those which have survived.

23 This English translation is by the Research Department of the Baha'i World Centre. For the Persian original, see: 'Abdu'l-Baha 1978: 159.

24 Shahanshāh Baygum's house is one of the very few houses owned by women mentioned on Najm al-Dawla's 1892 map of Tehran.

25 Ibn-i Aṣdaq delivered 'Abdu'l-Baha's *Risāla-yi siyāsiyya* (Treatise on Politics) to the Shah and notables of Tehran in the 1890s. See also Baha'ullah and 'Abdu'l-Baha 2005: 348.

26 Ḍiyā' al-Ḥājjīya contacted Mushāvir al-Mamālik (her cousin) to obtain travel documents for her and her daughters in 1913.

27 This English translation is by the Research Department of the Baha'i World Centre. The Persian original is: *az faḍl-i ḥaqq . . . ba maqāmī fā'iz shudī ka fakhr-i malaka-hā-yi 'ālam ast*; see Baha'ullah and 'Abdu'l-Baha 2005: 206–207.

28 The Persian is: *malaka-yi Landan har yawm ba ism-i ḥaqq ba kanīsa mīravad va ba gamān-i khud ba dhikr-i ḥaqq mashghūl ast valākin ḥaqq bar ghiflat-ash shahādat dāda va mīdahad cha ka az 'irfān-i ū maḥrūm u ba ism-ash mutamassik va hamchunīn sā'ir-i impirāṭūra-hā-yi 'ālam.*

29 For the English translation of this tablet, see Baha'ullah 2002: 88–96.

30 The Persian is: *tu-rā az bayn-i rabbāt-i ḥijāl imtiyāz dāda va bi-tāj-i vahhāj-i ʿirfān sar-at sarafrāz namūda.*
31 This English translation is by the Research Department of the Baha'i World Centre, see Aṣdaq 1999: 44. For the Persian original, see 'Abdu'l-Baha 1978: 59.
32 The Persian is: *bi-āncha akthar-i rijāl-i arḍ az ān ghāfil-and fā'iz shudī.*
33 For a similar statement by Baha'ullah in a tablet to Laqā'iyya, see Baha'ullah and 'Abdu'l-Baha 2005: 221.
34 Other Qajar Babi-Baha'i women include Shams-i Jahān Khānum, Fitna, daughter of Fatḥ-ʿAlī Shah's 13th son, Muḥammad-Riḍā Mīrzā, and Badr-i Jahān Khānum, Fatḥ-ʿAlī Shah's 48th daughter who became a Babi through Ṭāhira in Kirmanshah. On Shams-i Jahān Khānum see Cole 1998: 169–170; on Badr-i Jahān Khānum see Afnān 1999: 28.
35 It is important to note that Baha'ullah banned temporary marriage (*ṣīgha*), limited the number of wives to two, whilst strongly encouraging monogamy (which 'Abdu'l-Baha subsequently made binding on the Baha'i community), and gave women the right to divorce their husbands, see Momen 2005: 347–348.
36 This translation is by the Research Department of the Baha'i World Centre. For the Persian original, see 'Abdu'l-Baha 1978: 139.
37 For a discussion of similar classes and women propagators of the Baha'i religion (sing. *muballigha*), see Momen 2005: 363.
38 The Persian is: *umīd chunān-ast ka dar muddatī qalīla ān kanīzān-i ʿazīz-i ilāhī dar dalā'il-i manqūla va maʿqūla bi-qismī mahārat yāband ka har yik dar muqābil-i ʿulamā' . . . bi-dalīlī qāṭiʿ vu bayānī vāḍiḥ u burhānī lāmiʿ vu nuṭqī balīgh u kalāmī faṣīḥ lab bigushāyand.*
39 This English translation is by the Research Department of the Baha'i World Centre. For the original Persian, see 'Abdu'l-Baha 1978: 79–81.
40 For a general discussion of the tablets to these families, see Samandarī 1998.
41 For more on Samandar, see Balyuzi 1985: 191–215 and Samandarī-Khushbīn 2002: 61–76. For more on Nabīl ibn-i Nabīl, see Balyuzi 1980: 387–402, and Samandarī-Khushbīn 2002: 86–92.
42 Arabic headings: e.g. B96: *huwa al-nāṭiq min malakūt al-bayān* and, B119: *huwa al-nādī amām al-wujūh*; Persian titles: B97 and B118: *bi-nām-i khudāvand-i yiktā.* Most of 'Abdu'l-Baha's tablets open with the Arabic heading, *huwallāh* (He is God).
43 It was in the late 1860s/early 1870s that a distinct Baha'i community began to emerge under the leadership of Baha'ullah from the remnants of the Babi community which had been severely decimated by the late 1850s.
44 In a similar tablet to the wife of the prominent Qazvin Babi-Baha'i, Ḥājjī Ibrāhīm-i Khalīl, Baha'ullah says that many women have heard his call and answered it, whereas the prominent men (*rijāl*), heroes (*abṭāl*) and the learned (sing. *ʿālim*) are largely heedless of this day. In another tablet to the same woman, Baha'ullah says that the people of Iran (*khalq-i Iran*) are all deprived of knowing God because they cling to illusions (sing. *mawhūm*). At the end of the tablet, Baha'ullah praises her and the other female Baha'is for having faith. These unpublished tablets are in the family archives of Ibrāhīm Khalīlī.
45 Baha'ullah was imprisoned in 'Akka from 1868–1870, and was thereafter confined within the walled city until 1877, when he moved to a house in the countryside outside 'Akka called Mazraʿa. This tablet must, therefore, date from some time between 1868 and 1877.
46 In a similar tablet to Nuṣrat, daughter of Ḥājjī 'Abdu'l-Karīm of Qazvin, and wife of Ḥājjī Ismāʿīl, son of Ḥājjī Ibrāhīm-i Khalīl, 'Abdu'l-Baha praises her father and mother and calls on her both to give thanks for such a lineage and to

arise to serve the women of the community. This unpublished tablet is in the family archives of Ibrāhīm Khalīlī.

47 Ma'ṣūma Farhādī was the daughter of Ṣāḥib Khānum and Āqā Mihdī Farhādī. She visited Haifa on pilgrimage in 1899–1900, see Balyuzi 1985: 209 and Samandarī-Khushbīn 2002: 58–60. Ṣāḥib Khānum was the daughter of one of the earliest Babis of Qazvin, Ḥājjī Asadullāh Farhādī, who was martyred in Tehran, having been accused of involvement in the killing of Ṭāhira's uncle. Ṣāḥib Khānum became a follower of the Bab during his lifetime and subsequently became a follower of Baha'ullah. Baha'ullah composed a long Arabic tablet following her passing (*ziyāratnāma*), see ibid.: 78–81. Ṣāḥib Khānum's younger sister, Khātūn Jān Khānum, was instrumental in helping Ṭāhira escape house arrest in Qazvin and secretly transfer to the house of Baha'ullah in Tehran. Khātūn Jān Khānum was the recipient of Baha'ullah's *Lawḥ-i Bahā'*, see ibid.: 79.

48 *bihtarīn jāma-yi 'ālam az barā-yi imā'ullāh 'iṣmat ast, insha' Allāh kull ba ān muzayyan shavand.*

49 On the concept of the Covenant (in Persian Baha'i texts normally *'ahd* or *mīthāq*), see Smith 2000: 114–115.

50 *imā'ī mab'ūth gardand ka ḥujūbāt-i ahl-i imkān rā ba quvvat-i burhān-i 'aẓīm bar-dārand.*

51 Ma'ṣūma's mother, Ṣāḥib Khānum, is said to have had a good working knowledge of Arabic and to have copied the *Kitāb-i Aqdas* in her own hand, see Samandarī-Khushbīn 2002: 79. It is possible that she instructed her daughters to read Arabic.

52 In a similar tablet to the wife of Ḥājjī Ibrāhīm-i Khalīl, 'Abdu'l-Baha describes the pilgrimage of the addressee's son, Ḥājjī Ismā'īl, and calls on her to give praise to God for having been given such a son. This unpublished tablet is in the family archives of Ibrāhīm Khalīlī.

53 'Abdu'l-Baha refers to her family as *khānidān-i raḥmānī*. For a similar tablet containing praise of the family of Samandar, see tablet A87 in which 'Abdu'l-Baha refers to the family as *khāndān-i mubārak* (this blessed family). In Baha'i texts, the adjective *mubārak* is generally reserved for the members of the families of the Bab and Baha'ullah. 'Abdu'l-Baha praises the family for having responded to this new religion from the time of the Bab, and adds that the pages of the history are filled with their deeds, which will be remembered for eternity.

54 Baha'ullah appointed four Hands of the Cause of God (*ayādī amrullāh*): Mīrzā 'Alī-Muḥammad, 'Ibn-i Aṣdaq'; Ḥājjī Mīrzā Muḥammad-Taqī, 'Ibn-i Abhar'; Ḥājjī Mullā 'Alī-Akbar Shahmīrzādī, 'Ḥājjī Akhūnd'; and Mīrzā Muḥammad-Ḥasan, Adīb al-'Ulamā, 'Jināb-i Adīb'.

55 It seems that when her husband was away from Qazvin, Ṭarāziyya began to study Arabic and translate some of the Arabic tablets of Baha'ullah into Persian. She is said to have been one of the very few Baha'i women of Qazvin in her day who could recite Arabic prayers, see: Samandarī-Khushbīn 2002: 138–139.

56 Ṭarāziyya first tutored Baha'i girls informally in her home, but she disliked that traditional method, and she soon joined forces with others in Qazvin to establish a Baha'i-run school for girls. The Tavakkul school for girls was eventually established in 1909, see Samandarī-Khushbīn 2002: 138–139 and 393–394, and Momen's chapter in this volume.

57 The explanation of the circumstances in which the tablet was written is in Persian, and Baha'ullah's message to Sharīfa Baygum is in Arabic.

58 For a description of the circumstances of Nabīl ibn-i Nabīl's death, see Balyuzi 1980: 387–402.

59 *dar jahān-i āfarīnish chunān ṭulū' u jilva namāyand ka dhikr-i nisā'-i avā'il rā mansūkh namāyand.*
60 This is particularly poignant when we consider that five out of 'Abdu'l-Baha's nine children died in infancy.
61 *dar bāgh-i ilāhī ghars shud u ba bihisht-i barīn-i firdaws-i raḥmānī naql gasht.*
62 *maghmūm mabāsh, maḥzūn mabāsh, asīr-i andūh mabāsh. Īn ayyām bi-sar āyad u ba 'ālamī pur-i shahd u shikar dar-ā'īm.* Sharīfa Baygum visited 'Abdu'l-Baha in Haifa in 1899–1900.
63 For more information on the Baha'i community of 'Ishaqābād, see Momen 1991.
64 *dar mas'ala-yi 'adam-i ḥijāb bayn-i imā' al-raḥmān.*
65 There is a second tablet from 'Abdu'l-Baha to Sādhijiyya, A75.
66 For a concise history of the Baha'i communities of western Iran, see http://www.northill.demon.co.uk/relstud/kirmnshh.htm. For a selection of the tablets of Baha'ullah and 'Abdu'l-Baha to the Jewish Baha'is of Hamadan, see Thābitī 2004: 60–66.
67 See Ishrāq-Khāvarī 2004: 22 for a tablet addressed to the Jewish Baha'is of Hamadan: *Hamadan, aḥibbā-yi ilāhī sulāla-yi haḍrat-i Khalīl-i jalīl.* Near the end of this tablet 'Abdu'l-Baha refers to the recipients as *aḥibbā-yi kalīmī* (Jewish friends). For a study of the Jewish Baha'is of Hamadan, see Thābitī 2004.
68 Ishrāq-Khāvarī 2004: 22: *muntaẓir-i ān-am ka yārān-i Hamadan u imā'-i raḥmān sabab-i nurāniyyat-i 'ālam-i insān gardand.*
69 Ishrāq-Khāvarī 2004: 232: *shukr-guzārī kun ka az nasl-i nafsī hastī ka dar dargāh-i ilāhī maqbūl ast u dar āstān-i muqaddas maḥmūd.*
70 Ishrāq-Khāvarī 2004: 338–339. The women pilgrims were Sāra Khānum, mother of Nūr al-Dīn Mumtāzī, and several female relatives of Ḥāfiẓ al-Ṣiḥḥa. Ṭāvūs, daughter of Ḥakīm Āqā Jān was another Jewish Baha'i woman from Hamadan who made the pilgrimage to Palestine. Ṭāvūs Khanum, who worked for many years as a midwife in Hamadan, stayed in Haifa for some time in the mid-late 1920s and nursed Bahiyya Khanum, see Thābitī 2004: 39–40.
71 It is interesting to note that this school was founded before the Tarbiyat school for girls in Tehran. For more information on the establishment of the Baha'i-run schools in Hamadan, see Thābitī 2004: 75–81. See Momen 2005: 359–361 for a discussion of the initiatives of women in the Baha'i community of Iran at the turn of the twentieth century to set up schools for girls.
72 Ishrāq-Khāvarī 2004: 133. See the same page for a poem in praise of the Mawhibat school for girls by Mīrzā Muḥammad-'Alī Shāyiq.
73 Ishrāq-Khāvarī 2004: 319; directors: Shahlā Raf'at, Ishrāqiyya Dhabīḥ and Mastūra Ḥaqīqī; superintendents: Māhī Iḥtiyātī, Mulūk Khādim and Maymanat Nāmī; teachers: Ṭūbā Maẓharī, Shams al-Mulūk Mawzūn, Ṣadr al-Mulūk Mawzūn, Shawkat Anvar, 'Izzat Vaḥīd, Qamar Anvar, Akhtar al-Mulūk Mawzūn, Batūl Raḍī. Ishrāq-Khāvarī (ibid.: 128–129) mentions a number of other directors of the Mawhibat school, including Maḥbūba Na'īmī, Ṭāhira Ittiḥādiyya and Naw-Ẓuhūr Baygum, wife of Fāḍil-i Shīrāzī.
74 These classes were called *maḥfil-i dars-i tablīgh-i nisā'* and *maḥfil-i tablīgh-i ināth.*
75 See ibid.: 355–356 for a tablet to another teacher at the school, Ṭūbā (presumably Ṭūbā Maẓharī), in which 'Abdu'l-Baha asks her to congratulate Ḥannā on her perseverance, and sends greetings to Tāvūs.
76 The Persian is: *imtithāl-i avāmir-i muqaddasa-yi Jamāl-i Mubārak namūda-and u ba tarbiyat-i aṭfāl-i ināth bar khāstand.*
77 The Persian is: *dar qarn-i sābiq banāt-i Irān ba kullī az ta'līm maḥrūm, na maktabī u na dabistānī, na mu'allimī na ustādī u na murabbī-yi mihrbānī.*

78 For a biography of Fāḍil-i Shīrāzī, which contains many details about his wife, Naw-Ẓuhūr Baygum, see Falahi-Skuce 2004.

79 It is interesting to note that (c.1929) Ṣadr al-Mulūk was the first Baha'i from a Muslim background to be buried in the Baha'i cemetery of Hamadan, which suggests that up until that point only Baha'is of Jewish ancestry had been buried in the new Baha'i cemetery.

80 For a concise history of the Babi and Baha'i communities of the Isfahan area, including Najafabad, see Momen, online at http://www.northill.demon.co.uk/relstud/isfahan.htm

81 See Mudarris 2004: 430 for a picture of the ten women members of the Najafabad Baha'i Committee for the Advancement of Women taken in 1941.

82 This is a reference to the Baha'i Temple in Wilmette, Illinois, the site of which was dedicated by 'Abdu'l-Baha in May 1912.

83 This was Nora Crossley, one of the early Baha'is of England.

84 The Persian is: *mulāḥiẓa kunīd ka amrullāh ba cha daraja quvvat yāfta ka khānumī farangī gīs-i khvīsh rā fadā-yi mashriq al-adhkār mi-namāyad.*

85 The women named are: Baygum Khānum-i Vā'iẓa (presumably Zayn al-Muqarrabīn's niece), Gawhar Baygum, Munavvar Khānum, Maryam Sulṭān, Rabāba Sulṭān, Khānum Kūchak and the wife of the late Āqā Muḥammad Ḥasan.

86 For details on the Baha'i martyrs of Najafabad, see ibid.: 369–409.

87 For biographies of a number of early Zoroastrian Baha'is of Iran, see Farīdānī 2002 and Safīdvash 1999. For a discussion of the conversion of Zoroastrians to the Baha'i Faith, see Vahman's chapter in this volume.

88 Most of the Zoroastrians who converted to the Baha'i Faith in Iran and India seem to have done so either in the last years of Baha'ullah's life or during the period of 'Abdu'l-Baha's leadership (1892–1921), see Maneck 1990.

89 These numbers refer to individual tablets written by 'Abdu'l-Baha as numbered in *Yārān-i Pārsī.*

90 *sabab-i shādmānī-yi dil u jān gardad va nafḥa-yi ḥayāt damad va jān u vujdān-i yārān ḥayāt-i tāza yābad.*

91 In one tablet (157) 'Abdu'l-Baha describes one of this tablets brought back by a pilgrim as a prized gift (*armaghān*).

92 Some Baha'i scriptures (including Baha'ullah's *Kitāb-i Īqān*) were printed in Bombay as early as 1882.

93 Many Baha'is of a Muslim background had also performed the Muslim Ḥajj and continued to use the title Ḥājjī, even after conversion.

94 In the Qajar period, *mulla* signified a learned, literate man with knowledge of religious scripture, and was accordingly used by Muslims and non-Muslims alike.

95 The title *mihtar* is found in at least 45 tablets, and *sarvar* in less than ten.

96 Tablet 48 is addressed to: *sā'ir-i aḥibbā-yi ilāhī-yi islām u zardushti.*

97 Tablets 34, 61, 170, 173, 208, 236, 244, 256, 258, 298, 299, 331, 380, 405, 415, 440, 444, 516, 560, 579, 595, 599, 655, 657, 664 and 709.

98 E.g. Jināb-i Kharman (Kharman Hurmuzdyār), the first Zoroastrian woman to become Baha'i in Yazd, who converted her mother (Parī), sisters (Dawlat, Sarvar, La'l and Murvārīd), brother (Isfandiyār) and maternal aunt (Mihrbānū) to the Baha'i Faith. Kharman was instrumental in the conversion of many other Zoroastrian women to the Baha'i religion in Yazd and the surrounding villages, and she helped establish regular meetings of Zoroastrian Baha'i women. For more details on the Hurmuzdyār sisters, see Farīdānī (2002), 388–392 and 410–412.

99 The title *ustād* was also sometimes used for women, see Farīdānī 2002: 393–396 and 399–401 for the biographies of two women, Ustād Gulchihr Mihrabān and Ustād Khudāparast Khudādād, two Zoroastrian Baha'i women who taught at the Baha'i-run school for girls in Yazd, Madrasa-yi Hūshangī.

100 Most of the terms used to designate 'wife' are of Arabic origin and are the same as those used in tablets to women from Muslim and Jewish backgrounds: *ḍil'*, *ḍajī'*, *zawja*, *ḥaram* and *qarīn* or *qarīna*.

101 More than twenty of these tablets were sent via various relatives of the Bab (Afnāns) residing in Yazd, Shiraz and Bombay: tablets 76, 85, 88, 94, 101, 102, 378, 388, 393, 431, 435, 512, 514, 518, 519, 520, 526, 527, 562, 566, 646, 687 and 692.

102 63, 108, 130, 267, 301, 307, 363, 371, 373, 385, 386, 387, 503, 649 and 702.

103 118, 184, 223, 338, 389, 390, 392, 401, 402, 403, 530, 552, 555, 565 and 660.

104 221, 577, 579, 656 and 708.

105 For more on these American women, see Armstrong-Ingram 1986. In a tablet to the Baha'is of Bombay (511), 'Abdu'l-Baha mentions the imminent arrival of a number of female American and European Baha'is to the city to help propagate the religion. This is probably a reference to the visit of Lua Getsinger and Mrs. Stannard. Another early western Baha'i to visit India and Burma (1904–1905) was Sydney Sprague, who was fluent in Persian, and who later taught at the Tarbiyat School for boys in Tehran and who married a niece of 'Abdu'l-Baha. Sprague left a brief by fascinating account of his journey to India and Burma, see Sprague (1986). Sprague was visiting the Baha'i communities of the Indian sub-continent at the same time as Jināb-i Adīb, Mīrzā Maḥram and one of the first French Baha'is, Hippolyte Dreyfus.

106 'Abdu'l-Baha sent many prominent Baha'is to Bombay to promote unity in the community, they included: Maḥmūd Zarqānī, Ibn-i Aṣdaq, Jināb-i Adīb and Āqā Mīrzā Maḥram. Mulla Bahrām also visited Bombay to propagate the Baha'i Faith among members of the Parsee community.

107 'Abdu'l-Baha may have used these standard Arabic Baha'i invocations in order to familiarize the Zoroastrian Baha'is with the Baha'i scriptures which contain much Arabic vocabulary.

108 These tablets are mostly referred to as, *munājāt-i ṭalab-i maghfirat* ('prayer for forgiveness'), but in they are also entitled, *ṭalab-i āmurzish, khvāhish-i āmurzish* and *ṭalab-i ghufrān*.

109 71, 77, 113, 127, 214, 240, 255, 282, 295, 332, 335, 377, 391, 396, 425, 465, 466, 470, 483, 484, 493, 507, 523, 572, 575, 576, 577, 581, 588, 600, 610, 614, 633, 634, 635, 636, 645, 646, 664, 674, 675, 702 and 728.

110 *munājāt dar ḥaqq-i man istashhada fī sabīlillah, Jināb-i Āqā Gūdarz.* For details on Jināb-i Gūdarz and other Zoroastrian Baha'i martyrs from the time of 'Abdu'l-Baha and following the 1979 Revolution, see Farīdānī 2002: 426–431 and Safīdvash 1999: 87–88 and 150–151.

111 See Khiandra 1988: 167–169 and 219–226 for more information on these women.

112 Some examples are tablets 112, 255 and 347.

113 This was perhaps more true of India, where women were elected to local Baha'i councils as early as the 1920s, see Khiandra 1988: 219.

114 E.g. 279, 327, 361, 501 and 622.

115 Shīrīn: 185, 415, 651; Gawhar: 272, 383, 422; Murvārīd: 518; and Gul: 618.

116 30, 157, 327, 334, 352, 356, 361, 420, 422, 618 and 622.

117 417 is addressed to Murvārīd Bahrām, and 497 is addressed to Dawlat Iran, both of whom visited 'Abdu'l-Baha in Haifa. Dawlat Iran visited Haifa twice, once in 1906 and again in 1912.

118 E.g. 534, 564 and 700.

119 *dar nihāyat-i faṣāḥat u balāghat ast mānand-i āb-i ravān, salīs u faṣīḥ u balīgh.* For an example of some of the poetry Shīrīn Mihrabān sent to 'Abdu'l-Baha, see Farīdānī 2002: 402–403. In another tablet (498) also addressed to Shīrīn Mihrabān, but sent to Bombay, 'Abdu'l-Baha praises the quality of English poems she has composed, and signs the tablet 'abdul-Baha abbas' in Latin letters. Shīrīn Mihrabān of Bombay (Dawlat Iran's daughter) was, in 1936, the first woman to be elected to the National Spiritual Assembly of the Baha'is of India and Burma.

120 Shīrīn Mihrabān also taught Baha'i children in the village of Khurramshāh, see Farīdānī 2002: 401–404.

121 For a discussion of the development of the Baha'i community in India, see Smith 2005.

122 Both these tablets are very similar to several sent to the female relatives of Ibn-i Aṣdaq, Samandar and Nabīl ibn-i Nabīl.

123 *chunān'iṣmat u 'iffat u pākī u ṭahārat u āzādagī u nijābat u danā'ī u ma'rifat yāband ka sabab-i 'izzat-i abadiyya-yi nisā'-i 'ālamiyān gardand.*

124 See Sprague 1986: 15–20 for a description of the Bombay Baha'i community which was chiefly composed of Baha'is from a Zoroastrian background. Sprague's account shows that there were separate meetings for Baha'i women in Bombay as early as 1904.

125 *ānān sabab-i nijāt-i tu gashtand u tu rā az asīrī dar dast-i dastūrān rahānīdand.* For a similar anti-clerical tablet addressed to a group of Zoroastrian Baha'is, see tablet 264.

126 For another tablet sent via a female pilgrim, Bībī Fīrūza, see tablet 360.

127 *jināb-i Burzū bi-zūr-i bāzū az 'Abdu'l-Baha nāma bi-jihat-i har yik az khvīshān u muta'alliqān khvāst.* For a similar tablet addressed to three sisters of a male pilgrim, see tablet 619.

128 *īn āvāra ṣad mashāghil rūz u shabāna . . . chigūna mukhābira bā sharq u gharb tavānad u bā har yik az aḥibbā' ra'san mukātiba kunad.*

129 *dar nazd-i yazdān a'zam parastish u 'ibādat tarbiyat-i kūdakān ast ba ādāb-i kamāl-i insāniyyat.*

130 E.g. 31, 164, 261 and 698.

131 E.g. 154, 340, 464 and 511.

132 E.g. 31, 55, 59, 98, 189 and 328.

133 E.g. 107, 261 and 426. In a tablet addressed to a group of Baha'is in Maryamābād (644), 'Abdu'l-Baha explains that there is no time to write, but that a letter has been requested and so he is writing to them. He complains that his tongue is lacking, but adds that his feelings for them are complete: *zabān qāṣir ast valī iḥsāsāt-i qalbiyya kāmil.*

134 E.g. 107, 154, 328, 426 and 537.

135 9, 77, 112, 213, 282, 295, 391, 396, 435, 507, 523, 572, 581, 610, 625, 634, 636, 645, 646, 674 and 675.

136 E.g. 465: Shahriyār Surūsh *zīrak u bā-hūsh būd*, Nūshīrvān Bahrāmshāh *ba rāz-at āgāh*, Gul Bānū Fūlād *ba 'ināyat-at dilshād.*

137 *īn gawhar-i girān-qaymat dirakhshandagī-sh dar qurūn va a'ṣār tā abad al-ābād.*

138 It is thought that all the Zoroastrians of Qazvin converted to the Baha'i Faith, see Maneck 1990.

139 *ba nazdīkī khvāhīd dīd ka Daylam u Tajīk balka Amrīk u Afrīk rā āftāb-i khāvar-i Irān rawshan namāyad.*

140 *maqām-i 'āli-yi ān buzurgvār dar in ẓuhūr vāḍiḥ u āshkār gardīd.*

141 *tā ān dhillat-i kubrā badal ba 'izzat-i 'uẓmā gardad.*
142 *ṣadr-nashīnān az shiddat-i ghiflat ba ṣaff-i na'āl uftādand va sākinān-i ṣaff-i na'āl bar ṣadr-i jalāl nishastand.*

Bibliography

'Abdu'l-Baha. (2002) *Tadhkirat al-vafā'*, Hofheim, Germany: Baha'i Verlag.

'Aḍud al-Dawla (Sulṭān Aḥmad Mīrzā). (1997) *Tārīkh-i 'Aḍudī*, ed. 'A. Navā'ī, Tehran: Nashr-i 'Ilm.

Afary, J. (1996) *The Iranian Constitutional Revolution, 1906–1911: Grassroots Democracy, Social Democracy, and the Origins of Feminism*, New York: Columbia University Press.

Afnān, A. (ed.) (1999) *Chahār risāla-yi ta'rīkhī darbāra-yi Ṭāhira Qurrat al-'Ayn*, Darmstadt, Germany: 'Aṣr-i Jadid.

—— (2001) *'Ahd-i a'lā: zindigāni-yi haḍrat-i Bāb*. Oxford: Oneworld.

'Alā'i, 'A. (1974) *Mu'assasa-yi ayādī-yi amrullāh*, Tehran: Mu'asassa-yi Millī-yi Maṭbū'āt-i Amrī.

Amanat, A. (1989) *Resurrection and Renewal: The Making of the Babi Movement in Iran, 1844–1850*, Ithaca: Cornell University Press.

Anṣārī, 'A. (1970) *Zindagāni-yi man va nigāhī ba ta'rīkh-i mu'āṣir-i Iran u jahān*, vol. I. Tehran: Āftāb.

Arbāb, F. (1969) *Akhtarān-i tābān*, vol. I. Tehran: Mu'assasa-yi Millī-yi Maṭbū'āt-i Amrī.

Armstrong-Ingram, R.J. (1986) 'American Baha'i Women and the Education of Girls in Tehran, 1909–1934', in Smith, P. (ed.) *In Iran, Studies in Babi and Baha'i History* vol. 3, Los Angeles: Kalimat Press.

Aṣdaq, R. (1987) *Yik 'umr, yik khāṭira*, Copenhagen: np.

—— (1999) *One Life, One Memory*, trans. Shahbaz Fatheazam, Oxford: George Ronald.

Baha'ullah. (2002) *Summons of the Lord of Hosts: Tablets of Bahá'u'lláh*, Haifa: Baha'i World Centre.

Baha'ullah and 'Abdu'l-Baha. (1998) *Yārān-i Pārsī*, Hofheim, Germany: Baha'i Verlag.

—— (1999) *Āyāt-i bayyināt*, Dundas, Ontario: Mu'assasa-yi Ma'ārif-i Baha'i.

—— (2005) *Payk-i rāstān*, Ra'fatī, V. (ed.), Darmstadt: 'Aṣr-i Jadīd.

Balyuzi, H.M. (1980) *Bahá'u'lláh the King of Glory*, Oxford: George Ronald.

—— (1981) *Khadijih Bagum: The Wife of the Bab*, Oxford: George Ronald.

—— (1985) *Eminent Baha'is in the time of Bahá'u'lláh*, Oxford: George Ronald.

Bāmdād, M. (1968) *Ta'rīkh-i rijāl-i Iran*, vol. IV. Tehran: Zavvār.

Banani, A. (2004) *Tahirih: A Portrait in Poetry. Selected Poems of Qurratu'l-'Ayn*, Los Angeles: Kalimat.

Brookshaw, D.P. (2004) 'Letters to Baha'i princesses: Tablets revealed in honour of the women of Ibn-i Aṣdaq's household', in *Lights of 'Irfan*, 5: 19–41.

BWCRD (Baha'i World Centre Research Department) (1982) *Bahiyyih Khánum, The Greatest Holy Leaf: a compilation from Bahá'í sacred texts and the writings of the Guardian of the Faith and Bahíyyih Khánum's own letters*, Haifa: Bahá'í World Centre.

—— (1997) *Women: Extracts from the Writings of Baha'u'llah, 'Abdu'l-Baha, Shoghi Effendi and the Universal House of Justice*, Wilmette: Baha'i Publishing Trust.

Cole, J.R.I. (1998) *Modernity and the Millennium: The Genesis of the Baha'i Faith in the Nineteenth-Century Middle East*, New York: Columbia University Press.

De Vries, J. (2002) *That Babi Question You Mentioned: the origins of the Baha'i community of the Netherlands, 1844–1962*, Leuven: Peeters.

Falahi-Skuce, H. (2004) *A Radiant Gem: a biography of Jinab-i Fadil-i Shirazi*, Victoria, Canada: Trafford.

Farīdānī, S. (2002) *Dūstān-i Rāstān: ta'rīkh-i ḥayāt u khadamāt-i Bahā'iyān-i Pārsī*, Hofheim, Germany: Baha'i Verlag.

Garlington, W. (1997) 'The Baha'i Faith in India: A Developmental Stage Approach', *Occasional Papers in Shaykhi, Babi and Baha'i Studies*, 2. Online at: http://www.h-net.org/~bahai/bhpapers/india1.htm

Ishrāq-Khāvarī, 'A. (2004) *Ta'rīkh-i amrī-yi Hamadan*, ed. V. Rafatī, Hofheim, Germany: Baha'i Verlag.

Khāvarī (Mīrzā Faḍlullāh Shīrāzī). (2001) *Ta'rīkh-i Dhū'l-Qarnayn*, vols I and II, Tehran: Sāzmān-i Chāp va Intishārāt-i Vizārat-i Farhang va Irshād-i Islāmī.

Khianra, D. (1988) *Immortals*, New Delhi: Baha'i Publishing Trust.

Maneck, S.S. (1989) 'Tahirih: A Religious Paradigm of Womanhood', *Journal of Bahá'í Studies*, 2.2: 35–48.

—— (1990) 'The Conversion of Religious Minorities to the Bahá'í Faith in Iran: Some Preliminary Observations', *Journal of Bahá'í Studies*, 3.3: 35–48.

Milani, F. (1992) *Veils and Words: The Emerging Voices of Iranian Women Writers*. London: I.B. Tauris.

Momen, M. (1991) 'The Baha'i Community of Ashkabad: its Social Basis and Importance in Baha'i History', in S. Akiner (ed.), *Cultural Change and Continuity in Central Asia*, London: Kegan Paul International.

—— (2003) 'Usuli, Akhbari, Shaykhi, Babi: The Tribulations of a Qazvin Family', *Iranian Studies*, 36: 313–337.

—— (2005) 'The Role of Women in the Iranian Baha'i Community During the Qajar Period', in R. Gleave (ed.), *Religion and Society in Qajar Iran*, London: RoutledgeCurzon.

Mottahedeh, N. (1998) 'The Mutilated Body of the Modern Nation: Qurrat al-'Ayn Tahirah's Unveiling and the Iranian Massacre of the Babis', *Comparative Studies of South Asia, Africa and the Middle East*, 18: 38–50.

Mudarris, F. (2004) *Ta'rīkh-i amr-i Baha'i dar Najafabad*, ed. V. Rafatī, Darmstadt, Germany: 'Aṣr-i Jadīd.

Rouhani Ma'ani, B. (1993) *Asiyih Khānum: The Most Exalted Leaf entitled Navvab*, Oxford: George Ronald.

Safīdvash, 'I. (1999) *Tanī chand az pīshgāmān-i Parsī-nijād dar 'ahd-i rasūlī*, Dundas, Ontario: Mu'assasa-yi Ma'ārif-i Baha'i.

Samandar, K. (1975) *Ta'rīkh-i Samandar va mulḥaqqāt*, Tehran: Mu'assasa-yi Millī-yi Maṭbū'āt-i Amrī.

Samandarī, M. and V. (1998) 'Mujmalī darbāra-yi alvāḥ-i nāzila ba iftikhār-i khānidān-i Samandarī u Nabīlī', in *Khūsha-hā'ī az kharman-i adab u hunar*, vol. IX. Darmstadt, Germany: 'Aṣr-i Jadīd.

Samandarī-Khushbīn, P. (2002) *Ṭarāz-i ilāhī*, vol. I, Hamilton: Mu'assasa-yi Ma'ārif-i Baha'i.

Smith, P. (2000) *A Concise Encyclopedia of the Baha'i Faith*, Oxford: Oneworld.
—— (2005) 'Shoghi Effendi's Letters to the Baha'is of India and Burma during the 1920s', *Baha'i Studies Review*, 13: 15–40.
Sprague, S. (1986) *A Year with the Bahá'is in India and Burma*, Los Angeles: Kalimat Press.
Sulaymānī, 'A. (1973) *Maṣābīḥ-i hidāyat*, vol VII, Tehran: Mu'assasa-yi Millī-yi Maṭbū'āt-i Amrī.
Thābitī, H. (2004) *Vārithān-i Kalīm: ta'rīkh-i ḥayāt u khadamāt-i aḥibbā'-i Kalīmī-yi Hamadan*, Bundoora, Australia: Century Press.

4

BAHA'I SCHOOLS IN IRAN

Moojan Momen

From its beginnings, Baha'ullah made it clear that his religion was not just involved in improving the spirituality and morals of humanity but was also very much concerned with improving social conditions.[1] One of the main mechanisms for improving humanity's social conditions is stated by Baha'ullah to be education. Thus, for example, with respect to Baha'ullah's central goal of bringing about peace and unity in the world, he writes: 'Bend your minds and wills to the education (*tarbiyat*) of the peoples and kindreds of the earth, that haply the dissensions that divide it may, through the power of the Most Great Name, be blotted out from its face, and all mankind become the upholders of one Order, and the inhabitants of one City' (1983: 333–4). In general, Baha'ullah considers education as vital in the development of human beings. In a text from the 'Akka period, he states: 'Man is the supreme Talisman. Lack of a proper education (*tarbiyat*) hath, however, deprived him of that which he doth inherently possess . . . The Great Being saith: Regard man as a mine rich in gems of inestimable value. Education (*tarbiyat*) can, alone, cause it to reveal its treasures, and enable mankind to benefit therefrom' (1978: 161–2).

Having given such importance to education, Baha'ullah, in his most holy book, the *Kitāb-i Aqdas*, makes it a sacred obligation on parents to educate their children and if they are, for any reason unable to do this, he makes it a duty of the elected Baha'i councils in each locality, the 'Houses of Justice', to take over this task. Baha'ullah also raises the status of teachers to a high level in society and, for example, in cases of intestacy, the teachers (*mu'allimīn*) of the deceased are the only group of non-family inheritors among whom the wealth of the deceased is to be divided (Baha'ullah 1992: v. 20).

'Abdu'l-Baha shared Baha'ullah's concern for education. He regarded education as a high priority. He wrote: 'Every child is potentially the light of the world – and at the same time its darkness; wherefore must the question of education be accounted as of primary importance' (1978: 130–31). He was particularly keen for the Baha'is to set up schools in every town and village where the community was large enough to warrant this and for these schools to be functioning to the highest possible standards, morally and academically ('Abdu'l-Baha 1991: 276–87).

Education in Iran

The early history of the Baha'i Faith in Iran corresponded with a time when the inadequacies of the traditional educational system for the modern world were beginning to be realized and attempts were made to introduce modern education to the country. The traditional educational system was based on teaching by *mulla*s, who often had no formal training in educational methods. These taught, often in their own homes, a wide age range and all together, in a single classroom (*maktab*). They were not under any governmental control and did not have to meet professional requirements. A child might start as early as five years old and the first years were taken up with learning to read and write Persian as well as some arithmetic. There was a great deal of memorization of Persian poetry and large parts of the Qur'an. There were very few *maktab*s for girls. Fees were charged by the *mulla* and so most of the population was excluded from even this elementary education because of their poverty (Banani 1961: 86–7; Dustkhah and Yaghma'i: 807). Wealthy families often engaged a private tutor who taught much the same material in the family home.

The only source of secondary education was the *madrasa*, the religious college, which had as its objective the production of the *'ulama*, the religious class. Some other subjects such as astronomy, medicine and mathematics were taught at a few of these *madrasa*s but only using medieval texts and traditional methods. Some sons of government officials and merchants would attend these institutions for a few years before leaving to follow a secular occupation. The modern sciences and technologies were not being taught anywhere in Iran until 1851 when Nāṣir al-Dīn Shah's prime minister, Mīrzā Taqī Khān Amīr Kabīr, opened the Dār al-Funūn in Tehran. Even then the primary objective of this college was to improve the military capacity of Iran and the numbers of graduates from it were very small (less than 50 per year).[2]

A few schools run by foreign missionaries existed but these usually restricted their intake to their co-religionists. The American Presbyterian missionaries opened schools for Nestorian Christian boys and girls in Urumiyya in 1836 and 1838 respectively, and then in the Nestorian villages of that area. Later similar schools were opened in Tehran (1875), Tabriz and Hamadan for Armenians and other Christians (Waterfield 1973: 134–7). The French Catholic Lazarists were opening schools in Iran from the 1840s and established the St Louis School for boys in Tehran in 1862 and the St Joseph School for girls in 1890 (Waterfield 1973: 80–82; Faridani 2002: 6). Under an agreement with the Americans, the English missionaries confined themselves to the south of the country where they set up schools in the major cities there from the 1870s onwards (Waterfield 1973: 149–50). From the earliest period, there was alarm among the *'ulama* at the establishment of these schools which they feared would not only spread Christianity in Iran but also directly competed with their traditional role as *maktabdār*s (operators of traditional schools). As early as March 1857, the Shaykhi leader, Ḥājjī Muḥammad Karīm Khān Kirmānī was railing against Europeans 'building their schools, bringing their own teachers over and instructing the people from their own books, such that simple-minded children will be brought up according to the Christian religion' (Kirmānī 1967: 390; cf. partial trans. in Tavakoli-Targhi 2001: 72).

An Indian Zoroastrian mission headed by Manekji Sahib (Manekji Limji Hateria) had started small primary schools in Kirman and Yazd shortly after his arrival in Iran in 1854, and he later set up a boarding secondary school in Tehran in 1865. In 1898, the first Alliance Israélite school was opened in Tehran by French Jews; their school in Hamadan opened in 1900. From the 1880s onwards, small numbers of Muslim children attended these 'foreign' schools, but there was strong pressure against this, and the American Presbyterian girls' school in Tehran, for example, was only permitted on the condition that Muslim girls be excluded (Turābī-Fārisānī 1999: xi).

During the second half of the nineteenth century there were increasing calls among Iranian intellectuals, concerned about the fact that Iran was so far behind Europe, for the establishment of modern educational facilities in Iran. Individual reformers such as Malkam Khān and 'Abd al-Raḥīm Ṭālibzāda (Talebov) called on the government to provide universal schooling.[3] This debate did not yield any concrete results until the last few years of the nineteenth century. The first primary school with a modern curriculum based on Western models initiated by an Iranian was probably the Rushdiyya school in Tabriz that was founded in 1899, but this was closed down after local opposition (although it later re-opened). Then from about 1901, a series of private boys' primary schools were founded in Tehran, Tabriz, Rasht, Mashhad and Bushihr (Arasteh 1969: 70). Conservative members of the *'ulama*, such as Shaykh Faḍlullāh Nūrī opposed the schools, accusing those seeking to establish these schools of heresy and having 'Babi sentiments' and of trying to convert the children in these schools to 'Babism' (Āvāra 1923: 73). Something of the nature of this clerical opposition can be seen in the comments of Nāẓim al-Islām Kirmānī:

> With regard to the matter of schools, we saw that at first when these schools were being established, the people said: 'It is the Babis who are establishing these schools.' However later, after Ḥujjat al-Islām Āqā Sayyid Muḥammad Ṭabāṭabā'ī established the Islam School and this became widely known, then suddenly it was anyone who was saying bad things about schools who was now called a Babi. This is the condition of us Iranians . . .
>
> (Kirmānī 1967: 400)

A few *'ulama*, such as Shaykh Hādī Najmābādī, however supported the new schools.

Girls' schools faced even stronger opposition. Some of the *'ulama* even issued a *fatwa* stating that the existence of a girls' school is contrary to the principles of Shi'i Islam (Farīdānī 1999: xv). An attempt to found a girls' school in 1903 lasted only four days, another girls' school founded in 1907 was similarly forced to close. In 1908, the Nāmūs School for girls opened and was able to continue functioning partly because it ran from a private house. It was really only after the defeat of the reactionary forces in 1909 that it became possible to establish modern girls' schools openly. The second girls' school to open in Tehran (after the Nāmūs School) was Madrasa-yi Ta'īdiyya-yi Dūshizigān-i Vaṭan, founded in early 1911 by a Baha'i, Munīra Khānum Ayādī, the wife of Ibn-i Abhar (Muṣāḥib 1995: 2716). A short while later in May 1911, the Baha'i-run Tarbiyat School for girls was also founded.

In 1911, an Education Act passed by the Majlis made schooling compulsory in Iran, although this had little meaning as there were only a few, mainly private, schools and the government education budget was inadequate. It did, however, have the effect of making the founding of new schools easier and helped to nullify opposition from reactionary forces.

The Baha'i schools

In general, the Baha'is could be said to have been at the forefront of the advances in education that were occurring in Iran in the last decade of the nineteenth and the first decade of the twentieth century. When copies of Baha'ullah's *Kitāb-i Aqdas* and other writings began to circulate among the Baha'is of Iran during the late nineteenth century, they began to consider how they might put these injunctions regarding education into effect. This was particularly the case in some towns such as Qazvin where the Baha'i children were prevented from attending the local *maktab*s (Anon 1994: 29). Moreover, many Baha'is felt that they should leave behind the traditional Islam-based educational system and adopt a more modern approach to education based on curricula developed in the West. Both Baha'ullah and 'Abdu'l-Baha encouraged the study of modern sciences and arts which were not part of a traditional education.[4] The Baha'is were also keen to establish schools so that the emphasis on moral education in their scriptures could be adequately realized.

The earliest effort to establish a Baha'i school appears to have been in the village of Māhfurūzak in Mazandaran. Here Mulla 'Alī, the village *mulla*, had become a Baha'i while studying in Bārfurūsh. He gradually converted most of the village to the Baha'i Faith. Together with his very capable wife, 'Alaviyya Khānum, he set about trying to put the teachings of Baha'ullah into practice in the village. Among other initiatives was the institution of both a boys' and a girls' school in the village (this would, however, have been in the form a *maktab*, rather than a modern school). These schools must have been established before 1882, since in that year, Mulla 'Alī's activities came to the attention of neighbouring religious leaders, and he was denounced to the authorities, arrested, taken off to Tehran and executed.

In some of the larger towns as well, there was concern about the education of Baha'i children, especially in those places, such as Qazvin, where Baha'i children were prevented from attending the local *maktab*s (see above) or, for example in Hamadan, where a Baha'i child attending the Jewish Alliance School was subject to punishment when he failed to attend on a Baha'i holy day (Ishrāq-Khāvarī 2004: 116). Therefore efforts were made to set up education facilities for the children. At first these efforts were made on a purely individual and informal basis. Baha'is who had received a traditional Islamic religious education and who were no longer able to make a living this way became teachers of the Baha'i children. Thus in Tehran, Na'īm, who had been compelled to leave his home village of Furūshān, near Isfahan, and move to Tehran, was taken on by the Baha'i community as a teacher of the Baha'i children in the Sar Qabr Āqā quarter, where many Baha'is lived. In Ābādih, Baha'i *maktabs* were established, including one for girls set up by Qābil in Ābādih itself (at least early as 1898, Dhukā'ī-Bayḍā'ī 1965–70: 95) and another in the nearby village of Darghūk set up by Āqā Aḥmad (Dihqān 1999: 363).

The date of the start of the first modern Baha'i school in Iran, the Tarbiyat School for Boys is given differently in the various sources. Rafati states that the school began in 1315/1897 and was recognized by the government two years later (1989: 468). Māzandarānī (1974: 319), Ishrāq-Khāvarī (1969: 125) and Furūtan (1984: 47) state that the school began in 1317 (1899–1900). Bakhshāyish gives the date of the start of the school as 1317, which he equates to 1900 (cited in Thābit 1997: 53), while Muḥammad-'Alī Fayḍī states that the school was founded in 1317 (1899–1900) and recognized by the government in 1321/1903 (1986: 317). Āvāra states that the Baha'is of Tehran set about establishing the school in 1321/1903 (1923: 73). Insofar as these discrepancies can be reconciled, it appears that in about 1897, a small *maktab* was established in the Sar Qabr Āqā quarter of Tehran by Āqā Mīrzā Bābā Mu'allim Nayrīzī. Through the efforts and encouragement of a number of eminent Baha'is, especially Mīrzā Ḥasan-i Adīb and Ibn-i Abhar, and some non-Baha'is, this evolved into the Tarbiyat School under the headship of Āṣaf al-Ḥukamā probably in the latter part of 1317, which equates to 1900, but that it fell into grave financial and other difficulties in about 1903. Then Muḥammad Ḥusayn Mīrzā Mu'ayyad al-Dawla took over the school, placed it under the control of the Baha'i Central Assembly, revived its finances and moved it to a house owned by Dr. Muḥammad Khān Munajjim in the north of the city, at the same time obtaining government recognition for it (Thābit 1997: 34–6). In about 1906, Dr. Muḥammad Khān Bakhshāyish became the governor of the school. In about 1910, it moved to larger premises in Farmānfarmā Street (Shāpūr Street) and an American Baha'i, Sidney Sprague, was appointed headmaster, helping to move the school even further towards a modern Western system of education. By 1913, the boys' school consisted of six primary school years and two secondary years (at that time only the Dār al-Funūn provided complete secondary schooling) and over time further years were added. In 1914, 'Azizullāh Miṣbāḥ became head of the boys' school (Thābit 1997: 52–62).

Following the establishment of this school in Tehran, schools began to spring up throughout Iran wherever there was a substantial Baha'i community. 'Abdu'l-Baha was very insistent that Baha'i schools be established wherever possible, even in towns where there were other schools already. He stated that because education in childhood was so important for the formation of character and morals, it was important that Baha'i children attend Baha'i schools and be taught by Baha'i teachers (Ishrāq-Khāvarī 1964–72, vol. 5: 63–4, 89–90; Māzandarānī 1986, vol. 3: 338). He also was often asked to name these schools and usually named them after virtues or social principles. The Tavakkul (Reliance upon God) School in Qazvin (1906), the Ta'īd ((Divine) Confirmation, Assistance) School in Hamadan (1907), the Vaḥdat-i Bashar (Oneness of Humanity) School in Kashan (1909) and the Sa'ādat (Happiness) School in Bārfurūsh (Bābul, 1911) were among the earliest. It appears that formal government recognition of many of these schools was obtained through them being registered as branches of the Tarbiyat school in Tehran (Thābit 1997: 86–7). In 1909, the Persian-American Educational Society was formed among the American Baha'is with the express intention of assisting the Baha'i schools in Iran.[5]

A number of Baha'is also started schools which were run as private concerns. It is not clear to what extent Baha'i teachings influenced some of these schools. Shaykh Muḥammad-'Alī Hidāyat, a Baha'i from Mashhad, began some eight schools in Khurasan and Russian Turkistan (Māzandarānī 1974: 248–9). Only the schools in Mashhad and Darra-Jaz appear on the list below as there is some evidence that there was Baha'i influence in these schools. Bashīr al-Sultan started a school in Shiraz (Māzandarānī 1974: 563). Ṭā'ira Khānum was involved in the setting up of the Nawbāvigān School in Tehran (Arbab 1990: 26). Other private schools founded by Baha'is were much more clearly influenced by the Baha'i teachings and appear in the list below. In some large towns, such as Isfahan, where there was a substantial Baha'i community, no Baha'i school seems to have come into existence.

'Abdu'l-Baha was very insistent that, wherever possible, a girls' school be established as well as one for boys. Indeed in a letter to the Baha'is of Hamadan he writes: 'The school for girls taketh precedence over the school for boys, for it is incumbent upon the girls of this glorious era to be fully versed in the various branches of knowledge, in sciences and the arts and all the wonders of this pre-eminent time . . .' ('Abdu'l-Baha 1991: 284). With this encouragement, girls' schools started to be established side by side with boys' schools throughout Iran. From 1324/1906, Sayyid Baygum, the daughter of Sayyid *Ismā'īl* Sīnā, who became known as Mu'allima Khānum (1296/1879–?), began a *maktab* for girls in the Kūcha-yi Bāgh in the Sar Qabr Āqā quarter of Tehran as a branch of the Tarbiyat Boys' School (Māzandarānī 1974: 340–41; Sulaymānī 1975: 399; Arbāb 1990: 29). Through the persistence of Dr. Susan Moody and others, on either 1st or 2nd May 1911, a girls' school was inaugurated in the north of the city with 30 students and was called the Tarbiyat School for Girls.[6] However, this girls' school was not established without a great deal of difficulty. The financial situation in Iran was poor at this time and there was some opposition even within the Baha'i community. There were cultural clashes between the senior Baha'i men who were on the Baha'i administrative bodies and the young American woman, Lilian Kappes, who was brought over to run the school. The following is a comment by 'Ishrat Midḥat, a woman teacher at the school:

> This young headmistress [Miss Kappes] wanted to make the school like an American school and to make it exemplary in every way, but the school committee was often opposed to what this young headmistress wanted to do and prevented her new ideas being implemented. And it may be that the committee was right for, at that time, the situation was not suitable for modern reforms.
>
> (Cited in Anonymous 1987)

After Kappes's death in 1919, she was replaced in 1922 by Dr. Genevieve Coy, a highly trained educationalist (Armstrong-Ingram 1986: 188–99; Momen 2005: 359–61). While there had been Western women in Iran for some time, the wives of diplomatic staff and the American and British women missionaries for example, these had tended to maintain their own social circles and not to mix with the generality of Iranian society. These American women, however, mixed with the members of the Baha'i community and with a wider circle. Apart from the importance of their educational activities, they acted additionally as role models, especially for the girls in the Baha'i schools, showing how women could have a more active social role (Momen 2005: 362; Coy 1926: 52–4).

From the larger cities and towns, the network of Baha'i schools extended into those villages where there were large numbers of Baha'is. Here the difficulties were even greater, indeed many thought it pointless to even try. When Shahāb Shahmīrzādī went to the remote village of Īvil in Māzandarān, he entered into discussions with the Baha'i local spiritual assembly about starting a school. At the instigation of the local clerics, he was arrested by the governor of the area and taken off to Kiyāsar the centre of the district.

> The governor asked Shahāb: 'Are you the person who has come to Īvil?' He replied: 'Yes.' The governor said: 'Look my friend! How

> do you hope, here in the middle of the jungle, to convince these wild and ill-behaved people, who are a hundred centuries removed from education and civilisation and spend their days from dawn to dusk in the paddy-fields up to their waists in mud and water accompanied by cows, of the benefits of education and knowledge or that Moses or Jesus or Muḥammad or Baha'ullah has commanded this or forbidden that? They are not able to understand such matters. I have heard that you are planning to start a school there.' Shahāb replied: 'Although I am a teacher by profession, I had no intention of starting a school there but after I went there, the people there suggested a school and a teacher and so I have said to them that when I go further into Mazandaran, I will try to find a teacher and send him to them.' The governor said: 'What an optimist you are! I have been to Īvil. There is no possibility of a school there. Governors have come to the Chahārdānga district and tried to set up a school here in Kiyāsar which is the centre of the district and has almost 500 families, most of them having wealth and land, and they have failed. Two years ago, A'ẓam al-Vuzarā was the governor here. He really tried hard in this regard and spent fifty *tūmān*s of his own money for the furniture of the school. They constructed tables and benches. But he was not able to get the children to come to school for even a day. After he left, they used the furniture of the school for firewood . . . What do these people know of education and training?' Then he pulled out a piece of paper and said: 'Look, when you see what the learned (*'ulama*) of these parts have written [complaining of Shahāb's activities in trying to set up a school], what expectations can you have of the ordinary people?'
>
> (Īqānī 2001: 96–7)

In all, the Baha'i schools in Iran must have accounted for more than 10 per cent of the estimated 24,000 children in primary education in Iran and a similar proportion of the 2,392 students enrolled in secondary education in 1918–19.[7] It is very difficult to create a full list of all of the Baha'i schools across Iran because no there is no systematic record of them. Table 1 is a provisional attempt.

The Baha'is faced formidable obstacles in establishing their schools. In many places, after fifty years of hiding and keeping a low profile following the Babi persecutions, the establishment of a Baha'i school was the first occasion that the Baha'is stepped into the public arena. The schools thus became the visible sign of the existence of a Baha'i community in each locality and therefore often bore the brunt of the hatred engendered in the masses of Iranians, who had grown up fearing and hating the 'Babis' for no particular reason other than that this was what they were taught by their religious leaders and elders. Opposition to the Baha'i schools was

Table 4.1 Baha'i Schools in Iran

Locality	*Name of school*	*Dates of founding*		*Numbers*	*Prim/Sec*	*Priv/Community*
		Boys' School	*Girls' School*			
Tehran	Tarbiyat (boys)	1900		700	PS	C
	Tarbiyat (girls)		1911	800	PS	C
	Dūshizigān-i Vaṭan		1911	110	P	P
Ḥasanābād, Tehran[8]		X	X		P	C
Ja'farābād, Tehran		X	X		P	C
Bāqirābād, Tehran		X	X		P	C
Mashhad[9]	Dānish	1912	1912		P	P
Bushrū'iyya, Khurasan			c.1930		P	C
Ḥiṣār, Khurasan[10]		1923	1923		P	
Darra-Jaz, Khurasan[11]	Mas'ūdiyya				P	
Tūn (Firdaws)				20	P	
Sangsar[12]	Ḥusayniyya	1910			P	C
			1916?	180	P	C
Shahmīrzād	Taraqqī				P	
Bārfurūsh, Mazandaran[13]	Sa'ādat-i 'Umūmiyya	1912		40	P	C
Sārī, Mazandaran	Sālāriyya, later Ḥaqīqat, then Ta'īd	1906		60	P	PC
'Arab Khayl, Mazandaran	Mulk-i Jahān	1919	1919	20	P	PC
Bihnamīr, Mazandaran		1916	1926	30	P	C
Tākur, Mazandaran		1913	1913	30	P	P
Kafshgar-kalā, Mazandaran		1919	1919	60	P	C
Chāla-zamīn and Sarūkalā, Mazandaran		1927	1927	20	P	C
Māhfurūzak, Mazandaran		1923[14]	1923	20	P	C
Bur Khayl Arata, Mazandaran	Himmat	1925	1925	35	P	
Īvil, Mazandaran		1923	1923	120	P	
Rawshankūh, Mazandaran	Millī	1935		10	P	C
Sangar Kahumat, Gilan		1915			P	P
Khusha, Gurgan[15]		1967	1967	50	P	P
Uskū, Adharbayjan				60		
Saysān, Adharbayjan		1915	1933	700	P	C
Qazvin[16]	Tavakkul (boys)	1906		101	P	C
	Tavakkul (girls)		1909	96	P	C

Ishtihārd					P	
Jāsb, Qum		c.1921	c.1921		P	C
Kashan	Vaḥdat-i Bashar (boys)	1909		200	PS>8	C
	Vaḥdat-i Bashar (girls)		1916	180	PS	C
Arān, Kashan[17]	Maʿrifat Bashar	1914	c.1932		P	C
Qumrūd, Kashan					P	
Ardistān[18]		before 1906	?1913			
Najafabad, Isfahan[19]	Tarbiyat – became	c.1910	c.1917	400	P	C
	Saʿādat School	c.1917				
Dīzīj, Isfahan[20]		1941	1941	20	P	C
Sulṭānābād						
Shāhābād, Sulṭānābād[21]		before 1928			P>9	
Hamadan	Taʾīd	1907		300	PS>9	C
	Mawhibat		1909	300	PS>9	C
Nayrīz, Fars[22]	Mīthāqiyya	1920	1922	80	S	C
Ābādih, Fars[23]	Tarbiyat	1908	1908	100	PS>9	P
Sarvistān[24]			1921		P	
Yazd[25]	Tarbiyat-i Dūshizigān		1911		PS>9	P
	Hūshangī		1921	120	P	P
	Tahdhīb		1927	120	PS>9	P
	Tawfīq	1930		150	P	C
Mihdīābād, Yazd		before 1921	X	20	P	C
Maryamābād, Yazd[26]	Rustamī		X		P	C
Taft, Yazd[27]			X		P	C
Ḥusaynābād, Yazd		1917			P	C
Manshād, Yazd					P	C
Rafsanjān, Kirman	ʿIṣmatiyya		1920	60	P	C
Zāhidān[28]		late 1920s			P	C

Notes: X indicates where a school is known to have existed for the specified gender but the date of its founding is not known
Prim/Sec column – refer to whether this was a primary and/or secondary school;
>9 indicates up to the ninth form (i.e. class 3 of secondary only)
Priv/Community column – refers to whether the school was owned and run by a private individual or whether it was owned and run by the Baha'i community through the local assembly.
There are a number of possibilities for additions to this list. There is a reference in a letter from ʿAbdu'l-Baha to a school started by Mīrzā Maḥmud Dāmghānī but it is not clear where this school was (Tablet of ʿAbdu'l-Baha in ILMMAAA vol. 84, p. 398). There was also a branch of the Tarbiyat School in the Sar Qabr Āqā quarter of Tehran run alongside the main Tarbiyat school (Sulaymānī 1961: vol. 5, p. 269). There may have been a school in Vadqān, near Kashan (Sulaymānī 1975: vol. 9, p. 315). After the girls' school in Ābādih was closed in 1927, Bahiyya Ābādihī, one of the teachers there went to the village of Kūshkak and taught there for three years before moving to the village of Ṣufād where she taught for two years but it is not clear whether this took the form of a formal school or private lessons for these children (Dhukāʾī-Bayḍāʾī 1965–71: vol. 2, pp. 95–6).

often encountered from local Islamic religious leaders, who would stir up the populace against these schools, and from local officials, who would refuse the necessary permissions and certifications. The Baha'is took whatever steps they could to mitigate the opposition. For example, no classes on the Baha'i Faith were taught in these schools. Those pupils who were from a Baha'i family would have separate Baha'i classes, often outside the school, on Fridays (see Rāstānī 2000). The schools were careful to follow all government decrees relating to the curriculum (even when these were not mandatory for private schools), including giving classes in Arabic, the Qur'an and Islam.

Despite these measures, opposition to and attacks on the Baha'i schools occurred. In Sangsar in 1921, for example, a mob incited by the local Islamic religious leaders burst into the school and burnt it down (Māzandarānī 1974: 302–3; Ḥaqīqatpajūh 1988: 9). In Najafabad, near Isfahan, the Baha'is had to set up barricades to prevent a mob descending upon the school with hammers and picks to tear it down in 1910 and 1911 (Mudarris 2004: 108–9). In Ābādih, a girls' school was established in 1908, but when in 1913, the newly appointed governor of Fars province, Ḥājjī Mukhbir al-Salṭana Hiyādat, was passing through Ābādih, the local religious leaders went to him and complained about the presence of the girls' school, saying that it was against the *shari'a*. The governor summoned Ḥājjī 'Alī Khān, the founder of the Baha'i schools in Ābādih, and said to him: 'We have not even been able to establish a girls' school in Shiraz. To do this in Ābādih is premature.' And he compelled Ḥājjī 'Alī Khān to close the school (Anonymous 1993: 33). The pupils of almost all of these schools faced a certain degree of harassment on their way to and from school.

In spite of these obstacles, the network of Baha'i schools in Iran grew in number and each school grew in size. Initially most of these schools were primary schools but in later years, secondary years were added to those in the cities. The Vaḥdat-i Bashar School in Kashan, for example started as a primary school in 1909 with six primary years; a secondary year was added in 1913–14 (Māzandarānī 1967–82, vol. 5: 283). The Tarbiyat Boys' School in Tehran was the only indigenous school in Tehran, apart from the Dār al-Funūn, to have all 6 secondary years of schooling. Apart from the American School, it was also the only school to offer English language classes in addition to Persian, Arabic and French that were on the government curriculum. The following letter from Sydney Sprague, dated 9 June 1910, gives some details of the operation of the Tarbiyat School for boys:

> Now I will try to answer your questions about the Tarbiat school: We have at present 270 pupils, about 50 new ones having come to us during the past two months, for the school has really a very fine reputation in Persia. It is claimed by everybody as one of the very best. Several new schools have been founded here since the granting

of the constitution and though liberally helped by rich Persians, none of them equal ours. The other day a professor from the Doral-Fonoun (Shah's University) came to our school to examine the boys in arithmetic, algebra and geometry. He had been sent by the government to visit all the schools. After examining carefully each class, he told me that our school in Teheran had such bright and intelligent boys and that in mathematics we were 'way in advance of other schools'. One of the reasons why we make greater progress is that our school program is based on that of the American schools. When I came to Tarbiat school two years ago, I found its program was like that of all other Persian schools. For instance, mathematics would be taught but three days a week and then all the children who studied mathematics would be put in one room and taught at one time, though some might be advanced and others far behind. The first thing I did was to arrange the pupils in classes according to their ability and degree of advancement and have them study mathematics, English, Arabic, etc., every day in the week. Ours is the only school in Teheran, I believe, which has such a program and that is one of the reasons why it makes greater progress.

It takes eight years for a boy to finish the school and get his diploma. A boy is necessarily about seven years old when he starts going to school. During the first three years he must study Persian and a little mathematics, geography and history. Then when the boy has a good ground work in Persian, he may start either in English or French. Mirza Farajullah Khan is the French teacher and a very good one, and I am the English teacher assisted by Fariborz who came with me from Acca. During the five years of the advanced course the boys study one of these languages, so that when they leave they are able to converse, write and translate. They study ancient and modern history, foreign and Persian, mathematics, physics, chemistry, etc. They all, of course, must study Arabic. I teach also some physiology and botany to my advanced classes in English.

We have eleven teachers now. We have a president of the school, Dr. Ata-Ollah Khan, whose duty is to visit the school each day for an hour and report to the committee which meets every week. This servant, as you know, is the superintendent, and has a help, Mirza Yousaf Khan, who keeps the books, etc. There are also two servants. We have a good size school building for which we pay twenty toumans a month, but it is too small for our growing school and I hope next year we will be able to buy a big piece of land and build for ourselves. Another place we need is a place for boys to live who come to us from other cities. I am anxious to have dormitories with rules and regulations like our boarding school in America. We have started a boys' club of the older boys in the school, which

> meets every week, and I hope we can have a room for that some day where we can have English and French magazines and books.
> (Sprague 1910: 5–7)

Some of the practices in these schools were innovative for Iran. 'Alī-Muḥammad Dirakhshāniyān, who was head of the small school in Kafshgar-kalā in Mazandaran, was unusual in not administering any corporal punishment to the child (beating on the hand or bastinado were the usual formal punishments in Iranian schools and cuffs on the head were frequently given informally) (Īqānī 2001: 83). Some of the schools in Mazandaran, such as those of 'Arab-Khayl, Kafshgar-kalā and Bihnamīr, were co-educational, which was again unusual in Iran (Īqānī 2001: 63, 74). Other features of these schools that made them unique among the schools being founded throughout Iran at this time was the prominence given to physical education in the

Figure 4.1 The Sa'ādat School in Bārfurūsh (Bābul), Māzandarān, 1925. The teachers are, left to right (seated): Mīrzā Rūḥullāh Khān (Khādim), headmaster, Mīrzā Furūgh Baṣṣārī, Mīrzā 'Abd al-Vahhāb Baṣṣārī. Standing behind them is Mīrzā Majd al-Dīn Jalīlī, the school attendant (*farrāsh*). And on the other flank, left to right: Aḥmad Thābitīān, Yūsuf-'Alī Īqānī, Mīrzā Javād Jānfishān. The picture was taken at the house of Sayfullāh Thābitīān, which was next to the Bārfurūsh Baha'i Centre, where the school was housed.

Figure 4.2 Public speaking (*mashq-i nuṭq*) class at the Tarbiyat School for Girls, Tehran, 1933. The two teachers of the class were Rūḥangīz Fatḥ-i Aʿẓam, seated in the centre, and Miss Adelaide Sharpe, seated second from right.

Figure 4.3 Participants in Bahaʾi children's classes (*Dars-i Akhlāq*) in Tehran with their teachers, in a photograph taken on 13 August 1933.

Figure 4.4 A group of pre-school girls at the Tarbiyat School for Girls in Tehran, circa 1930.

curriculum (Coy 1926: 51–2) and the emphasis on English as the Western foreign language to be learned, whereas most Iranian schools were teaching French. French was also taught in the last three years of the Tarbiyat secondary school in Tehran during the Pahlavi period because this was required by the national curriculum, but English was taught in the last three years of the primary school and through all six years of the secondary school (Coy 1926: 51). This emphasis on English was partly on the instructions of 'Abdu'l-Baha (1991: 272) and partly the natural result of bringing in American Baha'is as teachers. One result of this was that the Baha'i students graduating from these schools would tend to then proceed to the American University in Beirut (and sometimes universities in England and the United States) for their higher education rather than the French universities favoured by most other Iranian students. Thus the Baha'i students in Beirut came to form quite a large, distinctive and prominent part of the student population at the American University (see Hollinger 2006).

It is difficult to know to what extent the innovations and standards set by these Baha'i schools influenced the development of education in Iran. There are, however, reports to indicate that in some towns, the Baha'i schools were regarded as the best schools in the town. Thus for example, in 1913, it was reported that of 33 students from the Tarbiyat Boys' School presenting for their government final school examinations at the Board of Education, 30 passed, while of the 300 students presenting from other schools only 10 passed (Anon 1913: 114). Similarly, the Minister of Education in 1923 is reported to have called the Tarbiyat Girls' School the best girls' school in Tehran (Coy 1926: 50; see also Sprague 1910: 5–7). It would therefore seem natural that the other schools would seek to emulate these Baha'i schools to some extent.

It was an invariable feature of these schools that although they were founded by Baha'is, often owned by the Baha'i community (i.e. the local Baha'i assembly in each area), and the teaching staff were either all Baha'is or the majority were Baha'is, nevertheless, the school was open to pupils of any religious community. The proportion of Baha'i children among the students attending these schools varied from place to place. In Tehran in 1932, the Tarbiyat Boys' schools had six primary and four secondary years with 541 students, of which 339 were Baha'is (63%), 175 were Muslims (32%), 21 Christians (4%), 4 Jews and 2 Zoroastrians. Of the 26 teachers, 20 were Baha'is (77%). In the Tarbiyat Girls' School, six primary and five secondary years were offered. Of the 719 students, 359 were Baha'is (50%), 352 were Muslims (49%) and 4 were Jewish. There were 35 teachers (*Baha'i World* 1936: 117). In 1926, all of the teachers in the girls' school were Baha'is (Coy 1926: 53). These schools were highly regarded in each locality and many of the children of the notables of each locality attended them (Farmaian 1992: 49; Banani 1961: 96). Even Riḍā Shah's own son and two daughters attended the two Tarbiyat schools in Tehran.

For an independent assessment of these schools, we can turn to Onera A. Merritt-Hawkes, a English journalist from Manchester. She travelled through Iran in 1933 and wrote of her visits to three Baha'i schools. In Yazd, she visited the Hūshangī and Tarbiyat-i Dūshizigān Schools:

> At Yezd I visited two girls schools run by the Bahais because the government would not provide enough. The head of the first school was an unmarried woman who had a married assistant. I sat talking to them in the small, neat, clean and charming courtyard while we had cold sherbet in bright yellow glasses that stood on glass plates and cucumbers which were dipped into iced vinegar. When a Bahais [*sic*] man appeared the children over eight raced away to get their chadars, which were neatly folded up on shelves. The teachers said that Bahallullah [*sic*] had wished the veil to be abolished, but they thought that neither men nor women were yet ready and that it would be ten to twenty years before either could look at the other without lascivious and passionate thoughts.

The students in one class were sitting round an octagonal pool in which goldfish were carrying on an anti-mosquito crusade. The pupils belonged to all the local sects, but most of them had a leather case with a charm round their necks, some of the cases green to make them yet more effective.

The other Bahais school, equally neat and tidy, was run by a remarkable woman, Hadji Bibi Sorghra,[29] whose face was thin, refined, full of eager enthusiasm. She very early became a widow and, having no children, went, in spite of her relations, to Tehran, where she lived with a Bahais family and attended school. That was fifteen years ago when the caravan took twelve days to do the journey. When she returned she realized how badly a school was needed in her own town and started one herself. Now she can do more because helped by Bahais funds, but she said pathetically:

> 'I am sorry we are doing so little. I learnt too long ago to be modern or to know much. Bahallullah said mankind had two wings, one was man, and one was woman, and it could not fly without both. I know by my life that that is true, but in Persia to-day few know that, so that my country goes slowly.'
>
> I was sorry that I had to go on to Kerman without seeing her again, for she was like a flower that had never had an opportunity to open.

(Merritt-Hawkes 1935: 144–5)

In 1913, the women's journal *Shikūfa* published a list of the girls' schools in Tehran. This showed the Tarbiyat-i Banāt School (Tarbiyat School for Girls) to be the third largest girls' school in the capital with 117 students (17 of whom had scholarships). The Dūshīzigān-i Vaṭan School had 110 students (67 of whom had scholarships) and was the fourth largest girls' school in the capital (Afary 1996: 182–3). Some further information about the Baha'i schools in Iran can be gleaned from papers of the Ministry of Education that have been published. Among the published documents is a report on the Mawhibat Girls' School in Hamadan for 1920 by Jalāl Ulfat (the Baha'i superintendent of the school). The following is a summary of the information that it contains:

> Headmistress: Maḥbūba Khānum [Na'īmī], born in Tehran, educated at the Tarbiyat and the American School in Tehran, started work in 1337/1917, monthly salary 25 *tūmān*s, taught English, Arabic and Mathematics.

Superintendent: Qamar Khānum [Anvar] (aged 20), born Hamadan, educated Alliance (Jewish) School in Hamadan, employed 1914, salary 7 *tūmān*s.

Five other teachers are named with salaries ranging from 3 to 6 *tūmān*s, aged between 16 and 23, all of them born in Hamadan and having been educated either at the Alliance or Mawhibat Schools. They gave the following lessons: writing, dictation, Persian, Arabic, mathematics, English, history, geography, science.

The School had 144 pupils ranging in age from 6 to 14 in one elementary year and six primary years. Its budget was 90 *tūmān*s. It paid no rent for its premises. Its income from its students was 36 *tūmān*s and the shortfall was made up from merchants and physicians of the town. This gave the school a balanced budget. The furnishings of the school were judged adequate but it had no teaching equipment.

(Turābī-Fārisānī 1999: 54–6)

Information about other Baha'i schools can be gleaned from published Ministry of Education tables for 1925:

The Tarbiyat School for Boys had 10 years (more than any other school in Tehran) and 350 primary pupils (more than any other school in Tehran) and 40 secondary pupils.

The Tarbiyat School for Girls had 6 years and 134 pupils (13 of them having free places).

Dūshizigān-i Vaṭan School had 5 years and 48 pupils (25 of whom had free places).

(Turābī-Fārisānī 1999: 61, 64, 65)

Even in the village schools, it was possible to maintain a wide curriculum. Most of the village schools in Māzandarān, for example, had classes on Persian language and literature, history, geography, mathematics, accounting (*siyāq*), dictation, science and health and hygiene (Īqānī 2001: 64, 74, 86, 103, 120, 130).

The Baha'i community also opened a number of kindergartens (sing. *kūdakistān*). In Tehran there were two, the Mīthāqiyya and the Āmādigī, which prepared children for the Tarbiyat schools and were closed down by the authorities at the same time as the Tarbiyat Schools. In Hamadan, there was a kindergarten that prepared children for the Baha'i schools there. In Qazvin, there was a kindergarten held in the home of Ḥājjī Ismā'īl Khalīlī. In Kirman, there was the Himmatī kindergarten established in

1932 by Bilqīs Mishkiyān. It had some 50 boys and girls. It was closed in 1934 at the same time as the other Baha'i schools. Bilqīs Mishkiyān then went to Yazd where she set up another kindergarten which operated from 1934 to 1938. The following is a description by the English non-Baha'i journalist, Merritt-Hawkes, of the Himmatī kindergarten in Kirman in 1933:

> It was very difficult to get about Kerman as there was only one droscha in the town, the few cars were appallingly bad and to walk between 9 a.m. and 5 p.m. in June was to court disaster. Because the chauffeur made a mistake, I had to walk a mile to the school run by the Bahais. I arrived dusty and tired out, but everything unpleasant was forgotten when I looked at the charming Persian woman, immaculately clean and tidy, and her thirty happy, clean pupils. She was a widow with three children, who had studied modern methods in Turkestan and had come to Persia after the Russian revolution.
>
> The children were from two to six years of age, paying only two rials a month, the local community of Bahais subscribing the remainder of the expenses. Each child had its own towel and on arrival washed its hands and nails and had its head examined. That doesn't sound much in Europe, but in Kerman it took your breath away. No corporal punishment was allowed; if a child did not behave, after being given several chances, it was sent away. That attitude of kindness to one another, of kindness to animals, the teaching that blows are not the only way to manage, was really startling in a land where corporal punishment, although theoretically abolished in the schools, was still considered the only practical discipline . . .
>
> Those children were gay and jolly, they all had shoes, most of them had stockings and they were learning to use a hand kerchief. They would not, like their parents, feel it necessary to wipe their noses on every post. That would make a pleasanter Persia! I suddenly realized that the inventor of handkerchiefs had been one of the world's greatest benefactors . . .
>
> I did not want to leave this place of happiness and hope, to go into the streets where the children's eyes were covered with flies, where their habits were cruel or disgusting.
>
> (Merritt-Hawkes 1935: 152–3)

The closure of the Baha'i schools

Riḍā Shah had instituted a policy of standardization and Iranianization of all social institutions in the country. As part of this, for example, he forced the American missionary schools and all other foreign schools in 1928 to conform to the curriculum set by the Ministry of Education. In 1937, Riḍā Shah's government was to nationalise all foreign primary schools and in 1939, the secondary schools also. Indigenous private schools such as the Baha'i schools came under increasing Ministry regulation also with increased emphasis on uniformity. 'Alī-Akbar Furūtan, the headmaster of the Tarbiyat Baha'i Boys' School, reports that for some time prior to 1934, the officials of the Department of Education had been harassing the school trying to find fault with it (Shahriyārī 2006: 28).

Sometime in 1934, the National Spiritual Assembly of Iran, which had only recently been established, was instructed by Shoghi Effendi that all Baha'i institutions, and specifically the Baha'i-owned schools should apply the Baha'i law that all work should be suspended on the Baha'i Holy Days. Furūtan and Dr. Yūnis Khān Afrūkhta, who were both members of the Baha'i National Assembly, obtained an appointment with 'Alī-Asghar Ḥikmat, the Deputy Minister of Education, in order to explain the situation to him. Ḥikmat refused to accept this explanation, insisting on a rigid observance of government regulations.[30]

On Thursday, 6 December 1934, the Baha'i schools were closed in observance of the Baha'i Holy Day of the anniversary of the Martyrdom of the Bab, according to the lunar calendar. When the school reconvened on Saturday 8 December, the following letter was received at the Tarbiyat School for Boys from the Ministry:

> 17 Ādhar 1313 [8 December 1934]
>
> . . . The Ministry of Education hereby nullifies the license of that school, which was issued on 26/3/10 [17 June 1931]. As of this date, you are no longer permitted to operate this high school.
>
> (signed and sealed) 'Alī-Asghar Ḥikmat
> Deputy, Ministry of Education
>
> (Furūtan 1984: 47)

The following dispatch, dated 15 December 1934, from the British Ambassador, H. M. Knatchbull-Hugessen, gives some further information about this episode:

> The Persian press announced on the 9th December last that the Ministry of Education had closed on that day the 'Tarbiat' schools at Tehran, owing to 'failure to comply with the instructions of the Ministry of Education.' The 'Tarbiat' schools belong to the Bahai community and are two in number, one for boys and the other for girls. The former, which has been in existence for thirty-six years, has about 700 boy pupils and the latter 800 girls. The closure has therefore affected about 1,500 students, whose ages range up to

20 years, and a number of teachers. Similar steps were taken by the local authorities in Hamadan, Kazvin, Sultanabad, Kashan and Yezd, and, I believe, some other towns which possess Bahai schools.

The head munshi of this Legation, Mirza Abdul Hussein Khan Naimi, is himself a Bahai. I have obtained from him a report on the whole circumstances of this somewhat remarkable action by the Persian Government, and the following facts are taken from his report.

The Bahais, as a matter of religion, hold nine days of each year sacred, and abstain from my work on those days. The present head of the Bahai religion, Shoghi Effendi, who lives, I believe, at Haifa, has enjoined the most strict observance of these days on his followers in every country. The Bahai schools in Tehran were therefore closed last year on the 28th Shaban, 1352 (the 17th December, 1933), the anniversary of the martyrdom of the Bab, one of the most important of the nine Bahai days. A few days later the Ministry of Education asked in writing the reason for the closure of the schools. The board of directors of the schools, who are appointed by the Bahai National Spiritual Assembly every year, explained the reason in writing. The principal of the boys' school was then summoned to the Ministry and told that the letter was not acceptable and must be taken back. He refused to do so, saying that it was not his letter; but a few days later the Minister sent back the letter in an envelope.

About last May the Ministry addressed to the schools a further letter, referring to the fact that the schools had been 'closed without reason' last year, and warning them that if the same thing were to happen this year the schools would be definitely closed down. The matter was referred to Shoghi Effendi, who, in reply, said that, although Bahais should subject themselves completely to the Government's orders in all matters connected with the programme of instruction and the general administration of the schools, they should nevertheless not fail to observe Bahai religious rules and not work on the specified days. The Bahai community were therefore determined not to give in, and declared themselves ready for death or martyrdom rather than obey the order not to close the schools. They therefore closed the schools on the anniversary of the death of the Bab . . .

The Bahais argue that they have had to support their schools, beginning from about thirty-six years ago, by a large subvention, without the least encouragement from the Government; and they state that their schools have always been well managed and have attracted the children of the best families of Tehran. Naimi considers that only about one-half of the children attending the schools were Bahais, though all the staff were, as a rule, of the Bahai faith. Religious propaganda was forbidden in the schools, as in all other schools in Tehran. As for the ban against closing the schools, the Bahais point out that all other schools of Tehran close occasionally in similar circumstances; it often happens, for instance, that a school is closed as a mark of respect on the death of a prominent dignitary.

. . . Naimi also informs me that the Government are now endeavouring to induce the teachers who formerly taught at the Tarbiat schools to transfer to other schools in Tehran, and to secure places for the pupils in other schools; even though the latter were previously said to be full.

The American College of Tehran is following these developments with great interest. It remains to be seen whether the Government will insist on that college keeping its schools open, for the first time in its history, on Christmas Day. I have heard no reports of interference from any of the British schools in the south.

I shall not fail to report any further developments which may follow. One member of the staff of the American College advances the theory that his Highness Feroughi [the Prime Minister] is really the cause of the opposition to the Bahais. I am inclined to wonder whether this curious assertion of governmental authority is connected with His Majesty's visit to Turkey; if so, we must, I suppose, expect a general attack on all forms of foreign instruction on the lines of the Turkish model.[31]

The government then proceeded against the other Baha'i schools in Iran, especially in the cities and towns, closing them down one by one in the course of about a year. Because it was regarded as a private school, the Tarbiyat-i Dūshīzigān School in Yazd, which was owned by Ḥājjīya Bībī Sughrā, continued to function until she closed it down herself when she retired (Hidāyatī 1992: 30–31). Some of the Baha'i schools in the villages, however, escaped closure, probably because the government did not even realise they were Baha'i schools and there was nothing, in any case, in those villages with which to replace them. Thus for example, eight of the village Baha'i schools in Mazandaran continued to function after 1934, and indeed one of them (at Rawshankūh) did not even start until 1935. These village schools did not in the end close but were voluntarily handed over to the government and became government schools, the last of these probably being the school at Bur Khayl Arata in 1948 (Īqānī 2001).

By the time of the closure of the Baha'i schools in 1934, most larger towns and cities had government schools to which the children could transfer. However this was not always a smooth process. In Kashan, the Muslim pupils attending the Baha'i Vaḥdat-i Bashar school were able to obtain places at the local government school immediately, but the Baha'i pupils were barred and spent almost a year without schooling until the Jewish Alliance school accepted them. In Yazd, the Baha'i pupils went to the English missionary school and the Zoroastrian school.

In the smaller towns and villages, the problems were greater, especially for the girls. Here, the local Baha'i communities often decided to continuing schooling their children informally. Thus after the closure of the Baha'i school in Ābādih, Bahiyya Ṣafā'ī went to the nearby village of Kūshkak and taught the children there for three years before going on to the village of Ṣufād and teaching the Baha'i girls there for two years (Dhukā'ī-Bayḍā'ī 1965–70: vol. 2, p. 95–6). The Baha'i National Spiritual Assembly also concerned itself with making sure that adequate facilities were available in all villages where there was an appreciable number of Baha'is. In several of the villages around Sulṭānābād, for example, where there were appreciable numbers of Baha'is and no schools, the National Assembly arranged for teachers to be resident in each village (their wages were paid for by the National Assembly) and for classes to be held in private homes. Such classes were established in villages of Shāhābād, Khalajābād, and Shāhzand. The children of non-Baha'i parents were also able to participate in these classes and sometimes children from neighbouring villages also came (Tavāngar 1997: 25). These arrangements were not, however, always stable or satisfactory. A Baha'i, Vujdāniyya Pārsā, for example, has written an account of her education in the village of Sangsar, near Simnan, in the years after the Baha'i school there was closed and arrangements were made to teach about 100 Baha'i and non-Baha'i girls in various homes around the village:

> In the years of my childhood, there was a government school for boys but none for girls. And so the Baha'i girls were forced to receive an education at a home school (*maktab-i khāna*). Thus, I had my first and second form education in the *maktab* of a Baha'i lady called Mu'allima Shahrbānū Fanā'iyān, then Mu'allima Subḥānī set up a better organized *maktab* which only went up to fourth form, but which was to some extent recognized by the Department of Education, since in the mornings some pupils were sent along to us by that department for learning national songs. In that same year, the Ministry of Education decided that girls should attend the boys schools and they should be educated together, but no-one was prepared to send their daughters to the boys' school. The following year, the girls' *maktab* closed and we two or three pupils studied at home with Varqā Vaḥdat for several months until, the National

> [Baha'i] Assembly sent Zīnat 'Askarī, the daughter of Mīrzā Ḥusayn 'Askarī Bushrū'iyya'ī, to Sangsar for the education of the girls. For one or two years, she was engaged in educating the Baha'i girls, and a few non-Baha'i girls, in houses rented from local Baha'is for this purpose. However, half way through 1319 Sh. (autumn 1940), she became unable to continue this service on account of illness and Bahīra Mumtāzī, who had, in the previous year succeeded in obtaining a certificate of completion of her primary education, as an independent candidate in the Simnan examinations, ran the school until the end of the year. The following year, I, who had just received my certificate of completion of my primary sixth form as an independent candidate, was given the task of setting up schooling for girls in the homes of the local Baha'is by the [Baha'i] Spiritual Assembly and teaching them. The following year (1322/1943), Ṭāhira Kiyānī was sent by the National Spiritual Assembly to Sangsar for the girls' school. After Kiyānī, the girls' school was continued by Mu'allima Subḥānī and Varqā'iyya Subḥānī until 'Aṭiyya Ḥaqīqī came to Sangsar and, with the help of female teachers and some of the young women organised the school on a better and more appropriate basis. [In 1330Sh./1951, the government established a girls' school in Sangsar, thus rendering these arrangements unnecessary].
> (Quoted in Ḥaqīqatpajūh 1989: 11; see also Haqiqi 1996: 27–30)

Similarly, Abū'l-Qāṣim Fayḍī volunteered to go to the small town of Najafabad, near Isfahan, where the Baha'is had similar problems following the closure of the Baha'i school. Within a few weeks of his arrival, some 20 classes totalling some 400 boys and girls had been set up in various Baha'i homes in the town (Fayḍī 1998: 155).

In conclusion, the Baha'i community in Iran was thus at the forefront of moves towards modern education in Iran. Its schools were among the first indigenous modern schools set up in Iran and they were providing a substantial proportion of the schooling available in Iran in the first two decades of the twentieth century. In two areas, the Baha'i community pioneered developments. The Baha'i community was taking education into the villages long before there were government schools in villages. In the area of girls' schooling also, the Baha'i community was starting up girls' schools in many towns and villages where there were no such facilities. The Baha'i schools maintained a high standard and it was not unusual for the Baha'i school in a town to be regarded as the best school and for the notables of the town to send their children there. The closure of the Baha'i schools appears to have been precipitated by a combination of Riḍā Shah's desire to impose a uniformity on the educational system and an enmity towards the Baha'is among certain individuals in the government.

Notes

1 I would like to express my thanks to Dominic Brookshaw and Seena Fazel for their suggestions and to Kaveh Hemmat for allowing me a preview of his paper 'Baha'i Schools and the Beginnings of Modern Public Education in Iran', presented at 'The Iranian Constitutional Revolution 1906–1911, Centenary Conference', Oxford, 30 July–2 August 2006, all of which enabled improvements to be made to this chapter.

2 Estimated from information related to the year 1891 given in Menashri 1992: 55 (i.e. that there were 387 students in 1891, taking between six and seven years to graduate – and allowing for some drop-outs each year). Banani states that only 15 students graduated in 1922 (1961: 108).

3 For a survey of the writings of nineteenth century Iranian intellectuals about education, see Menashri 1992: 27–45.

4 See for example statements by Baha'u'llah in *Compilation of Compilations* 1991, vol. 1, nos. 567, 568, p. 249; and the statements by 'Abdu'l-Baha, ibid, no. 601, p. 267; no. 617, p. 275; no. 619, p. 276.

5 *Bahai News* (*Star of the West*) 1/1 (21 March 1910): 12–3; 1/10 (8 Sep. 1910): 2–5.

6 Accounts by Baha'is of the founding and development of the Tarbiyat School for Girls can be found in issues of *Star of the West*, vol. 2, no. 18 (Feb. 1912): 12–3 (report by Lillian Kappes); vol. 4, no. 7 (July 1913): 114 (Dr. Susan Moody). See also Thābit 1997: 40, quoting a memoir by Dr. 'Atā'ullāh Bakhshāyish, and Armstrong-Ingram 1986: 188.

7 Menashri 1992: 60, citing Ministry of Education, *Annual Statistical Report*; see also Arasteh 1969: 74.

8 For this and next two schools: interview with Ashraf Shāhābādī, in Acuto, Italy, 3 July 2005.

9 Anonymous 2004: 38–9.

10 *Star of the West* 14 (Nov. 1923) 246.

11 Fu'ādī 1931: 128–130; Māzandarānī 1974: 248–9.

12 Māzandarānī 1974: 292; Dhukā'ī-Bayḍā'ī 1965–70: vol. 4, pp. 97–8; Haqīqatpajūh 1988: 9–12.

13 On schools in Māzandarān, see Īqānī 2001; Rastigār 1992: 37–8. On the school in Bārfurūsh, see also Sulaymānī 1961, vol. 5, p. 270.

14 Although, as indicated above, a traditional *maktab* was set up in the village by Mulla 'Alī Jān in the 1870s, this is the date of the setting up of a modern school.

15 Sulaymānī 1975: vol. 9, pp. 414–18.

16 Dabīr-Sayāqī and Ṣaffārī 2001, vol. 1, p. 72; Anonymous 1994: 29–34.

17 Māzandarānī 1974: 690, 719.

18 Māzandarānī 1975: 961–2.

19 Fayḍī 1998: 121–81.

20 Mīthāqī 1990: 26–27.

21 Interview with Ashraf Shāhābādī, in Acuto, Italy, 3 July 2005.

22 Rawḥānī-Nayrīzī 2002: 439, 449.

23 *Star of the West*, 2 (9 April 1911) Persian section 3, p. 3.

24 Sulaymānī 1964: vol. 1, p. 261.

25 On the schools in Yazd, see Sifīdvash 1999: 151–54; Hidāyatī 1992: 29–31.

26 Farīdānī 2002: 213.

27 Farīdānī 2002: 319.

28 Fu'ādī 1931: 459–60.

29 Ḥājjīya Bībī Sughrā. The details given here about her are essentially correct. She died in 1946.

30 Furūtan 1984: 48–9; Shahriyārī 2006: 28–30. Ḥikmat, although he later claimed that he was only acting on the Shah's orders in his action, was evidently much against the Baha'i Faith; years later when Shapour Rassekh had prepared an account of Iran's demography for the book *Iranshahr* which was published under the auspices of UNESCO, Ḥikmat, who at that time was head of the UNESCO national commission in Iran, deleted all references to the Baha'is in that report; Rāsikh 2005. See also Moayyad 1991 for further information about Ḥikmat's role in the closure of the Tarbiyat school.

31 Knatchbull-Hugessen to Sir John Simon No. 554, 15 Dec. 1934, File E7789/7789/34: FO 371 17917, see Momen 1981: 477–8. See also Moayyad 1991.

Bibliography

'Abdu'l-Baha. (1978) *Selections from the Writings of 'Abdu'l-Bahá*, Haifa: Baha'i World Centre.

—— (1991) *The Compilation of Compilations*, Prepared by the Universal House of Justice 1963–1990, vol. 1. [Sydney]: Baha'i Publications Australia.

Afary, J. (1996) *The Iranian Constitutional Revolution, 1906–1911: Grassroots Democracy, Social Democracy & the Origins of Feminism*, New York : Columbia University Press.

Anonymous. (1913) *Star of the West.*

—— (1987) 'Khāṭirātī az Madrasa-yi Tarbiyat-i Banāt', *Payām-i Baha'i*, 91: 15–16.

—— (1993) Shamma'ī darbāra-yi madāris-i Baha'i-yi Ābādih', *Payām-i Baha'i*, 164: 31–3; 166: 31–4.

—— (1994) 'Bunyān-i madāris-i Baha'i-yi Qazvin', *Payām-i Baha'i*, 173: 29–34.

—— (2004) 'Mu'allim-khāna-yi Dānish dar Mashhad,' *Payām-i Baha'i*, 294: 38–9.

Arasteh, A.R. (1969) *Education and Social Awakening in Iran 1850–1968*, Leiden: Brill.

Arbāb, F. (1990) *Khāna-yi muqaddas-i man*, photocopy of mss. in author's possession.

Armstrong-Ingram, R.J. (1986) 'American Baha'i Women and the Education of Girls in Tehran, 1909–1934', in P. Smith (ed.), *In Iran. Studies in Babi and Baha'i History*, vol. 3. Los Angeles: Kalimat Press.

Āvāra, 'A. (1923) *al-Kawākib al-Durriyya*, 2 vols. Cairo: Sa'āda.

Baha'ullah. (1978) *Tablets of Bahá'u'lláh revealed after the Kitáb-i-Aqdas*, Haifa: Baha'i World Centre.

—— (1983) *Gleanings from the Writings of Bahá'u'lláh*, Wilmette: Baha'i Publishing Trust.

—— (1992) *The Kitáb-i Aqdas*, Haifa: Baha'i World Centre.

Banani, A. (1961) *The Modernization of Iran 1921–1941*, Stanford: Stanford University Press.

Compilation of Compilations, The (1991) Prepared by the Universal House of Justice 1963–1990, vol. 1. [Sydney]: Baha'i Publications Australia.

Coy, G. (1926) 'Educating the Women of Persia', *The Baha'i Magazine (Star of the West)* 17: 50–55.

Dabīr-Siyāqī, M. and I. Ṣaffārī (2001) *Farhang va madāris-i sarzamīn-i Qazvin bar mabnā-yi ta'līmāt-i nuvīn*, Tehran: Nash-i Ḥadīth-i Imrūz.

Dhukā'ī-Bayḍā'ī, N. (1965–70) *Tadhkira-yi shu'arā-yi Baha'i-yi qarn-i avval-i Badī'*, 4 vols. Tehran: Mu'assisa-yi millī-yi maṭbū'āt-i amrī.

Dihqān, G. (1999) Addendum to Qābil Ābādihī, *Tārīkh-i amrī-yi Ābādih*, photocopied pages sent by the author.

Dustkhah, J. and Yaghma'i, E. 'Education.1.iii' in *Encyclopedia Iranica*, vol. 8: 207. Online at http://www.iranica.com/articles/v8/v8f2/v8f207iii.html (accessed 8 November 2005).

Farīdānī, S. (2002) *Dūstān-i Rāstān*, Hofheim, Germany: Baha'i Verlag.

Farman-Farmaian, S. (with D. Munker) (1992) *Daughter of Persia*, London: Bantam Press.

Fayḍī, A. (1998) 'Chahār sal u nīm dar Najafabad', in *Ba yād-i dūst*, Wilmette: National Spiritual Assembly of the Baha'is of the United States.

Fayḍī, M. (1986) *Hayāt-i haḍrat-i 'Abdu'l-Baha*, Langenhain, Germany: Baha'i Verlag.

Fu'ādī, Ḥ. (1931) *Tārīkh-i amrī-yi Khurasan: manāẓir-i tārīkhī-yi nihḍat-i amr-i Baha'i dar Khurasan*. Photocopy of typescript in Afnan Library, London.

Furūtan, 'A. (1984) *The Story of My Heart*, Oxford: George Ronald.

Ḥaqīqatpazhūh. (1989) 'Madāris-i Baha'i-yi Sangsar', *Payām-i Baha'i*, 103: 9–12.

Ḥaqīqī, 'A. (1996) 'Yādī az madrasa-yi dukhtarāna-yi Bahā'iyān-i Sangsar', *Payām-i Baha'i*, 203: 27–30.

Hidāyātī, R. (1992) 'Madrasa-yi dukhtarāna-yi Hūshangī-yi Yazd va du madrasa-yi dīgar', *Payām-i Baha'i*, 155: 29–31.

Hollinger, R. (2006) 'An Iranian Enclave in Lebanon: Baha'i Students in Beirut, 1906–40' in H.E. Chehabi (ed.) *Distant Relations: Iran and Lebanon in the last 500 Years*, London: I.B. Tauris.

ILMMAAA (Intishārāt-i Lajna-yi Millī-yi Mahfaẓa-yi Āthār va Ārshīv-i Amr). (133–134 BE/1976–7) photocopied series of 105 volumes from the Iranian National Baha'i Archives, Afnan Library Trust.

Īqānī, S. (2001) 'Tārīkhcha madāris-i Baha'i dar Mazandaran', unpublished MS.

Ishrāq-Khāvarī, 'A. (1964–1972) *Mā'ida-yi āsamānī*, 9 vols Tehran: Mu'assasa-yi Millī-yi Maṭbū'āt-i Amrī.

—— (1969) *Taqvīm-i tārīkh-i amr*, Tehran: Mu'assasa-yi Millī-yi Maṭbū'āt-i Amrī.

—— (2004) *Tārīkh-i amrī-yi Hamadan*, (V. Ra'fatī (ed.)), Hofheim, Germany: Baha'i Verlag.

Kirmānī, M.K. (1967) *Majma'at al-rasā'il-i fārsī*, vol. 1, Kirman: Chāpkhāna-yi Sa'ādat.

Kirmānī, Nāẓim al-Islām. (1967) *Tārīkh-i bīdārī-yi Irānīān*, 3 vols in 1, [Tehran]: Bunyād-i Farhang-i Iran.

Māzandarānī, A.F. (1967–82) *Asrār al-Āthār*, 5 vols. Tehran: Mu'assasa-yi Millī-yi Maṭbū'at-i Amri.

—— (1974, 1975) *Ẓuhūr al-Ḥaqq*, 9 vols, Tehran: Mu'assasa-yi Millī-yi Maṭbū'āt-i Amrī, vol. 8 (part 1) 1974, vol. 8 (part 2) 1975.

—— (1986) *Amr va khalq*, 4 vols, Langenhain, Germany: Lajna-yi nashr-i āthār-i amrī ba zabān-i fārsī va 'arabī.

Menashri, D. (1992) *Education and the Making of Iran*, Ithaca: Cornell University Press.

Merritt-Hawkes, O.A. (1935) *Persia: Romance and Reality*, London: Ivor Nicholson and Watson.

Mīthāqī, A. (1990) 'Madrasa-yi Baha'i-yi Dīzīj', *Payām-i Baha'i*, 124: 26–7.

Moayyad, H. (1991) 'Scholarly Dillettantism and Tampering with History: an Episode in the Baha'i History of Iran' in B.S. Amoretti and L. Rostagno (eds)

Yad-Nama: In Memoria di Allessandro Bausani, vol. 1: Islamistica. Roma: Bardi Editore.
Momen, M. (ed.) (1981) *The Babi and Baha'i Religions, 1844–1944. Some Contemporary Western Accounts*, Oxford: George Ronald.
—— (2005) 'The Role of Women in the Iranian Baha'i Community during the Qajar Period', in R.M. Gleave (ed.), *Religion and Society in Qajar Iran*, London: RoutledgeCurzon.
Mudarris, F. (2004) *Tārīkh-i amr-i Baha'i dar Najafabad* (V. Ra'fatī (ed.)), Darmstadt, Germany: 'Asr-i Jadīd.
Muṣāḥib, G. (ed.) (1995) *Dā'irat al-ma'ārif-i fārsī*, vol. 2, Tehran: Chāpkhāna-yi Shahr.
Rafati, V. (1989) 'Baha'i Schools', in *Encyclopaedia Iranica*, vol. 3, London: Rouledge and Kegan Paul.
Rāsikh, S. (2005) 'Khāṭira'ī āz marḥūm 'Alī-Ashghar Ḥikmat', *Payām-i Baha'i*, no. 303: 38–39.
Rāstānī, S. (2000) *Sayyid Ḥasan-i mu'allim va tārīkhcha-yi dars akhlāq*, Hofheim, Germany: Baha'i Verlag.
Rastigār, H. (1992) 'Madāris-i Baha'i-yi Mazandaran', *Payām-i Baha'i*, 154: 37–8.
Rawḥānī-Nayrīzī, M.S. (2002) *Lama'āt al-Anvār*, 2 vols. in 1, Bundoora, Australia: Century Press.
Shahriyārī, H. (2006) 'Ta'ṭīl-i madrasa-yi Tarbiyat ba ravāyit-i Jināb-i 'Alī-Akbar Furūtan', *Payām-i Baha'i*, 316: 26–34.
Sifīdvash, 'I. (1999) *Tanī chand az pīshgāmān-i Pārsā-nijād dar 'ahd-i rasūlī*, Dundas, Ontario: Association for Baha'i Studies in Persian.
Sprague, S. (1910) 'The Tarbiyat School, Persia', *Baha'i News* (*Star of the West*) 1.7: 3–7.
Sulaymānī, 'A. (1961, 1964, 1975) *Maṣābīḥ-i hidāyat*, Tehran: Mu'assasa-yi Millī-yi Maṭbū'āt-i Amrī, vol. 1, 2nd printing, 1964; vol. 5, 1961; vol. 9, 1975.
Tavakoli-Targhi, M. (2001) *Refashioning Iran: Orientalism, Occidentalism and Historiography*, St Anthony's Series. Basingstoke: Palgrave.
Tavāngar, 'A. (1997) 'Yādī az Bahā'iyān-i Shāhābād-i Arāk', *Payām-i Baha'i*, 210: 25.
Thābit, 'A. (1997) *Tārākhcha-yi madrasa-yi Tarbiyat-i Banān*, New Delhi: Mir'āt Publications.
The Baha'i World 1932–34 (1936) New York: Baha'i Publishing Committee.
Turābī-Fārisānī, S. (1999) *Asnādī az madāris-i dukhtarāna az mashrūṭa ta Pahlavī*, Tehran: Sāzmān-i Asnād-i Millī-yi Iran.
Waterfield, R. (1973) *The Christians in Persia*, London: George Allen and Unwin.

5

BAHA'I HEALTH INITIATIVES IN IRAN

A preliminary survey

Seena B. Fazel and Minou Foadi[1]

Baha'i scriptures place considerable emphasis on physical health, based on the belief that the spirit and body are closely interrelated. Hence Baha'is believe that the human body is a vehicle for spiritual development of individuals and 'the throne of the inner temple' (Bab 1978: 95), and that 'the bounty of good health is the greatest of all gifts' ('Abdu'l-Baha 1978: 151). The science of medicine is considered 'the most noble of all the sciences' (*ashraf al-'ulūm kulli-hā*) according to Baha'ullah's main text on health, the Tablet of Medicine (*Lawḥ-i ṭibb*) (Baha'ullah 1978: 222–227). Further, Baha'i scriptures recommend that individuals who are unwell seek advice and treatment from 'competent physicians' (*al-hudhdhāq min al-aṭibbā'*) (Baha'ullah 1992: 60). Baha'i texts encourage a lifestyle characterised by refinement, moderation, freedom from addictions, the consumption of healthy foods and a strong discouragement of smoking (Fananapazir and Lambden 1992: 18–65; Schaefer 2004). Baha'ullah's most important work, the *Kitāb-i Aqdas* (c.1873) has a number of health-related directives, including forbidding the use of opium,[2] 'any substance that induceth sluggishness and torpor' (interpreted by 'Abdu'l-Baha as meaning hashish and related substances), and alcohol,[3] stipulating that the dead should not be buried more than an hour from the place in which they died,[4] and the abrogation of the Shi'i practice of taking temporary wives (*ṣīgha*) (which would have reduced the risk of sexually-transmitted diseases[5]) (Baha'ullah 1992: 88, 75, 62, 66, 41). Furthermore, there are a number of laws aimed at promoting cleanliness: water to bathe in should not have been used before, and the public pools in Iranian baths or private courtyards were not allowed: 'In truth, they are as sinks of foulness and contamination' (ibid: 58). Rather the bather, 'instead of entering the water', should 'wash himself by pouring it over his body' (ibid). The regular washing of one's body and the clipping of nails is also emphasized (ibid: 58, 75, 57). An example of the Baha'i view of the interaction of body and spirit is that 'Abdu'l-Baha states that external cleanliness has a 'great influence upon spirituality' ('Abdu'l-Baha 1978: 147).

Researching health initiatives in the Iranian Baha'i community is limited by a paucity of sources. What little exist suggests that the two main contributions were the building of public bathhouses and the establishment of two hospitals. In addition, allied institutions were established such as a nursing school, a college for doctors' assistants, various outpatient clinics, and a modern old people's home. These initiatives were characterised by some innovative practices, which were probably influenced by Baha'i beliefs.

Bathhouses (*ḥammām, garm-āba*)

There is a long tradition of public baths in Iran, particularly after the arrival of Islam. The Zoroastrian reverence for water precluded public baths, although there are reports that Vologeses (r.484–488) ordered their construction, incurring the wrath of Zoroastrians priests in the process (Floor 1989: 863). With Islam, bathing became an integral part of a believer's life. For Muslims, water was used for ablutions before ritual prayer and for purification. Further, bathing in natural springs and spas was prescribed by traditional doctors and the clergy for good health.

In the nineteenth century, bathhouses were common in major cities. Tehran is reported to have had 146 public baths, and there were approximately 30–50 each in Isfahan, Kirman, Shiraz, Qazvin and Kirmanshah (Floor 1989: 863–864). Such bathhouses had common features. They were built below ground level in order to retain heat during the winter and remain cool during the summer. Their design was characterised by three separate spaces. First was a changing room (*rakht-kan*), which was reached by a narrow corridor. Here, there were benches where bathers would undress and leave their towels and clothes. At its centre was a fountain with a small pool of cold water for bathers to wash their feet. The second part consisted of a steam-room (*garm-khāna*) with a marble or tile floor, which was heated by means of covered flues, and where bathers spent most of their time, washing and socialising. The third section was the *khazīna*, which was a water-filled basin of approximately three by three metres and used underground heating. After washing themselves in the steam room, bathers would immerse themselves in the *khazīna* several times, a practice called *ghusl* ('total ablution'). Up to ten people could enter the *khazīna* simultaneously.

The water of the *khazīna* was changed infrequently, perhaps one to three times a year, and hence is invariably described as smelling fetid. More importantly, it became a public health hazard and the source of infectious diseases, in particular those of the skin, eyes, and gastro-intestinal system. Further, Dr. Edward Dobson of the Church Missionary Society reported in Kirman: 'it is quite a usual thing to go after acquiring an infectious disease' (Morton 1940: 217–18). Hence it is thought to have become 'one of the major sources of infection' (Floor 2004: 62). Children were at particular risk. If accessible, the public used them once every two to three weeks (Ibid.). Foreign visitors to Iran report the disgusting state of these *khazīna*s and, in particular, how local people ignored the dangers of immersing themselves in them (ibid: 865–866).[6]

The bathhouses played an important social role and people would stay there for up to five hours at a time. Besides places for relaxation, they were social venues where people of different social backgrounds could chat and gossip. However, wealthy individuals had baths built in their homes. Bathhouses were not common in smaller villages, and people had to either wash at home or travel to a town with one. Genders did not mix. Separate bathhouses existed for women in some places, or women and men used the same venue at different times (with priority generally given to men). People of non-Islamic religions were considered unclean and were not allowed in the public bathhouses (ibid: 866).

Baha'i communities around Iran started building bathhouses from around the early 1900s. These initiatives do not seem to have been part of a national strategy but rather as local responses to being prevented from using public baths after their conversion to the Baha'i religion. In addition, Baha'ullah forbade Baha'is using the *khazīna* in the *Kitāb-i Aqdas* (Baha'ullah 1992: 58, verse 106). There appear to have been two innovations introduced by Baha'is. The first was the use of a shower in place of the *khazīna* and all Baha'i bathhouses shared this feature (this is suggested by Baha'ullah in the *Kitāb-i Aqdas*). The second innovation was the building of bathhouses inside Baha'i-run businesses and factories. Furthermore, Baha'i bathhouses were open to all people, regardless of religion.

The first public Baha'i bathhouse was built by a physician, Dr. Ḥusayn Khān Ḍiyā' al-Ḥukamā, in Ābādih, a small town near Shiraz ('Abdu'l-Baha 1973: 32–33), in the first decade of the 1900s (Ḥaqqjū 2006). He received encouragement from 'Abdu'l-Baha for his efforts, who stated in a letter to him that he was the first person to have built a bathhouse with a shower. In addition, 'Abdu'l-Baha stated that the Baha'is should celebrate that at last they had been able to rid themselves of bathing in the 'dirty pit, meaning that malodorous *khazīna*' (*chāla-yi kithāfat ya'nī khazīna-yi karīha-yi pur-'ufūnat*) (Abdu'l-Baha 1973: 33).

There is no compendium of Baha'i bathhouses. However, records suggest that there were bathhouses built by Baha'is in all the major cities and towns in Iran. In Tehran, the first Baha'i-built bathhouse, Ḥammām-i 'Azīzī, was built by 'Azīzullāh 'Azīzī followed by Ḥammām-i Manshādī and Ḥammām-i Mīthāqiyya, and later others. In some cities, Baha'is were persecuted for building bathhouses. In Tabriz, the *mulla*s of the city banned Muslims from using the Baha'i-run *ḥammām*, and claimed that the water was not considered clean (*kurr*) according to Islamic law. In Najafababad, the Muslim clerics forbade building public baths with showers because they deemed it impossible to perform the full ablution or *ghusl* under the shower (Mihrābkhānī 1999: 41). There were two bathhouses in Najafabad, one of which is apparently still in use (Ḥammām-i Nūr) (Mudarris 2004: 306). In Yazd, local Baha'is used a private financing scheme to finance the building of a bathhouse, and a company was formed and shares were sold to Baha'is. This left a shortfall of three thousand *tūmān*s that was met by an individual donation (Yiktā 2000: 71–72). Yazd was a city notorious for persecuting Baha'is, and it was reported that in 1940 some local Muslims attacked the furnace stoker of the recently built Baha'i bathhouse, who happened not to be a Baha'i, and threw him into a local kiln (Afnān 1997). Baha'is were subsequently accused of this murder, which led to a short period of imprisonment for the nine members of the local assembly of the Baha'is there, and a harsher sentence for the owner of the bathhouse, Mr Sulṭān Nīk-Ā'īn, who was imprisoned for seven years (ibid). Some anecdotal evidence suggests local people other than the Baha'is regularly used these bathhouses. In Shāh-Riḍā, a small town in the Isfahan province, it is reported that after a period of opposition from local people, some of the town's notables started to use the Baha'i bathhouse (Safīdvash 2005). In Najafabad, the Muslims did so discreetly (Mudarris 2004: 43). Baha'is also built a bathhouse with a shower in the first decade of the twentieth century in Khusf, Khurasan, called Ḥammām-i Mīrza Ja'far (built by Mīrza Ja'far Rafsanjānī), reportedly used by both Baha'is and Muslims (Nakhāī 2006). Apart from the introduction of showers, another possible innovation of the Baha'i community is the building of bathhouses at places of work. These occurred in the few instances where Baha'is had opened businesses or factories, and bathhouses were built for all the employees (the majority of which were not Baha'is).[7] Some of these were later donated to the town municipality.

Medicine in nineteenth- and twentieth-century Iran

Until the twentieth century, medicine was still predominately Galenic in nature, based on the traditional schools of Persian medicine of Ibn Sīnā and Rāzī (Faghih 1989: 100), and mostly practised by traditional healers who used a range of therapies including phlebotomy (blood letting), cupping, and the use of leeches, potions and herbs (Paykī 1990: 196). Iran was subject to periodic epidemics of infectious disease with high rates of mortality and little intervention by public institutions. In particular, cholera and plague frequently gained entry through ports on the Persian Gulf, such as Basra (in Iraq), Bandar 'Abbas and Bushihr, and there are reported deaths of entire villages and towns (Elgood 1951: 550–572). There were seven major cholera epidemics between 1820 and 1903 (Floor 2004: 18). In addition, famine was not uncommon and in its wake came infectious diseases. Foreign embassies reported many of these public health problems (ibid: 567–570). The attitude of the general public towards modern medicine was generally sceptical in nineteenth-century Iran. For example, a riot is reported to have taken place when a retail pharmacy was opened in Tehran at the end of the nineteenth century (Ebrahimnejad 2005: 412). Travelogues of foreign visitors delineate the widely held superstitions at the time. These included giving a person suffering from fever a piece of paper or an egg with intentionally illegible writing on it, having the sight of a pregnant donkey or goat for pain relief, and wearing a diamond necklace to remedy epilepsy (Paykī 1990: 196–198). When modern smallpox vaccination was introduced from 1910 onwards (Kotobi 1995: 282), it was resisted because it was thought to make the recipient demonical (*jinn-zada*). Even though a penalty was set for its refusal, this was ineffective (Paykī 1990: 201–203). Furthermore, the campaign of vaccination in 1911 was focused solely on Tehran dwellers, and involved the use of largely ineffective vaccines (which had degraded on their 10-day journey from Europe) (Kotobi 1995: 282). In addition to traditional healers, fortune-tellers, magicians and their like were consulted by the general public for health problems. The belief in evil spirits as the cause of diseases was widespread and suspicion towards modern medicine common. Partly as a consequence of this, medical doctors used a combination and parallel practice of traditional and modern medicine (Ebrahimnejad 2005: 413).

Repeated epidemics of cholera, plague, small pox and other contagious diseases realized the need for hospitals and during the reign of Fatḥ-'Alī Shah (r.1797–1834), a number of small hospitals were built. 'Abbās Mīrzā (1789–1833), the heir apparent and governor of Adharbayjan, played a central role in the hospital building programme because he thought that the defeat in the war against the Russians was caused partly by a small population brought about by high mortality (Ebrahimnejad 2005: 410).

The reign of Nāṣir al-Dīn Shah (r.1848–96) brought with it institutional changes initiated by the reforming prime minister, Mīrzā Taqī Khān, Amīr Kabīr. These included the creation of the first modern polytechnic, the Dār al-Funūn, where modern medicine was taught (established in Tehran in 1851) and a military hospital (ibid: 412, 402). The first modern public hospital was built in Tehran sometime in the 1850s and known as Marīḍkhāna-yi Dawlatī ('state hospital') (Ebrahimnejad 2004: 58–59).[8] It accommodated 200–300 patients according to a 1865 manuscript (ibid: 82), although in 1924 is thought to have had a nominal capacity of fifty beds (Floor 2004: 194). The hospital, though, was poorly managed and lacked sufficient resources, and was subsequently called by the people 'the cemetery of the living' by Carla Serena in 1883 (Ebrahimnejad 2004: 82). After many decades of changing management, including the British embassy and the Anglo-Iranian Oil Company, the government regained direct control of the hospital in 1940 and renamed it Bīmāristān-i Sīnā. Later, the management of the hospital was handed over to Tehran University, which continues to run it to this day. The other modern hospital in Tehran was the Bīmāristān-i Niẓāmī (the military hospital), which was built during Nāṣir al-Dīn Shāh's reign.

This hospital also had a poor reputation (Paykī 1990: 210–211). In the second part of the nineteenth century, there were also other hospitals outside Tehran: the Dār al-Shafā ('house of healing') in Mashhad (c.1867), a state hospital in Simnan (1884), the Raḍavī hospital in Mashhad (c.1881), and hospitals in Kirman and Yazd. There were likely to have been other hospitals that have not been recorded in sources (Ebrhaminmejad 2004: 69–74). Hospitals also existed in Anzalī, Tabriz, Hamadan, Khurramshahr, and Malāyir (Floor 2004: 195). By 1924 there were three government hospitals in Tehran: the state hospital, the Vazīrī hospital that was built around 1903 by a private charity (Ebrhaminmejad 2004: 74) and had thirty beds (Floor 2004: 194), and a hospital for women, which was established in 1918 with 20 beds (ibid: 195).

Apart from the College of Medicine in the Tehran Polytechnic (offering a five year curriculum), there was a pharmacological college (three year course) and a school of midwifery (also three year curriculum) at the Polytechnic, and in 1915 an American missionary school of nursing was established in Riḍā'iyya (Faghih 1989: 102). The College of Medicine was transformed to the first medical school in 1905 (Madrasa-yi Ṭibb) under the influence of a Frenchman, Dr. Schneider (Kotobi 1995: 281).

Due to the poor condition of the public hospitals, private companies such as the Anglo-Iranian Oil Company, the army, police, and Christian missions established their own organized health care and brought in foreign doctors to work in them. The best known were an American hospital founded by the Presbyterian mission (1893) and a small Russian hospital sponsored by the Russian Orthodox mission[9] – both in Tehran (Sajjādī 1990: 260–1). The American mission also built several other hospitals, including a women's hospital in Tehran in 1897 and by 1920 operated seven hospitals. The poor were treated free of charge. It is reported that there were 11 physicians on their staff, of which two were women (Floor 2004: 198).[10] By the 1920s, there were 21 hospitals in total, with a total of 906 beds, which include 10 hospitals operated by foreign missionaries (650 beds) (Faghih 1989: 100). Infant mortality ran at 250 deaths per 1000 live births[11] and, in non-pandemic years, 270 persons died annually from smallpox (ibid: 103).

Baha'i-run hospitals

Educational levels were relatively high among the Baha'is, and the study of medicine was particularly popular. A good number of Baha'is studied at Tehran's Dār al-Funūn, the only university of the time, and a small minority went to European universities, particularly French ones. One of the first Baha'i doctors, Sayyid Muḥammad Nāẓim al-Ḥukamā (1853–1920), who converted to the religion in his twenties, is notable in that Nāṣir al-Dīn Shāh appointed him as head of the medical team of the royal guard (Sulaymānī 1950: 371, 374, 393). Another well-known Baha'i physician, 'Aṭā'ullāh

Bakhshāyish, was awarded a government medal for his services to the needy and sick as he stayed in Tehran during its periodic cholera epidemics to work at the Baha'i-run Ṣiḥḥat hospital (Thābit 1987: 24). Other well-known Baha'i doctors included Arasṭū Khān-i Ḥakīm (1877–1934) and Yūnis Khān Afrūkhta (1869–1948), who both worked at Ṣiḥḥat hospital.

Ṣiḥḥat hospital (Bīmāristān-i Ṣiḥḥat) was the first hospital founded by Baha'is in Iran.[12] In 1908–1909 three Baha'i physicians, Arasṭū Khān, 'Atā'ullāh Bakhshāyish and Muḥammad Khān-i Munajjim (1855–1920), all graduates of the Tehran medical school, decided to open a hospital (Thābit 1987: 23–25). The project was financed by the above doctors together with private donations from Baha'is, the sale of hospital shares, and the Spiritual Assembly of the Baha'is of Tehran but, despite this, had funding problems. The sale of hospital shares to raise finance must have been a novel development for any business at the time. Unlike the state hospital, Ṣiḥḥat received no government aid and was free of charge to most patients.

After advice from real estate experts, a property in a prime Tehran location, Khīābān-i Lālazār, was initially rented for two years. It was extensively refurbished, furnished with modern equipment and opened in June 1909. Initially, there were ten beds. Shortly after, four more beds were added after a donation from a non-Baha'i princess (whose name is unknown) (Anon. 2004: 29–31). On her recommendation and most likely funding, a hospital telephone line was connected. Later, another bed was added making a total of 15 beds. Treatment was offered free to patients, and only patients with sufficient means paid a small amount towards the cost of any surgery which was used to fund hospital expenses (Anon 1911a: 5).

The mission statement for the hospital, prepared by the hospital managers, was based on a letter they received from 'Abdu'l-Baha shortly after its opening (ibid: 5; Thābit 1987: 25). The statement went as follows:

- Service to mankind, regardless of race, religion and nationality,
- the dignity and respect of patients should be of paramount importance,
- to serve mainly the poor and those who due to poverty cannot afford medical treatment,
- to assist physicians in Tehran and surrounding areas if they are having diagnostic difficulties,
- hospital staff must aim to use the best medical treatment available at the time and to consult colleagues in the West for advice and direction.

As stated in the mission statement, other doctors could refer patients to Ṣiḥḥat for additional tests and diagnostic advice. Furthermore, should a patient need a surgical operation outside the expertise of their own doctor, they could be admitted to the hospital for the appropriate surgery. Another innovation was the setting up of specialist wards, and, in particular, a women's ward around 1909. At the time in Iran, the treatment of women's health problems was unsatisfactory and state hospitals did not have separate wards for women (Elgood 1951: 599). In contrast, at Ṣiḥḥat hospital, a woman physician saw women in a specialist women's clinic and, if necessary, admitted them to a female-only ward. This physician was initially Susan Moody (1851–1934), an American Baha'i and a gynaecologist and obstetrician, who had specifically come to Iran to work in this hospital (Thābit 1987: 25). An American trained nurse, Elizabeth Stewart (d. 1926), who was also a Baha'i, joined the hospital staff. This was unusual at the time as nurses working in hospitals received little specialist training.[13] Later, another American gynaecologist, Sarah Clock (d. 1922), assisted Moody in her work. In addition to these three American women, Dr. Yūnis Khān Afrūkhta, a Beirut University graduate and general physician and surgeon, joined the staff in 1910 (ibid). The use of foreign and in particular American expertise was paralleled in some Baha'i schools in Iran, and Moody and Clock also worked in the Baha'i school for girls in Tehran.

The hospital had a busy daily outpatient department where health problems of men, women and children were assessed and treated, including minor surgical procedures. For the first few years, at least one doctor was present every day, and in so doing, closed their private practice for the day (Thābit 1987: 25). As the hospital became busier, all the staff doctors worked in the outpatient clinic every afternoon (Anon 2004: 31). Initially, non-Baha'i doctors were reluctant to send their patients to Ṣiḥḥat hospital for fear of being labelled Baha'i, losing their patients to other doctors, and out of prejudice that the place was 'unclean' (*najis*). Over time, the public's attitude towards the Ṣiḥḥat Hospital gradually changed and its reputation improved. One particular episode is thought to have contributed to this change. Around the time of World War I, there was an epidemic of influenza in Tehran and most doctors fled the city. However, it is reported that the medical staff at Ṣiḥḥat stayed behind and continued to admit and treat patients (Revell 1937: 485). The hospital closed sometime in the mid-1920s. Documents regarding the circumstances of its closure are currently unavailable, but one can assume that it was a considerable challenge to fund the hospital entirely from Baha'i sources. Personnel shortages may also be relevant: Munajjim died in 1920, Clock died in 1922, Afrūkhta left to America in 1924, and Moody left in 1925. Having been open from 1909 until the 1920s, Ṣiḥḥat compares favourably with other privately run hospitals in Iran at the time. A hospital in Kirman was built in 1904 by the governor and ceased to function within a year. The Mashhad hospitals were reportedly neglected and ceased to operate in the early twentieth century. A hospital in Qazvin (with 25–30 beds) functioned from 1916 until 1927, when it ran out of finances. A hospital in Hamadan (with twelve beds) was financed by a tax on transport, but did not have an inpatient or surgical service (Floor 2004: 196). No private hospitals were mentioned in the 1924 report by John Gilmour for the League of Nations (ibid).

Susan Moody, one of the key figures in the history of the Ṣiḥḥat hospital, was born in Amsterdam, New York, in 1851. Having looked after her brother's children as a 'spinster-mother', she studied medicine in her fifties, and then set up her own practice in Chicago. There she met some Baha'is, and studied the new religion with Isabella Brittingham, an eminent Chicago Baha'i, and converted in 1903. Through a lodger in her home, an Iranian Baha'i, Amīnullāh Farīd, she learned Persian and something about the culture and customs of Iran (Armstrong-Ingram 2003). In 1909, medical staff at Ṣiḥḥat asked the American Baha'i community for the assistance of a woman doctor, and Susan Moody volunteered for this task. She arrived in Tehran in November 1909. She set up the women's ward, personally cared for all the women patients, and arranged for a trained nurse from the US to come to work there. Elizabeth Stewart, who was also a Baha'i and a niece of Isabella Brittingham, went to work there in 1911 (Ma'ani 1993: 1102; Thābit 1987: 25).[14] As the workload increased, Moody asked another gynaecologist and obstetrician, Dr. Sarah Clock, an American Baha'i, to assist, and she arrived in Tehran in the winter of 1911 (Ma'ani 1993: 1101; Clock 1911: 6), remaining there until her death in January 1922. In addition to working at Ṣiḥḥat hospital, Moody established a 'flourishing' private clinic that was open to all women regardless of their ability to pay, and from 1910 worked as a teacher at the Tarbīat Baha'i girls' school in Tehran (Stockman 1995: 360; Armstrong-Ingram 2003). Moody and Stewart left Iran in 1925 for America, apparently due to an increase in anti-American sentiment in the country (Ma'ani 1993: 1102). Moody raised funds for the Baha'i school for girls and also nursed Stewart who was suffering from cancer, and who died in 1926. That same year, Shoghi Effendi, the head of the international Baha'i community, asked the American Baha'is to send one or two women to Iran, and that they should consult Moody about this. As a consequence, Moody returned to Iran in 1928, at the age of 77, with a younger teacher Adelaide Sharp. She limited her activities to her outpatient clinic. On her death in Tehran in 1934, hundreds of people attended the funeral (Revell 1937: 484). From a Baha'i perspective, it has been argued that she acted as an important role model for Baha'i girls and women. She was given the title of 'Handmaid of the Most High' (*amat al-A'lā*) by 'Abdul-Baha (ibid). Her work was acknowledged in an editorial in an unnamed Tehran newspaper in 1910:

> Doctor Moody – American lady – Not only does she know medicine but also gynaecology, obstetrics and women's diseases. Her good qualities and kind attributes, her love for her Persian oriental sisters, all are equal. Every day from morning till noon, she is in her office, No. 10 Avenue Aladauleh, receiving her patients for consultation, examination and treatment, excepting Friday and Sunday afternoon, when she goes to the hospital Sihhat (Hospital of Health), where she meets the patients of the higher and wealthier classes.

> We give the utmost thanks and gratitude to such a noble woman, to such a respected person, whose presence here is a great privilege to the country of Persia. On account of great care of this blessed person, the sick of all nationalities, Moslems et al., become healthy and well. We beg of God to keep this blessed and respected person with us.
>
> (cited in Revell 1937: 484–485, translated in original)

Apart from her medical work, Moody was heavily involved in the running of the Tarbīat Baha'i School for girls, and arranged for Lillian Kappes (d. 1920), an American Baha'i, to come to Iran to teach at this school. Moody felt that her work in improving women's health was inextricably linked to their education, and complained of the lack of even the 'simplest hygienic measures' in the homes of the sick (Armstrong-Ingram 1986: 187). The correspondence of Sarah Clock reveals a number of innovative school-based

Figure 5.1 A group of Baha'is, Tehran, ca. 1920. Top row, left to right: two unidentified men, Elizabeth H. Stewart, unidentified man holding a picture of 'Abdu'l-Baha, Ḥājjī Ghulām-Riḍā Iṣfahānī (Amīn-i Amīn). Bottom row, left to right: Mulla Bahrām Akhtar-Khāvarī, Dr. Susan I. Moody, unidentified boy, Sayyid Asadullāh Qumī (Mīrzā Mūsā Asadullāh Qumī), and unidentified man.

Figure 5.2 From left to right: unidentified man, Lillian Kappes, Dr. Sarah Clock, Dr. Susan Moody and (reclining on Dr. Moody's lap) Ṭā'ira Khānum.

health initiatives. The first was the teaching of basic health. Clock taught anatomy and physiology once a week at the Baha'i girls' school, and Stewart taught first aid and nursing once a week. Clock states that 'it is the only school in all this country where these things are taught in this way' (Platt 1916: 7–8). The second and possibly more interesting was a school-based vaccination programme.[15] Clock states that in 1920 some cases of smallpox had come to Moody's practice, and therefore they vaccinated 'about 200' girls, and that the girls 'behaved most beautifully', and that 'only two or three made any confusion'. Interestingly she added that 'the people are so ignorant they brought babies from the families for us to vaccinate thinking the other members of the family would contract small pox from those who had been vaccinated' (Robarts 1920: 3).

With the closure of Ṣiḥḥat hospital and the increase in the incidence of infectious diseases such as typhus, typhoid, and dysentery during World War II, many Baha'is, in particular the poor and those living outside Tehran, had limited access to medical care (Yazdani 2004: 42). In order to remedy this situation, the Local Assembly of the Baha'is of Tehran formed a committee in 1948–49, called Lajna-yi Ḥifẓ al-Ṣiḥḥa ('health committee'), which was charged with attending to the medical needs of Tehran's Baha'is and neighbouring towns and villages of Tehran (ibid: 45; Rāsikh 2005). The members of this committee consisted of general physicians, dentists and pharmacists, who volunteered their time free of charge. They spent weekends and public holidays visiting different places and attending to those in need of medical care (Yazdāñ 2004: 42–45). In many smaller towns, including Nāzī-ābād, Jalālābād and Khānī-ābād, non-Baha'is were also treated. In addition, they showed American public education films on the causes, prevention and treatment of infectious diseases including typhus and malaria, ways to purify drinking water and avoid insect bites (Rāsikh 2005). The committee effectively ceased to function as its members became increasingly involved in the second Baha'i-run hospital, Mīthāqiyya hospital, in the 1940s. Nevertheless, it was a good example of a grassroots public health initiative that did not cost any-thing to the Baha'i community.

Mīthāqiyya Hospital (Bīmāristān-i Mīthāqiyya)

In 1949, a Baha'i from Tehran, 'Abd al-Mīthāq Mīthāqiyya (d. 1981), purchased a building in Tehran to accommodate Baha'i university students who came from other cities. However, after discussion with his friends, the project became the building of a Baha'i hospital. Mīthāqiyya had become rich from real estate and decided to donate the building to the national governing council of the Baha'is of Iran, the National Spiritual Assembly. The Assembly approved the formation of a hospital and appointed a 'Directorial Council' to run its operations that consisted of nine physicians. Mīthāqiyya was chosen as the permanent member of the committee. Mīthāqiyya financed the project, including the purchase of medical and other equipment. Later, he purchased several adjacent properties to the hospital to convert to new medical and surgical wards, and bought two other large properties in order to set up a nursing school and a training college for doctors' assistants (Rāsikh 1996: 49–51).

The hospital was a private one and did not receive any government support. The mission of the hospital was to become a well-equipped modern hospital that was open to all. Although its initial funding came from one individual, medical staff and other professionals, such as civil engineers, offered their services for free. The hospital council allocated one bed for each minority that was free of charge: Armenian, Assyrian, Sunni, Zoroastrian and Jewish. Shi'i Muslims were entitled to use an unlimited number of beds free of charge.

Mīthāqiyya hospital was a relatively large hospital with 110 adult beds and 60 paediatric beds. Patient rooms were reported to be comfortable with modern amenities. There were several operating theatres for surgery and an obstetric ward. It had its own laboratories, radiology department, physiotherapy, rehabilitation and hydrotherapy facilities ('Azīzī 1998: 22–23).

There were a number of novel practices. A polyclinic for patients with health problems of any type was opened, and patients were seen free of charge throughout the day. The emergency room was open night and day, and was staffed continuously by doctors. A well-stocked pharmacy was open until 10pm. It had its own electricity generator in order to continue functioning during power cuts, which was reportedly unique for a hospital at the time. Hospital waste was discarded using two large furnaces, which was a new practice shared by some other local hospitals (ibid).

Initially the attitude of local people and the wider medical community was not positive and the hospital was half full. The hospital was considered 'unclean' (*najis*) in their opinion, based on the popular religious belief in the ritual impurity of non-Muslims. Even doctors without such prejudices were worried that their patients would be upset if they recommended admission there. However, several incidents are likely to have improved its reputation. Two are particularly noteworthy. The first was that a famous sportsman was admitted to the hospital around the mid-1950s. Maḥmūd Nāmjū, an Olympic gold medallist for weight-lifting, needed a tonsillectomy, which was arranged through Dr. 'Alī Rāsikh, one of the directors of the hospital, who knew Nāmjū's surgeon, Professor Jamshīd A'lam, and arranged for the operation free of charge (Rāsikh 2005). News about his stay there spread in the general public and Nāmjū received many visitors, including other sport personalities, during his stay. Another notable hospital admission, shortly after, was that of Ayatullah Zanjānī, an eminent cleric, for whom the minister of health, Professor Jahānshāh Ṣāliḥ, arranged admission for an abdominal operation without any fee. Interestingly this was thought to be because the state hospitals in Tehran were thought to be unsuitable for an eminent person, such as Zanjānī. Again, many clerics visited Zanjānī at the hospital and saw the facilities for themselves (ibid). Subsequently, non-Baha'i admissions increased, and non-Baha'i doctors started to use the hospital's operating theatres. New hospital wings had to be added to meet this additional demand. A final mark of its success was that the hospital was rated by the government as one of the best and given the certificate of excellence ('Azīzī 1988: 22). At the beginning of the Islamic revolution, the hospital was confiscated and transferred to the state.

Due to the increasing work of the hospital and shortage of staff, the hospital managers decided to found a private college for doctors' assistants (Āmūzishgah-i Bihyārī) around 1969–70 and also one for nurses (Āmūzishgah-i 'Ālī-yi Parastārī) around 1974 (Rāsikh 2005). Properties were purchased for these colleges – the nursing school was based in a large building on Kākh Avenue, Tehran. Teachers and tutors were mainly Baha'i academics from Tehran University who worked pro bono developing the school's curriculum and teaching. The course for doctors' assistants was for two years, and for nurses three years, and students received free board and lodging. The doctors' assistants college and the nursing school received the approval of the Ministry of Higher Education despite opposition from other government departments ('Azīzī 1988). The hospital council offered the service of a few of graduate doctors' assistants to state-run hospitals every year – a generous gesture considering the cost of training. At any one time, it is estimated that there were 100 doctors' assistants working at Mīthāqiyya hospital (Rāsikh 1996: 50). After some years, the nursing college introduced an entry exam as competition for places increased. This was the first time that an independent hospital had established ancillary institutions such as a doctors' assistants college and nursing school.

An old people's home was also established by Mīthāqiyya hospital around 1970 in order to provide long term care for those suffering from chronic disorders such as Parkinson's disease, stroke, and dementia and so that more beds were available for obstetric, surgical and other emergencies. In addition, elderly Baha'is who lived alone or needed nursing care could be admitted there. The hospital council rented a large house in a leafy North Tehran suburb (that belonged to a Baha'i who charged a modest rent) and transformed it to a modern old people's home. Facilities included a library, music room, and cinema. Several orderly staff and two qualified nurses were appointed to look after patients day and night. Running costs were met by donations from Baha'is, some of whom were residents (Rāsikh 2005). This was probably the first modern private old people's home in Iran. At the time of the Islamic Revoluton, there were between 15 and 20 residents in the old people's home. After the government seized the building, the residents were allocated to relatives and friends by the Spiritual Assembly of the Baha'is of Tehran (Qadīmī 2006).

Outpatient clinics

Three outpatient clinics were set up by Baha'is in the latter half of the twentieth century. The first of these was in Tehran, and was funded by an Iranian Baha'i who had emigrated to Sweden. The National Assembly of the Baha'is of Iran decided against building another hospital, but that a clinic on the east side of Tehran would be valuable. It was built at Khīābān-i Bihbūdī and named 'Aṭṭār clinic, after its benefactor Dr. Hūshang 'Aṭṭār, and managed by Dr. Manṣūr 'Aṭṭār, a paediatrician and brother of the benefactor. It was opened in 1973, and consisted of a general clinic, paediatric outpatients, and an eye and dental clinic. The clinic was free for the poor but those who were able to pay gave a small sum for medical treatment (Rāsikh 2005). Two years after the Islamic Revolution, the name of the clinic was altered, and is now called 'Atārud Clinic, and all the Baha'i personnel sacked ('Aṭṭār 2007).

The second clinic was built in a remote village, Tākur, in Mazandaran province (the ancestral village of Baha'ullah's father, Mīrzā 'Abbās Nūrī). As the village was far from a tarmac road, inhabitants had little access to medical services. The problem was brought to the attention of national Baha'i institutions and, eventually, authorities at Mīthāqiyya hospital volunteered to establish a medical centre in Tākur. Mīthāqiyya himself undertook to finance the project. With the aid of a Baha'i architect, civil engineer and others, a medical centre was built and staff recruited. One of the notable members of the staff there was Qudsiyya Ashraf (1889–1976), the first Iranian Baha'i woman to study abroad.[16] She was retired and living in Tehran when the hospital committee in Tākur requested her to work there. She agreed and for two and half years did so despite her poor health and refused a salary (Rāsikh 1996: 50; Rāsikh 2005). All the medicines and other consumables were delivered free fortnightly by the technical director of Mīthāqiyya hospital, Haqīqī, who transported them in his own car and also without being paid (Rāsikh 1996: 50).

A third outpatient clinic was built in Buyir Aḥmadī province (inhabited by mainly tribal peoples, located in central Iran between Shiraz and Isfahan) (Rāsikh 1996: 51). The clinic was established when Mr Mīthāqiyya heard of the plight of the local Baha'is there at one of the annual conventions for all Baha'is in Iran. Apparently the delegate from Buyir Ahmadī province said that between 60 to 90 per cent of the Baha'is from the towns and villages had made this request. Due to poor roads and no local medical provision, Baha'is had limited access to medical care. Mīthāqiyya funded a medical centre, which was built under supervision of staff from Mīthāqiyya hospital. The site chosen was located in a natural beauty spot next to a river, and a medical centre was built, which also provided for six inpatient beds. Retired Baha'i physicians were recruited (ibid: 51).

The outpatient clinics in Tākur and Buyir Aḥmadī are interesting health initiatives. It is not particularly surprising that Baha'is would attempt to address the needs of their co-religionists,[17] but the way that these clinics were set up is notable. Local Baha'is brought their problems to national Baha'i institutions, Baha'i networks were drawn on in order to build the medical centres, and retired health care staff was recruited, making them relatively cost effective ways to establish such medical centres. Despite this, the number of health centres was relatively few compared with the Baha'i schools, for example, reflecting most probably the high cost of running medical facilities.

Despite all these various initiatives, it is uncertain whether the overall health of the Baha'is was better than other Iranians due to the lack of appropriate comparative statistics. There is one study from 1970s that studied family planning among 245 Baha'i and Muslim couples from a variety of rural and urban settings. The research found lower rates of pregnancy and higher use of contraception in the Baha'is, even after matching for social class and age (Jensen 1986: 223, 230). The main focus of the study was educational levels, but nevertheless, it would appear that Baha'i women were exercising more control over their fertility than their Muslim counterparts.

After the Islamic Revolution

After the Islamic Revolution, Mīthāqiyya hospital and the other Baha'i medical centres suffered the same fate as other Baha'i ventures and were seized by the new administration. The Islamic Revolutionary Court in Tehran issued a writ stating that they had reviewed the license of Mīthāqiyya hospital and revoked the practising rights of its doctors. After further consideration, the Third Revolutionary Court issued the following verdict ordering the hospital's confiscation, which listed common falsehoods about the Baha'is:

> Central Islamic Revolutionary Court
>
> After reviewing the documents of the founders of Mīthāqiyya hospital, Professor Manoucher Hakim, Dr. Mash'u'llah Moshrefzadeh, Dr. Mohammad Afnan, Manouhar Qaem Maqami, Dr. Bahram Saraj, Dr. Aref Khadem, and Nosrat'u'llah Baghaie are members of Baha'i community who have been supporters of Pahlavi regime and have turned the hospital into an anti-Islamic propaganda centre. This large and well-equipped hospital uses its massive profit to help the Universal House of Justice in Israel, thus working for the aims of Imperialism and Zionism. With the School of Nursing they have established the first official Baha'i university in which 40 out of 87 students are Baha'is. The university's importance to Baha'i institutions is evident from the donation of two million riyals to the hospital. The hospital is under the auspices of the National Spiritual Assembly of Iran. The staff of the hospital consists of 290, of which 123 are Baha'is. The hospital also has donated a sum of 500,000 riyals for the building of the Teaching Centre in Haifa.
>
> (document reprinted in Martin 1984: 42, provisional translation)

One interesting aspect of this document is its listing of the number of Baha'i staff and students at the hospital and school of nursing: 123 out of 290 staff and 40 out of 87 students were Baha'is. After the hospital was seized and its Baha'i employees sacked, it was renamed Shahīd Muṣṭafā Khumaynī hospital and continues to exist. The government seized all the other health care centres and the college for doctors' assistants, and all Baha'i employees were expelled.

In summary, since the late nineteenth century, Iran's Baha'is were involved in a modest number of health initiatives. These included introducing showers to public bathhouses, and the establishment of some health care centres. The first such centre, Ṣiḥḥat hospital, opened in 1909 in Tehran, and included a women-only inpatient ward with female medical staff. The second hospital, Mīthāqiyya hospital, was opened in the 1940s in Tehran and built around it ancillary institutions including a nursing school, a college for doctor's assistants, and a modern old people's home. Although these hospitals introduced some modern practices, it is unclear to what extent they influenced other hospitals or the development of health care in general in Iran. Outside of these hospitals, the Baha'is built three clinics, and effectively marshalled the human resources available within the Baha'i community to make them function with little central funding. With the Islamic Revolution, these health care facilities are no longer run by Baha'is, and at least a couple of them continue to exist under different names.

Notes

1 We are very grateful to Dr. 'Alī Rāsikh for providing information about Mithaqiyya Hospital; Dr. Arthur Dahl of National Baha'i Archives, Wilmette, Illinois, for sending the letters of Sarah Clock; Dr. Namdar Baghaei-Yazdi and Heather Empey for their assistance with sources on vaccination; Rochan Mavaddat and Dr. Rahmat Kashet for providing some clarifications about Mithaqiyya Hospital; Mrs Parivash Afnan for sharing information on the Baha'i bathhouse in Yazd from her late husband's unpublished manuscript, and Jasmin Enayati and Dr. Stephen Lambden for helpful comments.

2 It is estimated that the prevalence of opium addiction reached 50 per cent in certain towns and cities in Qajar Iran (Floor 2004: 47).

3 Baha'ullah also forbids the production, handling and trading of these substances. Alcoholism in Qajar Iran was mostly confined to certain groups, such as the political elite (Floor 2004: 47).

4 This had potentially important public health implications. Floor explains, 'The practice to transport dead bodies to the Holy Cities (Karbala, Mashhad, Qom) was a public health disaster. The storage space was not properly closed off, and corpses were not embalmed or otherwise treated. They were just packed in felt and put on the back of mules. The situation was even worse en route and when the corpses arrived at the shrine for burial' (Floor 2004: 61).

5 It is estimated that 20–40 per cent of the population of Tehran had a venereal disease (Floor 2004: 33).

6 In 1914, the Municipality of Tehran introduced rules to improve hygiene in these baths, but these did not include changing the water (Floor 2004: 228).

7 An example is the bathhouse at the electricity generating plant established by Safidvash (Safidvash 2005).

8 Some sources report this as date for the military hospital, which became the civilian hospital when the new army hospital was built in 1874 (Floor 2004: 193).

9 This closed after World War I, as did the French and German medical work (Floor 2004: 198).

10 The first female physician is reported to have been Dr. Mary Smith, who worked in the American mission hospitals sometime from the 1880s (Floor 2004: 198).

11 Some foreign doctors working in Iran report infant mortality rates higher than 50 per cent (Floor 2004: 11).

12 We have not found any non-Baha'i sources on Ṣiḥḥat. It is also not mentioned in Floor's recent survey of hospitals in Qajar Iran (Floor 2004: 189–203).

13 In 1924, it is reported that there was one trained nurse working at the state hospital (Floor 2004: 194).

14 Stewart suffered from poor health, and went to Haifa sometime in 1921 for a few months, returning in much better health (Jessie and Ethel Revell papers, letter from Clock to Brittingham, 28 July 1921).

15 We have not been able to establish whether this was the first school-based vaccination programme in Iran, as it is possible that some mission schools had

instituted something similar. The first Pasteur Institute was opened in 1921 in Tehran, and started a more successful national programme (Kotobi 1995: 283). Even in 1934, Merrill-Hawkes states, 'It is hoped that smallpox vaccination will be compulsory in two years and also satisfactory, as vaccine is now prepared in Tehran' (Merrill-Hawkes 1935: 148).

16 In 1911, Qudsiyya Ashraf went to America to study education (Anon 1911b: 7–8). Upon finishing her course, 'Abdu'l-Baha encouraged her to go to Beirut to study midwifery. After training and then working in Beirut and Jordan, she returned to Iran and worked as head nurse in the main hospital in Abadan.

17 Non-Baha'i local people were also able to access these clinics.

Bibliography

'Abdu'l-Baha. (1973) *Mā'ida-yi Āsamānī*, vol. 5, Comp. and ed. A.H. Ishrāq Khāvarī, Tehran: Baha'i Publishing Trust.

—— (1978) *Selections from the writings of 'Abdu'l-Bahá*, Haifa: Baha'i World Centre.

Afnān, M.T. (1997) *Bī-gunāhān*, unpublished manuscript.

Anon. (1911a) 'Avvalīn rāpurt-i Bīmāristān-i Ṣiḥḥat', *Star of the West*, II.5: 4–5, Persian section.

—— (1911b) 'Ghodsia Ashraf Khanum, "Miriam"', *Star of the West*, II.7–8: 7–9, English section.

—— (2004) 'Guzārish-i sālāna-yi Bīmāristān-i Ṣiḥḥat dar Tihrān', *Payām-i Baha'i*, 299: 29–31.

Armstrong-Ingram, J.R. (1986) 'American Baha'i women and the education of girls in Tehran, 1909–1934', in P. Smith (ed.) *In Iran: Studies in Babi and Baha'i History* volume 3, Los Angeles: Kalimat Press.

—— (2003) 'Susan Moody' published online at the Baha'i Academic Resource Library; http://bahai-library.com/?file=armstrong-ingram_encyclopedia_susan moody (accessed 9 October 2006).

'Aṭṭār, M. (2007) Personal correspondence with Minou Foadi.

'Azīzī, Z. (1988) 'Bīmāristān va zāyishgāh-i Mīthāqiyya', *Payām-i Baha'i*, 102: 22–23.

Bab, The. (1978) *Selections from the writings of the Báb*, Haifa: Baha'i World Centre.

Baha'ullah. (1978) *Majmū'a-yi alvāḥ-i mubāraka-yi haḍrat-i Baha'ullah*, Repr. Wilmette: Baha'i Publishing Trust.

—— (1992) *Kitáb-i Aqdas: The Most Holy Book*, Haifa: Baha'i World Centre.

Clock, S. (1911) 'Letter from Dr. Clock', *Star of the West* II.3: 6.

Ebrahimnejad, H. (2004) *Medicine, Public Health and the Qajar State: Patterns of Medical Modernization in Nineteenth-Century Iran*, Leiden: Brill.

—— (2005) 'Religion and medicine in Qajar Iran', in R. Gleave (ed.) *Religion and Society in Qajar Iran*, London: RoutledgeCurzon.

Elgood, C. (1951) *A Medical History of Persia and The Eastern Caliphate*, Translated by Furqani, B. Tehran: Sipihr.

Faghih, M.A. (1989) 'Behdari', in *Encyclopaedia Iranica* vol. III, New York: Columbia University.

Fananapazir, K. and Lambden, S. (1992) 'Baha'u'llah's Tablet to the Physician: introduction, provisional translation and notes', *Baha'i Studies Bulletin*, 6–7: 18–65.

Floor, W. (1989) 'Bathhouses', in *Encyclopaedia Iranica* vol. III, New York: Columbia University.

—— (2004) *Public Health in Qajar Iran*, Washington, DC: Mage.

Haqqjū, B. (2006) Personal correspondence to Minou Foadi, 10 October 2006.

Jensen, M.S. (1986) 'Religion and family planning in Iran', in P. Smith (ed.) *In Iran: Studies in Babi and Baha'i History* vol. 3. Los Angeles: Kalimat Press.

Kotobi, L. (1995) 'L'emergence d'une politique de la sante publique en Perse Qajar, XIX-XX siecles: Un apercu historique de la vaccination,' *Studia Iranica*, 24: 261–284.

Ma'ani, B.R. (1993) 'The Interdependence of Baha'i Communities – Services of North American Baha'i Women to Iran', in *The Bahá'í World*, vol. 20, Haifa: Baha'i World Centre.

Martin, D. (1984) *The Persecution of the Bahá'ís of Iran 1844–1984*, Ottawa: Association for Baha'i Studies.

Merrill-Hawkes, O.A. (1935) *Persia – Romance and Reality*, London: Nicholson & Watson.

Mihrābkhānī, R. (1999) 'Sharḥ-i ḥāl-i Fayḍī: murūrī bar ayyām-i Bayrūt, Najafabad va Qazvin', in *Khūsha-hā'ī az kharman-i- adab va hunar* vol. X, Darmstadt: 'Aṣr-i jadid.

Morton, R. (1940) *A Doctor's Holiday in Iran*, NY: Funk & Waynalls.

Mudarris, F. (2004) *Tārīkh-i Amr-i Baha'i dar Najafabad*, ed. Rafatī, V. Darmstadt: Germany: 'Aṣr-i Jadīd.

Nakhāī, M. (2006) Personal communication to Minou Foadi, 12 October 2006.

Paykī, H. (1990) *Tihrān-i Qadīm*, Tehran: Quqnūs.

Platt papers (Orol Platt), National Bahá'ī Archives, United States, letter dated 20 November 1916.

Qadīmī, M. (2006) Personal correspondence to Minou Foadi, 12 October 2006.

Rāsikh, A. (1996) 'Yādī az 'Abd al-Mīthāq-i Mīthāqiyya, bānī-yi Bīmāristān-i Mīthāqiyya', *Payām-i Baha'i*, 199: 49–51.

—— (2005) Personal communication with Minou Foadi, in a letter dated 9 June 2005.

Revell, J.E. (1937) 'A Baha'i Pioneer of East and West – Doctor Susan I. Moody (The Hand-Maid of The Most High) *Amatu'l-A'lá*', in *The Bahá'í World 1934–1936*, vol. 6, Wilmette: Baha'i Publishing Trust.

Robarts papers (Ella Robarts), National Baha'i Archives, United States, letter dated 26 November 1920.

Ṣābirān, E. (2005) Personal communication with Minou Foadi, July 2005.

Safīdvash, R. (2005) Personal communication with Minou Foadi, July 2005.

Sajjādī, S. (1990) 'Bīmāristān,' in *Encyclopaedia Iranica*, vol. IV, New York: Columbia University.

Schaefer, U. (2004) *In a Blue Haze: smoking and Bahá'í ethics*, Rev. ed. Hofheim: Baha'i Verlag.

Stockman, R. (1995) *The Bahá'í Faith in America: early expansion 1900–1912*, Oxford: George Ronald.

Sulaymānī, 'A. (1950) *Maṣābīḥ-i Hidāyat*, vol. 3, Tehran: Baha'i Publishing Trust.

Thābit, A. (1987) 'Khadamāt-i pizishkī va darmānī-yi yārān-i ilāhī dar Iran va ta'sīs-i Bīmāristān-i Siḥḥat', *Payām-i Baha'i*, 95: 23–27.

Yazdānī, K. (2004) 'Raf'-i nīāzmandī-hā-yi dārmānī va bihdāshtī-yi Bahā'iyān sākin-i ḥūma-yi Tihrān: khāṭira'i az panjāh u panj sāl-i pīsh', *Payām Baha'i*, 299: 42–45.

Yiktā, F. (2000) 'Dāstānī az sākhtan-i yik Ḥammām', *Payām Baha'i*, 249: 71–72.

6

BAHA'I DISCOURSES ON THE CONSTITUTIONAL REVOLUTION

Kavian Milani

The early twentieth century witnessed a decline in the fortunes of autocratic monarchies. Tsar Nicholas II of Russia, Sultan 'Abd al-Ḥamīd of the Ottoman Empire, and Muḥammad-'Alī Shah of Qajar Iran were contemporaries whose autocratic reigns ended more or less simultaneously albeit under different circumstances. The Ottoman Empire fell, bringing about the Republic of Turkey, and the autocratic rule of the Tsar of Russia ended with the creation of a representative assembly, the Duma (1905), leading to the Bolshevik Revolution (1917) and the brutal death of Nicholas II. In Iran, the most autocratic and least modernized of these three lands, a constitutional movement in 1905 resulted in the granting of a 'constitution' by the ailing Muẓaffar al-Dīn Shah (d. 1907). His successor, Muḥammad-'Alī Shah, attempted to reestablish absolutism and defy the constitution. His reign of defiance ended in 1909, and he died a few years later.

During this period (and ever since), the Baha'i community was Iran's largest non-Muslim religious minority. In this study, I will argue that the Baha'is contributed both to the conditions that made the Constitutional Revolution happen, and to the development of the constitution itself. I will provide evidence that the Baha'is introduced debates over the need for a code of law, a constitutional government, consultative assemblies and the necessity for a parliament as early as the 1860s. During the reigns of Muẓaffar al-Dīn Shah and Muḥammad-'Alī Shah, and under the leadership of 'Abdu'l-Baha (head of the Baha'i community, 1892–1921), the Baha'is pursued two aims. First, they focused on the need to unify the fragmented Iranian society. Post-1906, attention was given to the increasing tensions between the parliamentary representatives of the people (*millat*) and the government (*dawlat*). As the ideological debt of the Constitutional Movement to the Baha'i Faith began to emerge as a central anti-constitutional polemic in the hands of the anti-constitutional forces, 'Abdu'l-Baha chose a course of political non-involvement for the Baha'i community as the revolution was unfolding. I will also argue that, in the writings of 'Abdu'l-Baha, there is clear evidence to show that political non-involvement was chosen (and was understood thus by Baha'is of the time) largely as an attempt to protect the nascent Constitutional Movement.

The Baha'i writings and constitutionalism

By the 1870s, occasional references began to appear in the writings of the Iranian intelligentsia of the nineteenth century to '*mashrūṭiyyat*' (constitutional government).[1] Baha'ullah had praised the constitutional form of government as early as the mid-1860s and continued to argue for it throughout his writings. Here some of the Baha'i writings on this topic will be presented in chronological order. In a tablet addressed to Queen Victoria (c.1868), Baha'u'llah commends her on her constitutional rule and the presence of a parliamentary system:

> We have also heard that thou hast entrusted the reins of counsel into the hands of the representatives of the people. Thou, indeed, hast done well, for thereby the foundations of the edifice of thine affairs will be strengthened, and the hearts of all that are beneath thy shadow, whether high or low, will be tranquillized. It behoveth them, however, to be trustworthy among His servants, and to regard themselves as the representatives of all that dwell on earth. This is what counselleth them, in this Tablet, He Who is the Ruler, the All-Wise . . .
>
> (Baha'ullah 1978a: 36)

In the *Kitāb-i Aqdas* (c.1873), Baha'ullah envisioned a legislative function for parliaments (sing. *majlis*) – the same nomenclature adopted for the Iranian parliament in 1906. The following is an example of a legislative matter delegated to consultative assemblies (parliaments):

> O members of parliaments [*ahl al-majālis*] throughout the world! Select ye a single language for the use of all on earth, and adopt ye likewise a common script.
>
> (Baha'ullah 1993: 88)

In the early 1870s, Nāṣir al-Dīn Shah issued an edict organizing the *darbār-i a'ẓam* (royal court) into individual ministries responsible for the affairs of state (Bakhash 1972: 139–167). Shortly after this in 1875, 'Abdu'l-Baha wrote a book on reform in Iranian society entitled *Risāla-yi madaniyya* (which is often referred to in English-language Baha'i sources as *The Secret of Divine Civilization*). This book was printed in Bombay in 1882 and distributed anonymously in Iran shortly thereafter.[2] In this work, 'Abdu'l-Baha outlines a reformist and modernizing agenda including the establishment an Iranian bureaucracy, military reforms, an honest and fair judiciary, improvement of the condition of peasants, the separation of powers, and an elected legislature.[3] Cole has argued that in this work 'Abdu'l-Baha proposes an 'egalitarian' social system:

> His program was egalitarian in the sense that he thought the masses should be able to elect their governmental representatives directly and that positions in the government and in the professions should be open to educated talent. It is a very different vision of society than that held by the more conservative Qajar nobles, with their hereditary privileges, their overtaxation of the people, their frequent lack of a modern education (or much of any education at all), their arbitrary and autocratic rule.
>
> (Cole 1988: 88)

Further, 'Abdu'l-Baha emphasized the necessity of the creation of a consultative body that acts as the 'the very foundation and bedrock of government' ('Abdu'l-Baha 1990: 17). Moreover, the introduction of elected members (*vukalā*) created a system of checks and balances *vis-à-vis* the appointed members (*vuzarā*). It should be noted that a 'check' in this setting is a constitutional rein on executive powers placed in the hands of the people, whereas 'balance' refers to the mechanisms that create a slow and deliberative process much like a Newtonian clock (Schechter, 1990: 274). Both elements are present in 'Abdu'l-Baha's writings.[4] The overall effect is to create a slow (and deliberative) process by introducing the notion of a popularly elected membership. 'Abdu'l-Baha is thus one of the first Iranian authors to argue for a popularly elected body and for a system of checks and balances in government. His reference to the king as father (*pidar*) invoked the language of mutual rights by the subjects (*ra'īyat*) through introducing a 'familial' relationship, and is most probably a first among Iranian authors ('Abdu'l-Baha, 1990: 11).[5] The immediate political context for 'Abdu'l-Baha's statement arguing for an elected membership on consultative parliaments was the attempt of the reformist prime minister Mushīr al-Dawla (in the early 1870s) to organize the *Dār al-Shūrā-yi Kubrā* ('great house of consultation') that he envisaged as an advisory council to the executive powers of the state. This body was established in 1871 and functioned until 1875 or thereabouts. Therefore 'Abdu'l-Baha was arguing that a democratically elected membership should be added to the composition of this rudimentary parliament.

In the ensuing debates over constitutionalism in the early twentieth-century Iran, one passage from Baha'ullah's writings became the centrepiece of the anti-constitutional discourse of Shaykh Faḍlullāh Nūrī and other conservative supporters of autocratic rule. In this passage, taken from the *Kitāb-i Aqdas*, and therefore composed at the beginning of the 1870s, Baha'ullah appears to predict the advent of a constitutional government in

Iran, through which, he says, power will fall into the hands of the people. Addressing Tehran, Baha'ullah writes:

> Erelong will the state of affairs within thee be changed, and the reins of power fall into the hands of the people [*sawfa tanqalibu fī-kī al-umūr wa yaḥkumu 'alay-ki jumhūr al-nās*].
>
> (Baha'ullah 1993: 54)

Leading anti-constitutional clerics (such as Shaykh Faḍlullāh Nūrī and Sayyid 'Alī Yazdī) are said to have recited these verses of the *Kitāb-i Aqdas* from pulpits inciting anti-Baha'i and anti-constitutional sentiments in their audience.[6]

The advent of democratic rule in Iran was consistent with Baha'ullah's vision for society. He taught the virtues of a constitutional government, and praised constitutional and parliamentary monarchy:

> Although a republican form of government profiteth all the peoples of the world, yet the majesty of kingship is one of the signs of God. We do not wish that the countries of the world should remain deprived thereof. If the sagacious combine the two forms into one, great will be their reward in the presence of God.
>
> (Baha'ullah 1978b: 28)

The Baha'i religion emerged out of the milieu of autocratic and despotic Qajar Iran, nevertheless it strongly advocated for a democratic and constitutional government. The Baha'i community in Iran anticipated constitutionalism, Baha'i scripture claimed historical 'agency' for it and the enemies of the Baha'i Faith in Iran associated constitutionalism, in unmistakable terms, with the weakening of the pillars of autocratic rule.[7] Baha'ullah's admonition against despotic rule is further evidenced from the following passage where Baha'ullah writes about the necessity for reform in Iran and the need for a parliament of the people to be established:

> O people of God! . . . Certain laws and principles are necessary and indispensable for Persia. However, it is fitting that these measures should be adopted in conformity with the considered views of His Majesty – may God aid him through His grace – and of the learned divines and of the high-ranking rulers. Subject to their approval a place should be fixed where they would meet. There they should hold fast to the cord of consultation and adopt and enforce that which is conducive to the security, prosperity, wealth and tranquility of the people. For were any measure other than this to be adopted, it could not but result in chaos and commotion.
>
> (Baha'ullah 1978b: 92–3)

These passages were written in 1890 (at the same time as the Tobacco Protests in Iran) and they strongly endorse checks on the power of monarchy through the establishment of an elected parliament representing the views of the people. Even at that late stage in Iranian history and in the thick of the Tobacco Revolt that many consider the 'virtual dress rehearsal' for the Constitutional Revolution, one does not find within the writings and pamphlets of the discontent a systematic pattern for reform. The Baha'i discourses on the Constitutional Revolution were premised on these two points that Baha'ullah raised in the above passage: firstly, the necessity of parliamentary rule, and secondly, the 'chaos and commotion' which would ensue if parliamentary rule did not come about.

Baha'i attitudes towards the Constitutional Revolution

There have been a variety of Baha'i discourses on the Constitutional Movement, which I will now discuss. This variety is described by E.G. Browne in a piece entitled 'Attitude of Baha'is towards Persian Politics.' He writes:

> The attitudes adopted by the Babi, or rather the Baha'i, leaders towards the Constitutional Movement in Persia is a matter on which I have not been able to satisfy myself. I have heard three views advanced. . . .
>
> (Browne 1995: 424)

The first of the three views expounded by Browne is one of sympathetic neutrality where the Baha'is (though in favour of the Movement) refrain from politics due to the fact that the goals of the Baha'i religion were 'wholly spiritual' and that if their 'support' for the Constitution became known it 'would tend to prejudice it in the eyes of the orthodox Shi'a' (Browne 1995: 424). The second view is the one referred to earlier where Baha'is presumed historical agency not only for the Constitutional Movement, but also 'the general awakening of Asia.' The third view is that Baha'is were 'opposed to the Constitution' partly because they wished to curry favour with the Shah and partly because of their gratitude to Russia. Browne does not examine the three competing alternatives, but he does conclude that 'from the Baha'is little active support or sympathy can be expected by the Persian Nationalist' (Browne 1995: 429).

Primary and secondary sources on the Constitutional Revolution have since marginalized the Baha'i involvement into inertness and inactivity or anti-constitutional sentiments. For example Kasravī is a prominent exponent of the Russophile myth. He has opined:

> . . . Baha'is were supporters of autocracy and the Azalis were supporters of constitutionalism.

> The story goes that after Mīrzā Ḥusayn-'Alī made a claim and created a sect the Russians supported him in Iran and the Caucasus. Baha'ullah also demonstrated Russian leanings in his writings . . . [later on] as the Russian Empire showed hostility towards constitutionalism the Baha'is distanced themselves from the movement and supported Muḥammad-'Alī [Shah].
>
> (Kasravī 1354: 291)

In reality the historical data is much more complicated than either Browne or Kasravī have conceded. It is curious that Kasravī attributes pro-constitutionalist sentiments to the Azalis, despite the fact that little is found in the writings of Yaḥyā Azal that can be interpreted as supportive of constitutionalism. Neither Browne nor Kasravī take note of the writings of Baha'ullah on constitutional governance cited above. Furthermore, a study of 'Abdu'l-Baha's letters to Persian Baha'is indicates that the events in Iran had been referred to as revolution (*inqilāb*) as early as 1905 (Māzandarānī 1982: 442–43). In non-Baha'i contemporary sources the preferred term seems to have been *bīdārī* ('awakening'), rather than *inqilāb*. In non-Baha'i texts, *inqilāb* began to be used to describe the revolution only after 1910, around the same time as the publication of Browne's *The Persian Revolution*. The fact that the Baha'is made use of the term *inqilāb* at such an early stage is significant because of its deliberate association with the language of the verse from the *Kitāb-i Aqdas* in which Baha'ullah spoke of the establishment of constitutional rule in Iran. It also suggests that Baha'is expected the revolution to result in much more sustained and profound changes in governance and the structure of society, even at a stage when Iranian intelligentsia and reformers did not have a clear ideological vision of where the 'awakening' was heading.

As mentioned above, the Baha'i discourse on the Revolution was not static and uniform during the 1905–1914 period. From 1905 to 1907 the Baha'is, while anticipating the advent of constitutionalism, refrained from active participation in the social unrest. By 1905, and in response to the commotion in Iran, 'Abdu'l-Baha had one of his earlier works, the *Risāla-yi Siyāsiyya* ('Treatise on Politics', written in 1892) reprinted in Iran (Āyati 1914: 164).[8] In it 'Abdu'l-Baha had presented a strong case for the separation of the functions of religion and politics. He reiterated the same theme repeatedly in letters that were sent to Iranian Baha'is during this period. 'Abdu'l-Baha attempted to navigate a particularly difficult course of political neutrality, as it was essential for the creation of a cohesive society, a prerequisite for sustainable democratic reform, which was 'Abdu'l-Baha's grand vision for Iran.

In support, Baha'is at the time commented that the surest way to safeguard the Constitutional Movement was for it not to be associated with the Baha'is or their religion.[9] Later Baha'i historians have argued along similar lines. For example, the historian Hasan Balyuzi writes:

> 'Abdu'l-Baha's counsel was far from ambiguous, and the whole issue was crystal clear. Yet it seems that Edward Browne could not see the question in its true light. The general tenor and tone of this note in the appendices to his book on the Persian Revolution bears out that regrettable fact. As a fervent admirer and supporter of the Constitutional Movement, Edward Browne ought also to have realized that the surest way of damning the same movement in the eyes of the public was to associate it in any manner with the Baha'i community. It would have been stampeded out of existence.
>
> (Balyuzi 1973: 92)

A survey of the texts written by 'Abdu'l-Baha to Persian Baha'is from 1905–1909 reveals that the Baha'is had been under tremendous pressure (by pro-constitutional forces) to join the nationalist fronts. The Baha'is in Iran were also clearly enthusiastic and interested in a more active stance. Nevertheless 'Abdu'l-Baha refrained from allowing Baha'is to interfere in politics prior to 1909 and in so doing spared giving the anti-constitutional forces the much needed anti-Baha'i rhetoric. The history of the Constitutional Movement was already replete with anti-Baha'i polemics by anti-constitutional forces. The leading supporters of autocracy such as Shaykh Faḍlullāh Nūrī would invoke anti-constitutional sentiments by linking the constitutionalists with the Baha'i Faith. Important examples of such linking are cited by both Browne and Kasravī.[10] The evidence that Nūrī quoted the verses from the *Kitāb-i Aqdas* provoking anti-constitutional polemics was presented earlier. The letters of Shaykh Faḍlullāh Nūrī, known as the *Lawā'iḥ*, follow similar polemics. Baha'is had been attacked by pro-autocracy forces from 1905–1909 in Kirman, Khurasan, Tabriz and Qum.[11] The forces of Muḥammad-'Alī Shah also often attacked the Baha'is, especially during his failed attempt to invade Iran. In one particular episode in Mazandaran, a number of Baha'is were killed early in 1912 because of their alleged association with constitutionalism.[12] Therefore the thesis that Baha'is were Russophile and had anti-constitutional leanings is not supported by a close examination of the sources. In fact the reverse is true and ample sacred texts suggested otherwise to Baha'is. The above is further supported by a study of the letters written by 'Abdu'l-Baha during this period. 'Abdu'l-Baha, however, strongly mandated the Baha'is to become agents of national unity, and to repair the fragmentation of the society. He also taught that obedience is due to constitutional governments (*ḥukūmat-i mashrūṭa*) and to just governments (*ḥukūmat-i 'ādila*) that protect the human rights of all men (*ḥuqūq-i 'umūm-i bashar*) ('Abdu'l-Baha 1921: 388).

Muẓaffar al-Dīn Shah was praised by both 'Abdu'l-Baha and the Baha'is for the granting of the Constitution in 1906. Furthermore 'Abdu'l-Baha praised the formation of the Majlis in the strongest of terms.[13] In a letter written after the death of Muẓaffar al-Dīn Shah, 'Abdu'l-Baha praised the late monarch and expressed the hope that his newly crowned son Muḥammad-'Alī Shah would follow in his footsteps. In fact, Muḥammad-'Alī did sign the Constitution and early in his reign he upheld it. Most of the contemporary historical accounts have treated Muḥammad-'Alī Shah as an anti-constitutionalist, which probably represents a later reconstruction of his early position. While there is little doubt that Muḥammad-'Alī was not a constitutionalist at heart, but it was only later that he moved towards an overt anti-constitutional position. His increasingly conservative stance came from the growing influence of Shaykh Faḍlullāh Nūrī and conservative members of the court, combined with the increased radicalization of the people and the Majlis; this process accelerated in the aftermath of the attempt to assassinate him. There is a letter dated June 1908 by the Muḥammad-'Alī Shah that demonstrates that he distanced himself from the constitutional government on grounds of the Babi and Baha'i influences on constitutionalism, and in order to prevent the Baha'is gaining religious freedom (Dawlatābādī 1992: 358–59). By 1908 Muḥammad-'Alī decided to reestablish autocratic rule and moved against the Majlis in June of that year. During the 'Lesser Autocracy' (1908–1909) the sharp rhetoric of anti-constitutionalist forces was continually directed towards the Baha'is. Nevertheless, the Baha'is maintained their political neutrality. Again, the historical narratives left by contemporary Baha'is indicate that their understanding was that the neutrality of the Baha'is was intended to protect the Constitutional Movement. It was 'Abdu'l-Baha's intention that Baha'is become agents of social cohesiveness in Iran, bridging the *dawlat-millat* divide, and this vision required that the Baha'is maintain a neutral political position. Finally, it should be noted that the Baha'is did not seek to move closer to the government of Muḥammad-'Alī Shah during the 'Lesser Autocracy'. One can conclude that both Browne and Kasravī have taken their data from 1905–1908 and ignored important evidence pre-1905 and post-1908.

How, then, can the Baha'i discourses towards the Constitutional Movement be understood? Were the Baha'is simply interested (or disinterested) bystanders? Or did 'Abdu'l-Baha have a vision of the needs of the country and did he present a master-narrative? A study of 'Abdu'l-Baha's writings during this period indicate two concerns, one the fragmentation of the Iranian society, and the other increasing foreign intervention. It was suggested earlier that in 'Abdu'l-Baha's writings composed during the period of 1905–1913 we find stress placed upon the necessity for unity and accord between the government (*dawlat*) and the people (*millat*). The overarching mandate for the Iranian Baha'is during these years seems to have been to attempt to bring the two closer. In early 1912, 'Abdu'l-Baha wrote in relation to 'the agitations in Iran and of the Iranians.' He states that since in the beginning of the Revolution, he had repeatedly given 'unambiguous expositions' to both parties indicating that 'the government and the people should blend together like honey and milk otherwise deliverance and success are impossible' and Iran would be ruined and that neighbouring countries would intervene in its affairs. 'Abdu'l-Baha then states that the Baha'is should endeavour to reconcile the government and the people, and be a cause of 'healing'. He adds that should they fail, they should withdraw altogether. He warns that the blood of a single Iranian should not be shed. He then states that, in private, he had given advice to the parties concerned but they had completely rejected it 'and intensified confrontations, disputes and the shedding of blood.' He concludes by saying that uninformed leaders and a company of the foolish had intervened in the affairs of state ('Abdu'l-Baha 1975: 173–176).

Herein is the key to the Baha'i discourses on the Constitutional Movement. No genuinely democratic movement would have been possible within the fractured Iranian society of 1905–1913. 'Abdu'l-Baha's often repeated solution was that 'the government and the people should blend together like honey and milk otherwise deliverance and success is impossible.'

'Abdu'l-Baha was aware of the developments in tsarist Russia especially in the aftermath of the 1905 Revolution, and the formation of the Duma. He saw developments in Iran and Russia as moving in a parallel direction. A study of the Russian revolution of 1905 and the first two sessions of the state Duma provides additional insights into 'Abdu'l-Baha's policies. In a text written in 1907, 'Abdu'l-Baha praised the formation of the Majlis in most glowing terms.[14] At the end of this piece he makes a reference to the Russian Duma, and the increasing 'conflict and opposition' between the people and the government. He warns Iranians not to act as the Russians had done once the parliament was formed. In fact the Russian revolution of 1905 and its 'new political order' had been defeated by the 1907 conservative backlash. One notes the development of an 'unbridgeable gap' in 1905–1907 Russia, due to the increased radicalization of the populace, especially the Russian peasants and workers, combined with the unyielding and autocratic positions of the Nicholas II. As John Morrison has pointed out, 'for the new system to work, a spirit of conciliation and cooperation was necessary from both sides' (Morrison 1999: 145). This was notably absent from both Russia and Iran during the first two parliaments. The state Duma was marred from its opening ceremony, when the Tsar's speech was met with disrespect. Contemporary sources describe the Duma as 'full of hate and malice.' Even the 'intelligentsia' was said to be 'swamped by the "boiling energy" of the "black masses"' (Morrison 1999: 146). The increasing radicalization in the first and second Duma created in Nicholas II an even fiercer dislike for any checks on his powers. The outcome was inevitable: he came to see the Duma and constitutionalism as the enemy itself resulting in the 1907 'constitutional coup.' 'Abdu'l-Baha's fears in this regard proved justified. The developments in Iran and Russia would remain parallel for some time, with conservative reactions following early constitutionalist success.

'Abdu'l-Baha's policy was consistent in this regard. On a later occasion (24 March 1913), during his stay in Paris, 'Abdu'l-Baha dispatched two

Baha'is[15] with copies of the *Kitāb-i Aqdas* and the *Kitāb-i Mubīn*[16] to visit two Iranian dignitaries resident in Paris to show them specific verses of Baha'ullah regarding Iran and other countries and reportedly instructs them as follows:

> Recite for them the exact verses and inform them that forty years before this revolution the Supreme Pen had openly predicted these happenings and these have been printed in Bombay twenty-three years ago and are now dispersed in all lands. The passages addressing the Ottomans are extremely harsh however the passages addressing Iran speak of calm and safety after significant upheavals. It is clear that that which has occurred to this point has been according to that which has been revealed by the Supreme Pen. This to such an extent that in Tehran and Shiraz when the enemies attempted to propagate a selfish agenda and attack Baha'is recited the *Kitāb-i-Aqdas* from the pulpits and said that this [Constitutional] Revolution and the current events are predicted in this book and the Baha'is have caused these commotions and uprisings to bring about its fulfillment. However from the beginning of the Revolution the clear utterances of the Centre of the Covenant ['Abdu'l-Baha] to Baha'is was of the nature that until and unless the government and the people become intermixed like milk and honey salvation and success are impossible. Iran would be ruined and it would eventually lead to the intervention of foreign powers in Iran. Therefore, O Baha'is endeavor to bring complete unity and healing between the government and the people and if you fail then withdraw altogether. Beware! Beware! Lest you cause the blood of a single Iranian to spill.
>
> (Zarqānī 1987: 197, provisional translation)

He repeatedly emphasized that Baha'is should avoid the shedding of any blood. Most of 'Abdu'l-Baha's instructions during this period as well as the three letters that Browne produced in *The Persian Revolution* reiterate the same point: 'Abdu'l-Baha was concerned that given the divergence of the government and the people, the Constitutional Movement will fail and foreign powers will meddle in Iranian affairs:

> As regards what you wrote touching the intervention in the affairs of Persia of the neighboring States, time upon time it hath been declared by the Pen of the Covenant that the Government and the People should mix together like honey and milk, else the field will be open for maneuvers of others, and both parties will regret it. But alas! The two parties would not give ear, but have brought matters to this perilous pitch!
>
> (cited in Browne 1995: 426)

'Abdu'l-Baha's most audacious plan for bringing about such an outcome occurred around July 1911. It was at this period time that 'Abdu'l-Baha encouraged the Iranian Baha'is to obtain membership in the Majlis (parliament). At this point in Iranian history the country had witnessed the vanishing of the autocratic rule (*istibdād*). The country was increasingly radicalized by a social democratic movement (referred to by 'Abdu'l-Baha as *inqilābiyyūn*, 'the revolutionaries', but known in Iran also as the political party '*Ijtimā'iyyūn*'),[17] which presented a generally progressive agenda with regards to education, individual liberties and land reform. Consequently the moderates (referred to as *i'tidāliyyūn*) became the new right. Growing tensions between the 'moderates' and the radicalized 'revolutionaries' led to the unfortunate developments of December 1911 that culminated in the collapse of the Revolution. In an important letter written in June 1911, 'Abdu'l-Baha wrote to Persian Baha'is and authorized the candidacy of a few prominent Baha'is. He states that with regards to the membership in the Majlis, the 'friends' should with all their might rise to the service of the government (*dawlat*) and the people (*millat*) and act with 'utmost honesty and well-wishing and purity and liberty'. He then asserts that 'the Hands of the Cause of God must at any cost become members of the Majlis' (*'Abdu'l-Baha* 1908: 263).

Again one notes the overarching theme of unifying the government and the people. As an aside 'Abdu'l-Baha's plans to have Baha'is (and in this text the 'Hands'[18] specifically) represent the Baha'i voice in the second Majlis never materialized. Prior to 1911 the Baha'is had been barred given that electoral law (passed on 1 July 1909) did not permit non-Muslims either to elect (Section II, 5, iv) or be elected (Section III, 7, i) (Browne, 1911: 386–87). During the tenure of the second Majlis a successful attempt was made to make the exclusive language less strict.[19] The law was changed to state that one's abandonment of Islam must be proven in the presence of a *shari'a* judge (Ittiḥādiyya 1996: 150–1). This was meant to set a less enforceable standard and clearly more difficult to challenge. The reason for this change was probably to protect the candidates of the Democratic Party from charges of abandoning religion and disqualification (as was the case with Taqīzāda). This text may have been written after a change in electoral law had been debated in the parliament creating possibilities for Baha'i candidates. The most accurate dating for this tablet is June 1911.[20]

The text of this letter makes it abundantly clear that 'Abdu'l-Baha desired that the Iranian Government and people become unified ('Abdu'l-Baha n.d.: 257–263). During this period the latent tensions within Iranian society had given rise to out and out factional infighting that lead to a paralysis in the day-to-day affairs of the country. Unfortunately for the Iranian nation the absence of the unifying presence of Baha'is caused increasing fragmentation and fractionation of the Iranian society until December 1911 when 'Abdu'l-Baha's repeated warnings of foreign intervention in Iran materialized when the Russian army invaded Iran and forced the annulment of the parliament.

In the aftermath of 1911 the parliament was not reelected until 1914. By 1913 the window of opportunity opened in 1911 had been closed. A possible factor was the internal dynamics of the Iranian Baha'i community. There is ample evidence that, by 1913, 'Abdu'l-Baha was receiving many cables and letters from Iranian Baha'is requesting permission to seek candidacy in the third Majlis. In 1911, 'Abdu'l-Baha had allowed only for the 'Hands of the Cause' to seek parliamentary seats, with the possible exception of Shaykh al-Ra'īs. He now faced the spectacle of many prominent Baha'is running in an election. 'Abdu'l-Baha possibly foresaw that this could have lead to undesirable consequences, where a small Baha'i community would have too many candidates running against each other, reducing the real chance of any Baha'i representation. More importantly much of the revolutionary fervour was lost. The coup had demonstrated that the Great Powers would always trump any genuine indigenous movement. The influence of the Great Powers had markedly increased in both the government and in the third Majlis. It was clear to 'Abdu'l-Baha by 1913 that the Iranian parliament would be stacked with representatives speaking for the interests of Britain and Russia. His post-1911 public statements and letters to individual Baha'is clearly demonstrate the disillusionment 'Abdu'l-Baha must have suffered. Hence in a 1913 cablegram sent from Alexandria Egypt to Muḥammad-'Alī Davā-Furūsh in Tehran, 'Abdu'l-Baha reversed the direct involvement policy set in 1911. The cable read: 'Seek divine good-pleasure, not membership in the Parliament' (Zarqānī 1987: 370).

Conclusion

The traditional approach involving either marginalization of the Baha'i role in the Constitutional Movement or ascribing anti-constitutional sentiments is not supported by a close examination of the historical sources. It is essential to note as background that Iranian Baha'is were subjects of the government and not citizens. The Constitutional Movement provided an opportunity for the Iranian Baha'i minority to make its presence felt. From the 1870s, the Baha'is had pursued a progressive vision for Iran outlined by Baha'ullah and 'Abdu'l-Baha. During the constitutional period (1905–1909), the Baha'is navigated a course of political neutrality even though the Baha'is as a whole were anticipating constitutional rule and expected it. By 1913 'Abdu'l-Baha, who had become disillusioned with the aftermath of the Iranian Constitutional Revolution, changed his directives to the Iranian Baha'i community. His disappointment is evident in the letters written after 1913. It can be said that the Iranian Baha'i community was unsuccessful in any long term and sustained generation of social cohesiveness in the nation.

In the aftermath of 1913, the Iranian Baha'i community adopted a course of political non-involvement. The much anticipated historical transition from subject to citizen did not materialize and Baha'is did not emerge as a force within Iranian politics. It is not surprising that the disappointment suffered by Baha'is in the aftermath of the Constitutional Revolution has proven determinative in the attitude of the Baha'is towards Iranian politics. The failure of the Constitutional Revolution has exerted a lasting effect on the Iranian Baha'i community.

Notes

1 The terms *mashrūṭiyyat* and *mashrū'iyyat* appear to have been coined by Mīrzā Yūsuf Khān Mustashār al-Dawla and Mīrzā Malkum Khān in the 1870s. According to Bayat they 'coined the terms "mashrūṭiyyat" (constitutionalism) and "mashrū'iyyat" (from *sharī'at*, the holy law) and argued that the two concepts, far from being incompatible, were in fact identical in spirit' (Bayat 1991: 38).

2 See Smith 2000: 308: 'Written in 1875, the work was lithographed in Bombay in 1882 and received wide circulation in Iran. It was published anonymously and not identified as a specifically Baha'i work – presumably to avoid prejudicing readers against its contents. The first English translation was published in 1910 in London as *The Mysterious Forces of Civilization.*'

3 See Saiedi 1993 for a study of the comparative political theory in this treatise. For a comparative analysis of the *Risāla-yi madaniyya* and Mustashār al-Dawla's reformist treatise, *Yik kalama* ('one word', 1870), see Cole 1998: 81–87.

4 Checks and balances are not to be confused, as they are quite distinct. See Schechter 1990: 272–6 for an exploration of these terms in the context of the United States Constitution.

5 For a discussion of the significance of 'Abdu'l-Baha's reference, see Tavakoli-Targhi 2002: 217–238.

6 See 'Alāqband n.d.: 123 and 201. Also see Kasravī 1974: 681 for similar anti-Baha'i and anti-constitutional polemics.

7 On the issue of historical 'agency' it is important to note that the relevant verses were well known to Baha'is before the 1905–1911 period. Some tablets written by 'Abdu'l-Baha suggest that the development of the Constitutional Movement in Iran was consequent to the Baha'i teachings enumerated above, see Māzandarānī 1982, vol. 4: 442–9. See also Browne 1995: 424 where Browne attributes the following words to a 'sympathetic and discerning journalist who spent a considerable time in Persia': 'Not only the Constitutional Movement in Persia, but the general awakening of Asia, was the direct outcome of this new spiritual force known as Bābism or Baha'ism.'

8 On 'Abdu'l-Baha's *Risāla-yi Siyāsiyya*, see Smith 2000: 273.

9 See Āyatī 1914: 165 and Afrūkhta 1983: 539.

10 See Kasravī 1975: 681 and Browne 1911: 168.

11 Āyatī, 1914: 172–176.

12 Janet Afary gives 17 July 1911 as the date when Muḥammad-'Alī Shah landed on the eastern Caspian shore in an attempt to retake power (Afary 1996: 321). According to Fāḍil Māzandarānī, the mob style attacks by anti-constitutional forces and provoked populace occurred in January 1912. See Māzandarānī 1974: 801–14 for a detailed account of these events.

13 For an English translation of a tablet of 'Abdu'l-Baha on the election of the first Majlis see http://www2.hnet.msu.edu/~bahai/trans/vol2/abparl/abconst.htm.

14 See text translated by Juan Cole, *Translations of Shaykhi, Babi and Baha'i Texts*, vol. 2, no. 7 (October 1998), online at http://www2.h-net.msu.edu/~bahai/trans/vol2/abparl/abconst.htm.

15 Mīrzā Maḥmūd Zarqānī and Āqā Sayyid Aḥmad.
16 One of Baha'ullah's tablets that includes passages addressed to the leaders of different countries.
17 Literally 'socialists'.
18 The *ayādī-yi amrullāh* ('Hands of the Cause of God') were individual Baha'is appointed by Baha'ullah to assist in the propagation and protection of the Baha'i Faith.
19 Ittiḥādiyya gives Shavvāl 1329 AH (October 1911) for the debates on this issue in the Majlis (Ittiḥādiyya 1996: 150–1).
20 Memorandum from Baha'i World Centre, Haifa, Israel dated 3 May 1998. I am grateful to Mina Yazdani for providing me with a copy of this letter.

Bibliography

'Abdu'l-Baha. (1908) *Makātīb-i 'Abdu'l-Baha*, vol. 2, Cairo: Kurdī.
—— (1921) *Makātīb-i 'Abdu'l-Baha*, vol. 3, Cairo: Kurdī.
—— (1975) *Makātīb-i 'Abdu'l-Baha*, vol. 5, Tehran: Mu'assasa-yi Millī-yi Maṭbū'āt-i Amrī.
—— (1982) *Promulgation of Universal Peace: Talks Delivered by 'Abdu'l-Bahá During His Visit to the United States and Canada in 1912*, Comp. H. McNutt, Wilmette: Baha'i Publishing Trust.
—— (1990) *The Secret of Divine Civilization*, translated by M. Gail, and 'Ali-Kuli Khan, Wilmette: Baha'i Publishing Trust.
—— (n.d.) *Majmū'a-yi Mubāraka*, Manuscript edition by 'Alī-Akbar Mīlānī. Digitally reprinted, East Lansing. Mi; H-Bahai, 2002; online at http://www.h-net.org/~bahai/areprint/ab/M-R/M/milani/milani.htm, accessed 6 October 2006.
Afary, J. (1996) *The Iranian Constitutional Revolution 1906–1911*, New York; Colombia University Press.
Afrūkhta, Y.K. (1983) *Khāṭirāt-i nuh-sāla*, Los Angeles: Kalimat Press.
'Alāqa-band, M. (n.d.) *Tārīkh-i Ḥājj Āqā Muḥammad 'Alāqa-band-i Yazdī*, online at: http://www.2.h-net.msu.edu, accessed 6 October 2006.
Āyatī, A.H. (1914) *al-Kawākib al-durriyya*, vol. 2, Cairo: Sa'ādat.
Baha'ullah. (1978a) *Proclamation of Bahá'u'lláh*, Haifa: Baha'i World Centre.
—— (1978b) *Tablets of Bahá'u'lláh Revealed after the Kitāb-i-Aqdas*, translated by Taherzadeh, H. et al. Wilmette: Baha'i Publishing Trust.
—— (1983) *Kitāb-i Aqdas*, Haifa: Baha'i World Centre.
Bakhash, S. (1977) 'The Evolution of Qajar Bureaucracy: 1779–1879' in *Middle Eastern Studies*, 7: 139–167.
Balyuzi, H.M. (1973) *E.G. Browne and the Bahá'á Faith*, Oxford: George Ronald.
Bayat, M. (1991) *Iran's First Revolution*, Oxford: Oxford University Press.
Browne, E.G. (1995) *The Persian Revolution of 1905–1909*, Reprint, Washington: Mage Publishers.
Cole, J.R.I. (1998) *Modernity and the Millenium: The Genesis of the Baha'i Faith in the Nineteenth-Century Middle East*, New York: Columbia University Press.
Dawlatābādī, Y. (1992) *Ḥayāt-i Yaḥyā*, 4 vols, Tehran: Firdaws Publishers.
Gail, M. (1991) *Arches of the Years*, Oxford: George Ronald.
Ittiḥādiyya, M. (1995) *Majlis va Intikhābāt*, Tehran: Nashr-i Tārīkh.
Kasravī, A. (1979) *Tārīkh-i Mashrūṭa-yi Iran*, Tehran: Amir Kabir.

Kirmānī, N. (1978) *Tārīkh-i bīdārī-yi Irānīān*, Sa'īdī Sīrjānī, A.A. (ed.), Tehran: Lawḥ.
Mallon, F. (1995) *Peasant and Nation: The Making of Postcolonial Mexico and Peru*, Los Angeles: University of California Press.
Māzandarānī, A. (1974) *Tārīkh Ẓuhūr al-Ḥaqq* vol. 8, Tehran: Baha'i Publishing Trust.
—— (1982) *Amr va Khalq* vols 1–4, Langenhain: Baha'i-Verlag.
Morrison, J. (1988) 'The State Duma: A Political Experiment,' in A. Geifman, *Russia Under the Last Tsar: Opposition and Subversion 1894–1917*, Oxford: Blackwell Publishers.
Mustashār al-Dawla. (n.d.) *Yik Kalama*.
Saiedi, N. (1993) *Risāla-i madaniyya va mas'ala-yi tajaddud dar Khāvar-i Mīāna*, Dundas, Ontario: Persian Institute for Baha'i Studies.
Schechter, S. (1990) *Roots of the Republic*, Madison: Madison House.
Shuster, W.M. (1978) *The Strangling of Persia*, Washington: Mage Publishers.
Smith, P. (2000) *A Concise Encyclopedia of the Baha'i Faith*, Oxford: Oneworld.
Tavakoli-Targhi, M. (2002) 'From Patriotism to Matriotism: A Tropological Study of Iranian Nationalism, 1870–1909,' *International Journal of Middle Eastern Studies*, 34: 217–238.
Vahman, F. (1995) 'Ta'thīr-i diyānat-i Babi va Baha'i bar nihḍat-i rawshangarī-yi Iran' in *Khūsha-hā'ī az kharman-i adab va hunar*, vol. 6, Switzerland: Landegg Academy.
Zārqānī, M.M. (1987) *Badāyi' al-Āthār*, 2 vols, Langehain: Baha'i-Verlag.

7

THE COMPARATIVE DIMENSION OF THE BAHA'I CASE AND PROSPECTS FOR CHANGE IN THE FUTURE

Eliz Sanasarian

During a memorial gathering for those killed in the Iran–Iraq war, Ayatullah Aḥmad Jannatī, head of the powerful Guardian Council, was quoted as saying: 'Humans who follow anything but Islam are the same as those animals who wander about and commit corruption.' In an immediate official press release, the Zoroastrian deputy to the Majlis (parliament), Kūrush Nīknām, criticized Jannatī's remarks in the strongest terms. His rebuttal had three distinguishing characteristics, all reflective of the past responses of officially recognized religious minorities and in this case particularly the Zoroastrians (Sanasarian 2000: Chapter 5). He cited Article 13 of the constitution which grants recognition to the Zoroastrian, Jewish, and Christian members of the society; he reasserted that the religion of Islam does not recognize such distinction among humans (elevating and separating Islam from those who speak in its name); and disputed the points raised in the lecture:

> I apologize from the wise spirit of our ancestors that they have been insulted in such a manner. Because not only they were not animals and caused no corruption, but on the contrary, with their intelligence and endeavor were the founders and spreaders of a culture and civilization of the time. Certainly, the followers of other non-Muslim religions are cultured and learned people. In the end, I would like to apologize from animals as well, because they are not the cause of any corruption on the earth. In fact, they might be concerned and disgusted by the corruption of some of us humans.

Within days, a criminal decree was issued and he was summoned to court. Reportedly, several university faculty had complained about his remarks. Mr. Nīknām was accused of defaming and spreading lies.[1] This event illustrates a host of critical issues in the ongoing saga of Muslim and non-Muslim diatribe in the Islamic Republic of Iran, regardless of whether they are officially recognized or not by the state.

Ayatullah Jannatī's remarks may be dismissed as the utterances of an extremist, not reflective of either the state or the society. This has often been the position of many, including some in the intellectual circles of the West. Therefore, it is important to first address this issue, namely why the dismissal is wrong, and even more significantly, what it tells us about the dismisser. Both are relevant to the scant treatment the Baha'i persecution (or even the persecution of Iranian Christian converts) has received by those who dismiss Jannatī-type comments. Next, this article presents a comparative analysis of major non-Muslim minorities and offers suggestions for potential change in the future.

The meaning and the cause

Ayatullah Jannatī was not a regular *mulla* seated in the corner of an isolated village mosque. He was the head of the influential Guardian Council and remained a powerful player in Iranian politics. Labelling non-Muslimness as some form of derision from the normal human has been made many times before by those in a position of political authority. A host of such commentaries were either verbalized or written before and since the inception of the Islamic Republican regime (Sanasarian 2000: 24–27). Ayatullah Muṭahharī, a professor of theology and a member of the Revolutionary Council, tried at some length to explain why and how this inferiority was perpetuated by the refusal to convert to Islam (Muṭahharī 1970: 202–4, 240–1, 243, 247). Ayatullah Khumaynī's comments were more virulent; he politicized the argument. Among his many written and verbal comments, we were confronted with 'Jewish thieves' and 'monsters' who planned to take over the Muslim world. Along with the Baha'is, Jews were the oppressors of the Muslim people. Zoroastrians were 'fire-worshippers' and 'an old and inveterate sect' and he was not alone in calling the Zoroastrians the derogatory term *gabr*. Finally, he saw them all as 'stray sects' plotting against Islam (Sanasarian 2000: 27–30).

Baha'is have historically been targeted so often that non-persecution has fallen outside the realm of the normal. Defamatory labels such as 'perverted . . . instruments of Satan and followers of the Devil and of the superpowers and their agents. . . .' were commonly used (Martin 1984: 65–66). They have been accused many times (along with the Jews), of spying and 'warring against God', and 'corruption on earth' (Sanasarian 2000: 120).

The name-calling and outrageous statements did not cease during Muḥammad Khātamī's presidency, but recognizably their frequency and intensity increased with the election of President Maḥmūd Aḥmadīnijād. During a sermon broadcast on Iranian television in November 2005,

Ayatollah Aḥmad Jannatī, referring to troubles in France, said: 'Whenever we wanted to punish some mercenary Baha'i spies here, they [the West] would scream that the minorities in Iran are neglected, are not paid attention to, that their rights are violated, that there is discrimination in Iran, and that human rights are violated.'[2] Ayatullah Ḥusayn Nūrī-Hamadānī in a speech in April 2005 said: 'Fight the Jews and vanquish them so as to hasten the coming of the Hidden Imam.' His comments were so outrageous that several local news outlets removed them shortly afterward. In a departure from past behaviour, Morris Mu'tamid, the Jewish deputy, protested Hamadani's statements during a speech delivered in the Majlis (Report 2005: 20–1). President Aḥmadīnijād's speeches also attracted much attention for their blatant anti-Jewish and anti-Israel content (Ibid., 23 & *Los Angeles Times*, 2 January 2006). Similarly, as in the years just before the revolution and in the early years of the Islamic Republic, these comments do not distinguish between Zionism, Judaism, and Israel. Rejection of any criticism coming mainly from a host of international human rights organizations has also been similar to previous years, with reversal of accusations, cultural rights claims, and accusations of political conspiracy.[3]

History has shown that engagement in such verbal dehumanization by political authorities (with or without religious garb) is not without consequence. The laws and policies enacted after the revolution were closely on par with their pronouncements and belief systems. But it has also been shown that there were others, covering a wide political spectrum (left, liberal, moderate/reformist Islamists, nationalist, secular, or some convenient combination thereof) who were soundboards for similar sentiments. They took it upon themselves to write about and claim expertise on minorities and even advise minorities what was in their best interest. The stereotypical views on non-Muslims, particularly of the Jews and the Baha'is, were not abandoned (Sanasarian 2000: 109). These stereotypes could often be categorized as bizarre. In a book entitled *Knowing Thy Self or the Secrets of Food*, the author states: 'The Jews consume much sesame [*kunjid*] and are therefore very shrewd [*zīrak*]' (Jazāyirī 1999: 273). The sentence appears out of nowhere, in the midst of a discussion on food and its effect on the body.

The stereotypical views of the religious minorities do not evaporate with any of the obvious factors and manifestations attributed to modernism and Westernism such as higher education, marriage to a Westerner, acquiring an academic position in the West, or even mingling with a minute number of people from minority religious backgrounds. Fundamental perspectives do not easily undergo a major transformation. 'Major transformation' here means not having or holding onto a sense of entitlement, a belief in one's own superiority over others based purely on pigmentation or ethnic/cultural/religious factors.

This is the domain of the subtle and complex, often belonging to the intellectual class. It is not by any means limited to the Iranian milieu; by most accounts this phenomenon has existed everywhere, including in the Western world. Jean-Paul Sartre, in a strong attack on the French intellectuals who harboured anti-Jewish views, argued that the bigot has strong convictions because he has chosen to be 'impervious'. The bigot's views, which are never limited to the Jews, are a combination of a concept of the world and a personal passion. The Jew-hater is not without contradiction, however; 'sworn enemies of Israel' tended to surround themselves with 'Jewish friends' (Sartre 1999: 98–9, 104). Similar trends have been experienced in cases of blacks in the United States and others. The intellectual bigot can rationalize, ignore, and skilfully distort facts for personal gain.

According to William Brennan, the use of demeaning terms has a profound effect, and for too long have been taken lightly in intellectual circles. He sees 'name-calling as a strategy for justifying massive oppression', yet he acknowledges the tendency of many to be dismissive of outlandish expressions, seeing them 'as the ravings of crazed individuals and fringe groups' (Brennan 1995: Preface). Humans have great capacity to justify their words, but language has the potential to spread 'deception, illusion, misinformation, and falsehood' as well as violence (Ibid., 2). Serious scholarship has shown that historically, violence against Baha'is and Jews (and to a lesser extent other religious minorities) has been perpetuated initially by words, sermons, and false pronouncements.

Words should be seen as a force with the potential of unleashing powerful energy, positive or negative. Name-calling and stereotypes, through repetition, become accepted as truth with 'fully elaborated systems of concepts, beliefs, and myths' (Ibid., 12).

> Behind almost every escalation of linguistic derision is some kind of ideology: that is a philosophy, a social theory, a set of interrelated ideas, concepts, beliefs, and values that generate and sustain the dissemination of dehumanizing terminology.
>
> (Ibid., 11–12)

The existent hostility against the Baha'is was fuelled by the energy of the Revolution and its ideological elements. These ideological elements, whether religious or left or nationalist (or whatever-ist), shared a specific concept of the Baha'i Faith. Yet, ideas and actions did not materialize in a vacuum. According to Moojan Momen, whilst religious accusations were a characteristic of the early years of the Baha'i Faith, non-religious accusations dominated much of the twentieth century. Both stemming from the propensity of the Iranian society to 'believe and endorse conspiracy theories' (Momen 2004).

Dehumanizing language clearly transcends societies, cultures, and nations. Perhaps more than any other group, stereotypical views of the Jews have received close scrutiny (Helmreich 1982). These elaborate discussions shed some light on the global dynamics of hatred and prejudice. They also help us in seeking realistic solutions to their reduction, wherever and whenever possible.

There are many causes of harbouring prejudice, often revolving around the unexplored needs of the individual and society. Some believe that clarification of our needs (naturally present in most people) can help reduce, soften, or alleviate the negative engagement with others. One determinant is the need for 'self-justification', the need to justify our situation (e.g. lack of accomplishment). There can be other needs such as status and power. Competition and conflict can also breed prejudice (Aronson 1999). Our unfulfilled 'wants' provide a ripe environment for the rise of prejudice towards others.

Marshall Rosenberg, whose studies of individual, community, and inter- and intra-group conflict have been priceless, identifies several basic human needs across cultures and nations. They are: the need for autonomy (e.g. to choose one's dreams and goals), integrity (e.g. self-worth), celebration (e.g. creation of life), interdependence (e.g. emotional safety, trust), play (e.g. laughter), spiritual communion (e.g. peace, harmony), and physical nurturing (e.g. shelter, touch). The pain of not expressing these needs has serious consequences for the individual, community and nation (Rosenberg 2003).

Hate differs from prejudice, but time and time again it has provided the impetus for destruction and violence. Gordon Allport identifies three major contributing factors to hate: the amount of frustration experienced by the individual, the nature of the learning process in family and society, and a tendency to make life simpler by adopting an exclusionist approach to human relations (Allport 1999). Again, all of these can be traced to unfulfilled, unrecognized, unappreciated needs.

The above experts would say that those dismissive of outlandish remarks must ask themselves, what is it *in them* that perpetuates tolerance of dehumanizing phrases about non-Muslims (or women, or any other category of people)? What is it *in them* which allows and makes room for verbal violence upon the innate humanity of others?

In a similar but slightly different form, Sartre calls it 'an attitude totally and freely self-chosen' (Sartre 1999: 98). From this perspective, those who arrogantly dismiss Baha'i persecutions, or play them down, or remain silent, have *chosen* not only to ignore facts and figures, but, more importantly, they have ignored the devastating personal, social, and economic consequences which have befallen a collectivity of human beings. Even those who engage in stereotypical comments to belittle and/or to remove the non-Muslims from the competitive forum have *chosen* to hurt by design and are culprits in dehumanization. The expressed belief that the Jews are not loyal to Iran, or that the Armenians can never be fluent in the Persian language, are two of the most commonly held stereotypes.

There are scholars, however, who do not view 'choice' as a central point. They see prejudice (and even hate) as an attitude deeply ingrained in sociocultural structures and recommend consciousness-raising combined with an

Figure 7.1 The nine members of the National Spiritual Assembly of the Baha'is of Iran. Disappeared August 1980, presumed killed.

expansive definition of humanity (Brennan 1995: 15). Some scholars feel we should go beyond a discussion of socio-cultural reasoning; prejudicial sentiments are simply an extension of kinship networks: 'Ethnocentrism and racism are thus extended forms of nepotism – the propensity to favour kin over non-kin' (van den Berghe 1999: 141). This is an interesting perspective because, at least in terms of both the group nature of prejudice and discrimination and the resulting hurt to the victim, ethnocentrism closely resembles favouring of kin over non-kin. Both religious and nationalist discourses in Iran have exhibited these tendencies.

Ironically, the literature on change and transformation of prejudice is thin. In an extensive review article, Eberhardt and Fiske show that motivating individuals to change is anything but easy. Generally, people are resistant to change. Most importantly, change requires a contemplative existence and time for introspection. Busy and stressed lifestyles, competition, need for recognition/fame and the like, militate against reflection and the resulting potential change. They then ask whether a target person (or community) can bring about attitude change. The answer is disappointing. Despite proposing tactics, recommending thinking strategies and increasing the target's ability to detect danger signals, the experts conclude that the role of the target person or community is quite limited in changing the prejudicial environment or persons (Eberhardt & Fiske 1999: 369–415). In other words, no amount of expressed loyalty to Iran on the part of a Jew and no amount of fluency in Persian on the part of an Armenian can change the stereotype

Figure 7.2 Munā Maḥmūdnijād, 17, was one of ten Baha'i women executed in Shiraz on 18 June 1983. The primary charge against her: teaching Baha'i children's classes.

of the person or the community. The authors identify two factors for the inability of the target group to bring about change: (1) lack of control over resources, which contributes to the lack of ability to openly express one's attitudes, and (2) many researchers have been members of the dominant group who have not been victimized by prejudice, and despite the altruistic tendencies of some, again, the target group's voice has been left out (Ibid., 393–4).

The above studies (and many more) cover the causes of prejudice, discrimination and even hatred; some offer practical advice and others tell us that change does not come easily. However, since every change has a contextual component, the next section offers a comparative outlook on the historical status of non-Muslim minorities and suggests that the seeds of change are inherently present in Iranian polity.

The comparative dimension

The most critical distinguishing feature of the Baha'i Faith compared to other non-Muslim communities is its late birth and rise in the Iranian landscape.

The timing, namely its rise in the nineteenth century, had three interrelated consequences. First, it brought to the fore urgently needed progressive ideas about human liberation, ideas which were more directly and clearly expressed than ever before. Second, it inevitably got entangled with political and historical developments of the nineteenth century in the region. Third, having risen from amongst Shi'i Muslims as a post-Islamic religion, it violated the Islamic belief that the Prophet Muḥammad is the last of the prophets. None of the other major religious communities ever had to face such an intense and revolutionary experience in Iran. (The revolutionary contents of their faiths were tested and tried, each differently, in centuries past. None were there to offer a new manifestation of spiritual and temporal life.) From the beginning the challenges confronting the Babi-Baha'i adherents were immense.

In addition to their post-Islamic rise, other lesser factors intensified 'conspiratorial fantasies' about the Baha'is (Momen 2004). Baha'is did not belong to any particular ethnic group; they spoke the same language, and could not be identified by their names or specific geographical location. They were, therefore, 'the enemy within' who were welcoming converts into their faith (Sanasarian 2000: 123).

Historically, other communities existed side by side for centuries. Cultural links between the Armenians and the Persian Zoroastrians have received close attention. Despite the conversion to Christianity by one community and conversion to Islam by the other, the geographical and cultural ties remained. The significance of lingering cultural links, which appear today in various forms such as in language and ritual, is familiarity. Though familiarity evolves like everything else, facets still linger. Armenians were seen (and they liked to be seen) as a distinct community and often enjoyed a relative cultural and religious autonomy. Assyrians and Chaldeans had less of a clear ethnic identity due to their complex historical, social, and political evolution and the interplay of various Christian denominations of the East and the West. Some from among them were less distinct compared to the Armenians. Significant numbers of Assyrians were fluent in Armenian or intermarried with Armenians. Many Chaldeans spoke Persian as their first language. These factors increased the assimilative aspect of their communities. Regional concentrations (Assyrians in Adharbayjan and Chaldeans in Khuzistan) entangled each group in regional tensions. Yet, ultimately, they were viewed as Christians and shared much of their legal and social status with the numerous Armenians. Wherever their home base, Assyrians and Chaldeans were seen as Christian subjects adhering to the rules of the local governorates. Physical violence against the Christian population varied from place to place. For example, historically more violence occurred in the Adherbayjan region where foreign powers, Kurds, Azeris, and Christians often clashed, compared to the Isfahan region. Ethnic Christians have not lived without discrimination and stereotypical labeling, but the consequences have been less lethal in comparison with the Jews and the Baha'is.

Jews with a distinct identity lived in Persia as far back as 539 BCE. Their presence, therefore, pre-dates any segment of the Christian population. Jews of the area wrote in Judeo-Persian, classical Persian in Hebrew letters. Their prose and poetry clearly show the synthesis between the Jewish and Persian cultures. During the Islamic era, they shared many discriminatory laws and practices with other non-Muslims. Despite being people of the book and despite close cultural ties with the Iranian landscape, the Jews suffered more intense persecution and periodic violence compared with either the Christians or the Zoroastrians. Scholars have offered a host of explanations, which can be summarized in the following:

> (1) compared to the Christian population, they did not have the same strong backing and overall protection or intervention from the Western powers (and some missionary groups), and this turned them into an easy target; or (2) the local Christians shared the Muslims' bias against the Jews for one (or a combination) of these reasons: (a) their strong religious views, (b) anti-Jewish European ideologies, and (c) as non-Muslims were forced into vocational specializations due to their status, fierce economic competition resulted, and there was an incentive to eliminate Jewish competition from the local scene.
>
> (Sanasarian 2000: 46)

Compared to the ethnic Christian population, Jewish-Muslim intermarriages and business ventures were more prevalent in the mid-to-late twentieth century. By most expert accounts, the reign of Muḥammad Riḍā Shah, with heavy emphasis on nationalism, economic development, and closer ties to the West and Israel, had a positive direct impact on the status of the Jewish minority (Haddad 1984: 50; Sitton 1985: 184).

Zoroastrianism was the ancient religion of the Persians and its influence continued into modern times. Zoroastrians suffered the same restrictions as other non-Muslims and, like the Christians, their treatment differed from one locality to another. Modern Iranian nationalism of the twentieth century revolved around a particular take on the Zoroastrian past. This was an all-encompassing nationalism with a glorified past, embracing all non-Muslims and aggrandizing Persianism. (An issue of tension, if not always dissension, with a variety of ethno-national Muslim communities of Iran, e.g., Azeri, Baluch, Kurd.) Zoroastrians did not have to prove their loyalty to the nation. Their main challenge had always come from Twelver Shi'i purists.

Despite a mixed history, several peculiarities persist. First, cultural characteristics manifested in language, national rituals (e.g., celebration of the Persian New Year), customs, food, the arts and entertainment, and humour provide a natural common milieu and a strong bonding across religion. Second, a general tendency among the non-Muslims to play down stereotypes and their historical suffering and valuing their interpersonal relationship with the Muslim population. The reasons for this are many. It could be related to the deep gulf between the society and the state as well as the complexity and versatility of the society.

Why have attempts to change failed?

There has been little change in the legal and social status of either the Baha'is, Iranian Christian converts, or the recognized religious minorities. Despite numerous official protests by various governments, the United Nations, Human Rights Watch, Amnesty International, and other non-governmental groups and organizations, the inferior status of non-Muslims has been maintained.

Several Christian organizations have tried to set up and be involved in interfaith dialogue. The stated purpose has often been to draw the Islamic authorities (or their proponents) into a conversation about peace and understanding across religious divides. Yet none of the speakers ever directly addressed specific gross violations inside the country, nor did they seriously challenge the government representatives. The Baha'i case was never brought up, nor were the bigoted inheritance law,[4] and of course there has been silence on the violent oppression of the student movement.[5] By avoiding 'sensitive' topics, these conferences and symposia give rise to a host of questions: What is it that various religious figures wish to accomplish by such get-togethers? Do they hope that by engaging religious authorities in a 'dialogue', they can facilitate change? If the answer is affirmative, then the next logical step would be to assess their impact. How effective have they been, with all their meetings inside and outside Iran, in reducing oppression? Have they been used? Have they saved lives? Is religious statesmanship more effective than the activities of secular human rights organizations? This study can only raise these questions, since based on surface evidence, these 'dialogues' have not helped to bring about substantive change.

Every community at certain points in history needs people of courage whose most important characteristic is taking a stand for what is right. Most people do not take a stand because they do not want to suffer a loss. It is more convenient to resort to bargaining, some deal making, and projecting a positive image. But this is the communication domain of the merchant class; where are the dictates of conscience? The merchant class seeks maximum benefit with maximum convenience. It does not operate based on principle.

There are lessons to be learned from other Islamic countries, particularly Egypt where there has been a consistent history of intellectual debate. During the last two decades, a number of intellectuals have risked their lives in defense of the Coptic Christians. Faraq Foda argued in an essay that the official discrimination against Egyptian Christians has encouraged an atmosphere of intolerance leading to attacks by Muslim fundamentalists. In his moving last essay, he wrote:

> Say that the country is now for the Muslims only, and I have the courage, and I am a Muslim, to put my finger in your eyes, for Egypt belongs to all Egyptians. . . . I feel sorry for my country, that it will protect my son Yasir because he is a Muslim and treat another boy unjustly because he is a Christian.
>
> (*New York Times*, 10 November 1993, A19)

He was assassinated shortly after the publication of his essay.

Professor Saad Eddin Ibrahim suffered imprisonment for his open and clear stand against the oppression of the Christians.[6] Professor Khaled Abou El Fadl, a deeply devout Muslim, has focused on a masterful and thorough study of Islamic ethos in order to demonstrate the many falsehoods present today in Islam's interpretation. He, too, has suffered much in the process.[7] Are there lessons to be learned here?

Prospects for the future

In any contemplation of the future, a clear separation should be made between the state apparatus and the society. Even if individuals cannot free themselves from prejudice, the structure and the institutions of the government must; it is the only way to govern a heterogeneous society.

The state has the power to defend and to protect its citizenry. An objective study of the Khātamī presidency in regard to religious minorities still awaits scholarship. However, observational evidence indicates some loosening of restrictions. There were reports of travels back and forth to Israel by Iranian Jews as well as the return of some Jews from Israel back to Iran. There were also hints of government contacts and possible future recognition of the state of Israel.[8]

The capacity of the state machinery to institute change is immense. The following changes can be made in the state domain. First and most critical is the removal of religious laws which clearly treat non-Muslims as second-class citizens. In this context, the Baha'is and Iranian Christian converts will be subject to the same laws as everyone else.

Second is the issue of official political representation in parliament. The recognized religious minorities have had representation for a century. Today, Armenians have two deputies (representing north and south). Jews, Zoroastrians, and the Assyrians and Chaldeans combined, each have one representative in parliament. It is unlikely that any of these groups would want to change the system. Tradition and historical precedence gives them a voice, however meagre. This gives them a sense of security and direct access to state authorities. If they desire, they may also be given the right to vote for other deputies representing their district.

Third is the important issue of the status of the Baha'is. Various non-Baha'i sources have asked the Iranian government to allow Baha'is to attend universities or to grant them some legal status as a religious minority.[9] There is, however, a stronger reason for recognition of the Baha'is within Islamic, rather than a secular, state milieu. Recognition of non-Muslims in history has always been dependent on the personal and pragmatic calculations of Muslim local leaders and political authorities. Different groups (outside the 'People of the Book') have been granted recognition in different time periods for different reasons. Although Hindus are not recognized in Islam, they were granted the status of *Ahl al-dhimma* ('the Protected People') in some parts of the Islamic world. In this context, let us not forget that the status of the Zoroastrians has been a contentious issue as well. The Qur'an mentions the Sabeans but not the Zoroastrians; yet, they have received recognition and legal status (Sanasarian 2000: 19–21). The significance of the Protected People status outside and in addition to the status of the People of the Book is the existence of legal precedence. If these recognitions were not a violation of Islam then, how can one argue that they are a violation of Islam now? Also, the recognition takes place in the context *not* of the People of the Book but the Protected People; this is the exact domain of the state. The state is there to protect its citizens regardless of their religious or ethnic backgrounds.

The issue of how to institutionalize the recognition should be resolved in a discussion with the Baha'is. In practice this may take the form of one or more deputies to the parliament (but its political format may not be favoured by the Baha'is), or formal and open reinstitution of the elected Baha'i national governing body, the National Spiritual Assembly, or a new form of representation developed in discussions with the Baha'i community that will give a fair voice to this valuable religious minority.

Evidence from other countries shows that the state apparatus can change much faster than the social one. In the case of Iran, the society has exhibited much flexibility and humanity. Interpersonal relations have always been valued across religious divides. The individuals in society provide a cushioning effect against the excesses of state authorities and reduce the harsh impact. This explains why the Baha'i persecution has not matched the virulent remarks against them. Yet, in the case of Iran, there is one very important optimistic force, namely the Iranian youth. Unlike the previous generation, who was fishing for identity, ideology, opportunity, and domination, this generation is embracing the world in order to challenge the religious political authority in Iran. For this new generation, any semblance of oppression is to be resisted, including judging personhood based on religion. As long as the resistance does not indulge in materialism and imitation of the West, appreciates local and national customs, values the lessons of history and dares to be creative, it will guarantee a future brighter than yesterday and more veracious than today.

Notes

1 These events were reported on several websites; see e.g.
http://www.emrouz.info/archives/2005/11/00553.php
http://www.irna.ir/fa/news/view/line10/8409010916131001.htm
http://www.sharghnewspaper.com/840830/html/iran.htm
http://raha.gooya.name/politics/archives/038930.php

2 The Middle East Media Research Institute, 11/11/2005, Clip No. 932. For video clip, see http://memritv.org/Search.asp?Act=S6&P3=2#

3 For details on past defences, see Sanasarian 2000: 159–61. For the more recent defences, see the last page of Bill Samii, RFE/RL, inc. on the following website: http://www.rferl.org/featuresarticle/2005/12/f2fee1ea-7de2-0205767c73f.html

4 The law of inheritance states that if there is a Muslim in the family of the non-Muslim, he inherits the entire estate. This has the effect of indirectly encouraging conversion to Islam out of greed, if nothing else. This is similar to the 'Law of Apostasy' which was in effect under the Safavid Dynasty four centuries ago. For an explanation of legal aspect of the law, see Ebadi 1994: 94–5. For a real case story of conversion, see Sanasarian 2000: 131.

5 The symposium which attracted much attention was held at the Cathedral of St. John the Divine during the visit of then President Khātamī to New York in November 2001. It was convened by the World Conference on Religion and Peace; Khātamī was the keynote speaker.

6 Ibrahim has written extensively on the subject. For a more recent piece, see 'Christians Oppressed', *The Wall Street Journal*, 18 November 2005.

7 He is the author of many books and articles of high calibre; for one example, see *Speaking in God's Name* (Oxford: Oneworld Publications, 2001).

8 'Israel Secretly Passes Maps to Iran', *The Jerusalem Post*, 8 November 2000; 'Khātamī Suggests Iran Might Eventually Recognize Israel', *Ha'aretz*, 13 November 2001; and 'Immigrant Moves Back "Home" to Teheran', *The Jerusalem Post*, 3 November 2005.

9 For one example, see *Le Monde*, 16 December 2005.

Bibliography

Allport, G. (1999) 'The Nature of Hatred', in R.M. Baird & S.E. Rosenbaum (eds) *Hatred, Bigotry, and Prejudice*, Amherst, New York: Prometheus Books.

Aronson, E. (1999) 'The Causes of Prejudice', in R.M. Baird & S.E. Rosenbaum (eds) *Hatred, Bigotry, and Prejudice*, Amherst, New York: Prometheus Books.

Brennan, W. (1995) *Dehumanizing the Vulnerable: When Word Games Take Lives*, Chicago: Loyola University Press.

Ebadi, S. (1994) *Tārīkhcha va asnād-i ḥuqūq-i bashar dar Iran*, Tehran: Rawshangarān.

Eberhardt, J.L. and Fiske, S.T. (1996) 'Motivating Individuals to Change: What Is a Target to Do?' in C.N. Macrae, C. Stangor, & M. Hewstone (eds) *Stereotypes and Stereotyping*, New York: The Guilford Press.

Haddad, H.M. (1984) *Jews of Arab and Islamic Countries*, New York: Shengold Publishers.

Helmreich, W.B. (1982) *The Things They Say Behind Your Back*, New York: Doubleday & Company.

Jazāyirī, G. (1999) *Asrār-i khurākī-hā*, Tehran: Amir Kabir.

Martin, D. (1984) *The Persecution of the Baha'is of Iran, 1844–1984*, Ottawa: Association of Baha'i Studies.

Momen, M. (2004) 'Conspiracies and Forgeries: the attack upon the Baha'i Community in Iran', *Persian Heritage*, 35: 27–29; Online at http://www.persian-heritage.com/currentissue/Issues/no35/english/pages/27-29.html (accessed 4 June 2006).

Muṭahharī, M. (1970) *'Adl-i Ilāhī*, Tehran: Ḥusayniyya Irshād.

Report on Current Condition for Jews in Iran, Human Rights and Torture (6 December 2005) Los Angeles, California: Iranian American Jewish Federation.

Rosenberg, M.B. (2003) *Nonviolent Communication: A Language of Life*, Encinitas, California: PuddleDancer Press.

Sanasarian, E. (2000) *Religious Minorities in Iran*, Cambridge: Cambridge University Press.

Sartre, J-P. (1999) 'The Portrait of the Anti-Semite', in R.M. Baird & S.E. Rosenbaum (eds) *Hatred, Bigotry, and Prejudice*, Amherst, New York: Prometheus Books.

Sitton, D. (1985) *Sephardi Communities Today*, Jerusalem: Council of Sephardi and Oriental Communities.

Van den Berghe, P. (1999) 'The Biology of Nepotism', in R.M. Baird & S.E. Rosenbaum (eds) *Hatred, Bigotry, and Prejudice*, Amherst, New York: Prometheus Books.

8

THE HISTORICAL ROOTS OF THE PERSECUTION OF BABIS AND BAHA'IS IN IRAN

Abbas Amanat

Since the rise of the Babi movement in Iran in the 1840s, and later as it evolved into the Baha'i Faith in the latter decades of the nineteenth century and the early part of the twentieth century, Babis and Baha'is were subjects of recurring waves of persecution and discrimination in their homeland. Though among the most telling, and shameful, features of Iran's modern history, these events remained by and large untold by modern historical scholarship and to a large extent forgotten by the majority of Iranians. And yet as much as they are victims of conscious or unconscious historical amnesia, they are inalienable parts of Baha'i collective memory and the Baha'i psyche. It is true that Iranians never committed an act of genocide against the Babis and/or the Baha'is. Nor did they in the course of their long history, as far as can be ascertained, commit 'ethnic cleansing' against other religious or ethnic groups (perhaps with the exception of the Mazdakites in the sixth century). Thus 'Babi killing' (*Bābī-kushī*), as a phenomenon in modern Iranian history, is not comparable in quantitative or qualitative terms to what European whites did to the endogenous peoples of the Americas, Africa and Australia or what the Ottoman Turks did to the Armenians or Nazi Germany to Jews, Slavs and Gypsies or Serbs to Muslim Bosnians. The claim of 20,000 Babi-Baha'i Iranian martyrs, which seems to have first appeared in European accounts about the Babis, cannot be statistically justified even if all the victims of uprisings of 1848 to 1850 are included.[1]

Yet Babi-Baha'i persecutions are of great symbolic and symptomatic significance for they reveal remarkable patterns in Iran's socio-cultural past and in turn in the shaping of modern Iranian identity after more than three centuries of Shi'itization first under the Safavids and later under the Qajars when Iran was facing the forces of Western hegemony in the nineteenth century. Moreover, the gruesome nature of these pogrom-like campaigns, their dynamics, the clerical and government elements that perpetrated them, the textual and legal justifications, and the psychology of the mob that participated in these acts reveals much about intolerance for diversity and non-conformity in Shi'i culture.

The scope and frequency of Babi-Baha'i persecutions still awaits a thorough and objective study (or studies) that could utilize available Babi-Baha'i sources, official reports and documents, clerical *fatwās*, accounts of Western observers and diplomatic dispatches. Without such a detailed assessment, any preliminary inquiry such as this one is bound to remain interpretive in identifying chief motives for such persecution and their causes. The Babi-Baha'i accounts, though highly valuable, often come close to martyrology and even hagiography, while the Muslim accounts are invariably tainted with hostility and distortions typical of the heresiographic genre. European reports, on the other hand, are rare and distant with their own cultural biases even though they constitute a very valuable source yet to be fully explored.[2]

Throughout the nineteenth century, there were frequent instances of anti-Babi campaigns instigated, or sanctioned, by the Shi'i clerical establishment, and condoned, if not actively colluded, by the Qajar and at times by the Pahlavi states. When such campaigns turned into a full-blown harassment, they often involved mob frenzy. Instances of random or pre-meditated individual or mass killings, torture, looting, long-term imprisonment, forced recantation, banishment, confiscation of property, forced divorcing and raping of Babi and Baha'i women and the taking of children into slavery were familiar scenes in the second half of the nineteenth century, and even into the early twentieth century.

One perhaps can detect in the reinvigorated persecutions of the Baha'is in the Islamic Republic, the long and disturbing shadow of this painful past that stretched from the Qajar (1785–1925) through the Pahlavi era (1925–1979), and beyond. Though active persecution largely subsided in the Pahlavi period, enmity and rejection endured, partly one may argue because of the Baha'is' own retreat behind the walls of communal isolation and their reluctance to remain, as once had been, at the forefront of social and intellectual modernizing trends in the Iranian society. In the middle decades of the twentieth century, acts of intimidation and harassment were not rare, even at the national level, as the events of the summer of 1955 demonstrate. But more abundant were conspiratorial suspicions, charges of immorality and sexual excess, allegations of spying and subservience to foreign powers, 'unpatriotic' sentiments, and the accusation that a handful of Baha'is had a sinister grip over key positions within the Pahlavi regime. Moreover, there was a cynical disdain particularly among the pro-religious intellectuals of the 1960s and later for Baha'i doctrine and the Baha'i social message.

These charges, politicized and moralized, increasingly outweighed the old labeling of the Babis as heretics, as the Baha'i community became more firmly established along doctrinal lines and the Baha'i identity more clearly defined. It was as though the branding of the heretical 'other' in the Qajar and Pahlavi eras transformed into an act of reaffirming a threatened and confused Shi'i 'self' at a time when social dislocation, acculturation, and political oppression under the shah left little else for the Shi'i majority to rally behind. Even the earlier positive perceptions of the Baha'is as advocates of modernity, models of moral rectitude and devotion to their faith, were overshadowed, if not entirely eroded, in this milieu of suspicion and cynicism. Remarkably, the new attitude toward the Baha'is was not confined to clerical circles. Nor was it limited to affiliate Islamic activist organizations (such as the Islamic Propaganda Society [*anjuman-i tablīghāt-i Islāmī*] of the 1960s and 70s and the more virulent Ḥujatiyya Society whose self-definition as an organization was the 'anti-Baha'i Society' [*anjuman-i ḍidd-i Bahā'iyyat*]). It was also rampant, and still is, among the 'secular' members of the Iranian middle classes, and even among the intelligentsia whose only commitment to ancestral religion often was, and still is, an almost ritualistic parroting of anti-Baha'i conspiratorial illusions.

My scope in this chapter, however, is limited to the Qajar period, for I try in the main to detect a historical pattern in recurring cycles of ant-Babi and anti-Baha'i violence and highlight its doctrinal, and societal dimensions. Such an inquiry, one hopes, may help a deeper understanding of the present plight of the Baha'is in Iran and grasp its implications for the evolving Islamic, and more specifically Shi'i, public culture of tolerance or intolerance. In another level dealing with the Baha'i 'question' may contribute to the understanding of the shaping of the Iranian identity and the process of internalizing the 'other' as an enemy within at a critical juncture in Iran's national gestation.

The Babis as heretics

One could trace back the genesis of the Babi persecution, even beyond the inception of the movement in Iran in the 1840s, to the recurring instances of maltreatment of non-conformists of various sorts at least since the late Safavid period (1501–1732), most distinctly in the massacre of the Nuqṭawīs and the expulsion of the Ḥurūfīs, in the new *dhimma* restrictions imposed on Jewish communities and later in doctrinal refutation and active persecution of the Sufi orders, such as the Ni'matullāhīs in the seventeenth century and again in the early nineteenth century, and in hostile treatment of the newly-emerging Shaykhi theological school.[3]

Directly related to these expressions of communal intolerance, and perhaps the most potent force behind the anti-*shari'a* drive was the rise to prominence of the Uṣūlī legal school in the latter part of the eighteenth century and its advocacy of active involvement in the affairs of the community. Under the auspices of such a pivotal figure as Āqā Muḥammad Bāqir Bihbahānī, better known as Vaḥīd (1706–90), and his students, a network of *madrasa* teaching circles, and consequently judicial courts, began to emerge in Iran. By the early decades of the nineteenth century the Uṣūlī network enjoyed enormous power and prestige which it managed largely to muster and maintain up to the present time despite the secularizing hiatus of the Pahlavi period. It is not a coincidence that Āqā Muḥammad ʿAlī Bihbahānī (Kirmānshāhī), Vaḥīd's son and successor, became perhaps the most vociferous advocate of the Islamic doctrine of 'the enjoinment of that which is good and the prohibition of that which is evil' (*amr bi-maʿrūf wa nahy ʿan al-munkar*); the Muslim individual obligation for communal vigilance against ideological and moral non-conformity. Known as the 'Sufi-killer' (*Ṣūfī-kush*), it was the *fatwā*s of this leading Uṣūlī which sent to death as heretics some celebrated Niʿmatullāhī Sufi mystics, albeit with the reluctant endorsement of the newly-established Qajar state.[4]

In contrast to the waning Akhbārī theological school, the Uṣūlī *ʿulama* (scholars, as they were generally known) viewed themselves, collectively, as the 'vicegerent' (*nā'ib*) of the Imam of the Age who was believed to be in 'occultation' and whose return was expected at the End of the Time. Under the auspices of influential leaders such as Mulla Muḥammad Bāqir Shaftī of Isfahan (d. 1843), the Uṣūlīs claimed to be the sole source of 'judicial authority' (*wilāyat al-qaḍā*) which they considered to be complementary to the 'governing authority' of the state. The Uṣūlī jurists' pro-active position was enforced through the network of teacher-student patronage, over the pulpit of the mosques, and the growing revenue drawn from religious dues, charitable endowments (*awqāf*), and private investments.

The rise of the Babi movement, and the claim of the Bab to be the 'gate' of the occulted Imam, and later the 'Imam of the Age' himself, was naturally treated by the Uṣūlī jurists (*mujtahid*s) with hostility, and viewed as a clear threat not only to their doctrinal legitimacy but to their social prestige and material interests. The threat of a messianic-apocalyptic faith seemed even more imminent because the Babis replicated in the cities the same *ʿulama*-bazaar symbiosis upon which rested the Uṣūlī *mujtahids*' popular base and economic strength. Many early Babis were either newly-graduated *mujtahid*s of the rival Shaykhi persuasion, or *mulla*s of middle and lower ranks, seminarians (*ṭalaba*), and artisans and middle and lower rank merchants of the bazaar.[5]

By the early 1850s the anxieties on the part of the high-ranking *ʿulama* engendered sufficient public suspicion and resentment of the non-conformist Babis to allow their denouncement as outright heretics punishable by death. This however could not be easily achieved. According to an Islamic legal principle, adherence to the new 'heresy', as it was now labelled, could only be proven beyond doubt through the examination of the heretical text (*qirṭās*) and upon unambiguous confession of the accused. Such was not readily available to the *mujtahid*s without the help of the government. The trial in 1845 of Mulla ʿAlī Basṭāmī, an early Babi emissary to the holy cities of

Iraq (stronghold of the Uṣūlī jurists), and the complication arising from inter-communal Shi'i-Sunni squabbling demonstrates the obstacles that stood in the way of arriving at a unanimous verdict of apostasy for the Babis without the approval of the state, be it Ottoman or Iranian.[6]

Moreover, the growing popularity of the Bab and his new creed, made guilty verdicts hazardous for the *mujtahid*s. In the 1847 trial of the Bab presided over by the *mujtahid*s of Tabriz, even the Bab himself could not be found unequivocally guilty of the charge of 'incorrigible heresy' (*irtidād-i fiṭrī*) despite the fact that he openly claimed to be the Imam of the Age and despite the *fatwā* (or *fatwās*) that declared him of such charge but failed to specify the grounds.[7] Indeed, according to Shi'i law there was not sufficient ground for refuting the claim to 'special vice-regency' (*niyāba al-khāṣṣa*) of the Imam of the Age and perhaps even to the claim of Imamate itself. Most of the *mujtahids*' reasoning was based on Shi'i *hadīth* and *khabar* literature notorious for their disputed authenticity and confusion in their chain of reporters (*isnād*). Even the final verdict of execution for the Bab, which in 1850 was extracted from the Tabriz *mujtahid*s by the sheer force of the agents of the premier, Amīr Kabīr, was devoid of any legal ground in support of the charge of heresy.

By contrast, in later years, upon the dissemination of the Bab's principal book, the *Bayān*, which declared a new 'revelation' (*ẓuhūr*) and a new prophetic cycle independent from Islam, ample grounds were found for denouncing the new heresy. The charge of apostasy, along with its corollary, 'combatant (*muḥārib*) against God and his religion', were the salient points in the apostasy *fatwā*s issued by the *'ulama* in the following decades, though in no instance known to this author did these *fatwā*s seek to establish any doctrinal ground for the charge of apostasy beyond confession of the accused in belief in the Bab (and later, in Baha'ullah, the prophet of the Baha'i Faith). Sheer admission of belief in the new prophets, often attested by refusing to publicly denounce and abuse the Bab (and Baha'ullah) even under duress, allowed any *mujtahid* of authority, usually independent of his colleagues, to declare the accused as an apostate (*murtadd*) who was 'outside the pale of religion (of Islam)' and thus subject to the legal punishment requested by the *shari'a*.[8]

Yet the legal ground for issuing apostasy *fatwā*s, and the potential power invested in the opinion of a single *mujtahid*, was not always concomitant with actualizing such potentials and enforcing the invested judicial power. By the late nineteenth century instances of 'Babi-killing' (*Bābī-kushī*) appeared with varying frequency and intensity. As the term suggests, 'Babi-killing' offered a sense of sacrificial frenzy to the participating mob, often as the climatic momentum to an anti-Babi-Baha'i campaign. The success of these campaigns depended as much on a climate of crisis created by the *mujtahid*s as on the government's willingness to enforce the *fatwā*s issued by the *mujtahid*s. In the eyes of the Babis and the Baha'is, however, any such campaigns of persecution to save the faithful from the 'devious sect' (*firqa-yi ḍālla*) was a horrifying experience in terror and carnage; what in Baha'i parlance was termed as 'agitation' (*ḍawḍā'*). Recurring episodes of agitation of course were distinct from the more familiar low-intensity imposition of 'restrictions' (*taḍ'īqāt*), which were accepted facts of life. Restrictions ranged from verbal abuse and the beating of Baha'i children and adults, enforcing the Shi'i rules of ritual impurity, and a ban on social gatherings, to regular extortion and intimidation, intrusion into private family life, and the occupation and illegal possession of Baha'i-owned properties.

In order for these long-standing discriminations in any given urban or rural setting to turn into a crisis of active persecution, some essential ingredients needed to be present; what may be called a pattern of interests and interactions. Compared to other minority communities, the Babi-Baha'is were in an even more disadvantageous position. Though the Jewish, Zoroastrian, Armenian, Assyrian and Ahl-i Ḥaqq communities often sustained verbal and physical violence, and were targets of active persecution, ranging from forced conversion to Islam to looting of their residential quarters, the pillaging of shops and businesses, and even killings, they still maintained a recognized *dhimma* status in the majority Muslim society and were somewhat protected by its safeguards. The Babi-Baha'is, on the other hand, though not as demographically concentrated as these recognized minorities in certain cities and city wards, clearly lacked any such status and thus persecutions directed toward them often revealed a far more virulent hostility on the side of the *'ulama*, the state, and the public. The Babi-Baha'is were not protected by the obligations towards the people of the *dhimma* because they were seen as a post-Islamic heresy whose very existence militated against the Islamic notion of prophetic finality. Hence they were easy and legitimate prey for all forms of discrimination, abuse, and aggression.

Looking at the anatomy of any cycle of Baha'i persecution, we can see an initial instigator, whether a lay person, a low-rank *mulla*, or a seminarian, whose self-serving motives, often financial or sexual, were covered up by real, or more often, bogus charges against an individual or a community of Baha'is. Flimsy though they often were, these charges were taken up by high ranking *mujtahid*s who found benefit in a new round of Babi-bashing; a convenient, and a perfectly 'legitimate' exercise not only to enhance popularity, assert leadership (*riyāsat*), secure ascendancy in the informal clerical hierarchy, and to square old accounts with rival colleagues, but more likely to gain ground against the increasingly vulnerable Qajar government and its provincial representatives. Yet beyond doctrinal justifications, which were conveniently revived at the time of crisis, or issues of inter-*'ulama* quarrels, or the turf war with the Qajar government, the high-ranking *'ulama* were also moved by a range of political, material, and other personal interests. Denouncing members of a Babi and later Baha'i mercantile or land-owning family often promised to bring expropriated property, a large bribe, or even possession of the female members of the household. One case in point is the conduct of the chief clerical figure, the Imām Jum'a, of Isfahan, in the famous case of the Ṭabāṭabā'ī brothers in 1884. Defaulting the payment of a large loan owed to this prosperous Babi-Baha'i merchant family, the Imām Jum'a joined the notorious *mujtahid* of the city and his old rival, Āqā Muḥammad Bāqir Najafī, in issuing an apostasy *fatwa* denouncing the Ṭabāṭabā'ī brothers. Upon their arrest and later execution, he and Najafī, in collaboration with the powerful governor of the city, Nāṣir al-Dīn Shah's son, the Ẓill al-Sulṭān, confiscated their substantial property while some of the women of their household were sent to the prince's harem under the pretext of protection.[9]

The conduct and the motives of the Qajar state either to condone, or at times actively collaborate, with the *'ulama* in their anti-Babi-Baha'i campaigns was the second facet in any unfolding scenario of violence. Briefly under Muḥammad Shah (1834–1848) the government of Ḥājjī Mīrzā Āqāsī, himself a Sufi by persuasion, toyed with the idea of tolerating the Babis as a potential weapon against the menacing power of the *mujtahid*s. Yet, upon the accession of Nāṣir al-Dīn Shah (1848–1896), and largely because of the Babi armed resistance in Mazandaran (1848–1849) and in Zanjan (1848–1850), the Qajar state concluded that the *Bābiyya*, as the movement came to be known, is a dangerous revolutionary menace to the state and the ruling dynasty and hence has to be eradicated in its entirety. This state strategy especially proved successful under the reformer premier, Amīr Kabīr (1848–1851) because the Babi resistance could be characterized as a heretical revolt not only against the state but the very principles of the Islamic religion. Like other authoritarian reformers of the Middle East in the nineteenth century, Amīr Kabīr was hostile toward a movement of dissent with a messianic creed and with popular backing. From his standpoint, the Babi revolutionary movement as much was a challenge to his hard-earned idea of centralized 'order' (*naẓm*) as were the *mujtahid*s and their religious conservatism. It was his government that for the first time used the public execution of Babis, among other methods by firing squad (as was carried out in the case of the Bab himself in Tabriz in 1850), as an effective means of installing terror into the hearts of the sympathetic public.

The policy of terror was even more fully enforced after the fall of Amīr Kabīr and in the aftermath of the unsuccessful Babi assassination attempt against Nāṣir al-Dīn Shah in 1852, an event of lasting consequence for the Babis and their relation with the Qajar state. The ensuing mass execution of the suspect Babi conspirators set new standards for cruelty and sadistic frenzy. To minimize the chances of Babi reprisal being directed against him, the shrewd premier, Mīrzā Āqā Khān Nūrī, divided up the Babi victims among all groups within and outside the government to include even the students of the royal polytechnic Dār al-Funūn, the princes of the royal blood, secretaries of the *dīvān*, and even the merchants of the bazaar. Each group dutifully put to death one or several of the assigned victims from among their own ranks. The 1852 incident was a turning point for it opened the door to sporadic but severe mass killings in the Iranian provinces and smaller communities in the following years and even decades.[10]

Nāṣir al-Dīn Shah's deep suspicion of the Babis never ceased to exist for the rest of his long reign, though it was somewhat relaxed. Despite repeated statements by Baha'ullah, the new leader of the movement, renouncing the Babis' early anti-Qajar stance and condemning violence, and despite his conciliatory gestures toward the monarch, the shah barely relaxed his suspicion. Baha'ullah and all other Babis and Baha'is were viewed as revolutionaries and agitators on the same footing as European anarchists. The Qajar government seized every opportunity to imprison, banish, torture, and execute individual Babis and Baha'is whenever its political interests and its waning popularity required. Often refusing to practice *taqiyya* (doctrinal dissimulation of their real belief), the Baha'is, to the extent that in late nineteenth century were distinct from the Babis (and more than the Azali Babis, who more often did hide their real beliefs), were targets of the government's chronic round-ups and incarcerations. So far as the shah was concerned, no differentiation was to be made between the Baha'is, the followers of Baha'ullah, who mostly refrained from anti-Qajar activities, and the more radical but less numerous Azalis. The latter faction (the clandestine followers of Mīrzā Yaḥya Ṣubḥ-i Azal, Baha'ullah's rival half-brother), in contrast to the Baha'is, had remained, at least in theory, loyal to the old Babi dual opposition to the Shi'i *'ulama* and the Qajar state. Some members of the Azali-Babi leadership however had been able to fully wrap themselves in the garb of the *'ulama* and even upheld the rank of *mujtahid*, hence remaining relatively protected from persecution. Yet despite some relaxation, the persecution of the Babis and the Baha'is was one of the very few issues on which Nāṣir al-Dīn Shah was not prepared to compromise at any cost, even in the face of the humanitarian pleas of the European envoys, and the Americans.[11]

By the final decades of the nineteenth century and with the growing dissention against the Qajar state, the charges of Babi subversion and conspiracy, were widened and brought with greater frequency not only against the Babi-Baha'is but against anyone with anti-despotic and anti-clerical proclivities. Being a Babi thus gained a broader meaning than strict adherence to the tenets of the Bayānī religion or the Baha'i Faith (though it is wrong to believe that Babi affiliation was a sheer pretext to justify suppression by the state of all forms of dissent). Before the Constitutional Revolution (1906–1911), Babism, whether in its Baha'i or Azali manifestations, was the most prevalent non-conformist voice of political and religious dissent which gave expression to intellectual and political modes of opposition.[12]

Far more detrimental to the Babi-Baha'i community than the government-initiated acts of arrest and execution, however, was the backing of the Qajar state for the *'ulama*'s anti-Baha'i crusades. To enforce their apostasy *fatwās*, the *mujtahid*s seldom could act independent of the government and without its final seal of approval. Although the boundaries of religious law (*shar'*) and the customary law (*'urf*) remained blurred before the judicial reforms of the 1920s and 1930s, referral of the apostasy cases to the government for implementing the penalty (*ḥadd*) was often an accepted norm. The provincial or central government could not easily refrain from such a task given the structural vulnerabilities of the Qajar state and its waning legitimacy in the face of European imperial challenges in the battlefield and in the marketplace. No government authority could afford ignoring expressions of zeal and adherence to the rudiments of the *sharī'a*, especially when the issue of apostasy was involved. The Qajars were often walking on ground which was much too shaky to afford any measure of ecumenical benevolence, least of all toward Babis and Baha'is especially when they were put on the spot by the *mujtahid*s and their allies.

Bouts of Babi persecution hence were a mixed blessing to the Qajar government. On the one hand, instances of anti-Babi unrest could, and sometimes did, get out of hand and result in urban riots with a spontaneous anti-Qajar flavour. On the other hand, the governors and their agents stood to benefit from anti-Babi campaigns not only by receiving large bribes to spare lives, or by expropriating the property of the victims, and taking possession of the female members of their households, but also for potential such unrest provided to distract the public attention from severe political and economic problems the state was grappling with. Predictably, the anti-Babi campaigns usually coincided with instances of famine and harvest failure, urban unrest, epidemics, and other provincial or national crisis and frequently served as scapegoats to cover for the failure of the state policy in the face of European political and economic intrusion or the instances of the hoarding of grain and other forms of profiteering by wealthy *mujtahid*s and their allies.

Drawing the public attention towards the evils of the 'devious sect' helped consolidate relations between the clergy and the government. Throughout the latter part of the nineteenth century, the Babi-Baha'i threat, whether real or perceived, served as a catalyst to strengthen the bonds between the *'ulama* and the state at every level. Contrary to the common misconception about the oppositional role of the Shi'i clergy, most members of the high-ranking *'ulama* found in the Qajar government a natural partner in the suppression of Babi dissent. While the highest ranking *mujtahid*s in Iraq, such a Shaykh Murtaḍā Anṣārī and later Mīrzā Ḥasan Shīrāzī, remained ambivalent about persecuting the Babi-Baha'is, and thus unwilling to issue apostasy *fatwā*s against them, the *mujtahid*s in Iran, most notably in Isfahan, Tehran, Yazd, Mashhad, and Qazvin, incited anti-Babi campaigns at the mutual benefit of the clergy and the city or provincial authorities. With the rise of political unrest in the provinces at the turn of the twentieth century and on the eve of the Constitutional Revolution (1906–1911), the Baha'is often became scapegoats for the *'ulama* to divert anticlerical criticism and as a means of collaborating with the Qajar state to quell public discontent. Recurring persecutions in Yazd in 1903 and in subsequently in Rasht, Isfahan, and elsewhere are cases in point.[13]

Yet beyond the state–clergy symbiosis and the mutual benefits in eradicating the 'bad religion', as any Persian manual of government would have advised ever since the Sasanian times, there was a third dimension to the recurring anti-Babi violence, that sociologically – and morally – remains the most troubling. More often than not the 'agitation' against the Babis, though instigated in the clerical quarters and backed, reluctantly or otherwise, by the state authorities, found an enthusiastic, and at times frantic, endorsement from the urban public. Too frequently the public was willing to follow the *mujtahid*s' violent vigilantes: the *lūṭī*s (street gangs), the *sādāt* (agitating bands of presumed descendents of the House of the Prophet), and the *ṭalaba* (religious seminarians of the *madrasa*s), would attack *en masse* the shops and houses of defenceless Babis and Baha'is, beat them, lynch them, and loot their often meagre possessions. One no doubt can detect in these crises patterns of rivalry among city wards and the chronic violence of their affiliated gangs. One can also observe in these outbursts of suppressed aggression all the instantaneous irrationality of the incited mob. Yet both these aspects should be seen as symptoms rather than the causes of a deeper socio-psychological phenomenon.

Predictably, coinciding with the Régie protest of 1891–1892, when a mass anti-imperialist protest movement against a European monopoly for the distribution and export of Iranian tobacco led to the repealing of the concession by the Qajar government, Iran witnessed some of the worst cases of anti-Babi-Baha'i violence. The cycle of killing and looting which began in Isfahan and its vicinity culminated in the Yazd massacres of 1901–1903. The Yazd episode, in particular, demonstrated an interaction among three parties: the *'ulama*, the government, and the incited mob.[14] The Yazd upheaval potentially could have led to the massacre of Baha'is in other urban centres, thanks to a modern telegraphic communication network, a mini press revolution, and greater clerical solidarity vis-à-vis the weakening temporal authority. Yet with the dawning of the Constitutional Revolution, and especially after the civil war of 1908–1909, there was a noticeable downturn in incidents of anti-Baha'i violence. This, despite the fact that throughout the period, the royalist *mujtahid*s Shaykh Faḍullāh Nūrī and his allies conducted systematic attacks against both the Babi-Azalis and the Baha'is for their support for the constitutional regime. During this period both the Babi-Azalis and the Baha'is were more assertive in voicing preference for the constitution, parliament, civil liberties, and tolerance; themes which outraged even liberal members of the clerical establishment. What reduced anti-Baha'i persecution on a massive scale, however, was the shifting tide toward secular modernity. The Constitutional Revolution largely removed from the sectarian stage the two old players: the Shi'i clergy and the Qajar state. The subsiding of active persecution allowed the Baha'is to become more visible, economically prosper and socially excel, especially after 1911 and through the 1920s, and to gain a greater popularity and following among the emerging modern middle class.[15]

For a predictable, if not pedestrian, explanation of the pattern of anti-Baha'i violence and persecution one may resort to a theory of 'class conflict' and glean some supporting evidence in the way the urban poor, and in particular the lower strata of the bazaar 'proletariat', targeted the nascent Baha'i 'bourgeoisie' of the cities; a mercantile class which successfully linked up to the emerging markets of international commerce and represented economic interests essentially at odds with the dying local workshop industry and its domestic manufacturers and distributors. This new bourgeoisie, it may be argued, had adopted 'Protestant work ethics' with a modernizing this-worldly view and a moral idealism equally at odds with the otherworldly ethos of Shi'i culture which ultimately viewed as detrimental to the spirit of the old bazaar-*'ulama* alliance.

The existence of a socio-economic chasm between the Baha'is and the Shi'i majority, especially in the movement's later development under Baha'ullah's leadership (which benefited from the backing of a small but active Baha'i mercantile community), cannot be denied. Nor one can underestimate the contrast between the emerging Baha'i socio-ethical worldview which was in contrast to the ethos of the Shi'i majority, at least in the decades before the Constitutional Revolution. Yet overt class analysis of the anti-Baha'i hostilities faces an immense body of contesting historical data. For one thing, the target of much of the Babi and Baha'i mistreatment in the cities, as in the countryside, was the indigenous population in the same urban centres and villages who were neither better nor worse off than their oppressors. Moreover, the appeal of the Babi movement, and later the Baha'i Faith, was to the artisans and manufacturers of the bazaar, the very same groups who suffered from the changing economic climate of their time. Thirdly, the socio-moral message of the Baha'is was often at the heart of their grass-roots proselytizing among the ordinary people rather than the political or commercial elites; a fact which moved the *'ulama*, the guardians of Shi'i conservatism, to act against the Baha'is in the first place.

Alternatively, one can treat the problem of the Babi-Baha'i persecution as a socio-cultural phenomenon rather than as a class conflict. This reflects on a greater, and more acute, crisis of confidence within the Iranian society and touches on a range of cultural and behavioral discourses. The Baha'is, it may be argued, were a sore point of non-conformity within a society seeking monolithic unanimity in the face of overwhelming threats from within and outside of its boundaries; a society fearful of loosing its perceived 'uniqueness' as the Shi'i 'saved sect' (*firqa-yi nājīya*) in the sea of geographic insignificance, in the face of territorial losses to the Western powers, and against the painful economic subordination to overseas markets. The anti-Babi-Baha'i sentiments, one may thus propose, was a communally reassuring and doctrinally admissible ritual of aggression to forge a sense of collective 'self' versus an indigenous 'other' at a time when the alien 'other' was too intimidating and inaccessible to be viewed as an adversary. Hence stood the dichotomy between the Shi'i 'saved sect' in the eschatological sense and the Babi-Baha'i 'wayward sect' (*firqa-yi ḍālla*). The hostility by which the latter was treated by the Shi'i majority points to a defensive mechanism triggered by the Baha'i fulfilment of a messianic prophecy and the promise of the establishment of a this-worldly paradise. Uṣūlī Shi'ism, which aims to forge a sense of exclusive self out of the fragile complex of the existing religious and social identities, tends to deny this post-apocalyptic scenario and the historicization of the advent of the Shi'i saviour. The corollary to this Shi'i particularism was the rejection of the indigenous modernity of the Babi-Baha'i worldview and its advocacy of universalistic inclusion. It was this unresolved clash of worldviews which set the stage for hostility and suspicion for decades to come.

Notes

1 The Baha'i sources often refer to '20,000 martyrs', yet there is not sufficient evidence to support such a figure. Even a liberal estimate of the Babis killed between 1848 and the early 1850s does not go beyond 4,000, see 'Abdu'l-Baha 1891: 47. Even though, this number is substantial, given that the total population of Iran at the time was about 6 million, with only 15 per cent residing in the large towns and cities. Even if we add all those Babis and Baha'is killed up to the late twentieth century, we reach a figure of around 6,000 at the highest. For an assessment of these figures, see MacEoin 1983: 235–237.

2 Much of the available research focuses on the formative Babi period. Later Babi and Baha'i history, and especially the persecutions of Babis and then later Baha'is from 1852 to 1979, remain largely untouched. A critical assessment of causes and consequences is particularly missing. For a typical Baha'i account see for instance the valuable but old school Malik-Khusravī 1972. Even the massive nine volume historical survey of Babi-Baha'i history by Fāḍil Māzandarānī largely revolves around a persecution narrative.

3 For instances of Nuqṭawī persecutions under the Safavid see Amanat 1996. For the dispersing of the Ḥurūfīs, see Bausani 1971, and Bashir 2002. For the Safavid persecution of the Sufi orders see Aubin 1970.

4 For the persecution of Ni'matullāhīs in early Qajar period, see Pourjavadi and Wilson 1978 and Amanat 1987: 71–83. For Muḥammad–'Alī Bihbahānī and his father, see Davānī 1983. For Shaftī's assessment of the *mujtahids*' judicial authority, see Amanat 1990.

5 For a social composition of the early Babi community, see Amanat 1989: 322–371.

6 For this trial, see Momen 1982 and Amanat 1989: 211–37.

7 For a report of the Tabriz trial, see Browne 1918: 248–55. For the context, see Amanat 1989: 385–93.

8 For apostasy in Islam, see Zwemer 1924, Madelung 1993 and Griffel 2000. For Shi'i law of apostasy, see 'Āmilī 1901. In his chapter on capital punishments, 'Āmilī enumerates conditions of 'incorrigible apostasy' (*irtidād-i fiṭrī*) and the due punishment for men and women. If a sane, adult, free male of Muslim

parentage intentionally turns apostate he is punishable by death. If a Muslim woman of the same conditions is turned apostate she is to be incarcerated, beaten, and forced to ware clothing of coarse fabric until she repents. If she insists in her apostasy, she is also punishable by death. The admission of the repentance of male apostates is disputed, see 'Āmilī 1901: 424–25. For more extensive debate, see Najafī Iṣfahānī 1981.

9 For this case, see Momen 1981: 274–77 and cited sources including Wills 1894/2004: 153–56.

10 For the Babi assassination attempt against Nāṣir al-Dīn Shah in 1852 and its consequences, see Amanat 1997: 204–17.

11 See, for instance, Nāṣir al-Dīn's response to British minister Ronald Thomson upon the arrest of the Babis (Baha'is) in 1882–83, cited in Momen 1981: 292–95.

12 See Amanat forthcoming.

13 See, for instance, Momen 1981: 363–98.

14 The harrowing account of terror, mob frenzy, and lynching that went on for several years after 1903 in Yazd and its vicinity as recorded in Mālmīrī 1979, is one of several examples of appalling mob action in modern Iranian history.

15 Ironically, the Babi-Azalis, who maintained a crucial presence at the early stages of the Constitutional Revolution and who were the chief advocates of an anti-Qajar and anti-clerical programme, were soon reduced to an insignificant minority. See Amanat 2007.

Bibliography

'Abdu'l-Baha. (1891) *A Traveller's Narrative Written to Illustrate the Episode of the Bab*, trans. and ed. E.G. Browne, Cambridge: Cambridge University Press.

Amanat, A. (1989) *Resurrection and Renewal: the Making of the Babi Movement in Iran, 1844–1850*, Ithaca: Cornell University Press.

—— (1990) '"Pīshvā-yi ummat" va vazīr-i mukhtār-i "bītadlīs-i" Inglīs: murāsala-yi Ḥājj Sayyid Muḥammad Bāqir Shaftī, Ḥujjat al-Islām, va Sir Jun Maknīl dar qaḍiyya-yi laskarkashī-yi Muḥammad Shah ba Harāt', *Irānshināsī*, II.1: 11–41.

—— (1996) 'The Nuqtawi Movement of Mahmud Pisikhani and his Persian Cycle of Mystical-Materialism', in F. Daftary (ed.) *Mediaeval Isma'ili History and Thought*, Cambridge: Cambridge University Press, 289–292.

—— (1997) *Pivot of the Universe: Nasir al-Din Shah Qajar of the Iranian Monarchy, 1831–1896*, Berkeley and Los Angeles: University of California Press.

—— (forthcoming) 'Memory and Amnesia in the Historiography of the Constitutional Revolution,' in T. Atabaki (ed.) *Building Modern Iran: Historiography and Political Culture in Twentieth Century*, London and New York: I.B. Tauris.

'Āmilī, B. (1901) *Jāmi'-i 'Abbāsī*, Bombay.

Aubin, J. (1970) 'Le politique religieuse des Safavides,' in *Le shi'sm imamate*, Paris: Colloque de Strasbourg, 1968.

Bashir, S. (2002) 'Deciphering Cosmos from Creation to Apocalypse', in A. Amanat and M. Bernhardsson (eds.), *Imagining the End: Visions of Apocalypse from the Ancient Middle East to Modern America*, London: I.B. Tauris, 168–186.

Bausani, A. (1971) 'Ḥurūfiyya', *Encyclopaedia of Islam*, New Edition, vol. III, Leiden: Brill.

Browne, E.G. (1918) *Materials for the Study of the Babi Religion*, Cambridge: The University Press.

Davānī, 'A. (1958) *Vaḥīd-i Bihbahānī*, Qum.

Fāḍil Māzandarānī, A. (n.d. [1944]) *Ẓuhūr al-Ḥaqq*, vol 3, Tehran.
Griffel, F. (2000) *Apostasie und Toleranz im Islam: die Entwicklung zu al-Gazalis Urteil gegen die Philosophe der Philosopher*, Leiden: Brill.
MacEoin, D. (1983) 'From Babism to Baha'ism: Problems of Militancy, Quietism, and Conflation in the Construction of a Religion', *Religion*, 13: 219–255.
Madelung, W. (1993) 'Mulḥid', in *Encyclopaedia of Islam*, New Edition, vol. VII, Leiden: Brill.
Malik-Khusravī, M. (1972) *Tārikḥ-i Shuhadā-yi Amr*, 3 vols., Tehran: Muassasa-yi Millī-yi Maṭbū'āt-i Amrī.
Mālmīrī, M.T. (1979) *Tārikh-Shuhadā-yi Yazd*, Karachi: Baha'i Publishing Trust.
Momen, M. (1982) 'The Trial of Mulla 'Alī Basṭāmī: A Combined Sunni-Shi'i *Fatwā* Against The Bab', *Iran*, 20: 113–143.
Najafī Iṣfahānī, M.H. (1981) *Jawāhir al-kalām fī sharḥ sharāyi' al-Islām*, Beirut: Dār al-Iḥyā' al-Turāth al-'Arabī.
Pourjavady, N. and Wilson, P.L. (1978) *Kings of Love. The History and Poetry of the Ni'matullah Sufi Order of Iran*, Tehran: Imperial Iranian Academy of Philosophy.
Wills, C.J. (1894/2004) *In the Land of Lion and the Sun*, London; 2nd ed. with a new introduction by Abbas Amanat, Washington D.C.: Mage.
Zwemer, S.M. (1924) *Law of Apostasy in Islam*, London: Marshall Brothers.

9

ANATOMY OF PREJUDICE

Reflections on secular anti-Baha'ism in Iran

H.E. Chehabi

No Prophet is accepted in his own country.
Luke 4:24

The Baha'i religion challenges one of the key tenets of Islam: that Muḥammad was the last of the prophets (*khātam al-anbīa*). It is thus as impossible for a Muslim believer to admit the divine mission of Baha'ullah, as it is for a Jew to recognize Jesus Christ as the Messiah, or for a Christian to concede that Mānī or Muḥammad were the recipients of divine revelations that superseded the message of Christ. In the Abrahamic tradition, a religion can make a place for preceding ones, but not for one that, implicitly, declares it to be obsolete. In the Middle Ages, Christians did not tolerate Muslims in their midst in Europe, as their expulsion from Spain shows, and in the nineteenth century the prophet Joseph Smith, founder of the Mormon religion, was killed by a lynch mob while jailed in Carthage, Illinois; his followers found peace and security only in distant and inhospitable Utah.[1] A traditional Muslim's hostility to the Baha'i Faith, a creed that is from the point of view of Islam by definition heretical, is therefore not astonishing.[2] But, as Chesterton reminds us, no heretic has ever thought of himself as a heretic (Chesterton 1923: 11), and a secular attitude to religion can be expected to entail a definition of religion that is not informed by the tenets of one *particular* religion. One widely accepted definition is that of Emile Durkheim, who defined religion as 'a system of beliefs and practices relative to sacred things, that is to say, things set apart and forbidden – beliefs and practices which unite into one single moral community . . . all those who adhere to them' (Durkheim 1965: 62). Consequently, 'there are no religions which are false. All are true in their own fashion' (Durkheim 1965: 15). Which means that a secular Iranian could be logically expected to grant the Baha'i religion as much respect, or, for that matter, disrespect, as Islam or the so-called 'recognized' minority religions of Iran.

The real mystery is therefore not believing Muslims' antipathy to the Baha'i Faith,[3] but secular and anti-clerical Iranians' frequent hostility to it. It is only a slight exaggeration to say that until very recently any discussion of the Baha'is and their religion that did not use abusive, disparaging, or at least sarcastic language was suspected of being an apologia, and that any writer or speaker who talked about Baha'is in respectful or even in a merely matter-of-fact way was suspected of being a Baha'i.[4] While secular opponents of Iran's Islamist regime are quick to condemn its human rights abuses, the murder of close to 300 Baha'is since the revolution has elicited relatively little public outrage from non-Baha'i Iranian defenders of human rights.[5] As late as 1998, while Iranians both inside and outside Iran waxed eloquent about 'civil' society, the killing of five Muslim-identified dissidents generated far more criticism than the contemporaneous renewal of attacks against Baha'is.[6] This silence was broken by Shirin Ebady, the winner of the Nobel Peace Prize in 2003, who in her keynote address to the Fifth Biennial Conference on Iranian Studies in 2004 said: 'the rights of the followers of other beliefs, people such as the Baha'is in Iran . . . are overlooked and neglected' (Ebady 2004: 18).[7]

Many secular Iranians find it difficult to approach the Baha'i religion in an emic way, in other words, to accept that the Baha'i Faith is a religion simply because Baha'is *act* like a religious community – and, one might add, have often paid with their lives for doing so. Looked at from a global perspective, new religions are not a rare phenomenon, and they are still sprouting up. Mormons were once reviled in the United States, but today they are respected members of the American nation, and are envied for their higher life expectancy and lower incidence of diseases. In Iran, the Ilāhī sect (an offshoot of the Ahl-i Ḥaqq that has effected a rapprochement with Twelver Shiʿism) has been growing since the revolution without eliciting the same negative reaction (Mir-Hosseini 1997: 175–176; 185–192), although it should be noted that no new members have been officially admitted to the Baha'i community of Iran since the revolution of 1978–79. Baha'is and their religion have been a somewhat taboo topic in Iranian studies, which is all the more astonishing as Baha'is are much more integrated into the mainstream of Iranian life than other, 'recognized', religious minorities.[8] One indicator of this is the much higher incidence of mixed marriages with Muslims among them. So why do so many secular Iranians evince misgivings about Baha'is?

A sober discussion of the place of the Baha'i religion in Iranian society is not helped by the fact that, as Denis MacEoin has pointed out, 'Baha'i studies' is a tiny field, whose practitioners are mostly either Baha'is or ex-Baha'is.[9] While one might agree or disagree with the implication that scholarship by Baha'is or ex-Baha'is on issues pertaining to the faith is *necessarily* biased, commitment, disillusion, and disappointment can confer a certain emotional charge to one's analysis, especially in our post-modern times when many reject the very possibility, or indeed desirability, of striving for objectivity.[10]

The object of this chapter is not state attitudes toward Baha'is, but social attitudes. This is not to say that state attitudes do not matter: Nāṣir al-Dīn Shah's Iran persecuted Babis and Baha'is, under Riḍā Shah all Baha'i-run schools in Iran were closed down, including the famous Tarbīat boys' and girls' schools in Tehran, and under the last Shah the Ḥaẓīrat al-Quds (the Baha'i community centre in Tehran) was partially demolished, and the state at times tolerated the most vicious anti-Baha'i propaganda and economic boycotts.[11] Under the Islamic Republic one Baha'i in a thousand has been executed for his or her religious beliefs, representing the largest proportion of any religious group. But state attitudes have been studied elsewhere,[12] for which reason here they are not mentioned except in passing.

It would seem that there are three basic secular anti-Baha'i lines of argumentation. The first asserts that Baha'is (and other religions and sects) are causes of division. On that basis, many go farther to claim that Baha'is have been used by foreign powers in ways that are harmful for the national interest of Iran. Finally, it is often asserted that Baha'is were disproportionately represented in the inner circles of power, the assumption being that those who were in key positions used their political influence to advance the interests of their community. We will look at these arguments in turn, before attempting an explanation of the phenomenon.

Anti-Baha'i arguments

Causing Division in the Nation

In this line of argument, Baha'is are considered as a manifestation of a phenomenon that also includes Shaykhis and Isma'ilis. One very influential proponent of this view is the prominent and highly influential Iranian historian Firaydūn Ādamīyat, who wrote in 1944:

> The innovations of the Bab caused religious dissension in Iran, and what greater calamity is there than when a nation wallows in religious beliefs and wastes its time on [religious] disputes that lack the slightest scientific value. . . .
>
> As long as Iranians do not come to see the truth behind the many rebellions that were staged in the country in the 13th century of the *hijra*, and as long as religious beliefs do not crumble as a result of familiarity with the modern sciences, these dangerous dissensions will not disappear.
>
> (Ādamīyat 1944: 258)

Similarly, Aḥmad Kasravī, wrote in the 1940s that Baha'ism was based on Babism, which was based on Shaykhism, which was based on Shi'i messianism, and since the latter was false, all that was built upon it was false as well (Kasravī 1996: 61–62).

Conspiracy Theories

Together with Jews and freemasons, Baha'is figure very prominently in Iranian conspiracy belief.[13] In the above-mentioned work by the historian Ādamīyat, he avers that Baha'is were first supported by the Russians and later by the British, and concludes:

> If the Babi and Baha'i religions had not acquired a political coloration, and if the hands of the foreigners had not watered its roots, they would certainly have been buried in the nooks and crannies of this vast land, like the thousands of other sects that spring up every now and then in this or that corner of Iran. Then, they would not have caused all this brouhaha.
>
> (Ādamīyat 1944: 258)

Aḥmad Kasravī, for his part, writes:

> It is indisputable that Baha'is are the enemies of the masses . . . and that they wish them ill from the bottom of their hearts. The reason is that they have suffered tremendously and in the past hundred years have not been able to gain freedom for themselves, which means that in order to achieve freedom they have to hope for the country's breakdown.[14]
>
> (Kasravī 1996: 99–100)

Unlike other anti-Baha'i writers, Kasravī acknowledges the suffering of Babis and Baha'is (Kasravī 1996: 50–51), but ascribes it to the 'people', who 'never miss an opportunity to harm them' (Kasravī 1996: 99).

The foundational text of the attribution of conspiratorial proclivities to Baha'is is a fictitious memoir attributed to Prince Dimitri Ivanovich Dolgorukov, who was Russian ambassador to Persia in 1846–54. In it, Dolgorukov purportedly describes how he created the Babi-Baha'i religion so as to weaken Iran and Shi'ism. This document is in many ways a functional equivalent of the *Protocols of the Elders of Zion* (which was first circulated in Iran in the late 1930s), and although it was soon shown to be a forgery,[15] it is still reprinted on occasion and referred to in anti-Baha'i polemics.

Ultimately, it is the Baha'is' patriotism that is impugned. While it is true that historically Baha'is have shown no xenophobia and that their leaders have no record of fighting the imperial powers, the Baha'i leaders' dealings with outside powers have to be viewed (and if one is so inclined, judged) in the context of their times, which were marked by widespread persecution in Iran.

It is ironic that while Baha'is were suspected of anti-Iranian activities in Iran, in neighbouring Iraq they were also suspect and liable to be arrested and killed ('Alīkhānī 1993: 70). Under the Ba'thists, sweeping pardons or exemptions from prison sentences invariably excluded 'those who [were] sentenced for cases of espionage, masonry, Bahā'iyya and sabotage' (al-Khalīl 1990: 135).

Prominence in the Shah's Regime

The final justification one often hears for anti-Baha'i sentiment is their prominence in key positions under the Shah. This view is common among secular critics of the Shah's regime but could be found even among people who occupied high positions in it. Thus in the summer of 1973, the influential Minister of Court, Asadullāh 'Alam, wrote in his diary:

> Today I went to the celebration of the birthday of the Imam of the Age at Gulistan Palace. Usually I do not attend the religious ceremonies of the Court, as I have no time. But this feast day I always attend, to distinguish myself from the Baha'is. These fatherlandless (*bī-vaṭan*) Baha'is have infiltrated all walks of public life. It is thought that half the cabinet is Baha'i, causing a lot of dissatisfaction among the people. General Ayādī, the Shah's personal physician, is known to be a Baha'i, which hurts the Shāhanshāh a lot.[16]
>
> ('Alīkhānī 1995: 166)

Oddly enough, it seems that there is not a single empirical study that would endeavour to ascertain the truth of this often asserted claim. One problem that arises is the definition of 'Baha'i'. Islam is in sociological terms a 'church': a person with at least one Muslim progenitor is considered a Muslim,[17] apostasy is potentially punishable by death, and one remains a Muslim whether one performs the duties of a Muslim or not. Baha'is, by contrast, are in sociological terms more akin to a 'sect', which is 'a voluntary association and admits only persons with specific religious qualifications' (Weber 1978: 56).[18] In other words, one normally chooses to become, remain, or cease to be a Baha'i, although one can also be expelled.[19] Many people of Muslim background, however, seem to project a Muslim understanding of community membership to Baha'is, whereby individuals are considered Baha'is if one of their parents happens to have been one, or if they themselves had been one at some point. Baha'is use the term *Bahā'īzāda*, meaning child of a Baha'i, for people with a Baha'i background who are not themselves members of the religious community, a term for which there is no Muslim equivalent.[20] With these caveats in mind, let us first look at the presence of Baha'is, real or imagined, in the inner circle of the Shah's regime, and then try to interpret the reactions they elicited.

It is true that some Baha'is occupied a few sensitive positions in the 1960s and 1970s. The best known was the Shah's personal physician, General 'Abd al-Karīm Ayādī. There were a number of other Baha'i army officers, and Baha'is were also numerous in the National Iranian Oil Company. Paradoxically, the fact that the Baha'i Faith was not officially recognized as a minority religion allowed its adherents to occupy positions of influence, since officially they were not members of a non-Muslim minority. While Farhang Mihr, arguably Iran's most prominent Zoroastrian before the revolution, could not become minister of finance and headed the ministry while the prime minister was acting minister of finance (Alphonse 2000: 78–107), Asadullāh Ṣanī'ī could become minister of defence. And while the Baha'i community of Iran revoked Ṣanī'ī's administrative rights within the Baha'i community (*ṭard-i idārī*) for having accepted a political (as opposed to bureaucratic) appointment, he continued to be associated in the public mind with his earlier religion, for reasons pointed out earlier.

Others who were associated with the religion were either *Bahā'īzāda*s, former Baha'is, or unconnected with the religion altogether. The best example for the first category was Prime Minister Amīr-'Abbās Huvaydā, one of Iran's longest-serving prime ministers (1965–1977). As Abbas Milani has conclusively shown in his recent biography, his father had been a Baha'i but had left the faith, and Huvaydā himself was not religious in any way while acting in a way that a Muslim whose faith is not strong is expected to behave in a Muslim society, in the sense that he did not make his disbelief public and paid lip service to Islam to the point where he actually went on a pilgrimage to Mecca (Milani 2000).[21] Fu'ād Rawḥānī, another high-level technocrat of those years who was the first secretary general of OPEC (1961–64), had been brought up as a Baha'i but had stopped identifying with it by the time he entered politics. In fact, in his post-revolutionary exile he wrote a book about the Qur'an (Milani 2005: 81–89).[22] Mahnāz Afkhamī, Iran's first minister of women's affairs, is the daughter of a Baha'i mother and a Shaykhi father, while Iran's first female cabinet member, Farrukhrū Pārsā, also widely rumoured to belong to the community and executed soon after the revolution in 1979, had no connection to it at all. Allegations such as 'Alam's that 'half the cabinet' was Baha'i are therefore fanciful and, given the persecution Baha'is have suffered since 1979, highly irresponsible exaggerations.

The most unpopular official identified with the Baha'i Faith was Parvīz Thābitī, a high-ranking official of the Shah's secret police, SAVAK, who was that agency's public face on account of his appearances on national television as a *maqām-i amnīatī* (security official). Thābitī had indeed been brought up as a Baha'i, but he left the faith and was not an active member of the community by the time of his employment with the secret police.

Even if Baha'is had been as numerous in the inner circles of the regime as was claimed, from a strictly secular point of view this should have been objectionable only if it could be proven that they were less qualified for the jobs they were doing than Muslim-identified Iranians, a contention for which there is no evidence. While Iran under the Shah was certainly not a meritocracy, one of the criteria by which those who served the regime were chosen was reliability, and given their precarious situation in society, Baha'is were trusted by the Shah. In fact, it could be argued that all those with a Baha'i connection were among the least corrupt members of the Shah's circle, and someone like Fu'ād Rawḥānī is still widely admired for his administrative skills and cultured personality. The one exception seems to have been General Ayādī, whose business interests raised eyebrows.

More fundamentally, however, the fallacy of the argument can be shown by turning it around. Even if we were to agree that half the cabinet was Baha'i, this means that the other half was presumably Muslim, since members of recognized minorities could not accede to cabinet positions. Why does the latter fact not lead to resentment against Muslims? Presumably because being Muslim is 'normal'. But the mere fact of considering the religious background of the majority 'normal' is tantamount to Othering those who are of a different religion, which shows that resentment against Baha'is cannot *result* from their prominence in the inner circles of power and in fact is what renders this prominence politically objectionable in the first place. After all, few, if any, people objected to the prominence of graduates of Dār al-Funūn and Alburz high schools in the political elite (Zonis 1971: 168–169). In other words, one finds the disproportionate presence of members of a minority in high office only objectionable if one has a low opinion of that minority to begin with. In the United States, for instance, Unitarians have been disproportionately represented in the Senate, without this ever becoming a political issue or leading to anti-Unitarian polemics. And this, although most Unitarians deny the divinity of Christ, a belief to which most Americans probably subscribe. There is of course the crucial difference that the United States does not have an established religion but that Iran does, but to the extent that an established religion entails discrimination against those citizens who happen not to adhere to it, one would expect an honest and intellectually coherent secularist not to invoke that constitutional arrangement in defence of a type of discrimination that violates the Universal Declaration of Human Rights, of which Iran is a signatory.

Anti-Baha'i *ressentiment* was also caused by the existence of a small number of very rich Baha'i businessmen, whose success was probably ascribed to their good connections. The most talked about were Ḥabīb Thābit and Hujabr Yazdānī.[23] While the former was generally well respected except by those who held his faith against him, few admire the business practices of the latter, which are deplored by many Baha'is in private conversation. But there were, and, more importantly, are, plenty of Muslims whose practices do not conform to traditional Islamic business ethics, and no one would impute such businessmen's ways to their religion. *Ressentiment* was also probably caused by the perception that Baha'is were generally better off than the rest of the population, a perception that was probably due to a somewhat greater awareness of hygiene and perhaps a higher level of education among Baha'is.[24] One might even wonder whether Iranian Baha'is' frequently *soigné* appearance may not have contributed to generating an elitist image of them.[25]

One final impetus for anti-Baha'ism is their perceived conservatism. Although a few men of Baha'i background did join the Tūda party and other leftist organizations, the community's disinclination to get involved in partisan politics was often interpreted as a preference for the status quo. In the 1960s and 1970s, for instance, criticism of the Baha'is in the Confederation of Iranian Students centred on this point.[26]

While the reign of the last Shah was in many ways a golden age for Iran's religious minorities, in the case of the Baha'is the picture is mixed. True, Baha'is did find easy employment in the oil company and in the army, but in the latter they had to contend at times with Muslim superiors who disliked them for their faith. One Colonel Mu'minī, for instance, was put under arrest at the garrison for a month as punishment for having allowed Baha'i recruits to go home for a religious holiday.[27] In academia Baha'is were present but occasionally viewed with suspicion. In the 1950s the Yale historian Firuz Kazemzadeh was denied a teaching position in Iran because of his faith (Frye 2005: 100), and in the 1970s at least one university was pressured by SAVAK to avoid appointing Baha'i professors if they were not indispensable, as that would elicit a hostile reaction from the students.[28]

Let us now attempt to explain the above attitudes.

Nationalism and anti-cosmopolitanism

I would like to suggest that the anti-Baha'i prejudices of many secular Iranians derive from the anti-cosmopolitan outlook of Iranian nationalism. I will first discuss Baha'i cosmopolitanism, then offer a few thoughts on Iranian anti-cosmopolitanism, and conclude with an alternative view of Baha'is' connection with Iran.

Baha'i cosmopolitanism

The Baha'i Faith is explicitly cosmopolitan in its orientation. It affirms the unity of mankind, equality of all races, gender equality, calls for an international auxiliary language (Esperanto was for some time supported), and even advocates world government. To the extent that it spread to the United

States very early and that many members of the second generation of Baha'i community leaders in Iran had enjoyed an American education (Hollinger 2006), the Baha'i religion spans the Western world and the Third World to a degree that Islam, which remains essentially a Third World religion,[29] does not. Moreover, Iran's Baha'is adopted English as their primary foreign language at a time when most other educated Iranians learned French, which gave them an early advantage in dealing with Westerners when English replaced French in Iran sometime after World War II. Moreover, at equal levels of religious observance and commitment, Iranian Baha'is are more at ease in their interactions with Westerners than Iranian Muslims, perhaps because they lack the concept of *nijāsat* (ritual impurity, a quality non-Muslims have in common with pigs and dogs according to many Shi'i *mujtahid*s, including Khumaynī), and it is perhaps precisely the effortless social ease with which Baha'is seem to bridge what leftists and nationalists perceive to be a gap between Westerners and Iranians[30] that breeds resentment: Hamid Dabashi, for instance, has disparaged their 'graceless universalism'.[31]

The cosmopolitan values of Baha'is find a reflection in the film *Bāshū*, whose writer/director, Bahrām Bayḍā'ī, is of Baha'i background without being an active member of the community.[32] The very idea of making an Arab-Iranian boy the main and title character of a film produced during the Iraq-Iran War and having that war as a backdrop, is bold and goes against the grain of Persian nationalism, which, although not espoused by the Iranian state during the war, went through a revival among secular Iranians in the 1980s. Bāshū faces skin colour prejudice, a reality of Iranian life few have acknowledged, and finds refuge with a strong and beautiful woman in Gilan. The film acknowledges the multilingual character of Iranian society, which most secular Iranian nationalists deplore or feign to ignore, but points out the practical usefulness of a common language for everyone when Arab-speaking Bāshū and his Gīlakī-speaking tormenters find out that they can communicate in Persian, an epiphany which puts an end to their fighting.[33]

Iranian nationalism and the internal other

Iranian nationalism, which has been espoused by a majority of secular Iranians, has contained strong xenophobic elements from the beginning.[34] While hostility to Arabs has been motivated primarily by the fact that many secular Iranians blame their country's backwardness on Islam, a religion they see as having been forced on Iran by Arabs, suspicion of Westerners has more tangible reasons, given the peculiar geopolitical situation in which the country found itself: while its sovereignty was recognized on paper, Britain and Russia continuously meddled in its affairs and manipulated groups within Iranian society for the purpose of furthering their own interests. Groups that cultivate trans-national ties, like Jews, freemasons, and Baha'is, are therefore almost by definition suspect to Iranian nationalists. The cosmopolitanism of Baha'is thus renders them a prime target for conspiracy theorists, who attribute 'anti-Iranian' proclivities to them. Even the worldly Amīr Asadullāh 'Alam asked rhetorically: 'Is it possible to be a freemason, an internationalist, a member of the CIA, a Baha'i, and still have the interests of his nation at heart?' ('Alīkhānī 1993: 362).

For Jalāl Āl-i Aḥmad, the theoretician of 'westoxication' (*gharbzadagī*), Baha'is embodied that affliction: 'Their westoxication and the services they render to the oppression and injustice (*ẓulm*) of the current government are so obvious that no further comment is needed'. He admits that Baha'is were oppressed for years and that their house of worship was destroyed, but adds that in the years since the nationalization of oil 'since our governments repress religion and need more westoxication, [the Baha'is] have become more active, and like any other *parvenu* minority have so lost themselves that I fear for their well-being'. He then recounts how, when the flood gates of the Diz dam stopped working on a 15th of Sha'bān (the birthday of the Twelfth Imam) and as a result electricity went out in some cities with a mixed Sunni and Shi'i population in Khuzistan, Shi'is, who were more assertive in such a setting, blamed the engine trouble on the Baha'is (Āl-i Aḥmad n.d.: 412). In Āl-i Aḥmad's novel *Nifrīn-i zamīn* ('The Curse of the Earth'; Āl-i Aḥmad 1967), a 'Jew who has become a Baha'i'[35] sets up a chicken farm near a village and is rumoured to want to import one-day-old chicks, artificially inseminate cows, and plant Dutch alfalfa. While the novel's narrator pokes fun at the old land-owner who sees a British conspiracy behind this, he does liken the chicken farm to a 'parasite that attaches to the bottom of a tree and derives nourishment from its water, soil, and fertilizer',[36] combining the old anti-Semitic topos of the greedy Jew who enriches himself *at the expense* of others with criticism of innovation as a sign of westoxication.

In his study of Iran's political elite in the heyday of the Shah, Marvin Zonis noted that 'in many respects, the Baha'is of Iran are subjects to the criticisms frequently leveled against the Jews in the West' (Zonis 1971: 275–34). Studies of gentile attitudes towards Jews often distinguish between anti-Judaism and anti-Semitism, where the first denotes merely disdain for Jews while the latter sees a danger in them. Iranian anti-Baha'ism is more akin to anti-Semitism, in that Baha'is are not only despised or pitied for adhering to a 'false' doctrine, but feared as the fifth column of sinister outside powers who threaten the cultural integrity of society. The link with anti-semitism actually goes farther than a mere parallel, for Baha'is are commonly associated with 'Zionism'. The reasons for this are well known. First, the world centre of the religion is in what is now Israel, a historic accident,[37] and second, a good number of Iranian Baha'is are of Jewish origin,[38] which, incidentally, worried many Jews when the conversions were occurring (Fischel 1934). Another factor is that the 'return' of Jews to the Holy Land was prophesied to coincide with the coming of the Messiah, and Baha'ullah claimed to be the fulfilment of the messianic expectation of the Jews. Connections thus do exist between Baha'is and Jews, and by expressing prejudice against Baha'is, a bigoted Iranian can kill two birds with one stone, as it were.

If the association of Baha'is with Jews has a factual base, that with freemasonry is quite absurd, as Iranian masons did not accept Baha'is and the National Spiritual Assembly of Iran did not permit Iranian Baha'is to join lodges. This has not prevented the appearance of the term 'neomasonry' to designate Baha'is (Afrāsīābī 1989). In sum, the Baha'i is the quintessential internal Other of the nationalist imagination.

Baha'is as carriers of Persian culture

While the cosmopolitan spirit of the Baha'i religion militates against a preferential attachment to the state of Iran by non-Iranian Baha'is or the espousal of an exclusivist nationalism by Iranian Baha'is, the fact remains that given the Iranian origins of both Babism and the Baha'i Faith, Iran is considered *Mahd-i Amrullāh*, the Cradle of the Cause of God, in which capacity it commands a certain degree of affection for Baha'is around the world. Moreover, there is good evidence that at least 'Abdu'l-Baha harboured feelings of Iranian patriotism bordering on nationalism. This can be seen in his *Risāla-yi madaniyya* ('Treatise on Civilization'), whose authoritative English title for Baha'is is *The Secret of Divine Civilization*. He writes that every effort must be made so that 'this blessed (*mubārak*) land of Iran becomes the centre of the manifestation of human perfections in all matters'. He asserts that 'in olden times Iran was the heart of the world and shone like a lit candle on the horizon', . . . 'the wisdom (*ḥikmat*) of its government astonished the great leaders of the world, its political laws were followed by the rulers of the four corners of the world, [and] the Iranian nation was distinguished among the nations of the world by their world-conquests, culture, and civilization', while Iran was the 'centre of science and arts (*funūn*), the source of industry and innovation, and the mine of human virtues'. 'The knowledge and intelligence of [Iranians] astonished the wise of the world', and although they were 'the noblest of nations (*ashraf-i milal*)', they had regressed to a pitiful state and were in dire need of reform ('Abdu'l-Baha 1984: 6–11).[39] This is hardly the language of one who despises Iran and its people.

The same is true for the Persian language, which is, together with Arabic, a sacred language for Baha'is, many of whose scriptures are written in it. In the diaspora, Persian language retention is higher among Baha'is (and Jews) than among Muslims (Adelkhah 2001: 23), and at a time when the spread and the knowledge of Persian has declined outside Iran,[40] it is Baha'i pioneers who carry the language to distant islands and awaken interest in it in the converts they make. When Samoans learn Persian or Ugandans celebrate *Naw-Rúz*, when South African parents name their daughter Ṭáhirih or American parents their son Badí', it is, in a sense, Iranian culture that is being diffused, albeit by means of an old-fashioned transliteration system. From the perspective of a pragmatic Iranian nationalist, Baha'is could be seen as ambassadors of Iranian culture, although Baha'is themselves might not see it that way. The role of women is particularly noteworthy here. At a time when most urban Muslim women kept to themselves, Baha'i Iranian women settled in the most inhospitable places to spread their faith. Even one who might sneer at their motivation should not but admire their courage and initiative. Awareness of this dimension of Babism-Baha'ism is slowly spreading in Iran, as the growing popularity of Ṭāhira, Qurrat al-'Ayn among Iranian feminists shows.[41] In 2001 a women's calendar published in Iran featured her picture and explained that she was 'an erudite poet, philosopher, and lecturer', adding that she 'was executed by orders of Nāṣir al-Dīn Shah'.[42]

Conclusion

In this chapter I have tried to show that for many Iranians, Baha'is constitute the internal Other. It is interesting that colloquial Persian and scholarly English designate the opposition between 'self' and 'other' in a similar way: Iranians speak of *khudī* and *ghayr-i khudī*, 'self' and 'other-than-self', words that have connotations not unlike those of 'self' and 'other' as used in scholarly discourse. It would seem that many secular Iranians are still wedded to a confessional conception of Iranian nationhood, one that follows from the fact that Iran in many ways conforms to the model of the 'nation-church-state' that Bryan Turner proposed to conceptualize the role of religion in state-building and nation-building in Europe (Turner 1988: 330). To be a 'true' Iranian, it would seem, one has to be at least *culturally* from a Twelver Shi'i background. In the words of Afsaneh Najmabadi, 'until recent years, and even now only as a small minoritarian voice, Iranian modernity has not openly and explicitly inscribed Baha'is in the category Iranian' (Najmabadi 2005: 299 n41). In this sense, Iranian nationalism is not different from, say, Polish or Lithuanian nationalisms, which never quite accepted Protestants or Jews as integral members of the nation. The fact that Muslim Iranian 'credocentricity', to coin a neologism by analogy with 'ethnocentricity', is hardly unique does not make it less objectionable. As John Boswell put it in his magisterial study of tolerance and intolerance in Europe, 'almost all prejudice purports to be a rational response to some threat or danger: every despised group is claimed to threaten those who despise it; but it is usually easy to show that even if some danger exists, it is not the origin of the prejudice' (Boswell 1980: 7).

Notes

I am grateful to this book's editors and to Abbas Amanat for their detailed comments on my first draft.

1 Matters are different in Eastern religions: Hinduism made the Buddha the ninth avatar of Vishnu, and in Korea, Vietnam, and Japan a plethora of new religions flourish alongside the established ones. See Lanczkowski 1974.
2 Although a Muslim believer might wish to ponder the fact that of all religions other than Islam, the Baha'i Faith is the only one which considers Muḥammad to have been a prophet of God and the Qur'an to be the word of God.
3 See Tavakoli-Targhi's chapter in this book.
4 This author was once asked after a lecture in which he alluded ever so briefly to the plight of Jews and Baha'is in Iran after the revolution whether he was Jewish or Baha'i. The answer, to put the kind reader's mind at rest, is: 'Neither'.
5 For notable exceptions, see Sanasarian 2000 and Afshari 2001.
6 In late 1998 over 500 Baha'i homes were looted in 14 cities throughout Iran, and an informal university in which Baha'i professors who had been purged from Iranian universities taught Baha'i youth who are barred from entering Iranian universities was closed down, their animators arrested.
7 Ebady has mentioned Baha'is on other occasions as well.
8 For a general study of Iran's religious minorities since the revolution, see Sanasarian 2000.
9 MacEoin 1990: 55–61. See also MacEoin 1991.
10 As defined by Max Weber in his seminal 'Objectivity in Social Science', in Weber 1949.
11 For an example see Muntaẓirī 2001: 94–96.
12 See chapters in this volume by Tavakoli-Targhi and Afshari.
13 See Chehabi and Ashraf forthcoming.
14 This is in the epilogue to the second edition of the book. For further discussion of Ādamīyat's penchant for conspiracy theories see Ibid.
15 [Iqbāl] 1949: 148; Kasravī 1996: 95–97; Mīnuvī 1963: 22–26.
16 The symbolic charge of 'Alam's presence may be greater than he acknowledges, for the 'Lord of the Age' is, after all, the Twelfth Imam, whose return Twelver Shi'is expect while Baha'is believe that his return was embodied in the mission of the Bab.
17 See, for instance, Makkī al-'Āmilī 1996: vol. 2, 192, where an apostate is defined as an individual, one of whose parents was a Muslim at the time of conception.
18 Note that 'sect' and 'church' are used here in the sociological sense; no pejorative connotation is intended for the former, and no Christianizing for the latter. It has to be kept in mind that both terms denote ideal types rather than categories – in other words, they are not standards *to* which religious organizations are compared, but *by* which they are compared. For an excellent introduction to the use of the two terms in the sociology of religion, see Swatos 1998: 90–93.
19 As time passes, it could be argued that the Baha'i community is perhaps moving towards the church model, and a distinct Baha'i identity divorced from actual practice may be emerging. But this is a matter for empirical investigation.
20 In recent times some 'Muslim-identified' Iranians without faith have begun calling themselves *Musalmānzāda*.
21 Huvaydā even refused to intervene with the authorities in 1955 when the Baha'is of Ardistān were in the danger of being massacred, and in the end Ḥabib Thābit sent Pepsi-Cola trucks to evacuate them. Personal communication from Abbas

Amanat, whose father had urged Huvaydā to do something.
22 Rawḥānī's pseudonym was Fāruq Sharīf.
23 On the former, see his autobiography Thābit 1993.
24 See for instance Fecharaki 1977: 89–91, where she shows that the Baha'i neighbourhood of Najafabad was better planned and generally more 'modern' than the rest of the town.
25 Baha'is share this trait with the Shaykhi sect, who are known in Kirman to dress more carefully and with greater attention to the strictures of good taste than non-Shaykhi (*'bālāsarī'*) Shi'is.
26 Touraj Atabaki, a former member of the Confederation, personal communication, 27 July 2006.
27 Maythamī (n.d.): 259–260.
28 Farhād Rīahī, vice-president for academic affairs of Āryāmihr University (now Sharīf University), personal communication.
29 On this point, see Keddie 1995.
30 On the occasional limits of such intercultural harmony in practice, see Cole 2000.
31 Dabashi 2000: 495.
32 On him, see Mottahedeh 1999.
33 This is further developed in Rahimieh 1996.
34 See, for instance, Bayat Philipp 1974.
35 The Persian is *yahūdī-yi bahā'ī-shuda*, Āl-i Aḥmad, 1967: 199.
36 Ibid.: 254 and 261. Botanists, of course, might quibble with this description of a parasite.
37 It could easily have been on Cyprus if the Ottomans had sent Baha'ullah to Cyprus and his half-brother Mīrzā Yaḥyā, Ṣubḥ-i Azal to Palestine rather than the other way round!
38 See Mehrdad Amanat's chapter in this volume.
39 On this work, see Cole 1998: 81–91.
40 The evidence for this contention is presented in Fragner n.d..
41 See, for instance, Milani 1992: 77–99.
42 Aḥmadī Khurāsānī 2001: first week of November.

Bibliography

'Abdu'l-Baha. (1984) *Risāla-yi madaniyya*, Langenhain, Germany: Lajna-yi āthār-i amrī ba lisān-i fārsī va 'arabī.

Ādamīyat, F. (1944) *Amīr Kabīr va Iran: varaqī az tārīkh-i siyāsī-yi Iran*, 2nd printing, Tehran: Bungāh-i Āzar.

Adelkhah, F. (2001) 'Les Iraniens de Californie: si la République islamique n'existait pas . . .', *Les Études du CERI*, no. 75.

Afrāsīābī, B. (1989) *Tārīkh-i jāmi'a-yi Bahā'iyyat – Nawmāsunī*, Tehran: Sukhan.

Afshari, R. (2001) 'Naqḍ-i ḥuqūq-i bashar-i Bahā'iyān dar Jumhūrī-yi Islāmī', *Irānnāma* 19: 151–164.

Aḥmadī Khurāsānī, N. (2001) *Iranian Women's Calendar*, Tehran: Nashr-i Tawsi'a.

Āl-i Aḥmad, J. (1967) *Nifrīn-i zamīn*. Tehran: Intishārāt-i Nīl.

—— (n.d.) *Dar khidmat va khīānat-i rawshanfikrān: matn-i kāmil va sānsūr-nashuda*. Tehran: Ravāq.

'Alīkhānī, 'A. (ed.) (1993) *Yāddāsht-hā-yi 'Alam*, vol. 2. n.p.: New World Ltd.

—— (ed.) (1995) *Yāddāsht-hā-yi 'Alam*, vol. 3. n.p.: New World Ltd.

Alphonse, L. (2000) *Triumph over Discrimination: The Life Story of Farhang Mehr*. Mississauga, Ontario: Regal Press.

Bayat Philipp, M. (1974) 'Mirza Aqa Khan Kermani: A Nineteenth Century Persian Nationalist', *Middle Eastern Studies* 10.1: 36–59.

Boswell, J. (1980) *Christianity, Social Tolerance, and Homosexuality: Gay People in Western Europe from the Beginning of the Christian Era to the Fourteenth Century*, Chicago: University of Chicago Press.

Chehabi, H.E. and Ashraf, A. (forthcoming) 'The Paranoid Style in Iranian Historiography', in T. Atabaki, (ed.), *Historiography and Political Culture in Twentieth Century Iran*, London: I.B. Tauris.

Chesterton, G.K. (1923) *Heretics*, New York: Dodd, Mead & Co.

Cole, J.R.I. (1998) *Modernity & the Millennium: The Genesis of the Baha'i Faith in the Nineteenth-Century Middle East*, New York: Columbia University Press.

—— (2000) 'Race, Immorality and Money in the American Baha'i Community: Impeaching the Los Angeles Spiritual Assembly', *Religion* 30.2: 109–125.

Dabashi, H. (2000) 'The End of Islamic Ideology', *Social Research* 67.2: 475–518.

Durkheim, E. (1965) *The Elementary Forms of the Religious Life*, trans. J.W. Swain, New York: The Free Press.

Ebady, S. (2004) 'Nobel Laureate: Keynote Speaker at the Fifth Biennial Conference on Iranian Studies', *ISIS News* 33. 1–3: 18.

Fecharaki, P. (1977) 'Les Bahaïs de Nadjaf-Âbâd', *Revue Géographique de l'Est* 17: 89–91.

Fischel, W. (1934) 'The Baha'i Movement and Persian Jewry', *Jewish Review* 7: 47–55.

Fragner, B.G. (n.d.) *Die Persophonie: Regionalität, Identität und Sprachkontakt in der Geschichte Asiens*, Berlin: Das Arabische Buch.

Frye, R. (2005) *Greater Iran: A 20th-Century Odyssey*. Costa Mesa: Mazda.

Hollinger, R. (2006) 'An Iranian Enclave in Beirut: Baha'i Students at the American University of Beirut, 1906–1948', in H.E. Chehabi (ed.), *Distant Relations: Iran and Lebanon in the last 500 Years*, Oxford: Centre for Lebanese Studies, in association with I.B. Tauris.

[Iqbāl, 'A.] (1949) 'Mā va khvānandigān', *Majalla-yi Yādigār* 5: 8–9.

Kasravī, A. (1996) *Bahā'ī-garī, shī'a-garī, ṣūfī-garī*, Cologne: Mihr.

Keddie, N.R. (1995) 'Islamic Revival as Third Worldism', in Keddie, N.R., *Iran and the Muslim World: Resistance and Revolution*, New York: New York University Press.

al-Khalīl, S. (1990) *Republic of Fear: The Inside Story of Saddam's Iraq*, New York: Pantheon Books.

Lanczkowski, G. (1974) *Die Neuen Religionen*, Frankfurt: Fischer.

MacEoin, D. (1990) 'The Crisis in Babi and Bahai Studies: Part of a Wider Crisis in Academic Freedom?', *BRISMES Bulletin* 17: 55–61.

—— (1991) *The Baha'i Community in Iran in the Twentieth Century*, Occasional paper no. 4, London: CNMES, SOAS.

Makkī al-'Āmilī, Shaykh Abū 'Abdallāh. (1996) *Tarjuma-yi lum'a-yi Damishqiyya*, (trans.) Shīrvānī, 'A. Tehran: Dār al-Fikr.

Maythamī, L. (n.d.) *Az nihḍat-i āzādī ta mujāhidīn*, vol. 1, Tehran: Nashr-i Ṣamadiyya.

Milani, A. (2000) *The Persian Sphynx: Amir Abbas Hoveyda and the Riddle of the Iranian Revolution*, Washington, D.C.: Mage.

—— (2005) 'Dar sūg-i farzāna'i farzāna'ī: Rawḥānī', in *Sayyid-i Sāya-hā*. Los Angeles: Ketab Corp: 81–88.

Milani, F. (1992) *Veils and Words: The Emerging Voices of Iranian Women Writers*, London: I.B. Tauris.
Mīnuvī, M. (1963) 'Sharḥ-i zindagī-yi man', *Rāhnamā-yi kitāb* 6. 1–2: 22–26.
Mir-Hosseini, Z. (1997) 'Breaking the Seal: The New Face of the Ahl-e Haqq', in K. Kehl-Bodrogi, B. Kellner-Heinkele, and A. Otter-Beaujean, (eds), *Syncretistic Religious Communities in the Near East*, Leiden: Brill.
Mottahedeh, N. (1999) 'Bahram Bayḍā'ī: Filmography', in R. Issa, and S. Whitaker (eds), *Life and Art: The New Iranian Cinema*, London: BFI.
Muntaẓirī, H. (2001) *Matn-i kāmil-i khāṭirāt-i Āyatullāh Ḥusayn-ʿAlī Muntaẓirī*, Ittiḥād-i Nāshirīn-i Īrānī dar Urūpā.
Najmabadi, A. (2005) *Women with Mustaches and Men without Beards: gender and sexual anxieties of Iranian Modernity*, Berkeley: University of California Press.
Rahimieh, N. (1996) 'Marking Gender and Difference in the Myth of the Nation: *Bāshū*, A Post-Revolutionary Iranian Film', *Thamyris* 3: 2.
Sanasarian, E. (2000) *Religious Minorities in Iran*, Cambridge: Cambridge University Press.
Swatos, W.H. (1998) 'Church-Sect Theory', in *Encyclopedia of Religion and Society*, Walnut Creek: Altamira: 90–93.
Thābit, Ḥ. (1993) *Sargudhasht-i Ḥabīb-i Thābit*, Costa Mesa: Mazda.
Turner, B.S. (1988) 'Religion and State-Formation: a Commentary on Recent Debates', *Journal of Historical Sociology*, 1: 322–333.
Weber, M. (1949) *The Methodology of the Social Sciences*, trans. and ed. E. Shils and H.A. Finch, New York: The Free Press.
—— (1978) *Economy and Society*, G. Roth, and C. Wittich, (eds), Berkeley: California University Press.
Zonis, M. (1971) *The Political Elite of Iran*, Princeton: Princeton University Press.

10

ANTI-BAHA'ISM AND ISLAMISM IN IRAN

Mohamad Tavakoli-Targhi[1]

Introduction

Over the course of the past 50 years, the Iranian political discourse has continually misrepresented the Baha'i religion as a foreign entity. This xenophobic attitude is the culmination of a relentless campaign of purposeful forgetfulness aimed at representing a religion that emerged in the second half of the thirteenth/nineteenth century from the heart of Shi'i academic seminaries and Iran's religious culture. The exile of the Babi and Baha'i leaders to Baghdad following the attempted assassination of Nāsir al-Dīn Shah in 1268 (AH)/1852 paved the way for alienating and 'Otherizing' this Shi'i-Iranian movement.[2] In the historical narratives that proliferated in the 1320s/1940s, its leaders were successively declared to be agents of the governments of Russia, the Ottoman Empire, Great Britain, and Israel – their ultimate goal: to infringe the 'religious and national unity' of Iran. The spread of these narratives, which misrepresented the Iranian Baha'is as outsiders, was concomitant with the height of a campaign aimed at the effacement of 'the Alter' in Iran's national policies and political practices. The persecution of Baha'is and Jews, the campaign against 'materialists,' and measures such as the political acts of terror that marked the 1320s/1940s may all be considered signs of instituting a policy of effacing 'the Other' into Iran's political culture. The decade that is recognized more than any other as the period in which popular movements blossomed was also an era that witnessed the public acceptance of 'conspiracy theories.' The diffusion of these theories, which suspected 'foreign hands' of directing Iran's affairs, was in and of itself a catalyst toward 'Otherization' and the cleansing of other religions and thought systems from Iran's religious and political life.

In Iran, ghettoization and effacement of 'the Other' was concomitant with self-praise and self-acclaim. Although anti-Baha'ism had, for the most part, subsided during the reign of Riḍā Shah, it was violently rekindled in the 1320s/1940s. Its peak in this decade was concurrent with the founding of an Islamist movement. This movement, which sought to construct an Islamic future for Iran, crystallized all the while being in direct conflict with the Baha'i religion. Throughout this confrontation, in which this same movement achieved the propagation and spread of Islam throughout Iran, Islamic organizations and publications maintained a conspicuous plan for the gradual genesis of a 'Shi'i public sphere.' This sphere became systematized by conjoining mosques, centres for religious mourning (*takāyā*), organizations, and homes that served as sites for religious ceremonies. It created a 'counter public' vis-à-vis the 'national public sphere,' which until then, had not only been receptive to public dialogue, the exchange of differing views and the birth of a new culture and identity in Iran, but also inclusive of the adherents of all religious traditions. In the course of propagandistic campaigns aimed at thwarting the spread of the Baha'i religion, this Shi'i sphere was transformed into a powerful force that in 1327/1948, under the leadership of Ayatullah Burūjirdī, succeeded in incorporating Islamic education into the curriculum of primary and secondary schools. The government and the royal court, which had both garnered religious legitimacy in the 1320s/1940s and the early years of the 1330s/1950s through their protection of the Shi'i public sphere, began to face a crisis of leadership in early 1334/1955. In that year, Ḥujjat al-Islam Muḥammad Taqī Falsafī waged a denigrating attack against the Baha'is on a radio program aired daily in Ramaḍān. Following these vilifications, Tehran's military authorities occupied and destroyed the Haẓīrat al-Quds (the administrative and devotional centre of the Baha'is of Tehran). The coordinated aggression against individual Baha'is and Baha'i institutions in all parts of Iran, which transpired a mere ten years after the Jewish holocaust in fascist Europe, drew the concern of the world's Baha'is to these Iranian citizens. The protest of Baha'i Assemblies throughout the world to the United Nations and the reaction of the international community in defence of the rights of Baha'i citizens alerted the Iranian government to the fact that, after the genocide of the Jews in Europe, the effacement of 'the religious Other' was incompatible with the new political protocol and the prevailing civil code of conduct.[3] With the government distancing itself from the anti-Baha'i policies of the clerical establishment, the joint state-clergy project became more and more inclined to internal opposition and dispute. The direct confrontation between the two in 1341–2/1962–3 was the culmination of a disunion that began after the occupation and subsequent destruction of the Ḥaẓīrat al-Quds.

In this paper, I will undertake a study of several of the interrelated dimensions of anti-Baha'ism and Islamism in the period between 1320–34/1941–55.

The *Otherization* of Baha'is

The mode of encounter with the Babis and Baha'is over the course of the past one hundred and fifty years may be divided into two general phases. In the formative phase, which commenced in the 1260s [AH]/1840s, the clashes with Sayyid 'Alī-Muḥammad the Bab, his followers and the Baha'is, were disputes deeply ingrained in issues of Shi'i eschatology. These initial confrontations laid the groundwork for changing the understanding of such concepts as 'the Lord of the Age' and 'expecting the advent of the Hidden Imam' (*intiẓār*) in Shi'i jurisprudence. In the second phase, which took shape around the 1320s/1940s, these disputes gave way to a political discourse declaring a genuinely Iranian religion that had emerged from within the heart of the land's religious culture, to be entirely a machination of colonialists and imperialists. This period, which was contemporaneous with an upsurge in Baha'i propagation activities, witnessed the formation of numerous Islamic institutions throughout Iran for the explicit purpose of contending with the Baha'is. Once established, these organizations immediately set out to publish and circulate their positions and views. In this public mobilization effort, the Shi'i clergy both laid the foundation for numerous organizations and established the political discourse that paved the way for the attainment of political power at the threshold of the 'Islamic revolution.' The 'Otherization' of Baha'is in the political discourse played a decisive role in the crystallization of the concept of a 'Muslim nation of Iran.' In doing so, the discourse accused all other religions of being party to a colonialist plot to destroy the 'unity of the Muslim nation.' Furthermore, it misrepresented all Iranians who were not Muslim or who did not share in the ideals of a 'Muslim nation' as outsiders and, what is more, agents of foreign powers.

The polemics of Ḥājj Muḥammad-Karīm Kirmānī (1225–88 [AH]/1810–71), the spiritual leader and exemplary guide of the Shaykhīs, provides an example of the first confrontations with the Babis. Kirmānī believed that Sayyid 'Alī-Muḥammad the Bab 'was the perpetrator of . . . innovations that contradicted the exigencies of Islam, Shi'ism, and their essential nature.' After listing the 'innovations' of the Bab, at the conclusion of his *Risāla-yi tīr-i shahāb dar rāndan-i Bab* (Treatise of the Flaming Bullet to Expel the Bab; 1262 [AH]/1845–6), Kirmānī advanced the following motives for the Bab's adherents: 'Some followed him for the purpose of gaining some position of leadership, others because they were infatuated with changing the government and the prevailing social conditions, some as an act of enmity towards any form of government, others to spread injustice and oppression in the world, and so forth' (Kirmānī, M.K. 1387/1967: 210–11). In Kirmānī's aetiology of the Babi movement, 'each person' joined the Babis 'due to some vain imaginary idea' and thus, 'made famous the cause of this worthless and deceptive man' (Kirmānī, M.K. 1387/1967: 220).

In his *Risāla-yi sulṭāniyya* (Treatise of the Monarchy; 1275 [AH]/1859), written at the request of Nāṣir al-Dīn Shah, Kirmānī elucidated the point that 'during the occultation, it is unlawful for men . . . to wage the sword and revolt (*bi-shamshīr khurūj kunand*).' He explained: 'In this way, we pronounced the Babis who instigated men to wage the sword and revolt and who took an oath of allegiance from these people, to be demons. Moreover, we wrote books against the Bab and against the waging of the sword before the advent of the Imam, peace be upon him, and published these works in various parts of the world' (Kirmānī, M.K. 1277/1860: 219–20). In these polemics, the Babis' revolts (*khurūj*) and their conflicts with the state were the basis for alleging them to be 'misguided, misguiding, and infidels.' Ḥājj Muḥammad-Khān Kirmānī (1263–1324 [AH]/1847–1906), the son of Ḥājj Muḥammad-Karīm Khān, proceeded to refute the Bab and his followers based on the same Shi'i standards (Kirmānī, M. 1342/1923: 262).

In suit with countless other *'ulama*, in his work, *Irghām al-shayṭān fī radd ahl-i bayān* (The Coercion of Satan: Refuting the Babis'; 1342 (AH)/1923), Shaykh Zayn al-'Ābidīn Nurī-Shah Ḥusaynī Tihrānī likewise explicated the differences between the Shi'a and the Babis on the basis of Shi'i criteria. In this monograph, written to refute *Al-īmān fī iẓhār nuqṭat al-bayān* ('Faith in the Manifestation of the Point of the Bayān'), Tihrānī set out to cite and disprove, one by one, all of the issues presented in that treatise. In seeking to draw attention to the changes the movement experienced during the ministries of Mīrzā Ḥusayn-'Alī Baha'ullah (d. 1892) and 'Abdu'l-Baha 'Abbās (d. 1921), Tihrānī wrote:

> That which can now be seen and heard from the Babi and Baha'i sects regarding the need for good manners and the observance of courtesy is all due to the fact that they have become aware of how erroneous the initial goals of their leaders had been. For this reason, they decided to change their methods. It reached the point where 'Abdu'l-Baha himself dreamed up the idea of inviting the divided nations of the world to universal peace; heedless of the fact that a world war was approaching and the very opposite of what he had desired would occur.
>
> (Ḥusaynī 1342/1964: 392, 396)

In his *Risāla-yi uṣūl-i dīn va kashf al-khaṭā-yi muslimīn* ('Treatise on the Principles of Religion and Disclosing the Errors of the Muslims'), Mīrzā 'Alī-Akbar Mujtāhid-i Ardabīlī Ḥājib al-A'imma regretted the fact that, 'We are observing how some of the cowardly and unprincipled abandon Islam and become Babis.' He then briefly cited and vehemently refuted the 'obscene' claims of the Babis and Baha'is. For the most part, these polemics were aimed at citing the Arabic mistakes in Babi texts and mentioning reports such as 'the immodesty and indecency of the Babi and Baha'i sects where men and women gather together in the same meeting, with the lights turned off, and commit adultery by having intercourse with each other's wives' (Ardabīlī Ḥājib al-A'ima 1334/1956: 313, 318). In these polemics, the active role of Qurrat al-'Ayn in the Babi movement was assumed to have been a sign of the immorality of the Babis.[4]

The works of Aḥmad Kasravī (d. 1324/1946) mark at once, the final stage of studying the common foundations of the two religions and the beginnings of a new form of religious criticism. In stark contrast to other trends that took shape in those years, of which *Yād-dāshthā-yi kinyāz dālgurukī* (the Memoirs of Count Dolgoruki) is the example *par excellence*,[5] Kasravī believed that Baha'ism was founded on Babism, which was founded on Shaykhism, which was founded on Shi'ism and Mahdism, and 'all of these have nothing save imaginary foundations.' Kasravī argued that Mahdism was incompatible with the laws of God (or better said, the laws of nature).

He explained that Mahdists 'imagine that the Mahdī will arise with an overwhelming force, transcend the natural laws of the world and carry out deeds that are beyond the abilities of other (normal) men.' On the basis of this presumption, they believe that the Mahdī 'will rule the world in a different manner and weed out its maleficent roots' (Kasravī n.d.: 70, 72–3). Kasravī believed that 'most of the Baha'i leaders are the same old mullas and in their discourse, they employ the same old style and rhetoric of the mullas' (Kasravī 1322/1944: 29–31).

As a result of the confrontations with the Babis and Baha'is, the expectation of the advent of the Mahdī, an advent which was believed to have been imminent, was gradually postponed to a more distant future. The delay of the Mahdī's manifestation caused his believers to become concerned for the future. It, furthermore, paved the intellectual path for the project of *vilāyat-i faqīh* (the governance of the jurist). Thus, in place of waiting for a tomorrow that would never materialize, the Shi'a were invited to take part in constructing an Islamic future.

Anti-Baha'ism in the Islamic public sphere

The Shahrīvar 1320/September 1941 resignation of Riḍā Shah paved the way for the emergence of political forces that had been suppressed under his rule. Consequently, the 1320s/1940s witnessed the rise of numerous Islamic councils and organizations throughout Iran to confront Baha'is, materialists, and supporters of Aḥmad Kasravī. Alongside political parties and local councils, numerous organizations engaged in Islamic propaganda and instruction.[6] Apace with these groups, other forces operating throughout the country likewise spared no effort in their respective areas of activity.[7] Together, these groups succeeded in transforming organizations, mosques, centres where the martyrdom of Imām Ḥusayn was mourned (*ḥusaynīya*), and neighbourhoods into an interconnected sphere for Islamic propagation and education. Yet, that which distinguished these educational gatherings from devotional meetings or recitations of the tragedies of Karbala was their long-term objective. The aims of these groups had crystallized for the explicit purpose of confronting 'Baha'i committees,' political parties, and civic groups. By means of Islamic instruction and publishing, these organizations were keen to become an obstacle for the progress of not only Baha'is, but any system of thought that was unrelated to religion. In this manner, with a united coalition of mosques, homes, and Islamic associations, a preventive campaign for building an Islamic future commenced. In the midst of these developments, publications such as *Ā'īn-i Islam* (the Religion of Islam), *Parcham-i Islam* (the Banner of Islam), *Dunyā-yi Islam* (the World of Islam), *Nidā-yi Ḥaqq* (the Call of Truth) played a significant role in Islamizing the public sphere.

The *Anjuman-i Tablīghāt-i Islāmī*, founded in the early 1320s/1940s, was one of the most active anti-Baha'i organizations. Its 'founder,' 'Aṭā'ullāh Shahābpūr, had been one of the permanent writers of the fascist periodical, *Iran-i Bāstān* (Ancient Iran) in the 1310s/1930s. Reflecting on his previous experiences, Shahābpūr confessed: 'For many years I was blind and incapable of comprehending the truth . . . At about the same time that I had become deluded by all the useless pride and haughtiness, I was blessed to see the light of truth. In a matter of a few hours, all of the pride and frivolity dissipated . . . I realized that happiness is found in Islam alone.' After gazing on 'the beauteous vista of truth' in Farvardīn 1321/April 1942, Shahābpūr published a leaflet entitled, *Ā'īn-i gushāyish-i rāh-i naw dar 'ālam-i haqīqat* ('The Means of Embarking on a New Path in the Realm of Truth') (Shahābpūr 1323a/1944: 274). This booklet was the first work published by the *Anjuman-i Tablīghāt-i Islāmī*. In its pages, 'explicating the significance of religiosity' and 'elucidating the truth of Islam to the world' were presented as being among the central objectives of the organization. The society sought to 'prove' the doctrine that 'each and every one of the religions existing today, with the exception of Islam, is either archaic, has been abrogated, is full of superstitions or is man-made. The true religion to which all must adhere is Islam' (Shahābpūr 1323b/1944). By 1322/1943, Jalāl Āl-i Aḥmad, Ni'mat Jahānbānū'ī (the editor-in-chief of the weekly periodical *Firdawsī*), 'Alī Akbar Shahābī, Muḥammad 'Alī 'Ilmī, Muḥammad Ḥasan 'Ilmī, 'Abd al-Raḥīm 'Ilmī and 'Alī Akbar 'Ilmī (the latter four being the managers of the 'Ilmī publishing house) were among the well-known 'friends' of the *Anjuman-i Tablīghāt-i Islāmī* (Anjuman-i Tablīghāt-i Islamī 1322/1944: 13, 21). In order to achieve the goals of the society, Shahābpūr solicited the intimate cooperation of the *'ulama*. He, moreover, encouraged them to author a few easy-to-understand books entitled *khud āmūz-i fiqh* ('Teach Yourself Islamic Jurisprudence'). Mujtahid Kamara'ī, Ḥabbat al-Islam Shahristānī, and Maḥmūd Ṭāliqānī were amongst the *'ulama* to have their books published by the *Anjuman-i Tablīghāt-i Islāmī*.[8] To procure the *'ulama*'s collaboration, the society mobilized a force to ensure the enforcement of 'the second supplementary article of the Constitution and the acceptance of five of the most distinguished *'ulama* as members of the (National) Consultative Assembly.' In this mobilization of 'Muslim brothers,' the *Anjuman-i Tablīghāt-i Islāmī* desired 'the government and the Assembly to enforce this significant article, on which depends the very salvation of all Iranians and Muslims' (Raḥīmīyān 1326/1947: 3). In order to accelerate the propagation of Islam, in 1326/1947, the society established *Dār al-'ulūm-i dīnī va 'arabī* (The Institute For Religious Sciences and the Study of Arabic) (Anonymous 1326a/1948: 3). Moreover, it published the weekly journal, *Nūr-i Dānish* (the Light of Knowledge; Mihr 1326/October 1947) and created 'a place where the pilgrims to Karbala could rest' (Shahābpūr 1326/1947: 1–2). In addition to educational leaflets, 128,000 copies of which were printed between Farvardīn 1321/April 1942 and Ābān 1323/November 1944,[9] the society published *Sālnāma-yi Nūr-i Dānish* (the Annual Report of the Light of Knowledge). This report, first published in 1324/1945, contained mostly letters of introduction written by Baha'is who had converted to Islam in the preceding 12 months. These letters were often accompanied by a letter of repentance, the text of which was similar to the following letter, printed in 1345/1966:

> I, Rahbar Zamānī, the son of the late Muḥammad Taqī; identification number 9; born 1318/1939; the son of a Baha'i; a resident of Himmat Ābād, near the city of Ābādih. After recognizing the truth and contacting a number of enlightened Muslims regarding the falsehood and worthlessness of the lost and straying sect, I now proclaim my hatred and intense aversion for it. I recognize the Islamic religion and the sacred law of Shi'ism as being the sole path of truth and the only eternal religion. I announce my belief in the finality of messengership and prophethood through Muḥammad bin 'Abd Allāh and my recognition of his successors, 'Alī bin Abī Ṭālib and his eleven descendants. They alone are my guides and leaders, the true and righteous Imams and the trustees of the Messenger of Islam.

This letter is similar to a repentance letter written by someone else who had introduced himself as having being 'a resident of the village of Bād-Ābād' (Anonymous 1345/1967: 231).

Between the 1330s/1950s and the 1350s/1970s, the *Anjuman-i Tablīghāt-i Islāmī* was one of the most active anti-Baha'i organizations in Iran. In the two decades preceding the revolution, this society became known as *Anjuman-i ḍidd-i Baha'i* (the Anti-Baha'i Society) and *Anjuman-i Ḥujjatīya*. Moreover, its leaders grew to become some of the most influential figures in the Islamic republic.[10]

The *Jāmi'a-yi Ta'līmat-i Islāmī* was yet another institution that sought to inhibit the growth of the Baha'i religion via the spread of Islamic training. This organization was founded in early 1322/1943 on the advice of the preacher, 'Abbās-'Alī Islāmī, and with 'the assistance of six scholars.' It soon reached the conclusion that the most effective means to achieve religious and social reforms was to promote religious education and not interfere in the prevailing political debates. At the end of 1323/1945, this society established seven night schools for the study of the religious sciences. In Khurdād 1325/June 1946, the number of such schools in Tehran had reached 24 and the number of students had reached 2,337.[11] By the end of 1326/1948, the number of night schools increased to 45 and the number of day schools reached 16 (Anjuman-i Tablīghāt-i Islāmī 1326/1948: 3). According to 'Abbās-'Alī Islāmī, in its 25 years of activity, the *Jāmi'a-yi Ta'līmāt-i Islāmī* founded 'more than 170 cultural institutions offering moral and religious instruction' (Islāmī 1362/1984: 24). In addition to its schools in Tehran, the society's academies were established mainly in those cities and villages where Baha'is were known to have instituted teaching initiatives of their own.

'In order to serve our native land and sacrifice in the path of the unerring religion of Islam,' the *Jāmi'a-yi Ta'līmāt-i Islāmī* gave special attention to the dissemination of pertinent news and information. Ḥusayn 'Abdullāhī, for example, reported in a letter to 'the Shi'i exemplary guides and highest authorities on religion and law' that on a trip to the villages near Isfahan, a preacher from Tehran, Mr. Ghulām-Riḍā Fīrūzīān, witnessed the educational activities being carried out by Baha'is in Qahva-Rukh, Isfahan:

> For many years, a Baha'i has been teaching the Muslim children to say 'In the name of God, the All-Glorious' instead of 'In the name of God, the Merciful, the Compassionate.' He has also been training them in the Baha'i teachings and not the teachings and laws of Islam. He has even been showing . . . these Muslim youth a different *qibla* to turn to for their prayers. What's more, several Muslim girls have been attending the school. In instructing them, he used only the books that contained the worthless Baha'i teachings. What is the cause of this horrible state of affairs?! Who is responsible?!

Continuing his report, 'Abdullāhī argued that,

> from our standpoint, all of the immorality and corruption in public life is due to the absence of religious educators in these different regions. If this negligence continues, it won't be long before this small number of simple-minded Muslims, residing in villages that have no access to religious sermons, forget who they are and become entirely different people!!

'Abdullāhī, 'a correspondent for religious newspapers [and] spokesperson of the Islamic publications' believed that the solution to these problems lay in pursuing the following steps:

> As soon as possible, the respected and esteemed Shi'i authorities on religion and law, in particular Ayatullah Burūjirdī and individuals

> such as Mr. Ḥujjat and Mr. Fayḍ Kathrullāh, need to choose a number of enlightened and serious students and charge them to organize sorely needed propagation projects and effective consolidation programmes in the villages surrounding the townships. Hopefully, by means of religious propaganda, they will put an end to the progress of these worthless and irreligious people.

'Abdullāhī went on to request,

> Ḥājj Shaykh 'Abbās-'Alī Islāmī, the founder and director of the *Jāmi'a-yi Ta'līmāt-i Islāmī*, who is himself an enlightened and serious man, to place certain officials in charge of ensuring that in all of the townships, a sizeable number of branches are organized to offer the society's classes. In particular, more consideration must be given to those villages that are situated in difficult to reach regions. Perhaps, by the will of God and the effort of these enlightened Muslims, associating with these outlaws of religion will cease and some of the illiterate farmers will be protected and safeguarded from the clutches of these makers of sedition.
>
> ('Abdullāhī 1326/1948: 2)

Following the publication of this letter, in a report, Mahdī Ṣadīqī announced some very good news:

> Praise be to God, as a result of a number of nightly speeches by Shaykh Ghulām-Riḍā Fīrūzīān, night school number six of the Isfahan branch of the *Jāmi'a-yi Ta'līmāt-i Islāmī* has been established. After a series of religious discussions with the above mentioned Baha'i teacher, he became doubtful of his beliefs. He closed his school and has left that village for now.
>
> (Anonymous 1326c/1948: 2)

This string of propagandistic reports was published in the *Dunyā-yi Islam* newspaper. Ghulām-Riḍā Fīrūzīān, who was the main source for the reports concerning the propagation activities of the Baha'is, was also the founder of the school for religious education in Qahva-Rukh.

In addition to propagation projects and programmes, the society also contributed to the composition of curriculum. Simultaneous with Ayatullah Burūjirdī's efforts to augment the religious studies curriculum of primary and secondary schools, Ḥasan-'Alī Gulshan, who served as director of schools for the *Jāmi'a-yi Ta'līmāt-i Islāmī*, authored the monograph, *Akhlāq-i Gulshanī*. This text was to be taught at the society's night and day schools. Gulshan was hopeful that 'the ministry of culture might also prescribe the teaching of this book in all of the relevant primary and second schools as part of the religious studies curriculum' (Anonymous 1326d/1948: 2). In the final months of Dr. Muṣaddiq administration, the rumour that Dr. Mihdī Ādhar, the Minister of Culture, was intending to close the *Jāmi'a-yi Ta'līmāt-i Islamī* and reinforce the Baha'i schools, played a salient role in stirring strong religious sentiments against his regime.[12]

The *Jam'īyat-i Madhhab-i Ja'farī* was yet another anti-Baha'i organization active in the 1320s/1940s. Writing on behalf of the association, Sayyid Murtaḍā Khalkhālī and 'Abd al-Ḥusayn Mu'taḍidī published an open letter in the Bahman 1326/February 1948 edition of *Parcham-i Islam*. In this letter, they sought to report on the ever-increasing influence of the Baha'is:

> Nowadays, in all of the ministries and all of the governmental offices, Baha'is occupy important and influential positions. They have infiltrated all of our religious, civil, and national affairs with their worthless religion. Little by little, the situation has escalated to the point where, in some places, individuals with like-minded principles have been advocating for their employment. This, despite the explicit text of federal laws that prohibit such hirings. By these means, they are now busy spreading their licentious and repugnant propaganda.

In this letter, the *Jam'īyat-i Madhhab-i Ja'farī* solicited 'the sacred and blessed court' of the Shah 'to discharge the Baha'is from governmental offices and ministries and to repress their protestations' (Khalkhālī 1336/1958: 3). Two months after the publication of this open letter, 'a Muslim' mentioned 'the poisonous propaganda' of the Baha'is and requested the National Consultative Assembly to 'issue [a] manifesto. These sorts of people are capable of continuing their spurious deeds to disrupt the order and security.' He called on the Assembly to use this manifesto to 'Tell them to cease and desist their treacherous plots as early as possible; otherwise, the day will come when the Muslim nation of Iran will settle its accounts with the enemies of Islam and you will be punished mercilessly.' Possessing a favourable view of 'the clerics,' the writer then issued the following warning:

> Honored clerics: every township must be diligent in ensuring that the poisonous propaganda of the Baha'is does not leave even the slightest effect on the people's morale, people who slip easily into ignorance. It is imperative to develop a system for propagation that is based on the exalted principles of religion, a system that will deepen the faith of the people in performing their moral duties, in carrying out community development, and in seeking further progress for themselves and their community. This system will awaken the people one by one, until such time as every Muslim is capable, by producing strong rational proofs and showing the power

> of Islam, to deliver a fierce blow to the mouth of those who oppose Islam.
>
> (Anonymous Muslim 1327/1949: 4)

The fundamental aim of many of the Islamic organizations and societies that were founded in this change-filled decade was delivering this same 'fierce blow to the mouth of those who opposed Islam.'

Yet another one of the Islamic organizations was *Jam'īyat-i Hay'āt-i Muravvijīn-i Madhhab-i Ja'farī* (the Association for Organizations of Promoters of the Ja'farī School). Formed in 1326/1947, it was a coalition of between 60 and 70 religious organizations based in Tehran.[13] At a convention starting on 20 Ādhar 1326/12 December 1947, Shaykh Mihdī Sharī'atmadārī 'asserted that according to the explicit text of the Constitution, one of the obligations of the nation and government of Iran is to contest and fight any and all any actions that may be construed as being anti-religious or anti-Shi'i (Anonymous 1326g/1948: 1). This association sponsored an abundant array of initiatives and programs. In a statement issued in Bahman 1326/ February 1948, it stated: 'With the exception of Islam, and in particular, the true sect of Shi'ism, if you hear the name of any other religion or sect in the world, you can be confident that it is entirely devoid of faith and beliefs. On the contrary, at its root, you will find some political organization or some shadowy and sinister faction . . .' (Anonymous 1326h/1948: 3).

Islamic publication and propaganda

Publications such as *Ā'īn-i Islam, Parcham-i Islam, Dunyā-yi Islam*, and *Nidā-yi Ḥaqq* played a significant role in amalgamating religious organizations and societies and establishing an Islamic public sphere. This sphere had blossomed through consociating institutions and Islamic publications. By being morally critical of the new values of a rapidly changing Iranian society, this sphere laid the groundwork for an Islamic alternative to the national public sphere. In doing so, it strategically employed new cultural innovations and institutions prevailing in the national public sphere, e.g. radio, cinema, theatre, school, university, (political) parties and various newspapers and magazines. Islamic publications depicted Iran as a 'Shi'i state' and declared its citizens to be the 'the Muslim People of Iran.' In this manner, through excluding non-Muslim Iranians from the national public sphere, they triggered the appearance of a special and distinct sphere. *Ā'īn-i Islam* was among the first Islamic newspapers to begin circulation in the 1320s/ 1940s.[14] *Parcham-i Islam* began circulation in Farvardīn 1325/April 1946 with 'Abd al-Karīm Faqīhī Shīrāzī as its editor-in-chief. It was among the most influential weekly periodicals. Baha'is were rarely attacked in the first issues of *Parcham-i Islam*. For the most part, they were dealt with indirectly. References could be found in the writings of columnists such as Ḥujjat al-Islam Najmābādī, Sayyid Maḥmūd Ṭāliqānī, Ḥasan Nīkū, 'Abd al-Ḥusayn Āyatī and Muḥammad-'Alī Shikārī.[15] However, beginning on 9 Mihr 1326/ 2 October 1947, *Parcham-i Islam* began to directly attack the Baha'i religion and its adherents. The paper explained this change in policy in a memorandum as follows:

> We at *Parcham-i Islam*, from our paper's inception to some time thereafter, had refused to engage in these kinds of discussions and had no desire to do so, since we live these days in a world in which a large segment of its people deny the existence of God and essentially have no faith in the fundamental principles of religion and the coming of the Day of Resurrection. Therefore, we saw no reason to discuss the Baha'is, the followers of a political and fabricated sect. However, recently it has been heard that in addition to not observing good manners, courtesy and respect, the Baha'is have also been committing mischief against and breaking the laws of our country. Therefore, from this week forward, by including facts about this sect in our paper, we will reveal the truth about this sect to our respected readers. We are hopeful that perhaps, God willing, it will also have an effect on those (Baha'is) who have strayed from the straight path and remain lost.

This change in policy was made precisely at a time when *Parcham-i Islam* had been forced to suspend its operations for a week as a result of financial difficulties. The headline on the front page of that week's issue of *Parcham-i Islam* read 'The Reasons for the One Week Suspension of Operations: Low Number of Subscribers [and] the Politics of Foreigners.' This headline suggests that a conflict against the Baha'is was the pretext to garnering the protection of the *'ulama* and provoking the paper's Muslim readership. In this article, Faqīhī-Shīrāzī warned the *'ulama*:

> This is the last time we remind the spiritual leaders of Islam, the distinguished *'ulama*, and the honored preachers who know themselves to be devotees of Islam and champions of its *shari'a*, that if we are forced to shut down this religious paper, all of our enemies will rejoice and the day will come when you will regret your present disregard, laxity, and negligence.

Further in the article, Faqīhī, who was in actuality a physician specializing in sexually transmitted diseases, described his ardent desire to serve as a journalist:

> Due to my religious obligations . . . I will begin to walk down this perilous road. As I have been reminded time and again, I have

> already learned this service from watching Christian doctors and the authorities at American hospitals do the same. The activities of the Baha'i doctors have forced me, despite all of the difficulties, to arise and undertake this sacred path of service.
>
> (Faqīhī-Shīrāzī 1326a/1948: 1)

Although Faqīhī-Shīrāzī had given voice to his desire to engage in the propagation of Islam before, his previous words had been fairly different:

> During my years of studying medicine, receiving training at hospitals, and finishing my hospital residency, I was fortunate enough to observe the ways in which Christian propagandists spread their religion. I closely studied their activities. Luckily, I learned the secrets of their resolve and perseverance. I realized that despite all of the challenges and obstacles they face in Iran, they have toiled and made a valiant effort to propagate the abrogated religion of Christianity. In those same days, I swore to myself that in addition to my lifelong spiritual responsibility to the medical profession, I would seize the first opportunity that presented itself to serve the true religion of Islam and would spare no effort, financial or otherwise, for this purpose . . .

In this account, written in Murdād 1326/August 1947, one finds no reference to 'the activities of Baha'i doctors' (Faqīhī-Shīrāzī 1326b/1948: 1).

The occupation of the Ḥaẓīrat al-Quds

The campaign against Baha'is intensified in the late 1320s/1940s and early 1330s/1950s. The Tīr 1326/July 1947 murder of engineer Shahīdzāda in Bābulsar and the 14 Bahman 1327/3 February 1949 killing of Dr. Sulaymān Birjīs in Kashan were amongst the consequences of this new phase of attacks.[16] Ayatullah Riḍā Gulsurkhī, presently one of the foremost leaders of the Shi'i seminary in Qum, participated himself in the killing of Dr. Birjīs. He recalled the circumstances of that event as follows: 'Dr. Birjīs was a Jew who had become a Baha'i. Perhaps more than a hundred Muslims had been killed at the hands of this man. This Dr. Birjīs would give the wrong medicine to those Muslims who were anti-Baha'i and kill them.' This report bears striking resemblance to another rumour apropos the selling of lethal drugs by Jewish-owned pharmacies to Muslim citizens. Originally, *Iran-i Bāstān* had spread this rumour in Tīr 1313/July 1934 to instigate anti-Jewish sentiments in Iran.[17] However, in the 1320s/1940s, it was actualized as the primary motive of Dr. Birjīs's killers. In recounting the murder of Dr. Birjīs, who had been asked to visit an empty house under the pretext of seeing a sick patient, Ayatullah Gulsurkhī recalled that,

> Eight people, including Mr. Rasūlzāda went and killed Dr. Birjīs. Then, they left the scene saying aloud, 'There is no god but God.' Of course, their primary instigator was the late Turbatī Vā'īẓ. After killing Dr. Birjīs, they went to the police and surrendered themselves. The officers took them to Tehran. I myself was included among the accused and my name was recorded as Riḍā Gulsurkhī in the file.
>
> (Anonymous 1370/1992: 183)

The murder of 'Abd al-Ḥusayn Hajīr[18] at the hands of Sayyid Ḥusayn Imāmī[19] on 13 Ābān 1328/9 November 1949 can be considered another indicator of the start of a harsher phase of opposition against the Baha'is. He was killed during mourning services for Imām Ḥusayn in the Sipahsālār mosque (Anonymous 1328/1950: 5, 15, 17). According to witnesses, the rumour of his being a Baha'i was the primary motive behind Hajīr's murder and the main reason why his killing constituted the most important element of the plans of the *Jam'īyat-i Fadā'iyān-i Islam*. It is believed that this rumour was spread by Abū al-Ḥasan Ḥā'irī-zāda.[20] In a report of the incident dated 25 Khurdād 1327/15 June 1948, a police detective wrote:

> Following a talk that he delivered two nights ago before a crowd of people at the Masjid Shah, Ḥā'irī-zāda met yesterday with Sayyid Abū al-Qāsim Kāshānī and a few of the leaders of the *Jam'īyat-i Fadā'iyān-i Islam*. He said: 'You are *Fadā'iyān-i Islam* (the Devotees of Islam). Don't be content with the reins of the government falling into the hands of someone who is a promoter of the Baha'i religion (*dīn*). This is the first conflict that will be initiated by Muslims and you must remain obstinate and ensure that your interests are always met.'
>
> (Tafrishī 1371/1992 2: 147–8)

In this manner, the opposition to Hajīr had taken on 'a more religious tenor than before.' Those who sided with Sayyid Abū al-Qāsim Kāshānī considered fighting against Hajīr the same as 'protecting religion and the Qur'an (Tafrishī 1371/1992 2: 161).

Widespread propaganda against the Baha'is served to accomplish the dismissal of some followers during the administration of Prime Minister Razm-ārā (Tīr 1329/July 1950 – Isfand 1329/March 1951). Shams al-Dīn Jazā'irī, the Minister of Culture in Razm-ārā's cabinet, in explaining the decision to discharge these employees, recalled that in every meeting with Ayatullah Burūjirdī, the latter requested him to take this message to the Shah: At the command of Shoghi Effendi, the Baha'is will begin demonstrating. This 'is the why the Muslims are complaining.' Ayatullah Burūjirdī's complaint was based on the fact that, in those years, the Bahai's had gradually

Figure 10.1 Mulla Falsafī supervising workmen in the act of destroying the dome of the National Baha'i Center in Tehran, 1955.

ceased dissimulating their faith, and had begun identifying themselves as Baha'is on their employment applications. After conveying Burūjirdī's words at a cabinet meeting, Jazā'irī said: 'The non-official status of the Baha'i religion was communicated to all of the provincial governors in a circular, but I decided to discharge the Baha'is working in the ministry of culture.' In determining how to carry out this decision, he recalled: 'First, I requested to see all of them. I told them to write "Muslim" in your departmental files and we will leave you alone because Islam judges by what is written, unless the contrary is proved.' However, his suggestion for religious dissimulation was not accepted by the Baha'is who for some time had been openly stating their religious identity:

> But the Baha'i teachers did not accept. Instead, they wrote two formal letters against me, one signed by Furūtan, the secretary of the Baha'is' Assembly and the other by Fatḥ-i A'ẓam, the chairman of the Assembly. They sent these letters to the office of the Prime Minister and its inspection department. In these letters, they declared my actions to be a violation of the right to religious freedom and a contravention of the charter of the United Nations.

In reaction to this protest, Dr. Jazā'irī noted: 'When this happened, I fired all of the Baha'i employees who were employed under contract. Moreover, I discharged all of the formal employees from the training staff and demoted them to administrative posts' (Anonymous 1334a/1956: 1, 4).

In addition to these forms of discrimination, Islamic organizations and Islamist forces began fiercely persecuting the Baha'is. These groups believed the Baha'is' assertion of their religious identity was tantamount to an affront to Islam. Consequently, some reached the decision to destroy the Ḥaẓīrat al-Quds, the administrative centre of the Baha'is of Tehran. Although the rumour of destroying the Ḥaẓīrat al-Quds had been circulating since Urdībihisht 1327/May 1948, it finally materialized on 16 Urdībihisht 1334/ 7 May 1955 under the direction of Ḥujjat al-Islam Muḥammad Taqī Falsafī, the famed preacher of Tehran. Falsafī served as the intermediary between Ayatullah Burūjirdī and the royal court. In his *Khāṭirāt* (Memoirs), he has recounted the circumstances surrounding the Ḥaẓīrat al-Quds' destruction in a manner that would find acceptance in post-revolutionary Iran (Falsafī 1376/1998).

On the heels of the public mobilization effort headed by preachers and religious lecturers, in Ramaḍān 1334/April–May 1955, Muḥammad Taqī Falsafī (on Radio Tehran) and Mr. Shukūhīda (on Air Force Radio) reminded listeners in their talks that, 'the danger posed by the Baha'is is greater than that posed by members of the Tūda [Communist] party' (Anonymous 1334b/1956: 1). In his memoirs, Falsafī recalls that his on-air lectures against the Baha'is took place after the mutual agreement between Ayatullah Burūjirdī and Muḥammad-Riḍa Shah had been reached. In an interview with a reporter from *Ittiḥād-i Millī* (National Unity) on 19 Urdībihisht 1334/10 May 1955, Falsafī stated the following regarding his meeting with Ayatullah Burūjirdī: 'Prior to the arrival of the blessed month of Ramaḍān, I had the privilege of visiting Qum. While there, I visited an extremely wearied Ayatullah Burūjirdī. He said, "Now that the oil issue has been resolved and the members of the Tūda party have been dealt with, we have to give some thought to the Baha'is and do something about them."' Based on Ayatullah Burūjirdī's recommendation, after this meeting, Falsafī met with Muḥammad-Riḍā Shah and told him: 'Ayatullah Burūjirdī believes that it is important to discuss the Baha'i problem, which is a cause of great concern to Muslims, in the talks that will be broadcast in Ramaḍān on the radio. Does His Royal Highness agree?' According to Falsafī, '(The Shah) fell silent for a moment and then said, "Go and say it"' (Falsafī 1376/1998: 190–1).

Thus, in Ramaḍān 1334/April–May 1955, Falsafī devoted his annual talks, delivered in Masjid-i Shah, to attacking the Baha'is. These lectures had been broadcast directly on the radio since Ramaḍān 1327/1948. However, in previous years, they had been dedicated to confronting the Tūda party. Falsafī's successive attacks against the Baha'is (and in particular, during the month of Ramaḍān) served to inflame anti-Baha'i sentiments. Immediately following the procession of religious mobs towards Yūsuf-Ābād Boulevard and their raid of the Ḥaẓīrat al-Quds with the approval of the Ramaḍān Security Council, Tehran's military governor occupied the Ḥaẓīrat al-Quds on 16 Urdībihisht 1334/7 May 1955. This act marked the height of the cooperation between the government and the clergy during the period of Muḥammad-Riḍa Shah's rule. In a statement, General Taymūr Bakhtiyār, the military governor, explained the operation in the following terms:

> Since the demonstrations and propaganda of the Baha'i sect have been inciting public commotion, as a means of maintaining public order, the security forces were ordered to occupy the propaganda centre of this sect which is called the Ḥaẓīrat al-Quds. We have done this to prevent, in every way possible, the destructive events that this sect may coordinate in the future.
>
> (Falsafī 1376/1998: 193)

According to a newspaper report published in *Iṭṭilā'āt*, after sunset that day, 'sweets were distributed to the people' in front of the Ḥaẓīrat al-Quds (*Iṭṭilā'āt* 8671–17 Urdībihist 1334; cited in Falsafī 1376/1998: 194).

After occupying the Ḥaẓīrat al-Quds, in a telegraph to the Shah, Ayatullah Sayyid Muḥammad Bihbahānī offered heartfelt thanks for 'using the army of Islam . . . to close a society that corrupts religion and government.' Bihbahānī considered that day 'a religious holiday' (*Iṭṭilā'āt* 8672–17 Urdībihist 1334, cited in Falsafī 1376/1998: 194). In his response, the Shah recalled: 'As you have repeatedly heard from us, we have always considered ourselves bound to enforcing the provisions of Islam and we will continue to desire this grace from God, the Most Exalted' (*Iṭṭilā'āt* 8673–19 Urdībihist 1334, cited in Falsafī 1376/1998: 194). Ayatullah Burūjirdī likewise proclaimed his 'joy' to Bihbahānī at the closing of the Ḥaẓīrat al-Quds and prayed that 'God, exalted be He, has protected the sacred religion of Islam and the Iranian monarchy from the harm of enemies and the mischief of agitators. May He forever protect His Royal Majesty for the sake of the Muslims' (Ibid.). In a letter to Falsafī, Ayatullah Burūjirdī likewise expressed his appreciation for Falsafī's 'valuable services' to 'not only the sacred religion of Islam, but all of the divine religions, as well as toward the Holy Qu'ran.' He stated that 'Baha'ism enjoys thorough influence in the system of government. Therefore, the most important issue is to purify this sect from all offices, ministries, and sensitive posts in the government' (*Iṭṭilā'āt* 8672–18 Urdībihist 1334 and *Kayhān* 3574–19 Urdībihist 1334, cited in Falsafī 1376/1998: 194–5). In an interview with *Kayhān*, Ayatullah Burūjirdī demanded the demolition of the Ḥaẓīrat al-Quds, the dismissal of Baha'is from 'governmental departments and agencies,' and the approval of a proposition to expel every Baha'i from Iran (*Kayhān* 3575–20 Urdībihist 1334, cited in Falsafī 1376/1998: 195). This request, composed of four articles, was presented to the office of the President of the Assembly on 19 Urdībihisht 1334/10 May 1955 by Sayyid Aḥmad Ṣafā'ī, a clerical representative from Qazvin.

In the introduction of this proposition, Baha'is were accused of being agitators and troublemakers who in 'wearing the guise of religion have revolted against the Muslim nation of Iran in every location of the country. Through various means, they throw people off the path of righteousness and chastity and away from the axis of godliness and piety. Furthermore, they spare no effort perpetrating any crime that will advance their sinister objectives.' Right at the height of the Baha'i persecutions, the authors of this proposition claimed that 'countless cases of murder, seditiousness, and other felonies committed in the past by members of this association have been filed with the judicial courts.'[21]

After the occupation of the Ḥaẓīrat al-Quds, 'security officials seized other Baha'i centres in numerous townships, including those of Rasht, Shiraz, Isfahan, Kirmanshah, Yazd, Kashan and Kirman.' On the heels of these occupations, individuals 'who had identified themselves as Baha'is on their employment applications were discharged from certain offices.' As the persecution of individuals who had been recognized as Baha'is intensified, some Baha'is were forced to write and publish letters of denial. The text of these letters was more or less the same:

> Notwithstanding the fact that I am a Muslim and my being a Muslim is apparent and in no need of explanation, some of my coworkers accuse me of being a Baha'i. Just as I denied being so in 1330/1951 in the newspaper, *Dād*, once again I wish to inform the public that I, 'Abdullāh Bayāt, an employee of a chintz-making factory in Tehran, ID no. 3494 (issued in Malāyir), apart from being a Muslim, have been and will continue to remain loyal to the Shah and my native land, 2/3/34 (24 April 1955).
>
> (Anonymous 1334d/1956: 3)

It is important to reexamine the words of Ḥujjat al-Islam Falsafī, who, as will be remembered, in acting on behalf of Ayatullah Burūjirdī, was responsible for employing the radio to provoke public sentiment against the Baha'is. According to Falsafī, in his radio talks of Ramaḍān 1334/April–May 1955:

> I lectured on the prophets in the first two days and then went after those Baha'is. The government didn't pay much attention to the first three lectures. But slowly, reports from security officials throughout the country reached the state, and the government realized that this problem has deep roots. On the other hand, side by side with the messages of the clerics and the exemplary guide, His Imperial Majesty also issued certain orders. The command to occupy the Ḥaẓīrat al-Quds was issued at once. Anyways, I am deeply thankful of the service rendered by both the people and the army who came and occupied the Ḥaẓīrat al-Quds in time.
>
> (Anonymous 1334a/1956: 1, 4)

In an attempt to further incite the masses to persecute the adherents of other faiths and ideologies, Falsafī spread the rumour that the Tūda party was developing close ties with the Baha'is:

> One of the members of the Tūda party came to me himself and confessed, saying, 'Since our activities had been prohibited, we began to organize circumcision parties, weddings, and mourning ceremonies. But they became aware of our plans. So, when we heard the Baha'is were planning a coup d'état for the coming year, we decided to join them in order to pull off something significant. To this end, to show just how interested we were in Baha'ism, we even wed their women according to own their customs and laws.'

Conscious of the international reaction to his anti-Baha'i measures, Falsafī began glorifying 'his holiness Moses and his holiness Jesus' in his lectures. Aware of the international sensitivities against the persecution of religious minorities, generated as a result of the Jewish holocaust in Hitler's Germany, Falsafī found himself with no other choice but to declare: 'I am fully cognizant of the rights of minorities as expounded in the Constitution and in the holy books . . .' (Anonymous 1334b/1956: 4). On the heels of the Baha'i international Assemblies' complaints to the Shah, the Prime Minister, the National Consultative Assembly, the Human Rights and Social and Economic Commissions of the United Nations, and the governments of Europe and the United States,[22] Falsafī exploited Cold War rhetoric and fear of the Tūda party's progress as a pretext for his attacks: 'We haven't been talking about religion. We have been discussing pseudo-religions.' In explaining this issue, he offered the following reminder: 'I told the Americans that the Muslims have campaigned against the members of the Tūda Party and now the members of Tūda have joined the Baha'is. If you choose to protect the Baha'is, it will be as if you are strengthening the members of Tūda, who are the enemies of America' (Anonymous 1334b/1956: 4). In this manner, the conflict against Baha'is was not only a campaign for safeguarding the unity of Iran, but was also understood as being part of the campaign against the worldwide spread of communism.

In late Ramaḍān 1334/May 1955, 'the distinguished *'ulama*, prayer leaders and likewise all of the preachers and promoters of religion' organized meetings for the purpose of 'settling once and for all the Baha'i matter' (Anonymous 1334e/1956: 1, 4). One of these sessions took place at the home of Ayatullah Khānsārī and was attended by Mr. Najafī Shahristānī, acting on behalf of Ayatullah Burūjirdī. At this meeting, the participants wrote a letter to 'His Imperial Majesty,' calling for 'the immediate implementation of the request of these three men.' It was decided that the three part request, which had also been included in the proposition brought forth to the National Consultative Assembly by Sayyid Aḥmad Ṣafā'ī, would be presented in person to the Shah by Shaykh Muḥammad 'Alī Lavāsānī, Mr. Najafī Shahristānī, and Ḥājj Bāqir Āqā Qummī. In an open letter, written in Khurdād 1334/May–June 1955 to General Fākhir Ḥikmat (the president of the National Consultative Assembly), *Nidā-yi Ḥaqq*, which played a vital coordination role within the various Islamic associations, warned that the plan of the Baha'is 'is to destroy the government and monarchy and tear down the foundations of the sacred religion Islam.' Further in the same letter, which spoke of the *'ulama* as the protectors of the monarchy, *Nidā-yi Ḥaqq* wrote: 'At present, the Iranian people demand that the best interests of the nation be kept in mind and the proper course for the Baha'is become clear, just as the proper course of the members of the Tūda party was determined. Since they are not harming us now, it is an opportune time to deal with them. Otherwise, they will harm us in the future' (Anonymous 1334f: 2).

In determining the proper course 'for members of the Tūda party,' the government had sentenced numerous leaders of the Tūda party to death and life imprisonment. The state's dealings with the Tūda party became a model for its confrontation against the Baha'is. In Ābān 1334/October 1955, in an effort to attract the attention of religious forces, the military governor orchestrated the birthday celebration of the Prophet Muḥammad at the Ḥaẓīrat al-Quds. Consequently, *Nidā-yi Ḥaqq* expressed its appreciation to General Bakhtiyār and requested that 'the National Consultative Assembly hold an even greater and more elaborate festivity to celebrate the birthday of his holiness the Hidden Imām – the Qā'im, the Lord of the Command and the Lord of the Age – on 15 Sha'bān [28 March 1956].' *Nidā-yi Ḥaqq* was hopeful that 'in that celebration,' Tehran's military governor 'coupled with an unparallelled display of Muslim strength would strike a dagger to the heart of the few minor and straying sects' (Anonymous 1334g/1956: 1, 4).

As much as anti-Baha'i forces had grown hopeful from observing Tehran's military governor's role in suppressing and dissolving the Tūda party, these developments were equally distressing to the Baha'is.

The sudden disengagement of the government and royal court from meeting the *'ulama*'s request to 'settle once and for all the Baha'i matter' annulled the historic union between state and clergy. The suppressive stance of the state in fighting the Babis and Baha'is coupled with their defence of Islam and Shi'ism had begun to crystallize during the reign of the Qajar monarchs, Muḥammad Shah and Nāṣir al-Dīn Shah. By promoting the campaign against Babis and Baha'is, the government was able to enjoy the protection and support of the *'ulama*. The triumph of the Usūlīs over the Akhbārīs had, moreover, transformed the Shi'i mujtahids into an autonomous source of religious authority. In the process of attacking the Babis and Baha'is, the *'ulama* became united and of one mind. During the rule of Riḍā Shah, the government and clergy had openly confronted one another. However, in the 1320s/1940s and early 1330s/1950s, the campaign against the Tūda party, which had been declared the enemy of Islam, caused the two sides to again become united. With the occupation of the Ḥaẓīrat al-Quds in Urdībihisht 1334/April 1955, the amity between the state and religious establishment reached its peak. However, the government's change of course at the height of the Ḥaẓīrat al-Quds crisis deeply offended the Shi'i *'ulama*, and in particular, Ayatullah Burūjirdī, who had been anxiously concerned with the growth in the number of Baha'is in his 'Shi'i country.' Thus, the clergy, who had been defenders of the monarchy until 1334/1955, gradually began to oppose the state. The event of 15 Khurdād 1342/5 June 1963 marked the continuation of a process that had commenced with the occupation of the Ḥaẓīrat al-Quds. Therefore, the occupation of the Baha'i National Centre can be regarded as both the peak of the cooperation between the royal court and the clergy and the beginning of the end of their collaboration.[23]

Conclusion

The 'Otherization' of the Babis and Baha'is, a process which had commenced with the publication of *Yād-dāshthā-yi Kīnyāz Dālgūrukī*, reached a new peak with the founding of Israel in 1327/1948. The Baha'i religion, which had established its international centre in Palestine in 1310 (AH)/1890 prior to the appearance of the Zionist movement, was now declared to be its agent. In this fashion, anti-Zionist political sentiments that supported defending the Palestinian refugees were confounded with anti-Judaism and anti-Baha'ism. Moreover, political analysts were alleging that the state of Israel was nothing more than a tool of the American regime. And with the government of Iran developing closer ties with Israel, anti-government and anti-American sentiments exacerbated the prevailing anti-Baha'ism, giving the religion an entirely political connotation. The Iranian identity of the Baha'is and their ties to the culture and land of their religion's birth had no place in this chain of scapegoating Baha'ism as 'the Alter.' The Baha'is were accused of being the instruments of Zionism, the agents of Imperialism, and the antagonists of Islam and Iran.

In this process of effacing and rewriting history to represent Baha'is as the instruments of Zionism, it was forgotten that Mīrzā Ḥabībullāh Āl-i Riḍā (Huvaydā), one of the Baha'i employees of the foreign ministry, had been the first Iranian to express concern (more even than any Arab politician) over the Zionists' attempts to 'increase their numbers in Palestine.' In a letter dated 17 Ṣafar 1341 (AH)/9 October 1922 to the foreign ministry, Āl-i Riḍā reported that 'multitudes' of Jewish Iranians 'have migrated from Iran to Palestine . . . and if something is not done immediately to address this problem, every Jewish Iranian, like single drops of water, will eventually be absorbed into the sea of Zionism' (Vilāyatī 1376/1997: 98 [document 17]). It is particularly noteworthy that the Iranian *'ulama* failed to appreciate the implications of the increasing numbers of Jews in Palestine until the midst of the crises of the 1320s/1940s leading up to the founding of Israel.

With anti-Baha'ism reaching its peak in the 1320s/1940s, the racist theories that had been exploited against the Jews were now also imputed to the Baha'is. For example, writing in *Parcham-i Islam* in Shahrīvar 1325/ September 1946, 'Abd al-Ḥusayn Āyatī noted:

> For some time, I had wondered why the Babis liked the Jews more than any other group and tried so hard to proselytize them. I had likewise wondered why people became so united after joining these religions, until I learned that they have much in common in terms of their methods and ways. In one respect, they have both made religion into a plaything, fabricating some absurd teachings and foolish words. In another, they are both so fanatical in their belief of these fabrications, despite the fact that they themselves know that they are artificial and empty explanations that they have invented, that I can go so far as to say that no other group in the world today can be characterized by as much ignorant fanaticism and foolish zeal as Baha'ism. In whatever country they reside, Babis and Jews commit involuntary treachery.
>
> (Āyatī 1325b/1947: 2)

Just as the accusation of betrayal against the Jews resulted in the movement to wipe them out of Europe, similar accusations against Baha'is caused the anti-Baha'i movement to become an inseparable component of an Islamist movement seeking desperately to establish a one-religion future for Iran. The economic boycotts imposed against Baha'is were an essential component of this Islamist movement. The first of such boycotts was imposed against 'the imperialist soft drink' Pepsi-Cola in 1334/1955. These economic boycotts played an important role in the formation of an Islamic political discourse.[24]

The comparatively high social and economic status of the Baha'is only added to the anxieties of the *'ulama* and the Shi'i authorities vis-à-vis an Islamic future in Iran. The propositions of state and local organizations doubled these concerns. Of these, the 16 Mihr 1341/8 October 1962 decision reached by the cabinet to include the phrase, 'the heavenly book' in place of 'the glorious Qur'an,' in the official governmental oaths was especially distressing. The Shi'i *'ulama* interpreted this ruling and other civil reforms as efforts aimed at subverting the Islamic identity of Iran. The *'ulama*, who had become unhappy with the Shah after the Ḥaẓīrat al-Quds incident, directly confronted the royal court after the passing of this proposition. As Ayatullah Sharī'atmadārī's letter of 21 Urdībihisht 1342/11 May 1963 to the *'ulama* of Kirman indicates, many of the *'ulama* believed that the government 'trie[d] by different means to strengthen some of the straying, misguided, and anti-Islamic sects, support[ed] their interference in various governmental matters, and entrust[ed] numerous sensitive and high-profile positions to them' (Sharī'atmadārī n.d.a: 55). Following up on this letter, Sharī'atmadārī reminded people that 'Iran has become the arena of activity for a party that is the agent of imperialism and the broker for Israel, a party that falsely calls itself a religion' (Sharī'atmadārī n.d.b: 58). In a Khurdād 1342/June 1963 manifesto to preachers, Islamic speakers and religious organizations, Ayatullah Khumaynī warned:

> Know that the danger facing Islam today is no less than the danger posed by the Umayyads. The tyrant's government, with all of its forces, assists Israel and its agents (the misguided and misguiding sects). It has handed the information media over to them. In the royal court, they receive whatever they want. It has opened positions for them in the military, the ministry of culture and all of the other ministries and given them all of the sensitive posts. Remind the people of the danger posed by Israel and its agents. In times of reciting mournful songs and beating on chests, remind them of the disasters that have afflicted Islam and its religious centres, the calamities that have beset the helpers of the Shari'a. Express your disgust at this treacherous government for mobilizing and sending several thousand enemies of both Islam and nation to London to participate in an anti-Islamic and anti-nation assembly. **These days, to be silent is to support the tyrant's government and to succor the enemies of Islam.**
>
> (al-Khumaynī 1376/1998: 124, bold emphasis in the original)

Moreover, in Khurdād 1342/June 1963, *Jāmi'a-yi Rawḥāniyat-i Iran* (the Society of Iran's Clergy) denounced Israel as 'the greatest base for the enemies of Islam and the foremost agent of imperialism in the Middle East.' They anticipated that,

> the Baha'is, who are the middlemen of the Israeli state in our government (don't forget that Haifa and 'Akka are centres for the Baha'is and amongst the most well-known cities of Israel), have infiltrated the most sensitive organizations in government and every day, their influence increases in all of the departments, even the prime minister's cabinet. They are especially active in the field of proselytization.

Later in this statement, which reflected the 'the goals of the clergy from the recent campaign,' it was emphasized that 'the clergy can never accept this great shame to be brought on the Muslims of Iran and can never tolerate the influence of the agents of Zionism and their middlemen, i.e. the Baha'is, in their government' (Jāmi'a-yi Rawḥāniyat-i Iran n.d.: 75). Ayatullah Sayyid Muḥammad Ṣādiq Rawḥānī, in a letter declaring unlawful the Shahrīvar 1342/September 1963 elections of the 21st National Consultative Assembly, accused the Assembly of covering up 'a sinister coup d'état plot that aims to veer and temper the very foundations of religion and state in a single instance:'

> Thus, in cooperation with Baha'is, Israel's agents, SAVAK, and women and men who the pen shies away from even mentioning, they initiate meetings in the name of the masses, organize assemblies and create committees that, on behalf of the people, introduce candidates who are home-born slaves or pathetic individuals seeking the rations of colonialism. Of course, these are not people from this country, but rather people from overseas and Israel.
>
> (al-Rawḥānī M.S. n.d. 5: 88)

The manifesto dated 21 Farvardīn 1342/10 April 1963 by 'the religious seminary at Qum' also requested 'all of the exemplary guides and, in particular, Grand Ayatullah Khumaynī' to do their utmost to 'protect' their ten 'requests,' number five of which called for 'cutting off the hands of imperialism and the Zionist agents from our country' (Ḥawza-yi 'Ilmīya-yi Qum n.d.: 117). Akin to countless other documents written by Islamists, *Bīyugrāfī-yi Pīshvā* (The Leader's Biography) which was drawn up in 1348/1969, accused Baha'is of being 'the agents of the inhumane Zionist organization and representatives of the Jews' (Anonymous n.d.a: 63). In this manner, 'imperialism's instruments and Zionism's agents' became the preferred synonyms for depicting 'Baha'is' as foreigners in the revolutionary discourse. Since the Israeli government was deemed the unchanging enemy of Islam, the progress of the Baha'is in advancing politics, economics, and Iranian culture, was presumed to be proof of the weakening of Islam. Therefore, in the two decades preceding the revolution, numerous spokesmen and Islamic protagonists emphasized above all else that 'Islam is in a very dangerous position.' For example, on 17 Shahrīvar 1346/8 September 1967, in a board meeting for the Ḥusayn School, Muḥammad Javād Bā-hunar warned: 'Today, religion is exposed to great danger. Day by day, the propaganda of the Baha'is increases. Wake up and be concerned with the plight of religion . . .' (Mīzbānī 1376/1997: 100, 107). According to this view, all of the cultural initiatives sponsored by the government, be it the Shiraz Art Festival or the decision to replace the Islamic calendar, were dismissed as attempts by 'the misguided and straying sects' and 'the instruments of imperialism and the enemies of Islam' 'to change the Islamic character of the country.'[25] In line with this 'revolutionary' view, the Baha'is were held responsible for even the abusive suppression of SAVAK (the Iranian Security and Intelligence Service).[26] In other words, the revolutionary and Islamist discourse implicated Baha'is as participants in all of the outrageous policies of the Shah's regime.

The anti-Baha'i movement, which coalesced with Islamic propagandistic activities in the 1320s/1940s, played a crucial role in transforming 'Islamic faith' into 'political confrontation.' Instead of undertaking an objective study of the principles of the Baha'i religion, Shi'i dogmatists and other Islamic protagonists insisted that the Baha'i religion was nothing more than 'a political religion' created by imperialist governments to debilitate Islam. Consequently, more than ever before, members of Islamic boards and anti-Baha'i associations grew concerned with the prospects of an Islamic future in Iran. The intensification of this distress proved to be the means of converting piety and faith into 'political awareness.' It was, moreover, critical in encouraging the synthesis of a campaign to protect Islam. Accordingly, the board and general meetings of anti-Baha'i associations became appropriate venues to win individuals over to such organizations as *Mujāhidīn-i Khalq* (People's Freedom Fighters), *Ummat-i Vāḥida* (One Community), *Ḥizb-i Milal-i Islāmī* (International Islamic Party), and *Hay'at-i Mu'talifa* (the United Organization).[27] Through associating the anti-Baha'i movement with the anti-Zionist, anti-colonialist, and anti-imperialist movements, the battle to cleanse Iran of its Baha'i citizens was transformed into a campaign to overthrow the Pahlavi monarchy. In the 'Iranian people's' movement 'to win their freedom,' the civil liberties of all Baha'is were taken captive at the hands of 'the Muslim nation.' As a result, in the second half of the twentieth century, Iranian civil society became party to a contradiction that lives on to this day.

Notes

1 This chapter is a translation (by Omid Ghaemmaghami) and adaptation of my 2001 article 'Baha'i-sitīzī va Islam-garā'ī dar Iran, 1941–1955', *Iran Nameh*, 19: 79–124.

2 For a comprehensive study on the foundations of the Babi movement, see Amanat 1989. For a historical analysis of the Baha'i religion, see Cole 1998.

3 See Rūḥīyyih Khānum 1970: 156–8. Also *idem* 1963: 788–94, particularly 789–91.

4 See Mottahedah 1988.

5 Firaydūn Ādamīyat claims that 'the author of this anonymous document is 'Alī Javāhir-kalām' (Ādamīyat 1361/1983: 456). However, he has not furnished any evidence for this claim. 'Alī Javāhir-kalām completed his studies in Tehran and Beirut and was fluent in Persian, Arabic, Russian, and English. He was also the translator of numerous monographs, including *Āthār al-Shī'a, Iran-i Naw* (Elwell Sutton) and *Tārīkh-i Tamaddun-i Islam* (Jurjī Zaydān).

6 These included the *Anjuman-i Tablīghāt-i Islamī* (Society for Islamic Propagation), *Jam'īyat-i Mubāriza Bā Bī-dīnī* (the Association for Fighting Irreligion), *Ittiḥādīya-yi Muslimīn* (the Muslim Brotherhood), *Jam'īyat-i Fadā'iyān-i Islam* (the Association of the Devotees of Islam), *Jāmi'a-yi Muslimīn* (the Society of Muslims), *Jāmi'a-yi Ta'līmat-i Islamī* (the Society for Islamic Education), *Jam'īyat-i Muravvijīn-i Madhhab-i Ja'farī* (the Association of Promoters of the Ja'farī School), *Anjuman-i Islamī-yi Dānishjūyān* (the Student's Islamic Association), and *Kungurih-i Javānān-i Islam* (the Islamic Youth Congress). See Anonymous 1325a: 2. After the murder of Ahmad Kasravī, *Jam'īyat-i Mubāriza Bā Bī-dīnī* (the Association for Fighting Irreligion) transformed into *Ittiḥādīya-yi Muslimīn* (Muslim Brotherhood). It had been formed through the efforts of Ḥājj Sarāj Anṣārī, Shaykh Qāsim Islāmī, Shaykh Mahdī Shar'īatmadārī, and some of the other *'ulama* for the explicit purpose of attacking Kasravī. One of the Brotherhood's objectives was to wage 'a rationalist struggle against all manner of irreligion and a scholarly battle with all publications that are or will be opposed to Islam, the Qur'an, and the true path of Shi'ism.' See Sayyid Muḥammad Mahdī Mūsawī, the general director of the Islamic Youth Congress, Mūsawi 1325: 3.

7 These included the *Kānūn-i Intishārāt-i Islāmī-yi Rasht va Babul* (Society for Islamic Publications in Rasht and Babul), *Anjuman-i Payravān-i Qur'an* (the Association of the Followers of the Qur'an), *Kānūn-i Nashr-i Ḥaqāyiq-i Islamī-yi Mashhad* (the Society for the Publication of Islamic Doctrines in Mashhad), *Jam'īyat-i Da'vat-i Islāmī-yi Gilan* (the Association for the Propagation of Islam in Gilan), *Jam'īyat-i Barādarān-i Islamī-yi Kirmanshah* (the Association of the Islamic Brothers of Kirmanshah), *Anjuman-i Mubāriza bā Khurafāt-i Isfahan* (the Society for Fighting Superstitions in Isfahan), and *Kānūn-i Tablīghāt-i Islamī-yi Shiraz* (the Society for Islamic Propagation in Shiraz). See al-Sādāt 1326/1947: 3.

8 Mujtahid Kamara-ī, *Rawḥānīyat va Islam va fiqh-i Islam bā madārik va nuṣūṣ-i aḥkām;* Ḥabbat al-Dīn Shahristānī, *Rāhnamā-yi yahūd va naṣārā*; Maḥmūd Ṭāliqānī (translator), *Rāhnamā-yi manāsik-i ḥajj.*

9 From Farvardīn 1321 to Ābān 1323, 128,000 copies of eleven education leaflets produced by *Anjuman-i Tablīghāt-i Islamī* were published. See Shahābpūr 1323c/1944: 3.

10 For a report on the role of the *Anjuman-i Tablīghāt-i Islamī* in the election of the members of the seventh National Consultative Assembly in Mashhad, see Anonymous 1373a/1995: 28–40. For information on the close working relationship between this society and SAVAK, see Rawḥānī 1373/1994: 17–27; Anonymous 1373b/1995: 123–5. Several of the historians of the Islamic Revolution have conjectured that the *Anjuman-i Tablīghāt-i Islamī* (the *Anjuman-i Ḍidd-i Baha'i*) is an 'imperialist' organization: 'The evidence for this faction being an imperialist group lies in the fact that at the peak of the Pahlavi dynasty, when SAVAK would not allow any religious group to remain active, the members of

this society (just like the Baha'is) were fully engaged in carrying out their propagandistic plans. These two opposing factions were working together in achieving their malicious imperialist objectives. Bahā'ism had prohibited its adherents from interfering in politics. The *Anjuman-i Ḍidd-i Baha'i* had likewise announced that interfering in politics was forbidden and had forced its members to take an oath stating they would not meddle in it. Moreover, Bahā'ism claims that the command to wage *jihād* has been nullified. The Society has likewise ruled out any form of fighting or *jihād* under the guise of a motto that would appear to be sacred, but in fact only causes the people to be deceived, i.e. appropriating the right to rule a state to the Lord of the Age alone.' – Anonymous 1365/1987: 111.

11 Anonymous 1325b/1947: 4; Anonymous1325c/1947: 4; Anonymous 1325d/1947: 3–4. See also, Anonymous 1326b/1948: 1, 3.

12 Regarding the Minister of Culture, Dr. Ādhar's order and the closing of *Jāmi'a-yi Ta'līmāt-i Dīnī*, see Davānī 1332a/1954: 1, 4; Davānī 1332b/1954: 1–2; Ghalla-zārī 1332a/1954: 1, 4; Ghalla-zārī 1332b/1954: 1, 4; Ghalla-zārī 1332c/1954: 1, 4.

13 These included *Hay'at-i Muḥammadī, Hay'at-i Mutavassilīn* (the Organization of the Supplicants of God), *Hay'at-i Murtaḍaviyūn* (the Organization of the Champions of Imam 'Alī), *Hay'at-i Anṣār-i Dīnī* (the Organization of Religious Helpers), and *Hay'at-i Pīr 'Aṭā'* (the Pīr-'Aṭā' Association). See Anonymous 1326e/1948: 2 and Anonymous 1326f/1948: 3.

14 According to Sayyid Muḥammad Taqavī, this paper, which began being published in Farvardīn 1324/April 1945 under the management and editorship of Nuṣratullāh Nūryānī, 'was miles ahead of the rest in the field of propagation' (Anonymous 1325e/1947: 2).

15 Najmābādī 1326/1947: 1, 3; Ṭāliqānī 1325/1946: 4; Shikārī 1326/1947: 3; Nīkū 1325/1946: 2; Āyatī 1325a/1947: 1.

16 Regarding Dr. Birjīs, see Anonymous 1317/1939: 8. Concerning engineer Shahīdzāda, see Anonymous 1326i/1948: 6.

17 On the occasion of the opening of Rāzī Hospital, the pharmacy of which had been donated to the hospital by Tehran's Jewish community, *Iran-i Bāstān* wrote, 'Today the Jews own the greatest share of Tehran's pharmaceutical market. As a result, dissatisfaction and worry prevails amongst the masses and in particular, amongst those who are intelligent and well-informed, because they are unable to determine whether activities of the Jews are reliable and sound considering the reality of the type of people the Jews are . . .' In this article, *Iran-i Bāstān* accounted Jewish Iranians, the oldest extant inhabitants of Iran, as outsiders: 'Rāzī Hospital is an Iranian-only establishment. Just as all of its employees are Iranian men and women and must remain Iranian, "the pharmacy," its most vital department must be under the watchful eyes of its astute director and be managed by Iranians. In other words, the medicine that is donated or sold by the Jews should not be accepted as reliable medicine since, as the old adage goes, there are wheels within wheels.' See Anonymous 1313/1935: 2, 11.

18 After attaining a post at the Ministry of Industry and later, the Finance Ministry, he became the Prime Minister on 23 Khurdād 1327/13 June 1948. He was familiar with French and Russian. His writings include, Hajīr 1322/1944, Izaak n.d.a, Izaak n.d.b and Hajīr 1308/1930.

19 Sayyid Husayn Imāmī (1303–1328/1924–1949) assassinated Ahmad Kasravī on 20 Isfand 1324 (1 March 1946).

20 Simultaneous with the spread of the rumour of Hazhīr being a Baha'i, another rumour began circulating in Tehran regarding his having become a Christian. See, 'Fawq al-'āda-yi bahman: Hajīr Masīḥī shuda va murtadd mī-bāshad,' in Tafrishī 1371/1992 2: 149, 127–8.

21 The proposition was presented in the following format: 'Article 1: The corrupt organization of the Babis and those who follow them, the Azalis and the Baha'is, are opposed to the security of the country and are hereby declared to be illegal; Article 2: Henceforth, membership in or association with this organization in any manner, is a felony. The violator will be sentenced to two years solitary confinement and will be denied his civil rights; Article 3: The immovable material assets of social centres or institutes associated with this organization or any revenues belonging to it will be transferred to the Ministry of Culture. It will be reserved for the founding of educational institutes and the promulgation of religious learning and the fundamentals of religious worship; Article 4: Individuals from this organization who serve in governmental departments will henceforth be discharged from their positions and will in no way be hired again'. From Anonymous 1334c/1956: 3.
22 See Anonymous 1349/1970: 789–91.
23 For more on this, see Muḥammad Taqī Falsafī's analysis, 'Rawḥānīyat va intikhāb-i al-sharrayn' in Falsafī 1376/1998: 112–17.
24 I intend to examine them in a forthcoming study.
25 For example, see Anonymous n.d.b: 470, 489.
26 See Anonymous n.d.c: 683. Citation from Anonymous n.d.c: 684.
27 See Anonymous 1359/1981: 172.

Bibliography

'Abdullāhī, Ḥusayn (1326/1948) 'Qābil-i tavajjuh-i āqāyān-i ḥujjāj-i Islam va marāji'-i taqlīd makhṣūṣan haḍrat-i Ayatullah Burūjirdī madda ẓilluhu al-'ālī', *Dunyā-yi Islam* 2: 58, 26 Day 1326.

Ādamīyat, Firaydūn (1361/1983) *Amīr Kabīr va Iran*, 6th edition, Tehran: Intishārāt-i Khvārazmī.

Amanat, Abbas (1989) *Resurrection and Renewal: The Making of the Babi Movement in Iran, 1844–1850*, Ithaca: Cornell University Press.

Anjuman-i Tablīghāt-i Islamī (1322/1944) *Yārān-i mā: sharḥ-i mukhtaṣarī az āghāz-i yik kūshish-i buzurg dar rāh-i Islam*, Tehran: Anjuman-i Tablīghāt-i Islamī.

—— (1326/1948) *Parcham-i Islam*, 2: 44, 20 Isfand 1326.

Anonymous (n.d.a) *Bīyugrāfī-yi pīshvā*, n.l.: Intishārāt-i Pānzdahum-i Khurdād.

—— (n.d.b) 'Nāma-yi Ayatullah Muḥammad-Riḍā Gulpāygānī dar 17 Khurdād va 27 Tīr 1357', *Asnād-i Inqilāb-i Islamī*, vol. 1.

—— (n.d.c) 'Matn-i i'lāmiyya-yi ḥawza-yi 'ilmiyya-yi Qum darbāra-yi Basīj-i javānān barā-yi mubāriza-yi musallahāna va shināsā'ī-yi muzdūrān-i rijīm-i shāh', *Asnād-i Inqilāb-i Islamī*, vol. 4.

—— (1313/1935) 'Yādi-gārī az ā'īn-i gushāyish-i Bīmāristān-i Rāzī yik anjuman-i bā-shukūh', *Iran-i Bāstān* 2: 22, 9 Tīr 1313.

—— (1317/1939) 'Īn pizishk rā ba 'ibādat da'vat kardand va sar-anjām bih ṭarz-i fajī'ī ū rā ba qatl risānīdand', *Firdawsī* 22, 26 February 1939/7 Isfand 1317.

—— (1325a/1947) 'Barādarān-i dīnī muttaḥid shavīd', *Dunyā-yi Islam* 5: 1, 18 Ābān 1325.

—— (1325b/1947) 'Jāmi'a-yi ta'līmāt-i Islamī', *Parcham-i Islam* 1:10, 9 Khurdād 1325.

—— (1325c/1947) 'Jāmi'a-yi ta'līmāt-i dīnī', *Parcham-i Islam* 10, 9 Khurdād 1325.

—— (1325d/1947) 'Jāmi'a-yi ta'līmāt-i dīnī', *Parcham-i Islam* 11, 16 Khurdād 1325.

—— (1325e/1947) 'Dunyā-yi Islam barā-yi cha intishār mī-yābad?', *Dunyā-yi Islam* 1, 20 Mihr 1325.

—— (1326a/1948) 'Dār al-'ulūm-i dīnī va 'arabī', *Dunyā-i Islam* 2: 57, 19 Day 1326.

—— (1326b/1948) 'Bāz-ham du shakhṣīyat-i mutaḍādd', *Dunyā-yi Islam* 53, 21 Ādhar 1326.

—— (1326c/1948) 'Dar khuṣūṣ-i qahva-rukh-i Isfahan', *Dunyā'yi Islam* 2: 60, 10 Bahman 1326.

—— (1326d/1948) 'Kitāb-i akhlāq-i gulshanī', *Dunyā-yi Islam* 58, 26 Day 1326.

—— (1326e/1948) 'Jam'īyat-i hay'āt-i muravvijīn-i madhhab-i Ja'farī', *Parcham-i Islam* 79, 12 Ādhar 1326.

—— (1326f/1948) 'Jam'īyat-i muravvijīn-i madhhab-i Ja'farī', *Parcham-i Islam* 80, 19 Ādhar 1326.

—— (1326g/1948) 'Majma'-i hay'āt-i muravvijīn-i madhhab-i Ja'farī', *Parcham-i Islam* 2: 34, 3 Day 1326.

—— (1326h/1948) 'Bayāniyya'ī ka dar jalasa-yi 'umūmī-yi 'aṣr-i 16/11/26 hay'at-i muravvijīn-i madhhab-i Ja'farī tavassuṭ-i Aqā-yi Sayyid Naṣrullāh Shujā'ī tanẓīm va qirā'at shud', *Dunyā-yi Islam* 63, 1 Isfand 1326.

—— (1326i/1948) 'Āyā duzdān dast ba tirur va kushtār zada-and?', *Mard-i Imrūz* 116, 27 Tīr 1326.

—— (1328/1950) 'Dāstān-i kāmil-i ḥāditha-yi ghamm-angīz-i qatl-i Hajīr, vazīr-i darbār-i shāhanshāhī . . .', *Kāviyān* 1, 19 Ābān 1328.

—— (1334a/1956) 'Az kay va chigūna va bā cha muqaddamātī vārid-i mubāriza bā Baha'iyān shudand?', *Ittiḥād-i Millī* 11: 366, 26 Urdībihisht 1334.

—— (1334b/1956) 'Kāmil-tarīn jaryān va fa'ālīyat-hā'ī ka munjarr ba ishghāl-i Haẓīrat al-Quds gardīd', *Ittiḥād-i Millī* 1: 365, 19 Urdībihisht 1334.

—— (1334c/1956) 'Matn-i ṭarḥī ka barā-yi taḥrīm-i Bahā'iyyat qarār ast taqdīm-i jalasa-yi 'alanī gardad', *Rawshanfikr* 93, 21 Urdībihisht 1334.

—— (1334d/1956) 'Mas'ala-yi Baha'i-hā', *Rawshanfikr* 95, 4 Khurdād 1334.

—— (1334e/1956) 'Ijmā'-i āqāyān-i 'ulama va vu''āẓ', *Nidā-yi Ḥaqq* 5: 37, 24 Khurdād 1334.

—— (1334f/1956) 'Nāma-yi sar-bāz ba Jināb-i Aqā-yi Ḥikmat, ra'īs-i Majlis-i Shūrā-yi Millī', *Nidā-yi Haqq* 245, 24 Khurdād 1334.

—— (1334g/1956) 'Jashn-i milād-i Haḍrat-i Rasūl-i akram dar farmān-dārī-yi niẓāmī-yi Tihrān', *Nidā-yi Haqq* 6: 7, 17 Ābān 1334.

—— (1345/1967) 'Īn-hā az rāh-i gumrāhī bāzgashta-and', *Sāl-nāma-yi Nūr-i Dānish* 21.

—— (1349/1970) 'The Bahá'í Appeal to the United Nations', *Bahá'í World 1954–1963,* Haifa: the Universal House of Justice.

—— (1359/1981) 'Sharḥ-i ḥāl-i Ghulām-Ḥusayn Ṣifatī', *Tārīkh-cha-yi gurūh-hā-yi tashkīl dihanda-yi sāzmān-i mujāhidīn-i inqilāb-i Islāmī,* Tehran: Sāzmān-i Mujāhidīn-i Inqilāb-i Islāmī, vol. 1.

—— (1365/1987) 'Ḥarba-yi takfīr 3; isti'mār va takfīr', *Ḥawza,* 16 Shahrīvar 1365: 93–120.

—— (1370/1992) 'Fadā'īyān-i Islam va Ḥawza-yi 'Ilmiyya-yi Qum', *Tārīkh va Farhang-i Mu'āṣir* 1: 2, 173–89.

—— (1373a/1995) 'Jam'īyat-hā-yi mu'talif-i Islāmī-yi Mashhad va sarnivisht-i intikhābāt-i dawra-yi hifdahum-i Majlis-i Shūrā-yi Millī dar Mashhad', *15 Khurdād* 4: 14, Bahār 1373: 28–40.

——(1373b/1995) 'SAVAK and the Ḥujjatīya Society', *15 Khurdād* 17, Zimistān 1373: 123–5.

Anonymous Muslim (1327/1949) 'Baha'i-hā cha mī-gūyand', *Dunyā-yi Islam* 2: 68, 21 Farvardīn 1327.

Ardabīlī Ḥājib al-A'ima, Mīrzā 'Alī Akbar (1334/1956) *Uṣūl-i dīn-i Muslimīn va kashf al-khaṭā-yi khānsārī*, n.l.: n.p.

Āyatī, 'Abd al-Ḥusayn (1325a/1947) 'Bāzīgarī-yi banī Isrā'īl sabab-i khvārī-yi īshān ast', *Parcham-i Islam* 23, 14 Shahrīvar 1325.

——(1325b/1947) 'Bāzī-garī-yi banī Isrā'īl sabab-i khvārī-yi īshān ast', *Parcham-i Islam* 1: 28, 28 Shahrīvar 1325.

Cole, Juan (1998) *Modernity and the Millennium: the Genesis of the Baha'i Faith in the Nineteenth Century Middle East*, New York: Columbia University Press.

Davānī, 'Alī (1332a/1954) 'Shīrīn-kārī-yi Aqā-yi Duktur Ādhar', *Nidā-yi Ḥaqq* 148, 31 Tīr 1332.

——(1332b/1954) 'Naqsh-i Vazīr-i Farhang dar inhilāl-i jāmi'a-yi ta'līmāt-i dīnī', *Nidā-yi Ḥaqq* 149, 7 Murdād 1332.

Falsafī, Muḥammad-Taqī (1376/1998), *Khāṭirāt va mubārizāt-i Ḥujjat al-Islam Muḥammad Taqī Falsafī, muṣāḥiba-hā Ḥamīd Rawhānī (Ziyāratī)*, ed. 'Alī Davvānī, Muḥammad Rajabī, Muḥammad Ḥasan Rajabī, Tehran: Markaz-i Asnād-i Inqilāb-i Islāmī.

Faqīhī-Shīrāzī, 'Abd al-Karīm (1326a/1948) 'Sabab-i yik hafta ta'ṭīl: sustī-i mushtarikīn – siyāsat-i bīgānigān', *Parcham-i Islam* 72, 9 Mihr 1326.

——(1326b/1948) 'Mubāriza-yi mā muqaddas va pīrūzī-yi nahā'ī bā Islam ast', *Parcham-i Islam* 66, 22 Murdād 1326.

Ghalla-zārī, 'Abbās (1332a/1954) 'Āqā-yi Vazīr-i Farhang īn-jā Iran va kishvar-i Islāmī ast', *Nidā-yi Ḥaqq* 150, 14 Murdād 1332.

——(1332b/1954) 'Taqlīl-i durūs-i sharī'at va Qur'ān', *Nidā-yi Ḥaqq* 152, 28 Murdād 1332.

——(1332c/1954) 'Duktur Ādhar cha shud?', *Nidā-yi Ḥaqq* 155, 17 Shahrīvar 1332.

Hajīr, 'Abd al-Ḥusayn (1308/1930) *Ḥāfiẓ tashrīḥ: tabvīb va taqsīm-i ān az rūyi maẓāmīn*, Tehran: n.p.

——(1322/1944) *Az Pītirzbūrgh tā Qusṭanṭiyya*, Tehran: n.p.

Ḥawza-yi 'Ilmiyya-yi Qum (n.d.) 'Matn-i qaṭ'-nāma-yi Ḥawza-yi 'Ilmiyya-yi Qum', *Asnād-i Inqilāb-i Islamī*, vol. 4.

Ḥusaynī, Zayn al-'Ābidīn Nūrī Shah (1342/1964) *Irghām al-shayṭān fī radd ahl al-bayān wa al-iqān*, Tehran: Maṭba'a-yi Marvī.

Islāmī, 'Abbās-'Alī (1362/1984) 'Tarḥ-i naw', *Dar guftār-i vu''āẓ: majmū'a-yi sukhanrānī-hā-yi jam'ī az dānishmandān va vu''āẓ-i mashhūr-i Iran*, 9th edn, Tehran: Intishārāt-i Khazar.

Izaak, J. and Mala, A. (n.d.a) *Tārīkh-i qurūn vusṭā yā jang-i ṣad-sāla*, trans. (1311) 'Abd al-Ḥusayn Hajīr, Tehran: n.p.

——(n.d.b) *Tārīkh-i milal-i mashriq va Yūnān*; trans. (1309) 'Abd al-Ḥusayn Hajīr, Tehran: n.p.

Jāmi'a-yi Rawḥānīyat-i Iran (n.d.) 'Hadaf-i rawḥānīyūn az mubāriza-yi akhīr', *Asnād-i Inqilāb-i Islamī*, vol. 4.

Kasravī, Aḥmad (n.d.) *Baha'i-garī*, Tehran: Kitāb-furūshī-yi Pāydār.

——(1322/1944) 'Pāsukh-i Bahā'iyān', *Parcham* 1:1, Farvardīn 1322.

Khalkhālī, Murtaḍā and Mu'taḍidī, 'Abd al-Ḥusayn (1336/1958) 'Millat-i Iran bīdār shavīd: Bahā'iyān dīn, madhhab, ta'aṣṣub, milliyyat, va nāmūs-i shumā rā az bayn mī-barand', *Dunyā-yi Islam* 2: 62, 24 Bahman 1336.

al-Khumaynī, Rūḥullāh al-Mūsavī (1376/1998) 'I'lāmiyya-yi haḍrat-i Ayatullah al-'uẓmā Aqā-yi Ḥājj Rūḥullāh 'alā ru'ūs al-muslimīm khiṭāb bih vu''āẓ va gūyandigān-i dīnī va hay'at-hā-yi madhhabī', *15 Khurdād* 15, Bahār 1376.

Kirmānī, Ḥājj Muḥammad-Karīm Khān (1277AH/1860) *Kitāb-i mustaṭāb-i sulṭāniyya*, Bombay: Kār-khāna-yi 'Abd al-Ghafūr.

—— (1387AH/1967) *Risāla-yi tīr-i shahāb dar rāndan-i Bab*, Kirman: Chāp-khāna-yi Sa'ādat.

Kirmānī, Ḥājj Muḥammad Khān (1342AH/1923) *Hidāyat al-mustarshidān . . . dar javāb-i ḥadiyat al-namla*, n.p.: Maṭba'-i Marvī.

Mīzbānī, Mahnāz (1376/1997) 'Shahīd Bā-hunar ulgū-yi mubāriza va āmūzish', *15 Khurdād* 26/7, Tābistān va Pā'īz 1376.

Mottahedah, Negar (1988) 'The Mutilated Body of the Modern Nation: Qurrat al-Ayn Tahirah's Unveiling and the Iranian Massacre of the Babis', *Comparative Studies of South Asia, Africa and the Middle East*, XVIII: 2: 38–50.

Mūsāvi, Sayyid Muḥammad Mahdī (1325/1946) 'Ḥaqā'iq āskhār mīshavad', *Dunyā-yi Islam* 1, 20 Mihr 1325.

Najmābādī, Ḥujjat al-Islām (1326/1947) 'Yik su'āl az Shoghi Effendi va payruvānash', *Parcham-i Islam* 63, 25 Tīr 1326.

Nīkū, Ḥasan (1325/1946) 'Shujā'at mawlūd-i diyānat va ummat ast', *Parcham-i Islam* 22, 7 Shahrīvar 1325.

Raḥīmiyān, Ramaḍān-'Alī (1326/1947) 'I'lām ba kuliyya-yi Musalmānān-i Iran', *Dunyā-yi Islam* 39, 17 Murdād 1326.

al-Rawḥānī, Muḥammad-Ṣādiq al-Ḥusaynī (n.d.) 'Matn-i i'lāmīya-yi Aqā-yi Ḥājj Muḥammad-Ṣādiq Rawḥānī', *Asnād-i Inqilāb-i Islamī*, vol. 5.

Rawḥānī, Sayyid Ḥamīd (1373/1994) *15 Khurdād* 4: 14, Bahār 1373: 17–27.

Rūḥīyyih Khānum (1970) 'The Guardian of the Bahá'í Faith', *The Bahá'í World, 1954–1963*, Haifa: The Universal House of Justice.

al-Sādāt, Ṣadr (1326/1947) 'Du nimūna az fadākārī', *Parcham-i Islam* 63, 25 Tīr 1326.

Shahābpūr, 'Aṭā'ullāh (1323a/1944) *Shahādat-i 'ilm va falsafa ba ahamīyat va khūbī-yi namāz va rūza: favā'id-i dīnī, rawḥānī, jismānī, akhlāqī, ijtimā'ī*, 3rd edn, Tehran: Anjuman-i Tablīghāt-i Islamī.

—— (1323b/1944) *Ā'īn-i gushāyish-i rāh-i naw dar 'ālam-i ḥaqīqat: nashriyya-yi yikum-i Anjuman-i Tablīghāt-i Islamī*, 4th edn, Tehran: Anjuman-i Tablīghāt-i Islamī.

—— (1323c/1944) *Majmū'i-yi intishārāt-i Anjuman-i Tablīghāt-i Islamī*, Tehran: Anjuman-i Tablīghāt-i Islamī.

—— (1326/1947) 'Yik pīshnahād-i muhimm va sūdmand: āsāyishgāh barā-yi zuvvār-i ḥusaynī', *Dunyā-yi Islam* 35, 20 Tīr 1326.

Sharī'atmadārī, Ayatullah (n.d.a) 'Haḍarāt-i Aqāyān-i 'ulama va ḥujjāj-i Islam (shahristān-i Kirman) dāmat barakātu-hum)', *Asnād-i Inqilāb-i Islamī*, vol. 5.

—— (n.d.b) 'Haḍarāt-i Aqāyān-i 'ulama-yi a'lām va ḥujjāj-i Islam va vu''āẓ-i Kashan dāmat barakātu-hum,' *Asnād-i Inqilāb-i Islamī*, vol. 5.

Shikārī, Muḥammad-'Alī (1326/1947) 'Guft u shinūd bā Baha'iyān', *Parcham-i Islam* 71, 26 Shahrīvar 1326.

Tafrishī, Majīd and Aḥmadī, Muḥammad-Ṭāhir (1371/1992) *Guzārish-hā-yi maḥramāna-yi shahrbānī (1327–8)*, vol. 2, Tehran: Sazmān-i Asnād-i Millī-yi Iran.

Ṭāliqānī, Sayyid Maḥmūd (1325/1946) 'Mahdī-yi maw'ūd', *Parcham-i Islam* 1: 17, 27 Tīr 1325.

Vilāyatī, 'Alī-Akbar (1376/1997) *Iran va mas'ala-yi Filisṭīn bar asās-i asnād-i Vizārat-i Umūr-i Khārija 1897–1937*, Tehran: Daftar-i Nashr-i Farhang-i Islāmī.

11

THE DISCOURSE AND PRACTICE OF HUMAN RIGHTS VIOLATIONS OF IRANIAN BAHA'IS IN THE ISLAMIC REPUBLIC OF IRAN

Reza Afshari

Appearing exotic or anachronistic to some, exhilarating or liberating to others, the 1978–79 Islamic Revolution, with its mixture of populism, religious zeal, and self-righteous indignation, should have triggered anxieties among international human rights advocates. That it did not do so immediately can be explained by a widespread antipathy towards the regime it overthrew, the outré character of its leader, Ayatullah Ruḥullāh Khumaynī, and the euphoric support he generated among the nation, itself in the throes of an undigested modernity and existential crisis, aggravated by the policies of a faltering dynasty. An ancient people empowering themselves were simply thrilling. However, by the early 1980s, the international human rights observers became alarmed, in particular about the regime's brutality towards the Baha'is. The Bahá'í International Community, the international representative of the Baha'is, did strive to bring the plights of the Baha'i citizens to the attention of the United Nations.[1]

In 1984, the Commission on Human Rights placed Iran under what is generally referred to as the UN special procedure and appointed a Special Representative to report on its human rights violations.[2] The Special Representative diligently drafted his reports, the UN passed its condemnatory resolutions, and Iranian diplomats offered denials, while the regime's clerics in Tehran rallied their multitudes and railed against the double-standards of the Western sponsors of those resolutions. This confrontational stand went on for a decade until Khumaynī died in June 1989.

There are recognized religious minorities, and there are the Baha'is

In twentieth-century Iran, the Baha'i self-explanation as a new faith went largely unnoticed. No official recognition was ever granted – not even a hint of the possibility of such recognition. Excluded from the category of the *dhimmīs*, the people of the book, the Baha'is and their faith were never allowed to become another shade in this discriminatory spectrum of the *dhimmitude* that, in the post-1979 Iran, was to be fitted into the constitution of a modern state. Since the new faith had originated within Iran's religious traditions in the 1840s, it became the living example of apostasy the zealots of the time had only heard of in Islamic legends of distant eras. Conditions were bad enough in the nineteenth century. The twentieth century added a new dimension, as the newly acquired sense of Iranian nationalism turned any manifestation of non-conformity into treason. Different political factions have often used the Baha'is as human fibers in the incessant spinning of conspiratorial theories, for which Iranians have huge appetites. The Baha'is' anguished voices vanished into the dark communal recesses of the larger society – hardly listened to on their own terms. Thus, their predicaments preceded the creation of the Islamic state by Ayatullah Khumaynī in 1979; the source of the anti-Baha'i prejudice lay within the society and its Shi'i culture.

By the late 1970s, the impressive rise of religiosity in certain quarters gave the clergy elite – and not only the political ones – overconfidence in propagating Islamic teachings. Amir Arjomand's interviews with some thirty clerics in 1977 convinced him 'of their absolutely unshakeable faith in the inevitable spread of Islam as the youngest of the world religions' (Amir Arjomand 1988: 213). Far from feeling threatened by any competing religion or ideology, they were by the late 1970s giddily arrogant in their own evangelical bazaars. Thus, the groundswell of Shi'i religiosity, creating a vibrant social space beyond the reaches of modernizing bureaucrats, could only bode trouble for the Baha'is, even though most of the newly formed Islamic associations probably had no particularly vicious anti-Baha'i obsession. But those who did could find an increasingly congenial environment in which to operate. In a much broader cultural context, anti-minority prejudices continued to hold sway in many localities, where Jews, Christians and Baha'is lived among Muslims not sufficiently influenced by the glittering modernization of the state educational system.

The political and cultural contexts of the anti-Baha'i actions in the Islamic Republic

For the Baha'is of Iran, the emotionally potent Shi'i symbols woven into the canvas of the rising populism appeared familiar and threatening. So were the casts of characters that kept creeping out of the dark shadows of local and national political landscapes. The Baha'is could easily recognize the signs and rhetoric that were often the harbingers of attacks on their persons, properties and holy places. For the previously marginal Islamic groups, Baha'ism (or *Bahā'ī-garī*, a pejorative term) was an *idée fixe*. Thus, the triumph of the Islamic revolution and the establishment of the *vilāyat-i faqīh* (the vice-regency of the Shi'i jurist) presented the most serious threats to the Iranian Baha'is in the twentieth century.

The Baha'is imagined the worst. The rhetoric of the radicalized clerics presented the Baha'i Faith as a political sect that engaged in counter-revolutionary and espionage activities for foreign enemies, especially Israel. Ironically, the only active anti-Baha'i organization in society, the Ḥujjatīya, was led by Shaykh Ḥalabī, a cleric who took the Baha'i Faith seriously and tried to confront it, at least in part, by religiously-inspired argumentation. Shaykh Ḥalabī could not ultimately reconcile himself with the Islamic revolution. The new image that Ayatullah Khumaynī was projecting among the faithful troubled him. But such ambivalence was not the case with many of the former Ḥujjatīya members and fellow-travellers. They saw the opportunities that the new rule offered them and succumbed to the temptations of personal greed and political power. They distanced themselves from Ḥalabī, made the clerically-dominated Islamic Republic Party (IRP) their new political home and found employment in the newly Islamized institutions of the state (Momen 1985: 296).

The Iranian scholar Mahmoud Sadri has written that the 'Hojjatiya exerted considerable, albeit indirect and unintended, influence on the education and world-view of the lay elite leadership of the 1979 Islamic revolution' (Sadri 2004). Sadri has also added a note of caution; 'Its detractors from the left and the right have played a pivotal role in perpetuating views that vastly exaggerate and distort the organization's influence and agenda through spreading myths and conspiracy theories about Hojjatiya' (Ibid.). The 'detractors from the left' refers to the Marxist Tūda Party that, while supporting Khumaynī, attacked the Ḥujjatīya as a reactionary force.

Interestingly, Ḥalabī had reportedly expressed dismay at the violence used by the Islamic forces against the Baha'is in the Islamic Republic. Sadri has observed,

> As the leaders of Hojjatiya were committed to non-violent, persuasive strategy in dealing with Baha'is, the Association did not take part in persecution of Baha'is in post-revolutionary Iran. For all Ḥalabī's animus against Baha'is, he was a disciplined pacifist. He was distraught by violence and repeatedly warned his followers: 'This is not the way, this is not our way.'
>
> (Sadri 2004)

Notwithstanding this post-revolution backtracking, Ḥalabī's footsteps could not be concealed. He helped to keep what he called the Baha'i heresy alive.

His esoteric argumentation was perhaps beyond the Islamist activists; his anti-Baha'i venom was contagious. Shaykh Ḥalabī could have convinced himself that he had carried his struggles against the Baha'i Faith by providing rational refutations in a nonviolent way. But his campaigns were against the defendants who, by the logic of the conditions imposed on them, were not in a position to respond freely. There could hardly be any rationality in a discourse obsessed with religious heresy, particularly in an environment in which the targeted faith had already been cast away. The conditions under which the Ḥujjatīya carried on its anti-Baha'i teaching and preaching were highly irrational because they took place within the culture's taboo zones. Not only the Baha'is could not freely engage their opponents in open debates and offer their own counter refutations, but also no Muslims dared to enter the taboo zones and defend the rights of the Baha'is to engage in whatever religious activities they saw proper to advance their missions in this life and the life hereafter.

In the chaotic early months of the revolution, the anti-Baha'i sentiments – not all of them the result of the Ḥujjatīya outreach – found a deadly outlet. While finding reliable information has become difficult, one can logically assume that the Ḥujjatīya ex-members and fellow-travellers must have taken an active role in persecuting and dispossessing the Baha'is of means and influence. When Muhammad 'Alī Rajā'ī, once a member of the Ḥujjatīya, became Minister of Education in mid-1979, the ministry issued a circular calling on all districts to dismiss their Baha'i teachers. His former Ḥujjatīya comrades in charge of the Ministries of Commerce and Labour could not have been less aggressive, even though their domains had fewer Baha'i employees than the Ministry of Education did.

At any event, the Baha'is were the most vulnerable, non-political citizens in the sense that they lacked official status as a religious minority. In the aftermath of the collapse of the bureaucratic state, they had no effective recourse to what was possibly the only available refuge that could provide some measure of protection for a religious minority: the sanctum of the highest Shi'i *'ulama*. The Jewish and Christian leaders could take their cases to senior Shi'i clerics, sympathetic or not, and request protection under the *dhimmī* rules. In fact, at the height of revolutionary turmoil, some Baha'is followed that custom and met with some clerics. Of course, no meaningful protection could be forthcoming, despite some perfunctory pronouncements.

Reference to the Baha'is as 'an organized espionage ring' was prevalent in the first decade of the Islamic Republic. Sometimes the newspaper announcements, as well as official pronouncements, gave the lie to the official claim that the Baha'i Faith was not a religion. If it was not a religion, why had some Shi'i clerics taken such pains to show that it was a misguided faith? The anti-Baha'i rhetoric was often constructed within the duality of good and evil, always referring to the Baha'i Faith as a wayward sect (*firqa-yi ḍālla*), in contrast to the *dīn-i mubīn-i Islam* (the sublime religion of Islam).[3]

In the 1980s, many Baha'is told the UN Special Representatives that 'it had constantly been made clear to them that, if they recanted their faith, all measures against them would cease and they could regain their posts and studies' (UN Doc. A/42/648:10). The Bahá'í International Community has accurately pointed to this fact 'among the strongest proofs that the persecutions were based solely on religious beliefs' (BIC 1999: 28).

Since the drafting of the Universal Declaration of Human Rights in 1948, the international human rights community expects that UN member-states enact laws and create judicial procedures to counteract many of the societal norms and behaviours that have traditionally proven detrimental to human rights. These traditional norms often affect particular categories of citizens, ascriptively singled out for unequal treatments based on gender, age, race, and religion. The international human rights norms require that the states take responsibility in harnessing societal intolerance and prejudices. The passage of laws and their enforcement against considerable popular sentiments have constituted a significant chapter in the evolution of human rights, particularly in places where human rights have gained cultural acceptance since 1948. The Islamic Republic has in some significant ways reversed the direction of that evolution by enacting laws and adopting judicial and extra-judicial procedures that give official sanction to the prevailing prejudicial norms and behaviours. The root cause of human rights violations of non-Shi'i Iranians lies in this intersection of culture and state power; the modern centralized state has an uncanny ability to use and abuse the culture of the society for its short-sighted advantage.

Some Baha'i observers outside Iran paid attention to Islamist rhetoric and feared the possibility of genocide. The Shi'i political clerics expressed fidelity to a theocratic Imamate, but they now inherited and ruled a state with Western-style institutions. The Islamic Republic was led by an almost saintly looking Ayatullah. However, in many ways the behaviour of this particular revolutionary state did not differ from the other revolutionary states that were set up by the nationalists or Leninists around the world. Of course, Ayatullah Khumaynī and his clerical associates were the products of a country that had endured more than a half-century of Westernization and modernization under the two Pahlavi shahs. In exile, Khumaynī himself was exposed to the nationalist and radical political discourses of the late 1960s and the 1970s. Competing with the mystiques of the twentieth-century revolutions, perpetuated by his young Marxist-orientated adversaries in the anti-Shah movements, Khumaynī borrowed from their terms and slogans and gave them an Islamic veneer. Between 12 October 1978, when he went to France, and April 1980, when he launched, à la Mao Zedong, the Islamic Cultural Revolution, his learning curve accelerated. Politically, he had become a bipolar man, a cross between a Shi'i Imam and an Iranian Lenin. He and his comrades-in-revolution, clerics such as Muḥammad Ḥusayn Bihishtī, had moved away from the Shi'i tradition of patiently awaiting for the reappearance of the Shi'i Hidden Imam and moved closer to the Leninist expectancy that human will could overcome any temporal obstacle and that history could be hurried along by the determination of political activists.

They forcefully pursued two interrelated goals: (1) elimination or pacification of any and all individuals and political groups who challenged the clerical consolidation of power, i.e., the establishment of the *vilāyat-i faqīh* as the central pillar of the Republic; and (2) Islamization of the society and the state. The success in attaining the first goal was perceived as a precondition for achieving the second one. The success in the second goal would provide legitimacy for the first one, by enabling the clerics to claim exclusive right to political power. At that critical stage, they did not care what the outside world thought about their human rights records of fabricated charges, torture and executions.

In the second year of their rule, the politically shrewd clerics moved aggressively and their actions corresponded somewhat with the twentieth century revolutionary patterns elsewhere. This parallel was hardly surprising, because their equally determined opponents were grounded in the politics and rhetoric of the twentieth century. They were fighting on the same terrain and for the same spoils. The revolutionary contexts of the time included the presence not only of the leftist groups and the Mujāhidīn, who were armed and ready to do battle, but also of a large, semi-secular middle-class population who could not be easily cowed. The clerics added their own Islamic jargon to actions that were motivated by the realities of the contemporary nation-state in the context of an illiberal political culture. Even in the goal of Islamization of the society, their fundamentalism differed from that of the genuinely conservative clergy elite who endlessly engaged in nit-picking the juridical points. The state expediencies and lack of a strict adherence to the Islamic *shari'a* prevailed. In a larger context, Khumaynī considered the survival of the Islamic state to be the central issue. During a critical legislative impasse in the Majlis (parliament) in 1987, he issued the infamous *fatvā*, which utilized Sunni Islam's principle of *maṣlaḥa* (public good) and stated unequivocally that the existence of the Islamic state superseded all Islamic ordinances. As Asghar Schirazi has observed, 'If a measure was in the interests of the state and Islam, it could annul all other Islamic ordinances, even prayer, fasting and the pilgrimage to Mecca' (Schirazi 1997: 64, 213). Khumaynī, like many modern authoritarian rulers, equated the political interests of those in power with the interests of the state and religion.

Again, the survival of the state was paramount. Khumaynī moved firmly to fashion the *vilāyat-i faqīh*, and the real or imagined internal enemies were overwhelmingly Muslims who had failed to appreciate its values or its applicability to a modern nation-state. Thus, the 'Baha'i problem' of the Shi'i clerics was not even marginally significant to either of the two main considerations mentioned above. The fact that the lives of religious minorities became fraught with danger was largely unrelated to these two central tasks.

Cleansing the public space of those un-Islamic signs and symbols – particularly those that had direct bearings on the legitimacy of the *vilāyat-i faqīh* – and imprinting the Muslim Iranians, especially the lapsed middle classes, with 'Islamic moralities' were far more central to Khumaynī's agenda than any other consideration or desire. Thus, political considerations, security requirements, or the state expediencies could not fully explain the suppressions of human rights of the Baha'is. The Baha'is presented no challenge to Khumaynī's consolidation of the Islamic regime, nor did they offer a competing political vision or an ideological group clamoring for a share in the state's power and influence. Those who did – such as the radical Islamic Mujāhidīn and the Marxist-Leninist groups – were violently suppressed, physically eliminated and driven into exile by their thousands.

In the first decade of the Islamic Republic, motivations for anti-Baha'i policies and actions originated in the clerics' aversions, whose roots lay in a pre-modern religious prejudice. The prejudice against the Baha'i citizens issued from their elemental dislike of a homegrown religious faith; more broadly, it had everything to do with an intolerant Shi'i culture that still prevailed in some sections of the society. Iran became a clerical state; yet, at certain critical conjunctions, the state expediencies trumped much of the Shi'i cultural paradigm. I argue that this dynamism explained the predicament of the Iranian Baha'is; therein also lay the reason the atrocities against them did not rise to the level of genocide. Serious and systematic attempts at the extermination of Baha'is would not have served the security interests of Khumaynī's state. After the victory of Islamic revolution, he did not direct the sharpest edge of his rhetoric against them; only the royalists, the secular leftists and the Mujāhidīn had a taste of his verbal vermin, followed by deadly bullets.

To the degree that politics or policies played a role in the persecutions of the Baha'is, they were related to non-security considerations. Whenever political factions were vying for power and trying to eliminate one another – as during the Banī-Ṣadr presidency, as will be shown later – the sufferings of Baha'is increased. There were wild accusations concerning the Baha'i political conspiracies. Khumaynī was shrewd enough not to believe the Islamic propaganda he and other clerics had spawned. Had 'the Baha'i problem' been perceived within the state security paradigm, the results would have been far more bloody and destructive than they were.

With the consolidation of the *vilāyat-i faqīh* and its relatively secure institutions under tight control of men loyal to Khumaynī and his successor as the Supreme Leader, the state expediency paradigm left a decreased number of societal spheres in the 1980s for independent actions by the populace, even less so for political activities by loyal groups not totally under state control. Now the radicalized clerics and their associates owned the state, although factions within the regime could still give each other hard times at the expense of the religious minorities. The time had long passed since the 1960s when they had been the thorns in the side of the shah's government by acting as vigilantes-provocateurs and readily throwing about the notion of apostates deserving to be killed with impunity. Now, they were the rulers, and as such they developed an awareness of the state expediencies.

The first decade's persecutions: incapacitating the formal Baha'i institutions by murdering their leaders

Since the early 1980s, the Baha'i representative officials, as well as Baha'i authors, have often expressed fear of looming genocide. The Baha'i human rights researcher Nazila Ghanea has stated that the Bahá'í International Community 'never explicitly accused the Iranian government of genocide against the Bahá'ís in Iran' (Ghanea 2002: 118). However, the Universal House of Justice has used the words 'The calculated attempt at genocide' in its message to Iranian Baha'is on 26 November 2003. Other derivatives of the term have been used by Baha'i authors and representatives. The chairman of the Baha'i National Spiritual Assembly of the United States informed the House of Representatives in 1984, 'Their barbarous aim is to be achieved either through the forced conversion of the Baha'is to Shiite Islam or through their extermination.'[4] This statement reflected the official position that called the anti-Baha'i actions 'a campaign of extermination' (Nash 1986: 255). Giving to exaggerations, another author saw the possibility of the elimination of 'an entire community of nearly half a million souls,' a genocide in the making (Sears 1982: 13–14). Even the historian Moojan Momen detected 'a specific and planned programme for the elimination of the Baha'i community' (Momen 2005: 224). The Baha'i case is now being discussed in genocide journals (Affolter 2005: 75–114). And most recently, some Baha'i authors have used the terms 'genocidal policies,' 'genocidal actions,' or 'suspended genocide.'[5]

Given the history of Iran's treatment of its Baha'i citizens and the panic-stricken aftermath of the violent Islamic revolution, these anxiety-laden concerns for the well-being of Iranian Baha'is were understandable. However, the actual persecutions that took place needed no such plan to proceed, nor did they need a closely coordinated blueprint for action. The attacks on Baha'is proceeded because there existed not a systematic plan, but a highly prejudicial attitude shared by the clergy, in particular the middle and lower rank *mullas*. The anti-Baha'i clerics across the country partook in a culture of collusion, more insidious and difficult to pin down and expose than any plan. That culture was conducive to plots that could easily be hatched by local cabals with a degree of certainty that no one in higher authority would object to such actions. The British journalist John Simpson, who spent some time in Iran in 1979 and 1986–87, probably concluded correctly when he said, 'As with many other things in Iran the persecution is neither officially sponsored nor officially condemned; the initiative is left with the more violent of the mullahs and the local *Komitehs*, and nothing is done to curb the excesses' (Simpson 1988: 216). He was referring to the first five years of the Islamic Republic that were the most alarming period for Baha'is. Even Ghanea seems to be dismissive of such observations (Ghanea-Hercock 1997: 7). Did Ayatullah Khumaynī and his associates formulate an official policy? Did they sponsor the persecutions of Baha'is from the highest echelons of the Iranian regime? Did all these terms – official policy, sponsorship, planned programme – mean the same thing? Perhaps, there was such a plan, but no direct evidence of it has surfaced – not yet. As is discussed later, the so-called blueprint that was articulated in 1991 had no visible impact on the restrictions that were already imposed. To assume the existence of a plan, uniformly executed across Iran, but without direct evidence of it, raises an important question for a credible academic historiography. More significantly, to assert the existence of such a plan makes the task of assigning responsibility and demanding accountability less complicated. However, the probability that the persecutions of Baha'is proceeded without a centralized policy or a definitive plan aimed at elimination should make them even more pernicious and, in the long term, more troubling not only to the Baha'is, but also to all Iranians who desire to see the Baha'is as citizens deserving equal respect and concern. To assume the existence of a preconceived plan is an indictment of the state; to assume that most of the violations of human rights of the Baha'is took place without such a systematic plan is an indictment of both the state and a significant part of the Iranian society and its illiberal culture.

We might reasonably assume that the anti-Baha'i clerics thought that they had to eliminate only the top representatives of the Baha'i Faith. With a tinge of polemic, Douglas Martin has written, 'Influenced, no doubt, by the role which they themselves play in Shí'ih Islam, the mullahs mistakenly believed that the Bahá'í Faith's survival in Iran depended on a limited number of leaders . . .' (Martin 1984: 49). We simply do not know – beyond doubt – if they believed this proposition or, more generally, what they thought they were doing. We do not know whether or not the leaders of the Islamic Republic Party, to whom Martin has referred, had discussed the issue and arrived at such a conclusion. The scattered evidence shows a picture of much messier actions than this rather simple image of an operation singularly intended to eliminate a limited number of leaders to achieve mass conversion.

Khumaynī's sporadic statements before the establishment of the Islamic Republic denouncing the Baha'is became increasingly frightening now that he was in power. Ghanea has written,

> He also made passionate appeals such as, 'The Koran and Islam are in danger. The independence of the state and the economy are threatened by a take-over by the Zionists, who in Iran have appeared in the guise of Baha'is'. Unfortunately, these attacks did not just remain verbal in nature. . . .
>
> (Ghanea 2002: 101)

Ghanea has added that 'the effect of Khomeini's direct and repetitive verbal attacks on the Bahá'ís may be traced as his enduring legacy on the fate of the Bahá'ís in Iran even today' (Ibid.). Khumaynī spoke these quoted words in 1962, when he and his ilk boosted the credibility of their attacks against the Shah's policies by reiterating conspiratorial evil designs of Zionism and Baha'ism. From the forbidden political space of the early 1960s, Khumaynī was throwing stones at the Shah's halls of power. After the establishment of the Islamic Republic, he was sitting at the centre of power handling a litany of life-and-death issues related to the survival of his authoritarian state, while being surrounded by deadly stone-throwers. Ghanea and other Baha'i scholars who take similar positions must cite the instances of Khumaynī's 'repetitive verbal attacks' after the establishment of the Islamic Republic. What can be said with certainty is that he did not stop the middle-rank clerics to unleash their invectives, when they did, against Baha'is.

The British author Roger Cooper, writing for a human rights group, was probably accurate in his 1982 observations: 'It is also worth noting that despite his reputation for outspokenness Ayatollah Khomeini has not personally made any inflammatory anti-Baha'i remarks since his return to Iran, as he has done in the case of Kurds, Americans and the Mojahedin. . . .' (Cooper 1982: 15). At least on one significant occasion when Khumaynī talked about the Baha'is, it was his enmity towards the US government's policies that framed his polemics. On 22 May 1983, President Reagan made an appeal to spare the lives of 22 Baha'is who had been sentenced to death in Shiraz. The number was reported by international Baha'i sources, although the names of the victims were not provided. As will be discussed shortly, the death sentences in Shiraz were passed by the middle-rank cleric Ḥujjat al-Islām Qaḍā'ī. Six days after Reagan's appeal, Khumaynī responded. What was noticeably absent in Khumaynī's rhetoric was Qaḍā'ī's incendiary, religiously-grounded denunciations of the Baha'is. More sarcastic than fanatic, Khumaynī's remarks cast serious doubt on Reagan's sincerity as a defender of humanitarian values, since he and the US government were encouraging Iraq to do things to Iran that even the invading Mongols of the Middle Ages had not done. He mockingly added that the President portrayed the Baha'is not as spies but as innocent victims quietly following their own religion, as if 'Iran has convicted 22 of them to death only because they engage in their religious rites.' He suggested that they must have been spies. As if addressing Reagan directly, the Ayatullah asserted, 'If they were not spies, you wouldn't say a word.' He then resorted to the clerics' run-of-the-mill explanations that 'the Baha'is are not a religion, but a Party, a Party that the British had formerly supported and now America is backing.' Then he compared the convicted Baha'is with the leadership of the Marxist Tūda Party, whom he likewise accused of being spies for the other superpower, the USSR. If they were not spies, he further implied, the Islamic court would not have taken actions against either of them. The courts would have ignored them, as they had done in the cases of other religiously-misguided people (Khumaynī 1985: 266–267).

Perhaps there was nothing in Khumaynī's expressed views that could have made a substantial difference in the behaviours of the anti-Baha'i factions or individuals capable of inflicting harm. As the inheritors of a long tradition of anti-Baha'ism, did clerics like Yazd's Ayatullah Ṣadūqī or Shiraz's Ḥujjat al-Islām Qaḍā'ī need encouragement or approval? The Ayatullahs' anti-Baha'i rhetoric most likely appeared as ordinary and familiar as the patterns of their prayer mats. The only way that Khumaynī could have made an impression and created an enduring legacy was if he had encouraged total tolerance towards the Baha'is, a policy which would have been against his nature. However, he must be judged by history as bearing the ultimate responsibility for the sufferings and deaths that the Iranian Baha'is have endured. He was well aware of the views the *mullas*, such as the hanging judge in the city of Shiraz, held towards the Baha'is.

Ghanea further has observed, 'Nevertheless, it was the government-sponsored nature of this institutionalized discrimination that was the most disturbing and enduring feature of the attacks' (Ghanea 2002: 101). This observation is correct; she also provides a proper context by adding that the Baha'is were not included among the recognized minorities in the constitution of the Islamic Republic. As I argue in this study, that non-recognition has been the fountainhead of 'institutionalized discrimination.' The official and officially uncoordinated persecution and attacks around the country flew from the legal non-recognition of this significant religious minority.

In the first five years of the Islamic Republic, the differences in the anti-Baha'i action between one city and another in terms of the timing and intensity did not indicate the presence of a definitive plan of action being effectively carried out across the country. For the city of Yazd, the summer of 1980 was the murderous period, whereas in Shiraz the murders began in earnest in the spring of 1981 (up to then, three Baha'is were killed) and reached its climax in the fall of 1982. In Hamadan, not one Baha'i was killed until June 1981. In Tabriz, three Baha'is had been killed by 29 July 1981, when the nine members of the Local Spiritual Assembly, the town's elected Baha'i governing body, were executed. In Tehran the killings and executions were also intermittent, a condition that made discerning any pattern indicating a preconceived plan of actions difficult: 19 in 1980, 20 in 1981, 9 in 1982, 3 in 1983, 15 in 1984, and 2 in 1985. One Iranian Baha'i killed was one too many; human rights scholars need not use terms such as extermination and genocide – or their derivatives – to show the gravity of what took place. The fact that such wanton executions took place at the end of the twentieth century has disgraced Iranian society and its Shi'i culture. Generally, in the first years of the Islamic Republic some Baha'is known to the local Islamic groups continued their activities for a number of months before being arrested. Many were arrested between 1982 and 1984. Many more were not arrested. Fear was in the air, but not the type seen in an environment of genocide in the twentieth century.

Perhaps no directive from Tehran's revolutionary clerics was needed, since there was a reservoir of determined hostilities among their counterparts everywhere. The initial threats emanated from fanatical men whose pre-revolutionary associations with each other had an enduring anti-Baha'i component. Led by a cleric or a group of clerics, these groups provided the nuclei of the revolutionary, grass-root committees (*kumītas*) in different neighbourhoods or districts. Then, a Central Committee was formed by the senior radical clerics to bring some sort of order to the activities of the committees and to consolidate power by flushing out the undesirable elements. The clerics brought the armed men of the committees into what they named the Revolutionary Guard Corps. These groups became the instruments that not only crushed the radical opponents of the clerical factions such as the Mujāhidīn, but also eliminated or pushed aside the less fundamentalist factions and individuals in the loose revolutionary coalition. That they could engage in such brutalities against the Baha'is, with or without orders from established central leaders, was due to the existence of a shared view concerning the Baha'i Faith. They knew intuitively perhaps that many of the senior clerics involved in the revolution approved of their actions. Their prolonged silence signalled approval.

Leaders such as Mihdī Bāzargān, the first Prime Minister of the Republic, whose political instincts would disapprove of such actions, had much larger battles to wage against the more radical factions. Some prominent Baha'is in Tehran did try to bring to the Prime Minister's attention the ongoing attacks on their lives and properties. Feeling insecure within the new regime, he failed to take any open action to deal with the rising atrocities. When he was removed and President Banī-Ṣadr became the official face of the new administration, the attitude of indifference did not change. He also lacked the moral fortitude to spend his limited political capital in defence of the Baha'is. When asked by foreign journalists why he would not intervene to protect a prominent Baha'i from being killed, he was quoted saying 'that his enemies were only awaiting a faux pas in order to mow him down, and what worse faux pas could he commit than to intervene on behalf of a Bahá'í' (Martin 1984: 52). Notwithstanding this convenient excuse, history will not be kind towards his moral blunder of remaining the President of the Republic while innocent Baha'i human beings were being killed only because they followed their own consciences.

Already some Baha'is had been killed during the tumultuous months leading to the victory of revolution. Afterward, all the nine members of the National Spiritual Assembly were abducted and executed in August 1980. The Baha'is moved quickly and selected their replacements, whose lives were tragically cut short in the notorious Evin prison on 27 December 1981. The Baha'i leaders in Tehran were not the last individuals who were mysteriously executed. Other Baha'i leaders were tortured and executed (UN Doc. E/CN.4/1987/23: 17). The so-called judicial processes and extra-judicial actions became indistinguishable; moreover, collecting information, interrogating the prisoners under torture and issuing the final verdicts all merged, often conducted by one or two persons. The killings of prominent Baha'is in December 1981 and January 1982, perhaps more than any other tragic deaths, shaped the Bahá'í International Community's narratives regarding the situation of the Baha'is in Iran in the 1980s.

Again, the city of Yazd showed the dynamics that were historically detrimental to the well-being of the Baha'is: a combustible admixture of an anti-Baha'i tradition (well-remembered, both within and outside the Baha'i community); an active anti-Baha'i group under the leadership of a long-time Baha'i-hater, Riḍā Pāknijād;[6] and a leading Ayatullah who gave strong legitimacy to the local anti-Baha'i activities. The small but vibrant Baha'i community was indeed unfortunate to face the fanatical Ayatullah Ṣadūqī, who was well-connected to the Khumaynī network of clerics. Unchained by the collapse of the Shah's bureaucratic regime, Ṣadūqī then found an opportunity to give vent to his long-festering anti-Baha'i feelings. The Iranian scholar Mehdi Abedi has referred to him as 'the most authoritative voice to be raised in defence of the killing, jailing, and excluding from public service of Baha'is' (Fischer and Abedi 1990: 61).

Having already declared the Baha'is deserving of death, Ayatullah Ṣadūqī publicly discharged his first volley in a Friday sermon in June 1980, calling 'on the public to turn in all Baha'is to the revolutionary prosecutor' (Fischer and Abedi 1990: 260). Shortly after, 15 Baha'is were processed through a show trial that was filmed for broadcast. Seven of them were executed on September 8. There were no apparent security, legal or political reasons for these bloody persecutions. One of the seven was an elderly farmer (Nash 1986: 280). Five of them, including the distinguished Nūrullāh Akhtar-Khāvarī, were in positions of leadership. The above-mentioned Baha'i-hater, Pāknijād, knew Akhtar-Khāvarī well, because he used to receive private tutorials in English from this polished Baha'i leader of the city. He made no move to save the life of his teacher (Fischer and Abedi 1990: 49). That the most active anti-Baha'i layman received English lessons from a well-known Baha'i was indicative of the convoluted Iranian realities. Even in the city of Yazd, a hotbed of anti-Baha'i fanaticism, the killings were uneven and less than systematic. The Local Spiritual Assembly was reconstituted after the execution of seven of its members in the summer of 1980. The biographical sketches of two members of Yazd's Spiritual Assembly who were arrested in May 1982 and May 1984 and subsequently executed indicated the continuing defiant presence of the Baha'i community in the city (Universal House of Justice 1994: 217–219).

Shiraz was another city with an unsavory historical record. Perhaps nothing more tragically revealed the reason that fanatical clerics and their lay supporters attacked the Baha'is than the senseless murders of ten of the female Baha'is who fell into the clutches of the inquisitors in Shiraz in late 1982. The intent could not be clearer: recant and return to Islam and their lives would be spared. The prosecutors did not even bother to discuss with the accused the normal charges of surreptitious political activities or espionage. The clerical prosecutor-judge engaged the vibrant Munā Maḥmūdnijād, only seventeen, in a discussion about God and spirituality. 'What harm did you find in Islam that made you turn to the Baha'i Faith?' (Roohizadegan 1993: 133). The women who were hanged on 18 June 1983 could have saved their lives if they had agreed to the persecutors' demand: 'I ask you to recant and come back to Islam. If you do, I will let you go' (Universal House of Justice 1994: 217–219). Only two days earlier, six Baha'i men had been executed in Shiraz. The city's Baha'i community, many of its members middle class and educated, experienced the ultimate meaning of the Islamic Revolution for themselves. A report from a Baha'i source stated, 'Soon it was impossible to buy flowers in the city as all had been purchased and sent to the relatives of the martyrs as an expression of sympathy' (Ibid., 181). These tragic and senseless killings created a climate of fear. It did not, however, resemble the kind of fear associated with the twentieth-century genocides.

These killings of the assumed apostates in different cities often lacked the main features of public spectacles in the traditional communities of the nineteenth century. There were a few reports of mob activities in some agricultural villages. However, there were some indications that even in the rural areas the random attacks on the lives of Baha'is failed to draw the folks into the melees. As one anti-clerical author has stated (without indicating his source), 'Mullahs in the province of Yazd complained bitterly about poor Muslim peasants who refused to identify Baha'i families or to participate in shedding their blood . . .' (Taheri 1987: 217). The tragic circumstances surrounding the burning and killing of a middle-age husband and wife, simple farmers, in a remote hamlet, dramatically related by the Baha'i author William Sears, showed that the locals remained passive as a few masked murderers stealthily completed their gruesome acts in the dead of night (Sears 1982: 3–9). Of course the local clerics and their associates possessed the Western miracle of television that could be used to create the virtual versions of the spectacles of communal solidarity of the nineteenth century. In the case of the seven murdered Baha'is in Yazd, some sections of the procedure were televised, and photographs of executions were published in the press. However, that particular broadcast of the film of the execution in Yazd created some negative reactions among the viewers (Fischer and Abedi 1990: 49; Nash 1986: 258). Afterwards, the gruesome scenes remained hidden from the public; they could no longer serve the purpose of solidarity-generating public rituals, as they did in the traditionally authentic communities, in which the public was both actors and spectators. The outsiders/insiders dynamism was not played out in public squares. This secrecy subverted the new rulers' claim to cultural authenticity. Under the Pahlavi state, the public sphere had been rendered far less communal, and the clerics could not revert to making it what it had been during the persecutions of the Babis and the Baha'is in the nineteenth century. Overall, in many cities the public remained largely passive, and that passivity has added another shameful page to the modern history of Iran.

More than 215 Baha'is, most of them with capabilities to lead and/or inspire, were killed or disappeared between the advent of the Islamic Revolution and 2005. An overwhelming majority of them lost their lives in the early years of the Islamic Republic, one hundred and seventy by the summer of 1984. The charges against them often included almost everything that the anti-Baha'is held in their conspiratorial phantasm, including espionage for the Great Satan, cooperation with the Shah's regime, and assistance to Israel. No credible trial ever took place. None could be charged with any real crime in a credible court. What was even more heart-wrenching was that many of them could have avoided execution if they had professed – nominally, as is often the case in repentance – to have accepted Islam. Preserving both their own personal dignity and the honour of their faith, they died tragically.

They were not all eminent leaders or renowned teachers of their faith at the national level. Many of them were the members of Local Spiritual Assemblies. Some were common folks such as Bahman Dihqānī, a farmer who lived in a village outside Najafabad, Isfahan province. He was stoned to death by a group of murderers in the middle of night on 15 November 1983. The women of the summer of 1983 in Shiraz went about their normal lives as most Iranian middle-class women did, as they also served their religion, until they suddenly saw their ordinary lives metamorphose into a nightmare ending on the gallows. These were ordinary people caught up in an extraordinary time, as ordinary as Raḥmānullāh Ḥakīmān, who used to be a government employee working for the Department of Agriculture in the city of Kirman for 28 years, until he was dismissed. His wife also lost her job. 'The family had to sell carpets and other household goods to raise some capital with which to open a small stationery store' (Universal House of Justice 1994: 199). He was arrested in December 1983 and died in prison under torture. The prison authorities buried him without the presence of his family.

A few exceptional individuals had achieved prominence. To mention only one, Professor Manūchihr Ḥakīm, a physician-scientist with international reputation, was assassinated in January 1981, without anyone claiming responsibility. The murder sent a shock-wave of fear and indignation across the large Baha'i community in Tehran. The funeral procession, with some four thousand well-dressed and dignified Baha'is marching behind the members of the National Spiritual Assembly and the Local Spiritual Assembly, signified more than a deeply-felt sense of mourning and loyalty to the faith. They revealed a courageous defiance and determination rooted in the faith. The

Islamic Revolutionary Guards resorted to their intimidating tactics, but the general climate within which the cortège proceeded and the burial service took place was not one of extermination or genocide. One must place this event against the larger political context in the city and the security priorities of the power-holders in the regime. The visibly defiant funeral took place midway between the summer of 1980 and the summer of 1981, a critical period in the tumultuous early history of the Islamic Republic. That period ended with the ousting of President Banī-Ṣadr. As discussed earlier, any groups or individuals who were perceived as presenting a serious threat to the establishment of the clerical rule bore the brunt of the combined forces of the Islamic Revolutionary Guards and the violent *Ḥizbullāhī* throngs, the self-designated partisans of God. But the Baha'is were not in their security-obsessed radar screen. The enmity towards them revolved around a different orbit.

There are some indications that from early 1980, continuing well into 1981, the spike in attacks on the lives of Baha'is took place against the background of an intensification of the bloody clashes between different groups in the revolution. The taking of American hostages was only an outward manifestation of those internecine conflicts. By then, the remnants of the well-known anti-Baha'i group, Ḥujjatīya, enmeshed with other radical Islamist groups, had a much larger battle to wage over political power and the control of lucrative resources. Nevertheless, their attacks on the Baha'is dovetailed well with their collective efforts to eliminate the competing power-centres and leaders such as president Banī-Ṣadr. Their goal was to make everyday administration of the country more difficult for their moderate political opponents, some of whom controlled, at least nominally, different parts of the administration. They also wished to boost their own traditionalist Islamic credentials by projecting themselves as the protectors of Islam. Banī-Ṣadr became president in January 1980. The innocent Baha'is found themselves entrapped in unprecedented political violence.

Banī-Ṣadr was impeached on 21 June 1981 and soon after escaped to France. Shaul Bakhash has observed that Banī-Ṣadr's main goal was to 'reassert the authority of the government and its formal institutions' (Bakhash 1986: 97). The men whose revolutionary excesses Banī-Ṣadr wished to curtail countered his measures by increasing the very same excesses. Their most effective weapon was to intensify what Banī-Ṣadr considered the lawlessness of the committees, the Revolutionary Guards and other powerful revolutionary institutions. In a short interval, the Islamic prosecutors and judges who almost uniformly opposed Banī-Ṣadr executed more than 900 of their political enemies, an overwhelming number of them during the last eleven months of his presidency.

Outside the regime, the bloody conflicts between the clerics and the radical opposition, in particular the Mujāhidīn, were heading towards an open war in the second half of 1980. Targeting the IRP alliance, and indirectly Khumaynī himself, the Mujāhidīn propaganda was relentless and effective among the relatively well educated Muslim activists in Tehran. The two trends, inside and outside the regime, converged in the Mujāhidīn uprising in June 1981. Its hit-and-run actions in streets, plus spectacular terrorist bombings, were met by the IRP's reign of terror that raged well into 1985. According to Abrahamian, during these four years, 12,250 political activists were killed and executed – 'three-quarters of whom were Mojahedin members or sympathizers' (Abrahamian 1989: 223).

Here a pattern suggests itself. If we separate the numbers of the Baha'is killed between 1978–79 and 1985 into two periods, before June 1981 and after, the noticeable increase in the second period parallels the sharp rise in the number of executions and killings that took place in the larger political arena. In some two years before June 1981, the number of Baha'is killed was 47. In the following two years, the number of Baha'is killed was doubled, reaching ninety-eight individuals by June 1983. From June 1981 to the end of 1984, the period of the greatest number of political killings in the twentieth-century Iran, 132 Baha'is were killed. The firing squads were cranking their guns in the prison yards, and amidst hundreds of the regime's political opponents who were being hastily processed towards execution, hardly any imprisoned Baha'i could hope to be spared. At the beginning of the reign of terror, as Bakhash observed, the executions were indiscriminate. 'Among those killed were two prominent bazaar merchants, Baha'is, and royalists already long in jail' (Bakhash 1986: 211). In the entire revolutionary year of 1980, 24 Baha'is were killed. In those critical two months of the summer 1981, just before and after the removal of the president, 25 Baha'is were executed in three separate prisons, some of whom had been languishing in prison for months; Dr. Masīḥ Farhangī and a few others were among the most prominent Baha'is of Iran (Nash 1986: 261). The number of executions of Baha'is dropped to seven in 1985.[7] The drop also paralleled the sharp decline in the numbers of executions of the much larger category of political prisoners. Obviously the peaceful and politically passive Baha'is could not be in the list of the regime's political opponents and were not targeted for destruction. The Baha'i prisoners found themselves in the revolutionary vortex, though they had played no role in its making.

It was after June 1981, in the second period of increased radicalization, that all possible inhibitions were removed, giving the most intolerant elements in the Islamic revolution open fields in all aspects of state operations including the prisons, where they practiced excessive torture to extract confession and forced repentance. Different methods of torture that the members and fellow travellers of radical political groups were subjected to could be easily extended to the Baha'i prisoners who were often kept in the same prison wards. The goal was the same: to break the resolve of the captives. Even the methods of torture had become all-encompassing. A Baha'i source observed in May 1984, 'Recent reports indicate that torture is being used not only to force recantations and conversions to Islam but also to extract false confessions of various fictive crimes, confessions which would 'prove' the old accusations that the Baha'is were Zionist or imperialist agents, foreign spies, or a political subversive group.'[8] Many of the political prisoners were forced to confess to a litany of similar charges (Abrahamian 1999; Afshari 2001).

This discussion does not mean to imply that executing the Baha'is was merely a part of the ongoing revolutionary violence that devoured thousands of Muslim Iranians. The motives for the executions of the Baha'is were distinct from those that compelled the ruthless clerics to annihilate the members of the Mujāhidīn and the leftist organizations. The pains and traumas the Islamic Republic inflicted on individuals belonging to a historically persecuted religious minority lacked any political and security logic and were also differently experienced. But the climate of crisis offered an opportunity to the anti-Baha'i elements in the regime to try to do serious harm to the Baha'is, what they could not probably have accomplished before and after that crisis. This larger political context is needed for an improved understanding of the sharp rise and then the significant decline in the number of executions of the Baha'is in this revolutionary period.

To claim that international pressure on the Islamic Republic was responsible for its changed behavior towards the Baha'is is to give too much credence to human rights campaigns conducted in New York and Geneva. For the sake of international human rights enforcement, one wished it were true. Why did they fail to stop the executions of the Baha'is in 1980–1984? In fact, the explanation of the Baha'i sources in that early period claimed no such success. 'Despite a growing international outcry,' one source stated, 'the rate of executions continued to grow through 1981.'[9] And another author accurately observed in 1982, 'The complete failure of outside opinion to have any effect on the repressive activities of the Islamic Republic regime is in itself further testimony to the fanatical and impervious single-mindedness of the Shi'ite clerics now ruling Iran . . .' (Nash 1982: 115). It was not until 1989 that internal reorientation took place and the regime became responsive to the UN Commission on Human Rights, largely due to the changed domestic circumstances. Months before that reorientation, the executions of large numbers of the Baha'is had stopped. To denounce the radical Islamists as irrational fanatics and then claim that the same bloody clerics stopped executing many Baha'is because of international pressure appears incongruous. To claim that the international campaigns aborted certain genocide is to engage in self-congratulation.[10]

Altogether between 1978 and 1984, 88 Baha'is in various, formal positions of leadership, mostly as members of Spiritual Assemblies, were killed – 21 of them in the first period and 57 of them during the reign of terror. This number was a small fraction of the numbers of the leading Baha'is. Before the formal disbanding of their organizations in 1983, those who served on the local Spiritual Assemblies were numbered about 3,600 individuals. The same source has stated that by adding the members of numerous committees and subcommittees who were 'directly involved in organizational activity,' the number could reach over 10,000 people.[11] Of course the anti-Baha'i persons in the regime who wished to know could easily find the whereabouts of hundreds of Baha'is who were active in their organizations.

Beginning with the reign of terror, the sharp increase in the number of imprisoned Baha'is also paralleled the increases in the number of political prisoners. 'Between May 1982 and May 1984 over 1,000 persons were arrested . . . This constitutes an almost fivefold increase over the number of Baha'is in custody in May 1982.'[12] Some individuals were released as others were arrested. By mid-1985 there were still more than 700 Baha'i prisoners. By then the consolidation of clerical power had been achieved. A drastic reduction of all categories of prisoners followed.[13] Still pressure was applied to extract some sort of repentance from their captives. The well-informed Mottahedeh observed at the time,

> As a condition of release Baha'i prisoners are now asked to sign a statement that reads: 'I, the undersigned, have undertaken not to have in my possession any book, pamphlet, document, symbol, or picture of this misguided Zionist, espionage group of Baha'is. If any of the above-mentioned article . . . is found on my person or in my home, this will be tantamount to being of those who "war against God" . . . and the attorney-general will be free to give a decision against me in the manner he sees fit.' So far no Baha'i prisoner has chosen to sign this strange document. . . .
>
> (Mottahedeh 1985: 388–389)

This rather peculiar wording perhaps indicated a larger trend covering all political prisoners. They were also asked to sign similar documents – differently worded to fit their former political affiliations and ideological inclinations – that appeared less than a clear statement of confession and repentance. This was a reflection of the changed conditions in prisons after 1984. Political prisoners referred to this period of relative improvement as the 'intermission.' It was associated with the reforms attempted by Ayatullah Ḥusayn-'Alī Muntaẓirī, then Khumaynī's designated successor; he had been alarmed by the excessive brutalities of the prison system. Prison wardens were replaced. The memoirs of the leftist activists who survived and were freed between 1984 and 1988 have described the new conditions in prisons, particularly in Tehran. It became clear that the authorities were willing to free as many political prisoners as possible, sometimes with a minimum formality of repentance. Many of them chose to sign such a 'strange document.'[14] Many refused. By the time that the 'intermission' ended in 1988, the majority of the Baha'is had been released. By 1989, around one hundred Baha'is

Figure 11.1 The House of the Bab, Shiraz, one of the most holy sites for Baha'is worldwide, before its destruction in 1979.

remained in prisons (Ghanea 2002: 126). That number would be further reduced in the early 1990s.

The increased bureaucratization of the state administration and the changes in the overall policies towards the outside world did not mean a significant attenuation of formal and informal capabilities – and malevolence – that could still harass and persecute the Baha'is, especially in provinces. Some of the worst cases occurred when particular individuals fell into webs of entanglements between local factions that remained impervious to the new imperatives of the increasingly bureaucratic ministries in Tehran. In December 1988, a Baha'i who had been imprisoned since late 1983 was executed. Another man had spent some two years in prison before he was killed in November 1988 (UN Doc. A/44/620, 2 November 1989: 23). Two military generals, who were charged with being Baha'i, were executed early in January 1989. They were already in prison serving seven-year terms. Sporadically, there were other death sentences. One such tragedy was the execution of Bahman Samandarī, a businessman from a prominent Baha'i family on 18 March 1992 (UN Doc. E/CN.4/1994/50: 29).

A few of the particularly unfortunate ones in this period included Ḥasan Mahbūbī, Bihnām Mīthāqī, Kayvān Khalajābādī, Bakhshullāh Mīthāqī, 'Alī

Figure 11.2 The House of the Bab in Shiraz was destroyed by Revolutionary Guardsmen in 1979 and later razed by the government.

Dhu'l-faqārī, Dhabīḥullāh Maḥramī, Mūsā Ṭālibī, Māshāllāh 'Ināyatī, and Ruḥullāh Rawḥānī.[15] Some of these men were executed; others remained in prison for a long time (UN Doc. A/52/472: para. 44). Two of them languished in prison until 2004, when they were let go. To illustrate a little further, Ruḥullāh Rawḥānī, a medical supplies salesman and father of four, was executed in July 1998, when the reformist President Khātamī was offering some hope for human rights improvement in the country. Authorities in the city of Mashhad had charged him, wrongfully, with the crime of converting a Muslim to the Baha'i Faith. Rawḥānī was denied due process of law and the service of an attorney, and his family remained unaware of the death sentence until after the execution.[16]

The case of Dhabīḥullāh Maḥramī attracted the attention of international NGOs, mainly because the charges against him kept changing, as different levels of the Islamic Judiciary became involved. Maḥramī was a Baha'i, who felt compelled in 1985 to sign an official form stating that he was a Muslim, most likely in order to keep his job in the city's Department of Agriculture. Like some other Baha'is who had signed a similar form, his 'conversion' was only a formality. For seven years he went about his life as if he were a Muslim. In the 1990s, the always intrusive local authorities became aware of his continued allegiance to the Baha'i Faith. Assuming that he had reconverted, they charged him with the crime of apostasy. The Iranian laws were silent on the issue of apostasy. Nevertheless, the absence of formal law did not prevent clerics from making reference to Islamic edicts concerning apostasy. The revolutionary court in Yazd convicted Mahrami on 2 January 1995. The capital punishment had to be approved by the Supreme Court in Tehran.

The case was revealing of the dynamics of the human rights discourse and practice in Iran during the 1990s. Human Rights Watch explained:

> The Supreme Court, ruling at a time when the country was under scrutiny at the UN Commission on Human Rights following visits to the country by two special rapporteurs of the Commission and the special representative on Iran, referred the case back to a civil court. The Supreme Court ruled that the Revolutionary Court was not the appropriate tribunal to address a case of this nature.
>
> But the authorities did not comply with the Supreme Court ruling. Instead, they introduced new charges of espionage and brought Mahrami for trial before a revolutionary court again, and in February 1997, the head of the Revolutionary Court announced that Mahrami had been sentenced to death on charges of espionage for Israel.
>
> (Human Rights Watch 1997: 13)

The details of what happened next were not clear, but he was apparently granted a Presidential amnesty that commuted his death sentence to imprisonment for life. Maḥramī became one of the two long-term captives of the regime. He was declared a prisoner of conscience by Amnesty International and died in Yazd prison in late December 2005.

With the benefit of hindsight, what took place in Iran was neither an extermination of the Baha'is nor an extinction of the Baha'i Faith. Sufferings were intolerable; however, the desire for their conversion, like many of the dreams of Islamic fundamentalists, failed. It is a testimony to the historical blindness of the ideological zealots that the Shi'i clerics could imagine that they might succeed in converting the Baha'i prisoners – the overwhelming majority of whom were unflinchingly faithful – to Islam. Most of the formal executions in prisons took place by the order of the Shi'i clerics in different cities. These clerics saw themselves as the inheritors of an enduring legacy of historical perseverance in the face of formidable adversaries. The gatekeepers of the Shi'i mythology failed to see the presence of a parallel tradition, much younger in age, driven by the same prophetic impulses. The *mulla* who listened to a Baha'i woman affirming her faith in terms of her personal devotion to the Baha'i prophetic figure could not actually hear the resonance of the Shi'i trances that invoked the name of the seminal figures of the griping Shi'i mythology. In an enlightened mind, it could have generated awe and sympathy; in that fanatical mind it perhaps created an outrage.

> 'How can I make you understand that my being exists solely for Bahá'u'lláh, the object of my hope and love is Bahá'u'lláh, and my heart is also of Bahá'u'lláh.' 'I will tear your heart out of your breast,' the judge replied. 'Even then that heart will cry out "Bahá'u'lláh!", "Bahá'u'lláh!", "Bahá'u'lláh!"' Zarin retorted. Later, she wearily reminded him of his first interrogation of her. '. . . I told you the first day I would not recant. . . .'
>
> (Universal House of Justice 1994: 184)

Zarīn Muqīmī, a graduate of Tehran University in English literature, was only 29 when this almost surrealistic exchange took place. The clerics were utterly incapable of understanding the minds of their Baha'i captives, or of walking even a few steps in their shoes. Had they done so, they might have recognized the futility of their expectation of conversion to Islam, even on a small scale. And of course their fanaticism had so awfully darkened their spirituality that it did not occur to them that showing mercy to a young, radiant woman or a distinguished, elderly physician would open a window to divinity's grace in the darkness of a bleak interrogation room in a god-forsaken prison.

The first and second decades: making the Baha'is suffer for their continuous adherence to their faith

While the elimination of top leadership threatened the Baha'i community's organizational capabilities as a faith with a cohesive membership, individual Baha'is were subjected to measures that could deprive them of means to sustain themselves and families economically and socially. Those who carried out the harassment and persecutions wished to destroy the conditions needed for their survival as a community with a distinct religious identity. However, it was far from clear to what lengths the leading clerics in charge of state institutions were willing to go on the path to get the Baha'is to succumb religiously and to forfeit their faith. Until early 1990s, it seems, the leading clerics had given no systematic thought to the issues related to the continuing existence of the Baha'is in Iran.

It was almost four years after the victory of the revolution – by then, more than 150 Baha'is had already been killed – that the Islamic Prosecutor General, Ayatullah Ḥusayn Mūsavī Tabrīzī, announced in August 1983 the disbanding of all administrative organs and public meetings of the Baha'is in Iran. He added that they were already illegal. The announcement came in the course of a largely incoherent interview. One of the charges he levelled at them was that some Baha'is gave news to foreigners. Perhaps, some informed Baha'is did not miss the irony that during the same interview he also indicated that the Ḥujjatīya, the most articulate anti-Baha'i group, was also disbanded for its opposition to Khumaynī. Less than a week later, the Baha'i representatives in Tehran publicly replied by informing the prosecutor, and anyone else who wished to read, that they would obey the order. They used the moment to issue an eloquent defence of the Baha'i Faith and conduct. Setting the record straight, their statement strongly rejected, in a language that was polite, graceful and defiant, the typical accusations that the prosecutor, reflecting long-held views among the Shi'i clerics, had leveled at the innocent Baha'is and their faith. The Baha'is demanded an end to persecutions and removal of restrictions in all aspects of their social and economic lives. The Baha'is in Tehran seemed battered, but by no means were they prostrate.

However, what preceded this rather informal statement by Ayatullah Mūsavī Tabrīzī had already been quite alarming to the common Baha'i citizens. Leaving the harassment and persecutions aside, they had to earn their living and provide for the education of the children, just like everyone else, in the country that was at war with itself and with a neighbouring state. With varying degrees of intensity in different localities, the anti-Baha'i clerics and their allies attacked Baha'is on all possible grounds and in all spheres of public life, from elementary education to professional occupations, from marriage ceremonies to cemeteries.

The attacks on cemeteries revealed the traditional pattern of religious animosity. Again in the city of Yazd, one of the early anti-Baha'i actions occurred when the 'public' unleashed its rage on the gravestones of the dead Baha'is. In almost all tradition-bound communities, both the living and the dead had religiously designated quarters; the most visible sign of otherness for the dead was of course a separate cemetery. Religious minorities have their own separate cemeteries. Reflecting the common zealotry of the Shi'i traditional society of the nineteenth century, the possessors of the divine truth ceremonially left the marks of that truth on the bodies of the apostates. They did the same to those who were already dead by desecrating their graves. That tradition was now being incorporated into a revolution that took charge of a nation-state.

In some other cities the Baha'i cemeteries were also attacked. The revolutionary gangs destroyed the beautifully maintained Baha'i cemetery in eastern Tehran. In many places Baha'i cemeteries remained closed, making it difficult for Baha'i families to bury their dead properly (UN Doc. A/43/705: 15). Cemeteries in other cities were confiscated. By the mid-1990s, the Bahá'í International Community kept the UN Special Representative Galindo Pohl well informed. 'It is said that the Baha'is must bury their dead on waste land specified by the Government and that they are not entitled to identify the graves of their loved ones' (UN Doc. E/CN.4/1995/55: para. 53). The intensities and scope of attacks on cemeteries seemed to vary from one city to another.

Other attacks included, in the words of a UN report, 'torture, arbitrary imprisonment, denial of education and employment, arbitrary seizure of homes and possessions, confiscation of community assets, and seizure, desecration and destruction of holy places' (UN Doc. E/CN.4/1987/23: 17). Religious meetings and classes were invaded and their activities repeatedly interrupted. The revolutionary gangs broke into the houses of some Baha'is, and in the prevailing chaos of the time no valuable possessions in the hands of 'the apostates' were safe. Some of the prosperous Baha'i businesses were taken over and bank accounts of known Baha'is were frozen and perhaps subsequently plundered by powerful individuals or groups. Licences for small businesses and shopkeepers were not to be renewed. The Baha'is were particularly vulnerable in small towns, where they could be easily identified. In such places it was unlikely that Muslim-owned businesses could dare to give them a helping hand in employment.

In the early months of the Islamic Republic, no grandiose official blueprint was needed for many of the attacks that were carried out against the Baha'is. However, with the establishment of the new regime's authority in different ministries and the state-owned companies and institutions, anti-Baha'i actions emanated from these ministers and institutions. By the mid-1980s as the waves of killings, kidnappings and tortures subsided, the anti-Baha'i discrimination began to be institutionalized, and the persecutions carried on by the state authorities, particularly in the ministry of education, became systematic.

The Baha'is were told that they could not manifest their faith, hold public meetings, maintain places of worship, teach their faith to their children in their own schools in an open manner, and disseminate their literature (UN Doc. A/44/620: 23). In early 1980s, the general perception of the Baha'is outside Iran was that their coreligionists inside were placed under considerable pressure to renounce their faith, or all their possessions would be confiscated (Sears 1982: 22–23).

The newly created Islamic institutions took over the offices of the National Spiritual Assembly and those belonging to the city's Spiritual Assembly, as well as other administrative and youth centres in Tehran. Under the Shah's rule, the Baha'i assets belonging to the community had managed to do rather well, despite the prevailing cultural prejudices. These well-endowed corporations and communal assets became the targets of the anti-Baha'i zealots in the Islamic Republic.

Particularly, the two companies that had performed valuable services to the community were taken over in early 1979. The Shirkat-i Nawnahālān's roots went back to the early twentieth century; it had become a multi-million dollar establishment engaged in range of activities, importing goods, offering loans for houses and students' education, assisting the elderly and other charitable functions. The second company confiscated by the Islamic revolutionaries was simply called the Umanā' ('trustees'). It was in charge of the significant shrines and some one thousand local religious centres, facilities and cemeteries. Cooper observed, 'The assets of both companies have been confiscated and their records seized, thus wiping out the savings and pensions of some 15,000 Baha'is and providing a "legal" basis for the confiscation of property' (Cooper 1982: 13). The seizure of other institutions followed. The well-founded and managed Mīthāqiyya hospital and the Baha'i home for the aged in Tehran were confiscated.[17] These takeovers seriously threatened the financial solvency of the Baha'i community in Iran (Nash 1982: 81–84).

According to one estimate, 10,000 Baha'is lost their positions in the state institutions and private businesses by 1984 (Universal House of Justice 1994: 203). The government also denied their pensions. The details of the positions and the nature of businesses were not provided.

> Some who had been dismissed from their posts had been required to reimburse the salaries or pensions they had received over the years of their employment. A circular from the Ministry of Labour and Social Affairs . . . stipulated that, 'The penalty incurred by those who belong to any of the misguided sects . . . shall be permanent dismissal from public office . . . and also from organizations that can be classed as governmental associations or offices.'
>
> (UN Doc. E/CN.4/1996/95/Add.2: para. 60;
> UN Doc. E/CN.4/1996/95/Add.2: para. 640)

If the Baha'i government employees wished to retain their jobs, they had to undergo the humiliation of a public recantation. Some did – a particularly traumatic experience for Baha'is – and suffered. The conditions for their survival in the private sector were also made difficult (UN Doc. A/43/705, at 14). A typical notice issued by the General Employment Office in December 1987 listed thirteen individuals whose jobs in banks were terminated because they belonged to 'the depraved Baha'i sect' (UN Doc. E/CN.4/1989/26, at 9). A person who had been involved in scientific research for many years related how she had been ousted from Tehran University, together with other Baha'i professors who were now trying to survive as truck drivers or flower salesmen (UN Doc. A/45/697).

The notices of dismissal were insulting in tone and devastating in their consequences; some bordered on the bizarre. One notice from a state-owned company in Tehran in April 1984 began by recognizing the diligence and competence of the employee, who was addressed as 'Excellency' (*jināb-'ālī*). It also praised the ways he comported himself during his entire service to the company. Then by coldly referring to an official circular coming from a higher authority about Baha'i individuals 'who according to a consensus among Muslims are outside Islam,' it dismissed the employee it had just highly praised (Universal House of Justice 1994; my translation).

A revealing example was a judgment issued by the Central Court of the Islamic Revolution, dated September 1983, approving the prosecutors' request for the annulment of licences of 32 Baha'i lawyers that it named. It explained in five sections the reasons that made the court agree with the request of the prosecutors. The court's statement was both incoherently rambling and venomous:

1 Before the victory of the Islamic revolution, this organization was diligent . . . on behalf of the Corrupters of the World to bring about cultural decadence and political and social corruption, and it . . . gave assistance and strength to the hated Pahlavi regime. As far as the recovered documents belonging to the deceased Shah reveal, he selected its leaders as his confidants and closest advisors. . . .
2 In economically plundering the country, in offering credit and support to the state that has occupied Palestine, and in cooperating with the hated Shah's regime, this foreign-built organization has ruined, like a devastating cancer, all economic aspects of this Muslim country, and it has elevated its cooperation with the Zionists to its highest level in disseminating the materialistic culture of the West and spreading the culture of prostitution.
3 After the victory of the Islamic Revolution and up to now, this anti-human network has implemented, secretly and surreptitiously, the hidden designs of the hellish organization (CIA). It has also acted with precision in the fabrication and distribution of rumours, suitably concocted for any situation by the Zionist sociologists and psychiatrists. At the same time and with all its possible abilities, it strove to create anxiety among people and make them feel negative towards the regime of Islamic Republic, using its agents who deceptively appeared . . . to be caring and Islamic.
4 The agents of this Party . . . tried in every way, including hoarding of goods needed by the people, to weaken and overthrow the Islamic Republic which faces the conditions of war [against Iraq].
5 The sincere cooperation of this organization with foreigners was so valuable to their masters that after the arrest of a few of their leaders, [President] Reagan, who is the head of the plunderers and modernized criminals of the twentieth century . . . spoke in their support. And the mass media of the global oppression created uproars, expressing sympathy and concerns that had never been shown for any of their other lackeys.[18]

The fanaticism of such a statement was self evident; in ferreting out imaginary evidence, e.g., hoarding of goods, it typified one feature of the judicial discourse in the Islamic Republic in the 1980s. There was hardly anything judicious in the court's ruling, no tinge of the law – Islamic or otherwise – no introspective illumination of fairness or justice, no consideration for the rules of permissible evidence, and certainly no religious grace. In its stark barrenness, there was not even a hint of the presence of a genuine anxiety about the ongoing struggle against the purported powerful external enemies, employing crafty insiders doing their dirty tricks. If the clerical prosecutors thought that the 32 Baha'is were really guilty of those wild conspiracies, surreptitious infiltration, and subversive machinations, they would have gone for the jugular – or at least something far more substantial than the revoking of licences – as they did for their actual political enemies. No matter what Khumaynī's minions thought they were doing, they were not that dimwitted to believe that Baha'is were responsible for all those crimes stretching for a few decades before and after the Shah's regime.

The language mimicked the propaganda tracts of the old anti-Baha'i circles. That propaganda was now disgracing judicial rulings, pages of the semi-official press, and even diplomatic dispatches. The regime's diplomats informed the UN about the faith as:

> a foreign-affiliated political movement established through the then tsarist Russia and Great Britain as a means to ensure their colonial interests and long-term objectives in Iran. All activities of this political movement, disguised as a religion, either directly or through other conspiratorial means, have been aimed at the subversion of the Governments in Iran and gradual obliteration of Islam as the established faith and unifying base of the Iranian people. Such subversive activities were only diminished during the latter period of the Pahlavi regime when they infiltrated all segments of the government and held high positions in the Army and the SAVAK, the Shah's notorious secret police. Most of the Shah's policies, in respect to both internal and external affairs, were practically formulated and executed by the Baha'is. This is despite their claim that Baha'is are forbidden to become involved in partisan politics or to hold any political post. The Baha'is also maintain that they are obedient to the Government of the country in which they live, and preach non-violence. Their brief history is, to the contrary, filled with long periods of riots and armed rebellion against the established Governments in Iran and other countries in the Islamic world.
> (UN Doc. A/42/648: 18)

Was this statement intended to reduce the fear of the international community and lessen its concerns about possible human rights violations in Iran? A human rights monitor, cringing at the sounds of these words, would immediately want to know how a government with the power to take lives had arrived at such conclusions about a religious community and what would result from them.

Pressures on the Baha'is remained more or less constant during the 1980s. The harsh conditions were only mitigated by the pervasive official corruption and inefficiencies. Different officials in different localities continued to block Baha'i employment in the public sector and to deprive them of their pensions. The harassment in private sectors also continued. Some examples were brought to the attention of the UN Special Representative on Iran. In October 1988, the government announced that it had confiscated the property of fifty Baha'is and 'invited the legal Muslim relatives of these Baha'is to contact the authorities' (UN Doc.E/CN.4/1989/26: 9). It was impossible for Baha'is to seek redress through the courts, since they had already been declared ineligible, as 'unprotected infidels' (UN Doc. E/CN.4/1987/23: 17). In September 1993, the court in the city of Shahr-i Rayy failed to impose a just penalty on two killers because the murdered man was, in the language of the verdict, 'a member of the misled and misleading sect of Baha'ism' (UN Doc. E/CN.4/1994/50: para. 162). Even the Baha'i victims of automobile accidents had to forgo any restitution for damages. For example, when the 'driver of the car was found guilty of involuntary manslaughter, the relatives of the victim were not entitled to receive compensation because the victim was a Baha'i. Instead, the defendant was sentenced to make a payment to a government fund' (UN Doc. A/51/479: para. 25). In the administration of justice under the clerics' control, the institutionalization of discrimination was almost unbridgeable.

There were reports of more ghastly discriminations. One described the tragic predicament of Firaydūn Shumālī, who was burned in a fire that was deliberately started in a factory where thirty Baha'is worked. Suffering a severe injury in one eye and undergoing hospitalization and surgery, he required a corneal transplant. The local Islamic Committee that had to authorize the operation refused to do so on the grounds that the eye of a Muslim 'could not be given to a Baha'i.' The man had to find a Baha'i cornea. The letter that forbade the transplant stated 'since Mr. Fereydun Shomali has personally confessed his connection with the Zionist Baha'i faction, the cornea graft is not to be performed for religious reasons' (UN Doc. E/CN.4/1988/24: 4). No verses of the Qur'an or passages of the tradition of the Prophet and the Imams were cited to explicate the religious reasons for the denial of the corneal transplant. Of course, the religious reasons could possibly be applicable only to an apostate who had challenged Islam, and not to a spy caught in the tangled web of a nation-state. The motivations for mistreatment and persecution were patently religious.

Education on every level became a major concern for the Baha'i families. Here one of the consequences of the denial of the right to religious freedom directly impacted the lives of the youths. As the Islamic Republic was consolidating its power, orders were issued for the dismissal of the Baha'i students from schools. Many families had to find ways to prepare their children at home and to enable them to take the state-administered examinations that were periodically offered to those who had for any reasons missed regular schooling. What slightly mitigated the discriminatory restrictions on public education, if not the accompanying agonies, was an unevenness in implementation. Some Baha'i students remained in schools and often endured pressures from teachers and school authorities. University students, even those who were close to graduation from medical colleges, were dismissed.

The increased bureaucratization following the Islamic Revolution and the gradual reversal of directions in the state institutions after 1989 appeared to ease the pressure on the Baha'is, but not to a tolerable level that could have created hopes for further improvements in a near future. In fact, the reversal of directions perhaps only managed to prevent adding new burdens to a slew of informal and formal constraints that had already been imposed and institutionalized. Of course, factional disputes within the regime always loomed as menacing. The UN Special Representative Galindo Pohl wrote in 1990 that the status of this religious minority was 'moving towards quite broad *de facto* tolerance' (UN Doc. E/CN.4/1990/24: 55). In fact, it could be better described as an enduring status quo that was already well in place by 1985. Notwithstanding this optimistic impression, the citing of human rights violations of the Baha'is continued to take up most of the space in Galindo Pohl's reports on religious minorities in the first half of the 1990s (UN Doc. A/47/617, 1992: para. 132). The scope of human rights violations far exceeded – and still does – the right to freedom of thought, conscience, and religion, but all of them emanated from the violations of religious freedom.

There were indications that by the late 1980s even some of the regime's Islamic ideologues complained about the absence of a coherent policy governing the often scattered anti-Baha'i activities. These were activities above and beyond the institutionalized discriminations and legal persecutions. A journal published by the Organization of Islamic Propagation sometimes reported on the anti-Baha'i actions in different towns and commented on what it referred to as the local Baha'i attempts to counter these actions. One typical report said that in the town of Simnan a 'group of people' destroyed the Baha'i cemetery. The town's Baha'is objected, and in response 'some of the people who attended the Friday prayers warned the Baha'is to refrain from burying Baha'i persons in that place.' Despite the warning, the news item added, a Baha'i woman was buried in the cemetery the following day. Offering its own 'observation,' the journal stated that such actions were 'inappropriate and uncoordinated' and could only benefit the Baha'is. How? 'It is evident that in accordance with their current strategy, the Baha'is are trying to counter these actions with the goal of creating recognition for themselves and gaining various concessions. They are often using the tactic of presenting themselves as victims and pleading for help.' It concluded that the Islamic Republic lacked a specific strategy for dealing with the Baha'is and stressed the urgent need for a unified, appropriate approach.[19]

The often-quoted memorandum issued in February 1991 by the Supreme Council of Cultural Revolution and approved by the Supreme Leader recommended that the Baha'is be placed under such conditions that in effect they might forfeit their faith. Baha'i official sources often refer to it as a 'concrete evidence' of the existence of a 'secret plan' to destroy the Baha'i community, or 'a secret blueprint' for the 'strangulation' of the Baha'i community. In fact, like many other memoranda in the Islamic Republic, declaring lofty Islamist policies, it did not change much in practice. The Council was formed by Ayatullah Khumaynī's order in the aftermath of the Islamization of the universities that had dramatically increased factional conflicts among those in charge of the ideological directions in higher education during 1981–1984.[20] One Baha'i source has claimed that it provided 'for the first time conclusive evidence that the campaign against the Bahá'ís is centrally directed by the government.'[21] It could perhaps be more accurately characterized as evidence, conclusive or not, that up to 1991 there was no 'secret plan' and that certain individuals within the regime wished to create uniformity in the often random anti-Baha'is activities around the country. There was a reference in the memorandum to another Baha'i-related meeting that the Council held in 1987, when the current Supreme Leader – then the President of the Republic – was the Council's director. Historians would have to wait for the minutes of that meeting to become available. However, can it not be argued that if the 1987 meeting had arrived at a unified policy towards the Baha'is, there would have been no need for a renewed deliberation? It was significant that the memorandum made no reference to any prior directives – from Khumaynī or his close associates – regarding the regime's policies towards the Baha'is. The Supreme Leader's reason for directing the Council to deliberate the issue in 1991 was 'that everyone will understand what should or should not be done.' The memorandum may indicate that at last he and some other power-holders wished to create a plan to cover, with more uniformity, all anti-Baha'i actions around the country. In practice, it had no discernible impact on the discriminatory and repressive patterns that had emerged and had been institutionalized since the mid-1980s.

The stated policy called on the government to deal with Baha'is 'in such a way that their progress and development are blocked.'[22] The practical significance of this memorandum was not clear, with the exception that it made the official denials of the persecutions even more unbelievable. Since the advent of the Islamic Republic 'their progress and development' had been blocked – to the degree commensurate with the regime's chronic corruption and inefficiencies and the society's more or less indifferent attitudes. Nevertheless, despite considerable physical pains, sufferings and anguish, the Baha'is of Iran were still a viable community of faith. Lost opportunities for growth had been painfully large. However, the sufferings have perhaps made them stronger.

By the mid-1990s, the 1991 memorandum had helped to focus the attention of the international community on the issue of denial of education to the Baha'i youths. In his discussions with Iranian officials, Abdelfattah Amor, the UN Special Rapporteur on religious intolerance, raised the issue. The Deputy Minister of Education denied to him that there existed a prohibition against university acceptance of Baha'is. 'He indicated that access by the Baha'is to higher education should not pose a problem provided that the Baha'is did not flaunt their beliefs in educational institutions' (UN Doc. E/CN.4/1996/95/Add.2: para. 63). Again, as far as the regime's technobureaucrats were concerned, Baha'is should not tell the truth. Not believing this assertion, Amor observed:

> Erosion of the standard of education was seriously affecting the Baha'i community. The directives of the Supreme Cultural Council of the Revolution [*sic*] concerning the level of education were quoted: 'They can enroll in schools provided that they do not declare their Baha'i identity. Preferably, they should enroll in schools with a strong and impressive [Islamic] religious ideology. They should be expelled from the universities . . . as soon as it becomes apparent that they are Baha'is.' The Baha'i representatives indicated that . . . they did not engage in proselytism, but, if questioned, would acknowledge their religious affiliation and could give explanations concerning their faith.
>
> (UN Doc. E/CN.4/1996/95/Add.2: para. 63)

When Maurice Copithorne, who succeeded Reynaldo Galindo Pohl as the UN Special Representative on Iran, visited the country in early 1996, the officials continued blaming the victims by complaining that Baha'is had been trying to establish for themselves de facto recognition as a religious minority, as if that in itself was an offense. They had done so by not accepting what was expected of them, that is, by avoiding all circumstances which would indicate that they were Baha'is. As an example, the officials referred to instances in which the Baha'is completed the section on various government forms, like passport applications, where the religion of the applicant was asked. 'It was suggested that to respond to such a question with the name of an unrecognized religion was attempting to obtain constitutional recognition for that religion' (UN Doc. E/CN.4/1996/59: para. 69). Thus, the officials complained that the Baha'is wrote the truth, instead of assuming a false Islamic identity. The official evasions and denials continued. Copithorne expressed his concern and reiterated 'his view that the situation for the Baha'is in the Islamic Republic can improve only if there is a significant change in attitude towards them on the part of the Iranian authorities' (UN Doc. A/51/479: para. 27).

The current decade of structural discriminations and the continued defiant existence of the Baha'is

By the end of the second decade of the Islamic Republic, the structural discriminations were understood and painfully experienced. Limitations on travel abroad were in place. The problems faced by Baha'i physicians and lawyers continued unabated. No bank credit was supposed to be made available to Baha'i applicants. Baha'i marriages and divorces were not legally recognized. The properties of a deceased Baha'i would go to the state if there were no Muslims in the family. The regime continued denying Baha'is their retirement pensions (UN Doc. A/44/620, 1989: 24). As late as October 1998, Baha'is were arrested for burying their dead without government authorization, which could not be granted if the deceased's religion was truthfully stated (U.S. Department of State 1999: 4). The nation-wide university system was a forbidden territory to the Baha'i youth, as was state employment, if they insisted on declaring their faith in bureaucratic forms. In 1999, at least six Baha'is remained on death row; 17 Baha'is were in prison with or without formal sentences (UN Doc. E/CN.4/1999/32: para. 42).

By the beginning of the third decade after the Revolution, the official treatments of Iran's Baha'is became even more contradictory. The intermittent persecutions continued; however, a notable feature of the third decade – at least until the election of the new hardline President in 2005 – was that a few discreet modifications in some of the long-standing restrictions took place. They did so without announcements and public acknowledgment, as if official recognition would have generated a new momentum for a real lifting of restrictions that had become institutionalized since the early 1980s. These modifications perhaps reflected the generally less controlled social environment that the middle-class Iranians experienced in the 1990s. Restrictions were not actually removed; enforcement became laxer, at least in some sections of the state bureaucracies. The Baha'is succeeded in receiving limited exit permits for traveling abroad. They began holding funeral ceremonies, and there seemed to be no limitations enforced concerning the number of people in attendance. It appeared also that the ban on religious ceremonies was allowed to lapse, even though nominally no more than fifteen individuals could attend, at any place and time, the Baha'i religious gatherings. At least on one occasion in early 2005 some Baha'is gathered in a park near Tehran to celebrate the first day of Riḍvān, a Baha'i holy festival, in spring 2005 (BIC 2005b: 13).

A general state regulation favorably affecting married conscripts began to be applied to the Baha'is as well (UN Doc. A/45/697: 61). Demanding further improvement, the Bahá'í International Community acknowledged that the government began in 1999–2000 to allow the state registration of Baha'is as husband and wife. 'This step should also allow such couples to register children of their marriage' (qtd. in Ghanea 2002: 149). Obviously no open classes could be publicly announced and held for educating children in Baha'i spiritual and moral values (UN Doc. A/47/617: para. 131). Classes were held privately, and the scope of what was supposed to be private began to expand. By the late 1990s, the nominal ban on the Baha'i students attending primary and secondary schools was also disregarded (UN Doc. E/CN.4/1995/55: para. 53).

However, the story of their denial of admission to the universities has gone through a number of macabre twists and turns. To allow them to live under constraints was one thing; to see that they actually achieved something as undeniably valuable as acquiring higher education for their youth was beyond the tolerance of some of the hardliners in the regime. In what was clearly an inhospitable sociopolitical environment, the Baha'is managed to set up in 1987 what they eventually called the Bahá'í Institute for Higher Education (BIHE). Classes were held in private homes and offices. At one point it had enrolled some 900 students who studied in classrooms as well as through correspondence. What is perhaps indicative of the time was that these efforts continued for more than ten years before some forces within the regime made an attempt to put an end to them.[23] Why they allowed these efforts to continue, and why they stopped it at that particular time we do not know. As usual one may suspect the workings of the factional conflicts. In September 1998, the security agents raided some five hundred private homes and offices, disrupted these remarkable educational efforts, and arrested at least thirty-six teachers and administrators.[24] They confiscated textbooks and laboratory equipment. Eventually, they freed all but four of the instructors who were sentenced to prison terms ranging from three to ten years. They were in Isfahan.

The prevailing contradictory environment has allowed the reactivation of the Bahá'í Institute for Higher Education. Had the secret plan to strangle the Baha'is culturally been operational, would the security agents allow this open defiance to continue? By 2001, entrance examinations were conducted to select the best students and classes were held in different major cities. It even managed to bring to Iran some Baha'i academics from North America, Europe and Australia as occasional guest lecturers. Again, a low-level persecution and harassment continued, but it seemed that the Baha'i dedication to higher education prevailed.[25] Again in August 2004 it was reported that the Baha'is received an order from governmental authorities to discontinue their educational activities and close the formal Institutes of higher learning.[26] Yet, it seems that the order was not enforced. A year later, it was reported,

> In the early morning hours of Monday, 15 August 2005, four Iranian intelligence agents entered an apartment where Mr. Sina Vahdati, the administrative head of the BIHE responsible for academic affairs, was residing. The agents confiscated certain Institute documents, of which they appeared to have had prior knowledge, and left after having questioned him for a few hours. Later, Mr. Vahdati was directed to go to the local intelligence office in Tehran the next day. When he arrived there . . . , he was dismissed and informed that he would need to return at a later date.
>
> (BIC 2005b: 18)

The vicissitudes in the regime's approaches to Baha'i educational endeavors must be bewildering to the striving Baha'i students who are caught in the webs of prejudices, contradictory attitudes, and bureaucratic ineptitude of the often fumbling officials.

A small lifting of burdens occurred in other aspects of life without actual removal of the structural impediments to the enjoyments of human rights. Now the Baha'is in Tehran were able to bury their dead in the undesirable Khāvarān cemetery, where they have built a morgue and a parking facility.[27] They continued to own businesses or to be employed by other businesses. Of course there are no statistics about the occupations of the Baha'is of Iran. Scattered references to occasional harassment indicate that many Baha'is managed to sustain their businesses, as well as to give employment opportunities to their co-religionists. In some business-oriented occupations, they could experience a kind of low-intensity persecution that could indeed hinder their growth and prosperity.[28] The Baha'is were found in all walks of life, as accountants, manufacturers of small consumer items, engineers, contractors, authors, and intellectuals in the arts, literature and film. There are talented, young Baha'i authors who publish their works in Tehran and click their pieces into the extensive Persian cyber-world, reaching many readers around the world.

The most prosperous Baha'is continued to own assets and properties. The Bahá'í International Community indirectly acknowledged this fact by, for example, reporting that during some judicial procedures – if they can be called such – the Baha'is did post deeds of property or business licences as collateral for their release. They also faced situations ranging from petty harassment to confiscation of properties, especially in the provinces. Judging by the examples that were presented by the Baha'i official sources abroad, the cases did not seem numerous, surely not on the scale of the chaotic early years of the Islamic Republic. Some confiscations flow from the greed and corruption of local officials who could, in the absence of legal sanction, give vent to their anti-Baha'i hatred and line their own pockets or the coffers of their Islamic organizations. The example of confiscation of the homes of six Baha'i families in an agricultural community (Kata, in Buyir-Aḥmad region) was most likely driven by the greedy men who saw an opportunity for grabbing properties.[29] Other acts did flow from the circumstances created by the violations of their right to practice their religion in all its dimensions.

A vicious circle was created. For example, the house of a Baha'i was confiscated because it was used by the Baha'i Institute for Higher Education for holding classes. An appeal to a higher court upheld the decision by restating that the owner had allowed his house to be used for the Baha'i classes. 'Such verdicts,' an authoritative Baha'i source observed accurately, 'demonstrate that the Iranian authorities continue to consider the Bahá'í Faith as an illegal movement and legitimize, through the courts, violations against the rights of Iranian citizens who are members of the Bahá'í community.'[30] There were a number of reports indicating that the Baha'is energetically demanded their human rights and sought restitution through the legal system, often with no satisfactory results. They retained lawyers, made appeals and persisted.

Buoyed by the seemingly more moderate attitudes of the bureaucratic side of the regime under the reformist President Khātamī, the Baha'i leaders perhaps felt they could try to remove some of the burdens of the structural constraints that have been the main features of the status quo since early 1980s. Surely they could not as yet formally elect the members to the Spiritual Assemblies, at the national or local levels; yet, a semblance of the Baha'i organizations was created, including a kind of alternative National Spiritual Assembly, appointed from abroad by the Universal House of Justice. The intelligence agents must have known about their activities. In July 2005, when two prominent Tehrani Baha'is traveled to Mashhad to 'attend to administrative matters,' they were promptly arrested by the local security agents (BIC 2005b: 10).

Community activities have been resumed at many levels, and Baha'i training classes have been held, presumably with some links to the Baha'is outside of Iran. The Bahá'í International Community reported that in 2002 seventeen young Baha'is who participated in a camp were detained and questioned. 'Reports about this incident in the Iranian press carried a negative slant, referring to the young Bahá'ís in a derogatory and vulgar manner' (BIC 2005a, Chapter III: 5). Who organized such camps and for what activities remained unexplained.

Was this camp related to the 'Rūḥī Institute'? This is an internationally run training system devoted to Baha'i education.[31] Was the above reference to the Iranian press related to a news item published in *Hamshahrī* on 14 November 2002, in which the newspaper referred, in a typically conspiratorial manner, to a training session conducted in the United Arab Emirates (Dubai)? The Tehran newspaper said that the National Assembly of Iran sent Baha'i adherents to Dubai to attend a training course offered by the Rūḥī Institute.[32] Apparently, some training took place. These are essential activities that must be protected in accordance with the international human rights obligations of the Iranian state; otherwise the right to freedom of religion has no substance. Instead, these Baha'i activities generated renewed persecutions on the part of the regime. The Bahá'í International Community reported that in August 2005, four Baha'is were detained in the city of Karaj. 'All these individuals had received training to promote the moral education of young Bahá'ís in Iran.'[33] No details were provided.

It is reasonable to assume that there is a link between the recent arrests and detentions and the increased Baha'i public activities in Iran. Twenty-three Baha'is were detained for a short period in many different localities in 2003. A year later, there were renewed hostilities in Yazd, where 'a number of Bahá'ís were arrested, detained, and interrogated; several were beaten in their homes; at least one Bahá'í-owned small business was set afire; and Bahá'í graveyard desecrated.'[34] The Bahá'í International Community has explained briefly what precipitated the renewed attacks:

> The events began when Bahá'ís approached the officials of the Intelligence Office in Yazd to present them with a copy of the letter that the Iranian Bahá'í community had addressed to President Khatami. The officials refused to accept it and ordered the Bahá'ís to stop its distribution. They replied that they would continue, as this was the only way that they could bring the history of their persecution and the violation of their basic human rights to the attention of the authorities. Later, they were told that if they did not stop, they would suffer the consequences of having the Iranian public rise against them. . . .
>
> (BIC 2005b: 4)

This typical bravado of discredited local Islamist officials has continued to associate their own criminal mindset with that of the entire public. The Bahá'í International Community has observed that 'it has been the experience of the Iranian Bahá'í community that many of their fellow countrymen [-women] respect and admire Bahá'ís for their ideals, good character and steadfastness. Negative attitudes towards the Bahá'ís are much more often expressed and fostered by government officials.'[35] Whether or not these Baha'i traits played a role in the changed attitudes, many Muslim Iranians may no longer easily accept the Islamist baseless political charges against what they have begun to see as a decent group of Iranians going about their lives in dignity and faith and being unjustly treated.

In other localities, sixteen Baha'is were imprisoned in July–August 2005. Between March and May 2005, 35 Baha'is were detained for relatively short periods – some for a week, other up to three months – in different cities, including Shiraz and Simnan. Some were prominent individuals from Tehran; some were ordinary people from the provinces. The Bahá'í International Community reported, 'Most were released only after having posted significant amounts of money, property deeds or business licences as bail' (BIC 2005a, Chapter III: 5). Only one of them remained in prison; he received a one-year sentence for distributing the open letter to President Khātamī.

In this period of macabre twists and turns in the persecutions of the Baha'is, one episode that took place in 2004–2005 deserves particular attention, since it can be clearly seen as a costly sequel to the denial of the right to religious freedom. Its depiction by the Bahá'í International Community has also revealed an important aspect of the discourse of human rights violations of the Iranian Baha'is within the larger international Baha'i communities. The event was related to the yearly entrance examinations for the universities.

In 2004, the office responsible for the entrance examinations announced that the application forms would no longer inquire about the students' religious affiliations. This change would have allowed the Baha'i aspirants to take the examination and, upon success, enrol in the universities. However, religion would be a subject matter on which the students' knowledge would be tested in the entrance examination. The procedure allowed each participant to choose Islam (apparently for Muslim students) or one of the recognized religions (for non-Muslim students) and then answer questions related to the selected religion. Because of their familiarity with Islam, most of the Baha'i students chose it. There were apparently some excitement and anticipation among the Baha'is who did well on the examination. It is worth quoting a passage from the Bahá'í International Community's explanation of the episode, because the information it provided was as important as the interpretation it offered.

> In August, however, when the examination results were mailed out, government authorities had printed the word 'Islam' in a data field listing a prospective student's religion. Officials cynically explained they did that on the assumption that choosing to take the subject test on Islam amounts to a de facto declaration of faith in Islam. Upon learning of the forced religious declaration, a group of Bahá'í students complained to officials at the Educational Measurement and Evaluation Organization (EMEO), asking if they could return the exam results with corrected information. A footnote in the letter conveying examination results said that incorrect names and addresses could and should be corrected and returned.... Bahá'í were told by EMEO officials that 'incorrect religion would not be corrected' on the forms.... Shortly after that meeting, Bahá'í students wrote a letter of protest to the EMEO. The students expressed, clearly, their objection to having been designated as Muslims after having been promised that they would not have to disclose their religion in order to take the entrance examination. At first, officials of the EMEO seemed to sympathize with their problem, even allowing Bahá'ís to fill out revised registration forms with no religious affiliations. However, even though some 800 Bahá'í students who had passed their examinations also met the new deadline for submission of the revised forms, only ten names were published in an EMEO bulletin on 12 September 2004 announcing which students had been admitted to university....
>
> In the end, out of solidarity with the rest of the 800 students who had been unfairly discriminated against, those ten Bahá'ís declined to register in the universities to which they had been accepted. And so, for the school year 2004–2005, Bahá'í young people were once again utterly deprived of access to higher education.

This straightforward explanation, proudly upholding the Baha'i dedication to remain truthful about their religious identity at any cost, was followed by some speculations.

> For Bahá'ís, the entire episode seems calculated to accomplish a number of government objectives. First, it apparently seeks to demoralize Iranian Bahá'í youth in an effort to induce them to leave the country. Second, it allowed Iranian authorities to identify by name those Bahá'ís with outstanding academic ability, who might at some point play a role in helping to revive the Bahá'í community's fortunes. And, third, it allowed the Iranian government to say to international human rights monitors that they had given the Bahá'ís a chance to enroll – and that it was the Bahá'ís themselves who refused the opportunity. . . . And so it is clear from the whole affair that the 1991 policy aiming at blocking the development and progress of the Bahá'í community remains in effect.
>
> (BIC 2005a, Chapter III)

The second speculation may perhaps be seen by some to stem from conspiracy theory. Again, this interpretation has attributed this rather bizarre – and perhaps bungled – episode to the policy associated with the secret blueprint of 1991. However, this event in and of itself and without further evidence did not show a serious intent at 'cultural cleansing.' If there was such a plan, would the regime have sympathetic officials in one of its cultural-educational organizations? Of course the interpretation offered here by the Bahá'í International Community assumed that they were just pretending sympathy in order to carry out a plot worthy of the Ministry of Intelligence. Could it not be said that those in charge of that sordid affair had, like many others in the corrupt and bungling bureaucracy, failed to create a coherent policy? Could it be assumed that they were themselves in the throes of factional conflicts and made contradictory decisions? Could it not be said that those particular officials ultimately failed to liberate themselves from the deeply-rooted cultural-religious prejudices by accepting the diligent Baha'i youths as deserving of an access to higher education?

Is everyone so beyond hope that we cannot even assume the existence of a few such officials in the educational side of the Islamic Republic? I would rather err on the side of caution here, only because I see the presence of a few Muslims sympathizing, however hesitantly, with the predicament of a few Baha'is to be one small step forward in the realization of the dream of equal acceptance of Iranian Baha'is in their own country, at least among their educated compatriots. My speculative questions here may be inaccurate in what they assume; nevertheless, I offer them because the official Baha'i speculations remain unconvincing. Here, as in many other areas of the state interactions with the Baha'is of Iran, we lack sufficient information to offer a less tentative analysis.

The Baha'is did not allow the incident to rest. On 15 November 2004, the Baha'i community in Iran addressed a letter to President Muḥammad Khātamī. After a proper reminder of the increasing 'injustice and infringement of their rights in various aspects of their lives,' the letter focused on the episode of the national entrance examination. It highlighted the disappointing outcome of the episode, i.e. the rejection of almost all of the Baha'i students who had succeeded in the examination. The letter stated clearly the compelling case of the violations of human rights of the Baha'i citizens, without making inferences to such notions as 'cultural cleansing.' Some of the Baha'is who were detained for a short period had persisted in distributing the letter to as many officials as they could find.

At any event, the institutionalization of discrimination has not been substantially altered, and the contradictory politics and attitudes have increasingly become glaring and disturbing. The official Baha'i assessment of the Iranian situations in 2005 was understandably alarming. 'The government is now attempting to prevent all Iranian Bahá'ís from participating in monthly religious gatherings as well as all other forms of community or group activities. . . . The Iranian Bahá'ís had, for all intents and purposes, been instructed to suspend any and all activities that go beyond observations of religious obligations at the level of the individual' (BIC 2005b: 15). The assessment claims that the Baha'is have been informed that should they continue engaging in public and/or collective activities, the government will withdraw the 'protection' it has supposedly provided for them. It has not been the first time that they have heard such threats, all of them in violation of international human rights laws. The future remains uncertain; what is almost certain is that the Baha'is will obey such an order to the degree that it will be enforced. It was not made clear who in the regime had issued it.

Concluding remarks

Many of the observations I have offered in this essay are more or less tentative. There is a dearth of detailed information with reference to the Baha'is in Iran. One wishes for some monographs and field studies in, say, Yazd and Shiraz. With the exception of Roohizadegan's memories of the early years of the Islamic revolution (Roohizadegan 1993), there are hardly any accounts written by those who have survived imprisonment and harassment – similar, say, to the scores of articles and books authored by reformist journalists and Muslim dissidents since the mid-1990s. Most of the biographical sketches that one finds are almost always about those who have lost their lives. Lacking are the individual stories that could give contours to the lives of the Baha'is. We know next to nothing about the warps and wefts of their realities, of the everyday ordinariness of their existence. We really do not know how they have lived since 1979 and how some of them have distinguished themselves in their fields.

However, it can be stated with a high degree of certainty that in the context of cultural relativistic debates, the UN provisions with regard to the right to freedom of religion are meant to protect individuals from precisely the kind of abuses discussed in this chapter. Left unprotected, those who are accused of having false revelations will suffer greatly at the hands of majorities from whom they have broken away in faith. Individual Muslims are free to feel that Islam is superior to other religions, but a contemporary state institutionalizing that superiority creates human rights violations far greater in scope than the violations of the right to religious freedom. Such a state lacks legitimacy among the people it relegates to inferior positions. International human rights law prohibits states from creating different categories for treating adherents of different faiths. International human rights law forbids a state to declare a faith illegitimate, leaving its followers unprotected under the law; a modern state's enforcement of the ancient concept of apostasy is utterly unacceptable.

Since the mid-1990s, human rights violations committed against the Baha'is have entered a chronic state, no longer acutely manifested in kidnappings, killings and plundering of properties. Of course for those who have suffered by losing their loved ones, by being dismissed from their jobs and by forfeiting their properties, the acute phase could not be brought to a meaningful closure without an open reckoning with the pains and abuses that the Islamic Republic has spawned. There must be serious accounts of responsibility, restoration of reputation and property, not to mention an official apology, compensation and reconciliation.

After the first decade, certain discriminatory practices resulting in serious human rights violations have become ingrained in the official-legal procedures, or simply in the enduring habits of a clumsy state bureaucracy. The most consequential sequels to the denial of the right to religious freedom have remained the absence of judicial equality and the lack of due process of law. In such a legal environment, prevailing greed and graft can also enhance the tendency of the extortionists to see a vulnerable Baha'i as possible sources of financial gains. Factional strife and cultural prejudice can at any time wreak havoc on the lives of some Baha'is. Their lives are impeded by the administrative and social constraints, imposed on them formally or informally. There are still endless official forms and questionnaires, asking about religious identity, affecting everything from employment and education to marriage and death. Remedies offered for certain impediments are most often ad hoc waiving of discriminatory procedures and rules that can at any moment be reinstated for particular cases or certain individuals. Thus, life remains uncertain for individual Baha'is. They also face, as do other citizens, difficult circumstances of the daily life in a country that is at best dysfunctional in its economy and administration and pathetically corrupt throughout.

It has become clear that by 2005 Baha'is could live within these confinements, without being too demanding or too visible. Their presence in the Shi'i country has been grudgingly accepted by the regime in general, but when that presence manifests itself in a conspicuous or aspiring way, it may provoke the angst of some officials within the regime or some influential zealots in localities. Their efforts to establish the Bahá'í Institute for Higher Education has presented such a 'provocation.' They live in a limbo – intolerable to them, as it should be to all Iranians – neither facing annihilation nor free to plan for their future with a reasonable degree of confidence and certainty.

During the Revolution, the broader Iranian communities have neither massively participated in nor overtly celebrated the attacks on the Baha'is; their historical responsibility – and shame – rests on their quiet indifference, bordering on passive acquiescence. It is an historic failure that can be explained by the prevailing religious/cultural prejudices.

Whatever purpose it serves to speak of a secret blueprint for the destruction of the Baha'i community in Iran, the Baha'i sources accurately portray – beyond unfortunate, but perhaps understandable, hyperboles – the essence of the Baha'is' sufferings and their human rights violations. These are serious and intolerable enough, hardly in need of embellishment by adding the borrowed categories of genocide, extermination, or the newly coined 'cultural cleansing.' The Baha'is' difficult existence in Iran emanates from their being denied the right to religious freedom. That they are not allowed to practice and disseminate their religion, its values and rituals, and maintain and strengthen their organizations openly and without fear – what is called the blocking of their development – stand in clear violation of international laws. From that basic denial of religious liberty flow the rest of the human rights violations.

Those who speak on behalf of Iranian Baha'is to the outside world should perhaps keep in mind the prospect of an attitude change among many Iranians, a change that would possibly prepare them to accept the Baha'is self-definition of the faith. It can perhaps be imagined for the first time that the historic vicious circle that turned the Baha'is into the scapegoats of the Iranian political narratives has come to a close. In recent years many ordinary individuals took part in elections and saw a possibility for reformist politicians to replace the Islamic hardliners. Iranian politics no longer seemed entirely preordained. Emboldened ordinary citizens demanded a greater voice in the affairs of the state, and when they failed, as in the 2005 elections for the president, they did not reflexively resort to the worn-out themes, blaming the undesirable outcome on outside forces and their domestic lackeys. The new generation has perhaps helped to limit the social scope for roving conspiracy theories, a limitation which can only help to create a healthier attitude towards their Baha'i fellow citizens. The Islamic revolution may have facilitated the acceptance of the self-definition of the Baha'i Faith.

Moreover, for many Iranians, the traditional toxic cultural vapours have lost their potency, particularly in Tehran. The Islamic Republic may have in fact prepared the ground for the demystification of the Muslims' 'Baha'i problem' in Iran, in such a way that a significant portion of the educated population may be willing to accept the Baha'is for what they are and what they believe. There are 45 million young people who will decide the future of Iran. After more than two decades of turbulence, the society that they are inheriting may not be exactly a 'post-Islamic society,' as some observers have named it, but it is far less inclined to recreate 'otherness' and demonize the targets in religious terms. There seems to be a growing tendency to put aside the notions of the sacred and the profane in forming one's views about society and how it should conceive its political institutions and societal relationships. If no person can be sanctified and empowered in a sociopolitical setting, perhaps no one can be demonized either. For many Iranians, the religious myths have lost their potency in drawing the lines separating the 'self' from the 'other'.

Notes

1 The Bahá'í International Community had a consultative status with the UN's ECOSOC.

2 'In fact,' asserts Nazila Ghanea, 'the skillful lobbying capacity of the BIC [Baha'i International Community], . . . cannot be overestimated in the profile given to this case at the UN' (Ghanea 2002: 201).

3 For example, see the advertisement placed by Mihrāb Qāsimnijād, who converted to Shi'ism and requested that his 'father and mother also convert to the *dīn-i mubīn-i Islām*' (*Kayhān*, 2 July 1994).

4 Prepared statement of James F. Nelson before Subcommittee of Human Rights and International Organizations, 2 May 1984.

5 If a threat of genocide ever hung over Iran's Baha'is, it was in 1981–84, when the regime was impervious to international pressure. That threat had significantly receded by the time the regime began to reengage Iran with the influential side of the outside world. Since early 1980s when the international human rights community focused on Iran, Amnesty International and Human Rights Watch, both of whom produced detailed reports, never used the term genocide, or any of its adjectival derivatives, to define the plights of the Baha'is. Nor did the UN Special Representatives make such a reference.

6 In Yazd the local cell of the movement that was later renamed Ḥujjatīya was in existence during the Shah's regime (Fischer 1980: 227).

7 For the names and the date of executions, see Universal House of Justice 1994: 229–235.

8 Prepared Statement of James F. Nelson before Subcommittee of Human Rights and International Organizations, 2 May 1984: 9.

9 BIC 2005a, Chapter IV: 2.

10 Momen writes 'that the Iranian government was intentionally and actively proceeding along the pathway towards a genocide but was stopped in its tracks by the vigorous international campaign waged by the international Baha'i community' (Momen 2005: 238). He assumes, 'By the start of the 1990s, however,

international pressure had grow [*sic*] so intense and Iran's own position had weakened so much economically and politically that the Iranian government was forced to reconsider its position' (Ibid. 226). As indicated above, much of the harms inflicted on the Baha'i community in term of loss of lives and imprisonments took place between 1980 and 1985. Thereafter, persecutions had become institutionalized and remained in place, with some lapses of enforcement in the later years of Khātamī's presidency, to the present day.

11 Prepared statement of James F. Nelson before Subcommittee of Human Rights and International Organizations, 2 May 1984: 15.

12 Ibid. 10.

13 Momen tries to draw parallels between Iran's 'suspended genocide' and the genocides that actually took place elsewhere and writes about 'thousands of Baha'is who have been imprisoned since the Islamic revolution' (Momen 2005: 228). The Baha'i official statements continue to provide accurate information. 'Since 1979, nearly 1,000 Bahá'is have been arrested and imprisoned' (BIC 2005a: 53).

14 For an explanation of the new trend, see Afshari 2001: 104–107.

15 UN Doc. E/CN.4/1993/41, para. 222; UN Doc. A/51/479, para. 24; UN Doc. E/CN.4/1997/63, para. 52; UN Doc. A/51/479, para. 24 and UN Doc. A/52/472, para. 27.

16 Statement by American Baha'i community, July 1998, online at http://www.prnewswire.com/images/todayhed.gif.

17 See Chapter 5 by Fazel and Foadi in this volume.

18 Printed in the daily *Iṭṭilā'āt*, 5 September 1983. Reprinted in Universal House of Justice 1994, my translation.

19 *Khabar-nāma-yi farhangī va ijtimā'ī*, no. 73, Day 15, 1368: 63.

20 The creation of the Council 'resulted in a further concentration of power in the hands of classical figures close to Khomeini. . . .' (Rahnema and Nomani 1990: 230).

21 BIC 2005a: 17.

22 An accurate translation of the memorandum is provided in BIC 2005a: 18–19.

23 Momen seems to attribute the closing of the BIHE in 1999 to a document issued by the Supreme Council of Cultural Revolution in 1991; he does not speculate why it took the state's security agents more than ten years to implement its directive and close the BIHE (Momen 2005: 227).

24 Ethan Bronner, 'Iran Closes "University" Run Covertly by the Baha'is,' *New York Times*, 29 October 1998.

25 BIC 2005a, Chapter IV: 1–3.

26 BIC 2005b: 18.

27 Reported from Iran by Muḥammad Khākpūr, BBCPersian.com, 1 September 2005.

28 For an example of a successful engineering company in Isfahan and the level of harassment, see BIC 2005a, Chapter III: 6.

29 BIC 2005b: 20–21.

30 BIC 2005a, Chapter III: 7.

31 The Ruhi Institute sponsors formal training courses to turn the participants who have some knowledge of the Baha'i Faith into tutors to be able to repeat the courses for others within their localities. See http://www.ruhiresources.org.

32 A translation of the *Hamshahrī* item was made available in *Research Notes in Shaykhi, Babi, and Baha'i Studies*, vol. 6, no. 2, December 2002 online at http://www.h.net.org/~bahai/notes/vol6/ruhi/ruhi.htm. Accessed 9 October 2005.

33 BIC 2005b: 11.

34 BIC 2005a, Chapter III: 5.

35 BIC 2005b: 7.

Bibliography

Abrahamian, E. (1989) *The Iranian Mojahedin*, New Haven: Yale University Press.

—— (1999) *Tortured Confessions: Prisons and Public Recantations in Modern Iran*, Los Angeles: University of California Press.

Affolter, F.W. (2005) 'The Specter of Ideological Genocide: The Bahá'ís of Iran', *War Crimes, Genocide, and Crimes Against Humanity*, 1.1: 75–114.

Afshari, R. (2001) *Human Rights in Iran: The Abuse of Cultural Relativism*, Philadelphia: University of Pennsylvania Press.

Amir Arjomand, S. (1988) *The Turban for the Crown: The Islamic Revolution in Iran*. Oxford: Oxford University Press.

Bahá'í International Community (BIC). (1999) *Iran's Secret Blueprint for the Destruction of a Religious Community*, New York: BIC.

—— (2005a) *The Bahá'í Question: Cultural Cleansing in Iran*, New York: BIC; online at http://question.bahai.org/003.php. Accessed 9 October 2005.

—— (2005b) 'Update: Situation of the Bahá'ís in Iran', New York: BIC.

Bakhash, S. (1986) *The Reign of the Ayatollahs: Iran and the Islamic Revolution*, New York: Basic Books.

Cooper, R. (1982) *The Baha'is of Iran*, London: Minority Rights Group.

Ghanea, N. (2002) *Human Rights, the UN and the Bahá'ís in Iran*, Oxford: George Ronald.

Ghanea-Hercock, N. (1997) 'A Review of Secondary Literature in English on Recent Persecutions of Bahá'ís in Iran,' in *Bahá'í Studies Review*, 7: 1–14 Online at http://www.breacais.demon.co.uk.

Fischer, M.J. (1980) *Iran: From Religious Dispute to Revolution*, Cambridge: Harvard University Press.

Fischer, M.J. and Abedi, M. (1990) *Debating Muslims: Cultural Dialogues in Postmodernity and Tradition*, Madison: University of Wisconsin Press.

Human Rights Watch. (1997) *Iran: Religious and Ethnic Minorities, Discrimination in Law and Practice*, New York.

Khumaynī, R. (1985) *Saḥīfa-yi nūr: majmū'a-yi rāhnamūd-hā-yi Imām Khumaynī* (vol. 17), Tehran: Vizārat-i Irshād-i Islāmī.

Martin, D. (1984) *The Persecution of the Bahá'ís of Iran, 1844–1984*. Ottawa: Association for Bahá'í Studies.

Momen, M. (1985) *An Introduction to Shi'i Islam*, New Haven: Yale University Press.

—— (2005) 'The Babi and Baha'i Community of Iran: a Case of "Suspended Genocide"?' *Journal of Genocide Research*, 7.2: 221–241.

Mottahadeh, R. (1985) *The Mantle of the Prophet: Religion and Politics in Iran*, New York: Pantheon Books.

Nash, G. (1982) *Iran's Secret Pogrom*, Suffolk: Neville Spearman Limited.

—— (1986) 'The Persecution of the Bahá'í Community of Iran, Ridván 1979 – Ridván 1983,' *The Bahá'í World*, Volume XVIII, Haifa: Baha'i World Centre.

Rahnema, A. and Nomani, F. (1990) *The Secular Miracle: Religion, Politics and Economic Policy in Iran*, London: Zed Books.

Roohizadegan, O. (1993) *Olya's Story: A Survivor's Dramatic Account of the Persecution of Baha'is in Revolutionary Iran*, Oxford: Oneworld.

Sadri, M. (2004) 'Hojjatiya,' in *Encyclopaedia Iranica*, volume 12, fascicle 4 available at www.iranica.com.

Sanasarian, E. (2000) *Religious Minorities in Iran*, Cambridge: Cambridge University Press.

Schirazi, A. (1997) *The Constitution of Iran: Politics and State in the Islamic Republic*, trans. John O'Kane. London: I.B. Tauris.

Sears, W. (1982) *A Cry from the Heart: The Bahá'ís in Iran*, Oxford: George Ronald.

Simpson, J. (1988) *Inside Iran: Life under Khomeini's Regime*, New York: St. Martin's Press.

Taheri, A. (1987) *Holy Terror: The Inside Story of Islamic Terrorism*, London: Sphere Books.

Universal House of Justice, The. (1994) 'The Persecution of the Bahá'í Community of Iran,' *The Bahá'í World*, vol. XIX. Haifa: Baha'i World Centre.

U.S. Department of State. (1999) 'Annual Report on International Religious Freedom for 1999: Iran,' online at http://www.state.gov.

INDEX

Page numbers in *Italics* represent Tables and page numbers in **Bold** represent Figures
Page numbers followed by {n} represent Endnotes

For Product Safety Concerns and Information please contact our EU representative GPSR@taylorandfrancis.com
Taylor & Francis Verlag GmbH, Kaufingerstraße 24, 80331 München, Germany

www.ingramcontent.com/pod-product-compliance
Lightning Source LLC
Chambersburg PA
CBHW071453110726
47908CB00003B/602

* 9 7 8 0 4 1 5 5 8 3 2 2 0 *